"Incisive . . . The most fun business book I have read this year. . . . Clearly there will be people who hate this book—which is probably one of the things that makes it such a great read."

—Andrew Ross Sorkin, *New York Times*

"Reckless and rollicking . . . perceptive and funny and brave . . . The resulting view of the Valley's craziness, self-importance, and greed isn't pretty. But it's one that most of us have never seen before and aren't likely to forget."

—Margaret Sullivan, *Washington Post*

"There are some books that are just too good to miss. . . . In his insider-tells-all book, García Martínez discusses everything from goofy stories to cultural secrets about some of the country's most powerful and influential businesses."

—*Atlantic*

"Michael Lewis was never a top Wall Street bond salesman, but in *Liar's Poker* he captured an era. *Chaos Monkeys* aims to do the same for Silicon Valley, and bracingly succeeds. Nothing I've ever read conveys better what it actually is like to be in the engine room of the start-up economy. There were moments I laughed out loud, something I never recall doing while reading about Steve Jobs."

—David Streitfeld, *New York Times Book Review*

"This year's best non-business book about business . . . García Martínez is a real writer. . . . A classic tale, well told . . . If you're in a startup or even plan to sue one, *Chaos Monkeys* is the book to read."

—John Biggs, *Techcrunch*

"Feels darkly true . . . García Martínez is brilliant at describing the relaxed yet self-centered attitudes of high-powered Californians."

—Hannah Kuchler, *Financial Times*

"Unlike most founding narratives that flow out of the Valley, *Chaos Monkeys* dives into the unburnished, day-to-day realities: the frantic pivots, the enthusiastic ass-kissing, the excruciating internal politics. . . . (García) can be rude, but he's shrewd, too."

—*Bloomberg Businessweek*

"An irresistible and indispensable 360-degree guide to the new technology establishment . . . Provides fascinating insights into the nature of the online and offline advertising worlds . . . Mr. García is not just a keen observer of corporate and social culture, but a thoughtful business and policy analyst armed with a highly refined detector for pretentious nonsense. . . . A must-read."

—Jonathan A. Knee, *New York Times*

"An unvarnished account (of Silicon Valley)."

—*CBS This Morning*

"Eye-popping."

—*Vanity Fair*

"Romps through Martínez's wild trajectory from Wall Streeter to pre-IPO Facebook employee, with the dramatic sale of his Y Combinator-backed ad-tech startup (to Twitter) in between."

—Jillian D'Onfiro, *Business Insider*

CHAOS MONKEYS

CHAOS MONKEYS

OBSCENE FORTUNE AND RANDOM FAILURE IN SILICON VALLEY

Antonio García Martínez

18 17

HARPER

An Imprint of HarperCollins*Publishers*

For information, address HarperCollins Publishers, 195 Broadway, New York, NY 10007.

First Harper mass market international printing: February 2017
First Harper hardcover printing: June 2016

ISBN 978-0-06-266979-7

16 17 18 19 20 QGM 10 9 8 7 6 5 4 3 2 1

Author's Note

The events described in this work, with the exception of one scene in New York, occurred between roughly March 2010 and October 2014, in and around the San Francisco Bay Area. This account is based on archived emails, Facebook posts and messages, tweets, and blog posts from the time. Any dialogue, if quoted from emails, texts, or messages, is verbatim. If quoted from conversation or phone calls, it's been reconstructed from memory. While these re-creations are not exact, I've done my level best to capture the spirit and significance of every scene depicted. To those who may have been present but feel I have misconstrued events, I invite you to write your own competing account. Together we may arrive at the set of mutually agreed-upon lies called history.

Note: Some names have been omitted to protect the truly guilty.

To all my enemies:

I could not have done it without you.

To Zoë Ayala and Noah Pelayo,

the only lasting products I have ever shipped.

Lastly, to Rachel Caïdor.

Lo prometido es deuda.

Contents

Prologue: The Garden of Forking Paths

> Had I been present at the creation, I would have given some useful hints for the better ordering of the universe.
>
> —attributed to Alfonso X, "the Wise," of Castile

FRIDAY, APRIL 13, 2012

The area housing the Facebook high command was a completely unexceptional cluster of desks, remarkable only for the pile of sporting equipment kept by Sam Lessin, one of Zuck's lieutenants. Similar clusterings, arranged like hedgerows, extended as far as you could see into either leg of the large L formed by Building 16 on Facebook's campus. The décor was standard-issue Silicon Valley tech: industrial shag carpet, exposed ceilings revealing ventilation ducts and fire-retardant-covered steel beams, and the odd piece of home-brewed installation art: an imposing Lego wall featuring the blocky murals left by employees, another wall papered with the vaguely Orwellian posters the in-house printshop churned out.

At the exact vertex of Building 16 was the "Aquarium," Facebook's glass-walled throne room, where Zuck held court all day. It jutted into the main courtyard, allowing passing Facebookers to snatch a glance of their famed leader while strolling to lunch. Its windows were reputedly bulletproof. Just outside the Aquarium's entrance was a makeshift foyer with couches and some trendy coffee-table book or another, which the ever-present scrum of waiting FB courtiers ignored as they made last-minute tweaks to presentations or demos. An adjoining minikitchen, like so many that littered the campus, stocked plenty of lemon-lime Gatorade, Zuck's official beverage.

Inside Facebook's campus, geography was destiny, and your physical proximity to Zuck was a clear indicator of your importance. Along the periphery of the L ran the exclusive conference rooms of Facebook's five business-unit leaders. Zuck's desk neighbors at that point were Sheryl Sandberg, the star chief operating officer (COO) of Facebook; Andrew "Boz" Bosworth, the engineering director who had created News Feed; and Mike Schroepfer, Facebook's chief technical officer (CTO). None of them were at their desks as I strode in from the courtyard that afternoon.

Unlike much of the user-facing side of Facebook, the Ads team was held at arm's length, as if it was a pair of sweaty underwear, in the next building over. That would eventually change, and Ads team members would occupy some prime real estate in and around Zuck's and Sheryl's desks. That was still a long way off, though, and every senior management meeting I was pulled into involved crossing the courtyard at ground level.

The centerpiece of this Facebook Champs-Élysées were the letters H-A-C-K, actually inlaid in the concrete slab that formed the courtyard and easily a good one hundred feet long. Angled to be readable on the Google Maps satellite image of campus, it appeared as the supreme Facebookian commandment.

My mission today was a meeting with Zuck, scheduled in Sheryl's conference room, which was named, for reasons I never discovered, "Only Good News." Skirting the pile of athletic equipment around the executive-desk cluster, I walked into the glass cube of the conference room, which featured a long, white table flanked by a score of pricey Aeron chairs, a flat-panel screen on one wall, and a whiteboard on the other. Most of the meeting attendants, except the two most important ones, were already seated.

Gokul Rajaram, the product management head of Ads and my boss, was slouched in his usual twitching, anxious knot; he took a nanosecond's break from his ever-present phone as his eyes rose to mine. Next to Gokul sat Brian Boland, a buzz-cut-and-balding guy you imagined had wrestled in college, and whom cozy, corporate life had made thick with age. Boland ran product marketing for the Ads team, the group that wove the thick packing layer of polished bullshit that any Ads product was wrapped in before being given to the sales team, who would then push it on advertisers.

Sitting at a remove and staring into his phone was Greg Badros, a former Googler who ran both Search and Ads, but seemed more absence than presence in either. Mark Rabkin, the engineering manager in Ads, and an early hire on the Facebook Ads team, was closest to me in rank and attitude. A close collaborator since my first days at Facebook, he resembled a less satanic version of Vladimir Putin. Elliot Schrage was in his usual perch, close and to the right of the table's end. Schrage held an elevated-sounding and vague title but was Sheryl's consigliere in all matters. In his fifties, wearing a button-down shirt and "business casual" slacks, he seemed out of place among the fleece-and-jeans-wearing techies; he could have been mistaken for a senior lawyer in a stodgy East Coast law firm—which is what he had been before joining Google and the Sherylsphere.

I took a seat toward the opposite end of the Sheryl intimates, and flipped open my Facebook-issue MacBook Pro to nervously remind myself of the meeting's script. The agenda was pitching Zuck on the three new ads-targeting ideas I had dreamed up, and which constituted a big monetization bet the company was (hopefully) soon to make.

Camille Hart, Sheryl's all-powerful executive administrative assistant, or admin, milled about and tapped away on her laptop, wrangling meeting participants.

"Where's Fischer?" asked Sheryl as she blew in through the door and took her seat at the end of the table.

No meeting could start without the minyan of Elliot Schrage and David Fischer, the entourage she had poached out of Google. Camille bolted out to find him.

Most everyone stayed silent, pecking at smartphones or laptops. Boland and Sheryl quietly conferred on the state of the slides we were presenting. We'd already prepitched her our products, tweaking the message to maximally appeal to Zuck. Any Zuck meeting around Ads required a bit of prechewing and spoon-feeding. The reason was simple: Ads were not something he cared about at the time, and I imagine he saw these meetings more as duty-bound drudgery than anything else. In one year in Facebook Ads, I had seen the famously micromanage-y founder and CEO in the Ads area precisely once: when he was walking around the building in a circle to get in his ten thousand daily steps. This stood in sharp contrast to the gossipy stories I had heard from product managers on the user-facing side of Facebook about the withering spotlight one lived in when working a product Zuck cared about.

In our premeeting meeting, Sheryl had let slip various hints about the best way to present our plans. She clearly knew her boss inside and out. Here was a woman who excelled in the role of gatekeeper and shepherd to difficult and powerful men, whether that role was chief of staff for the prickly US treasury secretary Larry Summers, or COO of and for Zuck. Between her ability to navigate and manage the mercurial and fractious political landscape of a complex organization like Facebook, and her ability to shape messages for Zuck, she was both de facto and de jure the person who ran Facebook Ads. As the debate about the future of Facebook monetization grew more polarized and heated, these meetings would resemble the Supreme Court of Sheryl, the one place where conflicting views could be aired with some hope of resolution.

In came Fischer: slim, dapper, and the best-coiffed man at Facebook. Originally one of Sheryl's reports at the Treasury Department, he had begun his career as a journalist at *U.S. News & World Report*, and then, as with many senior Facebook people, joined Google. As Facebook's vice president of sales and operations, he ran the entire sales team for Sheryl, and in my time at the company I rarely heard him utter anything other than corporate platitudes and MBA-speak (Stanford Graduate School of Business '02, *bien sûr*).

Greetings all around as Fischer took a seat to Sheryl's left near the head of the table, opposite Schrage. Executive admin's duty done, a satisfied Camille disappeared to wherever she lived at FB.

Noiselessly, Zuck padded into the conference room, staring at his smartphone, and sat down in the empty seat to Schrage's right. Now the meeting could really begin.

Sheryl kicked things off. "Mark, as you know we've been considering some new initiatives in Ads."

Way to understate things, Sheryl.

The company had announced its intention to go public months ago, and the IPO was imminent. Precisely when the company was opening itself to investor scrutiny, its revenue growth was slowing, and revenue itself was plateauing. The narratives the company had woven about the new magic of social-media marketing were in deep reruns with advertisers, many of whom were beginning to openly question the fortunes they had spent on Facebook thus far, often with little to show for it. A colossal yearlong bet the company had made on a product called Open Graph, and its accompanying monetization spin-off, Sponsored Stories, had been an absolute failure in the market. The company's senior leadership had called on the Ads team to dream up something fast to revive the lagging fortunes of the enterprise. This being Facebook, the initiatives originated not at the senior levels of the company but rather at the lower: random engineers who had conceived of a bit of cleverness, glib product managers (that would be your humble correspondent) who had managed to seduce a few people to their vision.

On the agenda this afternoon were three proposed products, each very different from the other. The first involved using Facebook's Like buttons—"social plugins" in Facebookese—as all-seeing eyes that would hoover up users' browsing behavior for fun and profit.

A bit of background for the nontechie: When you load a page in your browser, everything you see (and most of the things you don't) is not from the company whose ".com" address you've entered. The way the modern Web works, different elements come from different places. Every element you load, whether you like it or not, touches your browser, and is allowed to read data in the form of what's known as cookies.

The popularity of Facebook's Like and Share buttons meant Facebook was on something like half the Web in a mature market like the United States. As you browse the Web far and wide, from shoe shopping on zappos.com to news reading on nytimes.com, Facebook sees you everywhere, as if it had a closed-circuit TV on all city streets. Facebook's terms of service had so far prohibited the use of the resulting data for commercial purposes, but this bold proposal suggested lifting that self-imposed restriction. As ominous and powerful as that may sound, it was not guaranteed to succeed, as the actual value of that data was unknown.

I knew a thing or two about the value of Facebook data.

A year before, I had been hired as Facebook's first product manager for ads targeting, charged with converting Facebook's user data into money by whatever legal means available. This task had proved considerably more difficult than it sounds. For months, the targeting team and I had been testing and ingesting every piece of Facebook user data—posts, check-ins, shared links, friends, Likes—to see if it would improve the targeting and delivery of Facebook ads. Almost without exception, none of it increased monetization to a substantial degree. The miserable conclusion was that Facebook, though assumed to be a rich repository of user data, did not in fact have much commercially useful data at all. Social plugin data, despite its ominous and all-pervasive nature, might fall into that same depressing category.

The second and third proposals were more radical from a business, if not a legal, perspective and reflected this grim realization. The plan was to join the Facebook Ads experience to data generated completely outside Facebook. Thus far, all ads on Facebook used FB-only data, but this proposal would involve tapping into "external" data like browsing history, online shopping, and offline purchases in physical shops. Historically, Facebook had been a walled garden, in which advertisers could not use their data on Facebook or use Facebook data elsewhere. From the data perspective, it was as if Facebook was absent from the Internet ecosystem, off on some island under its own complete control. Via two different technical mechanisms—one roughly in keeping with the existing Ads system, another vastly more sophisticated—we were proposing to bridge that divide at last. Both proposals, at an abstract level, were equivalent; at the implementation and business level, however, they were vastly different, and required completely different approaches to the advertising market.

Zuck and Sheryl hated projecting PowerPoint decks, so somebody had printed out the slides I had prepared and stapled them into neat packets. Boland had summarized debates and meetings going back months in easy-to-parse bullet points on the first page. That's all anyone ever saw. My detailed technical schematics, with walk-throughs of data flows and outside integration points, were, as I suspected, completely ignored. Sheryl wouldn't have cared about the technical detail, and Zuck wouldn't have had the patience to go through it anyhow. As I observed more than once at Facebook, and as I imagine is the case in all organizations from business to government, high-level decisions that affected thousands of people and billions in revenue would be made on gut feel, the residue of whatever historical politics were in play, and the ability to cater persuasive messages to people either busy, impatient, or uninterested (or all three).

Boland did his breezy best walking through the summary slide, leaving out the endless debates concerning privacy and legal regulation that had eaten up countless hours of everyone's time. If ads already made Zuck drowse, then privacy trade-offs would have sent him keeling over off his Aeron chair. Whatever Zuck approved, we'd engineer the legal workings.

"So do we think using the plugin data will make us more money?" Zuck asked.

Boland and Gokul turned to me, the usual cue for the lowest-ranked but most-informed guy in the room—that is, the actual product manager—to pipe up and say something.*

---

* Facebook, given its size, was a relatively flat organization. There were still roughly three types of hierarchical characters in FB Ads at the time. First, the senior management level, whose members spent their lives in a blizzard of meetings interspersed with email breaks, and who formed a middle-management cadre between Zuck/Sheryl and everyone else. This was Gokul, Boland, Badros, and most everyone else in that room. Then there were the product and engineering teams, whose members usually spent their time on the engineering floor, hacking people and product. That's me and everyone else who actually built anything. And then, last, the sales and operations people, of which there was a small army, who occupied the unfrequented buildings on campus and the equally unfre-

My brain reacted like an old truck in winter, failing to start and cranking away futilely.

"Well, that depends . . . I mean, there are lots of things that affect monetization. We haven't really done the controlled A/B studies, as it's legally touchy, but it is possible that it's unique data in some way. Of course, there's also the issue of whether the Like button is even where we want it to be datawise, as—"

"Why don't you just answer the question?" blurted Zuck, cutting me off.

Panic breeds focus.

"I don't think it would move the needle much, given recent experience," I replied flatly.

Silence, as we all waited for what Zuck would say.

"You can do this, but don't use the Like button," he said finally.

The statement percolated through the room.

"So yes to retargeting, but no to using social plugins," reiterated Sheryl, more question to Zuck than assertion.*

"Yes."

And that's all he ever said about the matter.

What was still undecided was which of the two proposals Facebook would pursue. A year from this meeting and in this same conference room, with more or less the same

---

quented international offices. The lowest level, despite often being the face of Facebook to the world and bedecking themselves with fancy titles like "head of Facebook EMEA," had no real impact on what product got built, and were there mostly for show.

* "Retargeting" is ads-speak for the practice of showing a user ads based on what he or she has browsed on the Web. At its simplest, it's the creepy tactic of showing you an ad for a product you just eyed on Amazon or other online commerce site. At the time of the meeting described here, the targeting was more sophisticated than merely showing you a version of a product you've already seen, but the term was really code for predicating your experience on site A with things you've done on sites B, C, and D (and perhaps even done offline, in physical stores).

cast assembled, we'd finally decide that question. It would take Facebook an exasperating year to even decide to decide. The resulting decision, when it finally came, would see me ejected from Facebook, and change how Facebook made money for years to come.

But right then, on that Friday afternoon, I was giddy inside. The last two months of scheming had worked out. We could build this magic targeting device I had proposed that would combine the two great Internet data streams, Facebook and the outside world, and change everything.

I took one look at Gokul, who half nodded. Sheryl turned to the next item on the meeting agenda. This was her weekly meeting between her, the Ads team, and Zuck. Product reviews were packed into fifteen-minute slots. Other product managers had filed into the room during the brief discussion, and were waiting their turns. As discreetly as possible, I vacated the spring-loaded Aeron chair and slid out the door. I had my marching orders.

Part One

Disturbing the Peace

The great source of both the misery and disorders of human life, seems to arise from over-rating the difference between one permanent situation and another. Avarice over-rates the difference between poverty and riches: ambition, that between a private and a public station: vain-glory, that between obscurity and extensive reputation. The person under the influence of any of those extravagant passions, is not only miserable in his actual situation, but is often disposed to disturb the peace of society, in order to arrive at that which he so foolishly admires.

—Adam Smith, *The Theory of Moral Sentiments*

The Undertakers of Capitalism

> Commercial credit is the creation of modern times, and belongs, in its highest perfection, only to the most enlightened and best governed nations. It has raised armies, equipped navies, and, triumphing over the gross power of mere numbers, it has established national superiority on the foundation of intelligence, wealth, and well-directed industry.
>
> —Daniel Webster, US Senate speech, March 18, 1834*

NOVEMBER 2007

"Hey! What's going on with risk right now?"

I looked up from a row of four monitors covered in blue windows flowing with computer code, a financial matrix only a select few understood, but whose outputs made the

* A version of this quote was engraved on the bronze facade of the Moody's building in downtown Manhattan. Moody's was one of the credit rating agencies whose incompetence or illicit collusion with banks was partially responsible for the credit crisis.

world go round. The speaker was Jonathan Mann, "JMann" in the trading floor's argot. He had a golf club slung across his shoulders, his arms draped over its ends, a blasphemous image of Christ financial.

Credit spreads, the FICO scores of the largest companies in the world, were exploding, meaning the world's financial faith was withering. The crucifixion was an apt metaphor.

"Not sure. We'll look into it, JMann," I replied, barely looking up from my four computer screens. His bloodshot eyes fixed on me for a moment, then he retreated to his desk, which featured even more screens than mine.

JMann worked for Goldman Sachs trading credit indices, basically lumped-together sets of credit bets on large corporations, almost like mutual funds. Unlike in the world of stocks, prices in the credit world weren't determined by some vague premonition of future value, but on the perceived future probability of corporate death. In credit land, there were only ever funerals, no weddings or baby showers. By betting on death, we were the bookie undertakers, gambling on either this or that company living or dying.

JMann's malfunctioning index was not my real problem, though. General Motors was my problem. Southwest Airlines was my problem. Ford Motor Company was my problem. I looked over my screens at Charlie McGarraugh, the Yale math grad who traded airlines and auto companies, and whose quant manservant I was, building sophisticated pricing models for the abstruse derivatives that paid our bonuses, and maintaining the clean flow of data that gave us a view on this cutthroat world. As per usual on days like today, he was worked up into a lather screaming price quotes, either at people on the floor or into his phone headset. Rob Jackson, his junior trader, was next to him entering trades into a risk system, to be digested by the code I wrote, producing the pricing models that let traders navigate this precarious world, and guide yet more trades.

What was the value of the full faith and credit of United

Airlines? Whatever the fuck Charlie McGarraugh said it was, as he was the "market maker" in airline credit for Goldman Sachs. The broker of public perception, he was both the market's conduit and its lion tamer, buffeted by market forces out of his control, but also warping the market according to his predatory designs.

For two years now, Charlie had been betting on the demise of America's anemic auto industry, plus the death of several airlines. We were always just one Ford Pinto–esque safety recall, or several months of high jet fuel prices, away from a truly gargantuan windfall. One could easily imagine the sardonic grin on Charlie's pale face if news of a United jet crashing into a mountain were to flash across his Bloomberg terminal. Thanks to me, he could tell exactly how much money we'd make if that happened. But even with the growing housing credit crisis, industries like cars and planes remained creditworthy. The damn planes stayed up, fuel prices stayed down, and no one figured out what a piece of shit the 2008 Pontiac Vibe was.

Even amid the perpetual convulsions of fear and greed that possessed everyone on the floor, reason would occasionally out. Like a rock-bottom alcoholic contemplating his vomit-stained sheets through the haze of another post-bender hangover, you occasionally asked yourself: How did I get here? How could I do this to myself? Where was the humanity?

I joined Goldman Sachs after five flailing years in a physics PhD program at Berkeley. At the time, my graduate stipend (taxable as income!) was the princely sum of $19,000.

The average salary at Goldman Sachs in 2005 was $521,000, and that's counting each and every trader, salesperson, investment banker, secretary, mail boy, shoe shiner, and window cleaner on the payroll. One of the few things I took from my sordid grad student pad was a copy of Michael

Lewis's *Liar's Poker*, that classic of the Wall Street trading genre, for reference.

My job on arrival?

I was a pricing quant on the Goldman Sachs corporate credit trading desk.* That means I was responsible for modeling and pricing the various credit derivatives that the biggest credit-trading house in the world traded. We'll get into what a derivative is in a moment. More important at Goldman Sachs than the "what" was the "who."

Goldman Sachs was unusual among Wall Street banks in that it had mostly kept a partnership management structure. Hence, every incoming employee was hired by a specific partner, and you were that partner's boy. My feudal liege lord was a short, balding guy with an intense stare and oddly biblical name: Elisha Wiesel. Elisha was none other than the only son of Elie Wiesel, the famous Holocaust survivor whose horrifying *Night* is required reading for many American high schoolers. His father may have been a Holocaust luminary and a public intellectual, but his son was a vicious, greedy little prick.†

His lieutenant, my boss, was a Caltech mathematics grad

---

* "Quant" is short for some flavor of quantitative analyst or quantitative trader. These are the financial engineers who recycle the mathematics of fluid mechanics or probability for the world of filthy lucre. They absolutely litter Wall Street now, and some areas of finance, like the hyperfast world of high-frequency trading, couldn't exist without them. The most authentic view of their world was penned by a founder of the Goldman Strategies team, Emanuel Derman, in his classic *My Life as a Quant*.

† For fans of schadenfreude, life is a never-ending feast. When the Madoff scandal, the largest Ponzi scheme in American history, erupted in late 2008, it would turn out that the Elie Wiesel Foundation for Humanity had invested all of its assets with Madoff. Elie's son, Elisha, my boss, was the foundation's treasurer. This reminds me of the joke about mixed emotions being the sight of your mother-in-law driving over a cliff in your new Porsche. Shame about the loss to such a worthy cause, but as for the hit to Elisha Wiesel, well, couldn't have happened to a nicer guy.

from my home state of Florida. Ryan McCorvie ("RTM," per the three-letter acronym everyone was known by on the internal messaging system) was tall and gangly, with twiggy arms that emerged from a potbellied, ectomorphic body. His one flash of personal color was a tattoo of the infinity symbol on his forearm, studiously covered while at Goldman.*

There were other characters in this drama too.

The traders were crafty and quick-witted, but with little technical sophistication and the attention span of an ADHD kid hopped up on energy drinks and Jolly Ranchers. Their role was to trade with Goldman clients and other traders at rival firms, posting prices to buy and sell securities and their derivatives, all the while both hedging their books and making smart bets with the firm's money. It was like juggling flaming chain saws while dancing a jig on top of a speeding train.

The sales guys were complete tools, with a collective IQ safely in the double digits. Their only role was to woo and ply clients with potential trades, presenting the glib appearance of trading savvy and market control, and then skulking away to a trader and begging for a special price for a client trade.

And the quants, called "strategists" or just "strats" in Goldman-speak? Mostly failed scientists like me who had sold out to the man and suddenly found themselves, after

---

* But wait, schadenfreude-lover, there's more! My former boss RTM, as of January 2016, is currently out on bail while awaiting trial for the sexual molestation of minors. It's been alleged that he groped a group of young girls in a public pool. Innocent until proven guilty (of course). Already proven guilty is my former trader, Matt Taylor, who would also do a turn in the clink. He went rogue, and somehow fooled both Goldman's risk systems and me (his quant) by taking outsize positions in exchange-traded securities, risking billions of dollars of house capital in order to juice his returns, and his annual bonus. He did his time in the federal pen and now runs a pool-cleaning business in Florida. Such a sterling lot, my Wall Street colleagues.

making it through years of advanced relativity and quantum mechanics, with a golf-club-wielding gorilla called a trader peering over their shoulder asking them where their risk report was. We were quantitative enablers, offering the new and shiny blessings of modern computation to the old business of buying and selling. But giving sophisticated models and fast computers to traders was like giving handguns and tequila to teenage boys. The quants were there to make sure the guns were loaded, but also to make sure the traders didn't shoot themselves in the foot.

Though crucial to the drama, we weren't terribly appreciated. In fact, we were basically the traders' little bitches, and any quant who was honest with himself realized that. In time, we quants developed knee calluses from genuflecting to service the traders on whose profits our livelihoods depended.

The only time we quants shone was when some particularly hairy deal came up, and a befuddled trader dropped off a thick bond indenture document, pleading for help. Peering into these deals was like looking at the zoomed-in penetration shot in a cheesy porn video: you could barely tell which end was up, which part was which, or, more important, who exactly was screwing whom. The quant aspect, involving detailed matters of future risk and optionality, almost didn't matter in the end. One lacrosse-playing Penn graduate would agree on price via phone with another lacrosse-playing Cornell grad, and life would resume its speedy course to another deal.

Quants were the eunuchs at the orgy. The fluffers on the porn set of high finance. We were the ever-present British guy in every Hollywood World War II film: there to add a touch of class and exotic sophistication, but not really consequential to the plot (except perhaps to conveniently take some bad guy's bullet).

There were some rewards. When the markets presented an apocalyptic Boschian landscape, every Goldman grunt, sergeant, and general would close ranks and form a Greek phalanx of greed. Unlike almost every other bank on the street, Goldman could actually calculate its risk across desks and asset classes out to five decimals. The partners, who had much of their net worth wrapped up in Goldman stock, held tense meetings and came up with a plan to save the foundering ship. Favors were called in. Clients squeezed. Risks very quickly hedged and positions unloaded. Despite the mayhem (and all the promises of drama in *Liar's Poker*) I rarely saw anyone lose their cool for longer than two seconds. We bled, but others died, and you felt fortunate to have a front-row seat at the biggest financial show in a generation.

What's a derivative? Here, I'll create one for you. I just signed my name on a slip of paper. If my writerly reputation takes off thanks to the book that you (and hopefully a million other people) are holding in your hands, then that slip of paper becomes an autograph, and could be worth thousands in the sweet by and by. If, alternatively, I die in complete obscurity, that signature is worth zero; less than zero, you'd pay someone to dispose of it. The noteworthy details are that the derivative holds no intrinsic worth of its own, and rather derives its value completely from some other thing: in this case, my authorial renown. Also important is how wide its value can swing; a banker would call this "highly levered." It could be nothing, or it could be thousands. While the underlying value of my writing skill will fluctuate within a relatively narrow band even if I'm successful, in the improbable event of literary immortality, that derivative can be worth very much indeed (or nothing at all).

What's a credit-default swap (CDS) then? A CDS is like car insurance, except it protects a pile of money someone has lent, rather than a pile of glass and steel called an automobile. Some asshole keys your car and destroys $500 of value; the insurance contract pays you that amount. The thing gets stolen? The policy pays out the total value of the car. Credit-default swaps work superficially the same way. You lend someone money in the form of a bond. They don't pay you back, or pay you back only partially? The guy who sold you the CDS makes you whole again, and you recover what you lost by lending money.

Here the similarity ends, however.

Unlike with car insurance, with CDSs anyone can get a policy on your car, even if he or she has no material interest in it. In other words, people other than the car owner can insure it. Not only can they take out a policy, they can write one as well—that is, act as their own mini-GEICO—and offer to repay losses. If the price of insurance is too high given the risk, and badly mispriced in some way, then greedy market players will be happy to sell you some. Perhaps they know you keep your car in a garage in an otherwise dangerous neighborhood, and therefore insurance for you is needlessly expensive. Or perhaps the opposite: they're car thieves and plan on stealing it, and want to profit both from stealing your car and from cashing in the insurance claim on it. And so they buy a policy before they commit the theft. Wall Street does that too.

"Credit" is the third-person singular conjugation of the present tense of the Latin verb *credere*, "to believe." It's the most exceptional and interesting thing in the financial world. Similar leaps of belief underlie every human transaction in life: Your wife might cheat on you, but you hope otherwise. The online store you paid may not ship you your goods, but you trust otherwise. Credit derivatives are just the explicit encapsulations of such beliefs, in financial and contractual form, for corporate entities. Unlike other financial securities, such as shares of IBM stock or oil futures, a credit derivative is not even some theoretical value of a tangible good. It's the perceived value of a complete intangible, the perception of the probability of meeting some future obligation.

People often asked me in the early days of my tech career

how I had gone from Wall Street to ads technology. Such a person almost certainly knew nothing about either industry, or the answer would have been obvious. I did the same thing the whole time: putting a price on a human's perception, be it of a General Motors bond or a pair of shoes coveted on Zappos. It's the same difference either way; only the scale of the money pile changes.

For a random reason I'd soon forget, in early 2006 I walked onto the interest-rates trading floor inside Goldman's headquarters at 85 Broad Street, and detected the stomach-churning odor of fast-food grease. Two whole rows of desks, formerly occupied by tense traders speaking tersely into phones, were now occupied by what appeared to be a rowdy battalion of kids in their best Century 21 finery.* Crowds of traders, dressed in very *not*–Century 21 finery, surrounded them, like the beginnings of a lynch mob. Alan Brazil, the managing director for mortgage strategies at Goldman Sachs, was rationing out small, paperbound grease pucks, like a World War I commanding officer handing out munitions to his troops before an assault.

It was, of course, the White Castle burger-eating contest.

All trading turned from interest-rate swaps (minimum notional size: $50 million) to wagering on which young Goldman acolyte would down the most White Castle burgers in an hour. The betting structure was a typical Vegas-style over/under bet on how many burgers would be eaten without puking. The surrounding crowd turned into a howling, gesticulating mass of electrified greed, with the serious traders signaling to each other and actually writ-

---

* Century 21 is an endearingly retrograde discount department store housed just off the northern border of the Financial District in Manhattan. Its only real selling point was a $40 Hugo Boss shirt you had to try on (pins still in the fabric, and soon into you) right there on the floor.

ing down trades in notebooks, as they would million-dollar positions.

The odds-on favorite was a young analyst named Rich Rosenblum, who employed the Kobayashi technique to get the tiny grease pucks down.* This involved splitting them in half and dunking the bready, greasy mess into a cup of water to premoisten them for easier inhalation.

The underdog was a blond female intern from Princeton who looked like she weighed maybe as much as a dozen burgers. A circle of her friends piled into the over side of her betting book, betting on incongruously high numbers for her, all the while knowing her secret Princeton eating-club rap sheet—insider trading at its finest.

And there she went! Blowing past fifteen burgers, and approaching twenty, to everyone's surprise. At twenty-two she was tied with the going leader, Rich. Then, the unexpected: the fat Asian kid next to her, who was looking a bit queasy, started projectile-vomiting burger chunks. Alan Brazil, the old burger contest capo, instantly jumped in with a plastic garbage can to catch the mess. The blond girl's support crew, who had knowingly entered this burger black hole into the race for shits and profits, started madly waving their arms and egging her on to distract her from the puke-o-rama next door. If she tuned into the vomit monsoon, it could unleash an upchuck chain reaction! Alan wisely walked the Asian kid and the barf pail off the floor. Rosenblum's count reached twenty-six, as recorded on the leaderboard, but the blond Princetonian managed to get to the over side of her insider-trading racket's bet, which was all her betting syndicate needed. The crowd went wild as the hour expired, and

* Takeru Kobayashi is a pint-sized Japanese man who holds or has held most major records in the revolting "sport" of competitive eating. He pioneered such innovative speed-eating techniques as the dunking described here. He once ate sixty-four hot dogs in ten minutes at Nathan's Famous at Coney Island, in 2009.

just as quickly the entire riot disbursed as everyone hurried back to phones and risk reports. The trading floor smelled like the inside of a deep fryer for the whole day. Capitalism marched inexorably onward.*

Of course, the betting didn't stop at burgers. Analysts would be pressed into push-up contests, with over/under bets on the total. And so, on a random walk across the floor, busily engaged with the important work of capitalism, one could trip on a trading analyst and a particularly fit sales VP, faces red with exertion, sweating through their pressed shirts and pumping out their 237th push-up in an hour, with shouted bets raging all around.

On Friday afternoons, to shatter the preweekend slump, the entire desk would play an interesting game. Everybody chucked his or her corporate ID into a sack, and anted up something like twenty to one hundred dollars (higher ranks paid more). Then the head trader would remove the IDs one by one from the sack, calling out the names. The last ID in the sack got the entire pot. It was winner take all, and no splitting the pot at the end. When there were only twenty or so IDs left, things got *really* interesting: a mob formed, and trading started. People with IDs left in the sack sold their IDs to the highest bidder, selling out early and monetizing rather than risking elimination. Fair value for an ID is a simple calculation: if the pot is \$2,000 and there are 10 IDs left, then the option on one ID is just \$2,000 ÷ 10 = \$200. That's not the way the market traded, though; IDs would inevitably sell for a premium, and the closer the process was to a close (i.e., the smaller the number of IDs left) the higher the premium got on a percentage basis. Mentally, people were irrationally willing to overbid for a large payout, and the likelier the payout, the more they'd overpay. Also,

* And what became of Rich Rosenblum, he of the Rabelaisian burger stamina? He eventually made managing director at Goldman Sachs and rose to be its senior oil options trader. Capitalism rewards true talent.

there were structural forces at work: it was Friday afternoon in New York, and people wanted the cash to blow on the weekend. I bet that steak at Peter Luger tasted even better if it was bought with the trading floor's money. The winner would pocket (if he could) the thick stack of twenties and hundreds, and everyone would take back his or her ID. By five p.m., the trading floor was a ghost town.

To fans of irony, Wall Street provided endless delectation. The all-out, unfettered, and glorified pursuit of gain was like sex in pubescent adolescence: it was all you could think about, and all you wanted to think about. But there was corporate decorum to maintain all the same. We were doing God's work, remember. (God is certainly also doing Goldman's work, from the looks.) And so, after a particularly competitive round of Friday afternoon push-ups and ID bingo, a memo about office decorum went out to the entire floor. It boiled down to a reminder that betting was prohibited on the trading floor. It reminded me of that classic scene in *Dr. Strangelove* in which the character played by George C. Scott gets into a wrestling match with the Russian ambassador inside the control room at the Pentagon, and is sternly admonished: "Gentlemen, you can't fight in here. This is the war room!"

No fucking in the brothel either, dear comrades!

While on Wall Street, I had the good fortune to witness the tail end of an epochal historical transformation. Given my role in the derivatives markets, this transformation was something glimpsed from afar, but its impact was profound, and relevant to our story.

In September 2000, way before the events depicted here, Goldman Sachs acquired a decades-old company called Spear, Leeds & Kellogg. SLK was an old-school stockbroker and market-making firm that ran markets on exchange-traded stocks and options. It employed armies of traders and clerks, the sort of people in colored jackets busily gesticulating at one another across some mosh pit such as you see at the Chicago Mercantile Exchange. Those hundreds of traders were serviced by a couple of programmers with basic options-pricing models running on a few machines.

By 2007, those hundreds of traders were gone. Instead, there were two traders, twenty quants building and maintaining models, and hundreds of very fast machines running code. Those guys in colored jackets who still populate a few exchanges? Like the dinosaur fossils at a natural history museum, they're there only for show. They've been replaced by expensive blinking boxes housed as close as possible to the real exchange, and connected with the shortest cables one can buy, rent, or bury in the ground.

In this new world, the only speed limits were Moore's law and Einstein's relativity: the business logic was as fast as microchips can do math without melting themselves, and as fast as pulses of light can fly through fiber-optic cables. The key insight here is that what happened with SLK wasn't some exceptional niche piece of technological innovation, but a harbinger of what would happen to the entire world. In the future, anywhere nontrivial decisions took place, it would be computers talking to one another, with humans involved only in the writing of the logic itself. Finance saw the innovation first, because the stakes were high, and the value of an incremental computational advantage was very large.

To paraphrase the very quotable Silicon Valley venture capitalist Marc Andreessen, in the future there will be two types of jobs: people who tell computers what to do, and people who are told by computers what to do. Wall Street was merely the first inkling. The next place where this shift would be seen at whopping scale in terms of both money and technology (though I didn't realize at the time) was in Internet advertising. And after that, it would hit transportation (Uber), hostelry (Airbnb), food delivery (Instacart), and so on. To take the theory further, computation would no longer fill some hard gap in a human workflow process, such as the calculators used by accountants. Humans would fill the hard gaps in a purely computer workflow process, like Uber's drivers. But we're getting ahead of ourselves.

There's an additional lesson here.

This shift from humans to computers took place predominantly on the equity side of things. The debt side of the financial world, for various reasons, still traded in what amounted to open-outcry markets with humans talking to one another, whether through phones or instant messaging systems. It was capitalism at the speed a tongue can wag or hands can type. This was mostly because a company's debt is complex and multifarious, and entities like General Motors have hundreds if not thousands of different types of debt floating around the world's trading floors. Briefly, they are not what economists call "fungible," meaning interchangeable the way quarter-inch screws or bottle caps are.

Credit derivatives are different, though. Protection against General Motors' default is just that, a guarantee against a clear and one-time event. The only thing that varies, and even that in standardized time windows, is how long the policy lasts (e.g., three months or three years). To continue the car analogy, when an insurance company insures your jalopy, it doesn't take into account the infinite combinations of features, car colors, wheel rims, postpurchase modifications, and dangling air fresheners. It knows the make, model, year, and location of the vehicle, and the value insured. That's it. There are really only a few hundred types of car insurance when you break it down; likewise with credit-default swaps.

So why not trade CDSs on exchanges, as we do shares of Google? The question was raised in 2008 as the financial world burned. The internal chatter on the desk was that the government would exploit the crisis to regulate our Wild West market. Goldman (briefly) considered taking the initiative and self-regulating into exchange-traded markets instead. It decided against doing so, with reasoning I'd see again at Facebook: an incumbent in a market dominated by a few, with total information asymmetry, and the ability to make prices on the market rather than just take them, has little incentive to increase transparency. The bid-ask spread—that is, Goldman's difference in price when buying or selling the same thing—was huge on credit derivatives. Goldman made fortunes simply passing a piece of paper from its left hand to its right, from seller of risk to buyer of it. While trading on exchanges might have increased the overall volume of trade and hence profits, the openness would have eroded Goldman's privileged view of the credit markets, and opened it to upstart competition, not to mention financial scrutiny. Even if the open approach had increased the total size of the market, Goldman felt more comfortable owning a small market than merely participating in a larger one. Thus, many markets were and are inefficient, because that inefficiency is very profitable to those running the market, even if only in the short-term picture.

As I would eventually see, Wall Street and Silicon Valley possess surprising parallels.

I envy the religious. Their inner lives are so blessed. If you're Christian, do as the Gospel says, live a Christlike life, and salvation is yours. If you're Orthodox Jewish, wear all black and a Borsalino, check off your share of the 613 mitzvoth, and you can await the messiah with an untroubled heart. No gnawing sense of existential dread when staring at a godless, star-filled night sky.

Wall Street is even simpler than religion. Your entire worth as a human is defined by one number: the compensation number your boss tells you at the end of the year. Pay on Wall Street works as follows: your base salary is actually quite modest, but your "bonus" is where the real money is. That bonus is completely discretionary, and can vary anywhere from zero to a multiple of your base salary.

So, come mid-December, everyone on the desk lines up outside the partner's office, like the Communion line at Christmas Mass, and awaits his or her little crumb off the big Wall Street table. An entire year's worth of blood, sweat, and tears comes down to that one moment. And the entire New York economy marches to the beat of that bonus drum.

Without that number, your privileged place in the New York hierarchy goes away. Gone is the house in the Hamptons. Gone is the duplex on the Upper West Side. Gone is your kid's $30,000 preschool. And that's why Wall Street has that roach-motel quality: people check in, but rarely check out. By the time you've been through a couple of bonus cycles and seen that wad of cash hit your bank account in mid-January, you can't imagine a life without it—which is exactly how the senior management at the Wall Street banks like it. If Wall Street investment bankers were dogs, they would flaunt their expensive collars and leashes as marks of status, not realizing their true purpose. My collar was tiny in the scheme of things, but enough to rub my neck raw.

Such canine reflections were on my mind one day while reading the *New York Times* during a lull at the trading desk. To an active market participant, the *New York Times*' business section is so dated and slow to respond, it may as well be a history book. Which is why it was very random indeed that I noticed something on recently funded Silicon Valley startups. Given the pestilential news from the Street, an upbeat headline must have shone like a blinking fluorescent sign. Almost in passing, the article quoted the CEO of a company called Adchemy, which had just raised its third round of financing. The one-line description was something about using mathematics for advertising. Checking out their website, I noted there was an open position for something called a "research scientist." On an absolute whim, almost as a man enlists in the army or consents to a tattoo, I sent them my CV. Then I completely forgot about it.

A week later Adchemy's recruiter called and offered to fly me to California. With nothing to do but watch capitalism fibrillate, I accepted, and a few days later I was back in the Bay Area I had left three years earlier. Perhaps because I didn't really give a damn, I breezed through the gauntlet of interviews, rederiving the probabilities around the birthday paradox with a newly minted PhD named David Kauchak, and together with the VP of Research, filling a wall-sized whiteboard with some long-winded calculation or another. All I really remember is that I managed to cadge a Ford Mustang out of the rental agency, and once released from interview hell at six p.m. I still had a good three hours until my flight.

I then embarked on what had really drawn me to SF: I hightailed it to the Mission District, parked the rental in that somewhat dodgy neighborhood, and went to Zeitgeist for one of their Bloody Marys.* It was as epic as I remembered. I bolted the pint of vodka, chili pepper brine, tomato juice, heap of horseradish, and phallic arrangement of pickled string beans and two olives, and hopped back into the Mustang, barreling it to the airport. I forgot all about Adchemy.

A week later the company called to offer me the job. Capitalism, at least as engineered by my soon-to-be-former Goldman colleagues, was on life support. I had a gut intuition that the insulated and insular world of tech would be the last man standing in the coming collapse. So I haggled the Adchemy offer from the Goldman Sachs trading floor on my personal phone, while contemplating the starry Milky Way of Manhattan's skyline. I felt like the one guy inflating the life raft while everyone else was still bailing water on the sinking ship, and yelling "Aye, aye!" to the captain.

---

* Zeitgeist, if you'll excuse a geek reference, is like the bar on Tatooine in *Star Wars*. You can probably get hep B from using the toilets. On a sunny Saturday afternoon, its beer garden is the best hangout in San Francisco. You'll get high as a kite from the secondary pot smoke alone.

A week before my last day, I had lunch with the only senior person at Goldman Sachs who was not an inveterate asshole. Scott Weinstein had been my boss briefly, and in previous corporate lives had headed the electrical power trading desk business and the credit-default swap quant team, where I anxiously built models and calculated risk. He was older by a decade than most people at the managing director level, and had been at Goldman for going on twenty years, though he had never made partner. Due to some vascular reason, perhaps his smoking, his face bloomed in a tomato-red flush when excited, which was most of the time. Combined with his barrel-chested frame and fast, staccato speaking clip of indeterminate East Coast origin (Philly? Baltimore?), you got the feeling he was about to burst into some Scorsese-esque paroxysm of violence at any moment. He was about the only genuine person I ever met on the trading floor.

Sitting in the forty-seventh-floor Goldman Sachs canteen, with sweeping 360-degree views of Lower Manhattan and New York Harbor, we kibitzed about the various internal dramas the financial zombie apocalypse had caused. Finally, awkwardly, we got to the topic of my departure. I was a tiny fly on a big cow's ass at Goldman, but at least within my small circle, the news that I was leaving "the game" for some dodgy California startup was a topic of interest. Most people thought I was crazy.

"Don't you ever think about venturing out and doing your own thing, and not this big-company stuff, Scott?" I asked, gesturing at the cloud of worker bees around us, pounding their sensible salads before heading back to the trading hive.

"My parents ran a small family business, and I watched them go through all the stresses of that . . . the ups and the downs. The uncertainty of their lives was terrible on them. I could never imagine going through that myself. Goldman isn't perfect, but it'll be here a long time. I wouldn't want to live with the insecurity."

Within a few months, Scott Weinstein's two-decade-long career at Goldman would come to an abrupt end. His final gig had been at the bank loans desk, a business that had suffered considerable losses in the financial debacle. Things were tense in the bank loans group, and an argument between Scott and the head trader escalated into a vendetta. Scott was sacked—just like that. Scott quickly, as these things go, found a comparable role at another bank, but the irony of the security-seeking loyal employee getting the ax never left me.

In all my experience in both startups and large companies, including and especially at Facebook, I would always prefer—a hundred times prefer—being subject to the rigors of the market, the fickleness of luck, and the whims of users than to navigate the popularity-contest politics of a large company, surrounded by the mediocre duffers who've succeeded in life through nothing more than guile and appearances. Scott Weinstein's unfortunate example was the best advice he (or anyone else) has ever given me, and one that I ignored to my extreme peril.

A week after that lunch, I cleared out my belongings from the apartment I shared with my (now) ex-girlfriend, hopped into a convertible BMW, and drove into the setting sun for six days to return to California and the adventure awaiting me.

The Human Attention Exchange

> The spectacle is capital accumulated to the point where it becomes image.
>
> —Guy Debord, *The Society of Spectacle*

APRIL 24, 2008

"Count backwards from one hundred, but say every seventh number," ordered Officer Klein. Five feet two in her police-issue patent-leather shoes. I tried not to look at her uniformed and badge-decorated breasts. The etiolated state of my brain wasn't helping.

"100, 93, 86, 79, 72, 65, 58, 51, 44, 37, 30, 23, 16, 9, 2 . . . should I go into the negatives?" I asked solicitously. After years of using mathematics for a living, I could do this all night, even while three sheets to the wind.

"What level of education have you achieved?" asked Officer Klein.

I found that question telling.

Some police officers are bullies who enable their sadism via a badge. Most officers, however, are really just reactionaries, believers in some simplistic Manichaean duality of the universe, in which everyone is intrinsically good or evil. Sworn defenders of order, these officers protect property and its patrician owners from violence and thievery; they separate moral wheat from chaff, and discern the no-good criminal from the upstanding citizen. Such judgment is their calling, their vocation, with the full backing of whatever jerkwater town is paying for the uniforms and squad cars. To earn their leniency, you just have to be perceived as someone from the good side who has momentarily gone astray and ventured into the dark. Just a little nudge to put you back on the straight and narrow.

Which is what I did.

"PhD level. In fact, you can see my coworkers right here. We work at a venture-backed startup in the area. It's our company happy hour. I'm a research scientist there," I said, gesturing to the handful of Adchemy employees who had come out to watch the show of a new employee being arrested. I was trying to wear my respectability like a perfume.

Officer Klein stood there hesitatingly.

This was when her backup, a thick-necked, latter-day Bull Connor—the ur-authority figure who now stars in many a shooting video—stepped in.

"Sir, can we have you blow into this?" he ordered, proffering a piece of white plastic tubing as if it were one of the tequila shots I had just been downing.

Whether it be a Breathalyzer or a banana, you can't make eye contact with a man while going down on something. It's too weird. So I looked into the fuzzy distance while blowing into the law's little gadget.

Drumroll, please!

"0.91," declared Bull Connor.

Damnation. The Golden State's blood-alcohol limit while driving was 0.8.

This scene requires some explanation.

Every Thursday, a volatile nucleus of the youngest and most unattached Adchemists would stage a happy hour at one or another of the local watering holes. You'll believe me when I say that between bohemian grad school and dissolute Wall Street with corporate AmEx, I had done enough happy-hour liver damage to earn the dubious rank of lush. But these new capers were cataclysmic alcoholic implosions beyond any reason or planning. They left all of Friday and part of Saturday a smoking ruin. This was my first such outing, and my "good behavior" plan had evaporated the moment I made out with the cute Asian colleague at the bar. A round of tequila had followed an additional make-out session in the bathroom, which had led to things I couldn't then or now remember. Amid the swirl, I had noticed that my research colleague Dave, the suave bastard, had made off with the Asian girl. Twinges of Latin possessiveness tugging, I ventured out into the night to see where my prize had gone. Spotting what seemed to be their receding backs in the urban distance, I double-timed it after them, only to get disoriented in the unending commercial blah of downtown San Mateo. Retracing my steps, I found myself next to the BMW 3-series convertible that had driven me across amber waves of grain and purple mountain majesties, from East Coast civilization to this air-conditioned startup nightmare. Convinced that the car needed to be saved from inexplicable dangers, I decided to drive it closer to the bar, whose geographic location was now somewhat vague. Engine started, clutch popped, we were rolling.

In the Southern California of my birth, we are endowed by our Creator with the self-evident right to make U-turns.* In Northern California, matters are more regulated. I made

---

* While raised in the cradle of the Cuban exile in Miami, I was born in Southern California, making me more Californian than most Silicon Valley denizens.

an illegal U-turn on Third Street and back to the bar—upon which the blinking red-and-blues filled my periphery.

Bull Connor's face didn't fly into the grimace of triumphant but disapproving authority I had expected.

"So what happens now, officer?" I asked.

"You are above the California blood-alcohol level. You cannot drive," he stated flatly.

Evaluation time. I was over the limit, but not by much. If I acted like a whiny little bitch and insisted on a blood test at the station (my right under California law), he'd have to arrest me, stick me in the car, and drive me to the station. Then they'd have to set up the blood test. By the time all the crap was done, I'd be below the limit, and he'd have missed two hours at whatever DUI trap I had driven into, ruining his night.

Time for a gambit. Nothing to lose anyhow.

"How about I wait here with my fellow employees for an hour or so, until my level goes down?"

"If I let you do that, you're going to get right back in your car, and drive off."

This was progress. Before I was a perpetrator being castigated, now we were merely haggling.

"Well, officer, how about we call a cab, and you watch me get in it, and we call it a night?" I offered.

Officer Thick Neck thought for a moment. Then he nodded.

This was pre-Uber, so *dial, dial, dial motherfucker!* before they change their minds. The taxi drunkmobile pulled up, and with a wave to the gathered Adchemists and Officers Klein and Thick Neck, I was off. Eighty dollars later I was back in Cole Valley, San Francisco, in the cold bosom of the drafty Victorian I shared with two hippie chicks.

One week into my new Silicon Valley life, and the lesson was this: if you want to be a startup entrepreneur, get used to negotiating from positions of weakness. I'd soon have trickier situations to negotiate than convincing a cop to let me take a cab. And so will you if you play the startup game.

The next morning, I wasn't merely hungover, but was in fact still mildly drunk. The company all-hands meeting, wherein the entire company gathered to hear about new deals and employees, and generally to get pep-rallied by Murthy Nukala, the CEO, was scheduled for noon that day. I had to be there or risk having my coworkers file a missing persons report, as well as look like a pussy. My frazzled brain was slow to realize my car was still somewhere in San Mateo. One hundred and thirty dollars and too much sunlight later, I was standing beside my four-wheeled Bavarian steed at the scene of last night's triumph over the rule of law, and fifteen minutes later I was an acceptable five minutes late for the all-hands.

As I walked into the company-wide meeting, a murmur was heard from a corner of the assembled crowd, expressing either surprise or amusement at my being both alive and unincarcerated. The company rumor mill had been busy that morning. I probably looked as pickled and embalmed as I felt. Murthy launched into his weekly harangue. The wheels of capitalism ground ever on.

Every new form of media initially emulates the forms of the past. The first radio shows were merely people reading books on air, or playing instruments, with no use of clever sound effects or editing. The first TV shows were quiz shows that had originally appeared on radio, with mere headshots of the contestants. No sophisticated panning shots or jump cuts; simply the addition of a face to the spoken word.

Internet advertising has the same atavistic resemblance to the newspaper advertising that preceded it. The first such ads were run in *La Presse*, a Parisian paper, in 1836. Advertisement was originally a scheme to lower the paper's selling price and capture market share. A successful strategy, it was soon copied by all newspapers. The ads themselves were rectangular frames of advertiser-created content, placed either below or alongside regular content, and marked as distinct by their blocky frame and large, garish lettering.

Sound like an ad you saw on nytimes.com recently?

Of course, advertising isn't the only place where this happens. We refer to spacecraft as "ships" given their resemblance to the seafaring kind, and given the intellectual origins of space travel in the mathematics and engineering of marine navigation. This emulation is merely a result of the organic progression of our mad and clever species from one technological toy to another.

In the same way, marketers refer to websites and mobile apps as "publishers," a quaint reflection of the advertising world's origins in that of ink and newsprint. The "publisher" is simply the entity that brings the eyeballs to the auction block, whether via Pulitzer Prize–winning writing or a game in which you launch irate birds against antagonistic pigs. During the early days of Internet advertising, the publisher played a critical and powerful role. In the aughts, websites like Yahoo had an entire sales force (as newspapers still do) that sold those little squares of characters and images directly to advertisers. Many a fax and email flew around just to sell one "insertion order," in the industry argot (and a wonderful double entendre). The ability to target was nil; at best, one could indicate a certain part of the website for an advertisement to appear in (say, the movies section). Analytics and attribution—answering the question of who saw and eventually bought what—were equally nonexistent. The only difference between the Internet and highway billboards was that you didn't have to physically glue a poster somewhere.

By 2008, that had all changed, which is why a former

Wall Street quant like me was at Adchemy. A company called Right Media was allowing advertisers to segment users into specific clusters based on their actions on a given site (e.g., putting something in a shopping cart). Originating the notion of real-time data synchronization between the online world and specific publishers, Right Media even let you tag users that came to your site (or anywhere else) and find them again later. Acquired by Yahoo in 2007, it had developed the first "programmatic" media-buying technology; "programmatic" meaning media controllable via computers talking to one another, rather than humans talking to one another via sales calls. Additionally, one could target advertisements based on user demographics like age, sex, and geography. Media buying was no longer about putting a square on the automobile or real estate section, but about finding specific users anywhere and anyhow. All this data being generated, stored, and used, by both publisher and advertiser, made room for people who once priced credit derivatives to do the same for parcels of human attention instead.

Something else was going on.

In media, money is merely expendable ammunition; data is power. With this new programmatic technology that allowed each and every ad impression and user to be individually scrutinized and targeted, that power was shifting inexorably from the publisher, the owner of the eyeballs, to the advertiser, the person buying them. If my advertiser data about what you bought and browsed in the past was more important than publisher data like the fact that you were on Yahoo Autos right then, or that you were (supposedly) a thirty-five-year-old male in Ohio, then the power was mine as the advertiser to determine price and desirability of media, not the publisher's. As it turned out (and as Facebook would painfully realize in 2011, forming the dramatic climax of this book), this "first-party" advertiser data—the data that companies like Amazon know about you—is more valuable than most any publisher data.

This was a seismic shift that would affect everything about how we consume media, leaving publishers essentially powerless and at the service of the various middlemen between them and advertiser dollars, all in the name of targeting and accountability. If the publisher wasn't savvy enough to arm itself with sophisticated targeting and tracking before tangling with the media-buying world, then that world would come to them, in the form of countless arbitrageurs and data quacks peddling media snake oil. Which is why even august publishers like the *New York Times* live at the pleasure of the media supply-side technology, data management solutions, and advertiser technologies that ostensibly pay them. Of course, some very protective publishers like Facebook and Google, with unique media offerings, refuse to get arbitraged so openly, and to one degree or another, attempt to own the technical and business connection between them and the advertising dollars.

This is how online advertising works: money turns into pixels and electrons in the form of ads, which turn into a scintilla of attention in someone's mind, which after a few more clicks and electrons shuffling about, turns back into money. The only goal here is to make that second pile of money as large as possible relative to the first pile of money.

That's it.

Whether it be brand marketers trumpeting the new BMW X5, game developers getting players to spend real money on virtual goods, or someone selling an online nursing degree, the only difference is the time frame in which those different goals occur—in other words, the time between attention and action. If the time frame is very short, like browsing for and buying a shirt at nordstroms.com, it's called "direct response," or "DR" advertising. If the time frame is very long, such as making you believe life is unlivable outside the pricey mantle of a Burberry coat, it's called "brand advertising." Note that the goal is the same in both: to make you buy shit you likely don't need with money you likely don't have. In the former case, the trail is easily trackable, as the "conversion" usually happens online, usually after clicking on the very ad you were served.* In the latter, the media employed is a multipronged strategy of Super Bowl ads, Internet advertising, postal mail, free keychains, and God knows what else. Also, the conversion happens way after the initial exposure to the media, and often offline and in a physical space, like at a car dealership. The tracking and attribution are much harder, due to both the manifold media used and the months or years gone by between the exposure and the sale. As such, brand advertising budgets, which are far larger than direct-response ones, are spent in embarrassingly large broadsides, barely targeted or tracked in any way.

Now you know all there is to know about advertising. The rest is technical detail and self-promoting bullshit spun by agencies. You're officially as informed as the media tycoons who run the handful of agencies that manage our media world.

Here's something you may not know: every time you go to Facebook or ESPN.com or wherever, you're unleashing a mad scramble of money, data, and pixels that involves undersea fiber-optic cables, the world's best database technologies, and everything that is known about you by greedy strangers.

Every. Single. Time.

The magic of how this happens is called "real-time bidding" (RTB) exchanges, and we'll get into the technical details before long. For now, imagine that every time you go to CNN.com, it's as though a new sell order for one share in your brain is transmitted to a stock exchange. Picture it: individual quanta of human attention sold, bit by bit, like

* Marketers use "conversion" to indicate a sale, the way Mormons refer to souls saved.

so many million shares of General Motors stock, billions of times a day.

Remember Spear, Leeds & Kellogg, Goldman Sachs's old-school brokerage acquisition, and its disappearing (or disappeared) traders? The company went from hundreds of traders and two programmers to twenty programmers and two traders in a few years. That same process was just starting in the media world circa 2009, and is right now, in 2016, kicking into high gear.

As part of that shift, one of the final paroxysms of wasted effort at Adchemy was taking place precisely in the RTB space. An engineer named Matthew McEachen, one of Adchemy's best, and I built an RTB bidding engine that talked to Google's huge ad exchange, the figurative New York Stock Exchange of media, and submitted bids and ads at speeds of upwards of one hundred thousand requests per second. We had been ordered to do so only to feed some bullshit line Murthy was laying on potential partners that we were a real-time ads-buying company. Like so much at Adchemy, that technology would be a throwaway, but the knowledge I gained there, from poring over Google's RTB technical documentation and passing Google's merciless integration tests with our code, would set me light-years ahead of the clueless product team at Facebook years later.

If you had told me at the time I wouldn't have believed you, but one day I'd be writing the technical docs and running the integration tests for Google's biggest ad exchange competitor, Facebook Exchange. But I was far, far away from that during those dark days.

Knowing How to Swim

> An empty pageant; a stage play; flocks of sheep, herds of cattle; a bone flung among a pack of dogs; a crumb tossed into a pond of fish; ants, loaded and laboring; mice, scared and scampering; puppets, jerking on their strings; that is life.
>
> In the midst of it all you must take your stand, good-temperedly and without disdain, yet always aware that *a man's worth is no greater than the worth of his ambitions*.
>
> —Marcus Aurelius, *Meditations*

FEBRUARY 2010

It's not the rats who first abandon a sinking ship. It's the crew members who know how to swim.

By January 2010 it was abundantly clear that Adchemy was a complete failure, a hecatomb of human effort sacrificed at the false altar of Murthy's ego. Real-life experience is instructive, but the tuition is high.

The first sign of trouble was an externally visible one, a symptom that any suitably experienced startup practitioner could have detected: nobody from the early days of the company was still around other than Murthy. Every other single cofounder or early employee had left. As Vonnegut wrote in *Bluebeard*, never trust the survivor of a massacre until you know what he did to survive. And indeed in this case, Murthy wasn't a mere survivor, but rather an author of said massacre.

Like Stalin's USSR doctoring photos featuring former party favorites, removing the now-purged victims from its history, a startup will disappear the former founders and employees from its "Team" page online. The official history of the startup, at least as told by itself, will only ever mention the current leadership, and reweave some narrative about how the current team is the God-ordained combination of human talents that will take the startup to the stratosphere. This is utter tripe, but it's the party line you'll be told. Discreet inquiries on CrunchBase or LinkedIn, or emails to professional connections, tell the real tale.* Don't work for the survivors or architects of massacres. You'll live just long enough to regret it.

Here's a second sign: the startup makes money, lots of it. You heard right. This was another illustrative Adchemy problem, though a relatively rare one. Adchemy made software that automated and optimized the laborious task of running ad campaigns. In Silicon Valley, there's a piece of tech-speak called "dogfooding," which basically means using your own product.† The idea in this case was to have

* CrunchBase is the database of people and companies that's the who's who (if I can use that phrase without puking) of Silicon Valley. The parent publication of CrunchBase, *TechCrunch* (hence the name), is the day-to-day news and gossip rag of the Silicon Valley carnival.

† The origin of the term "dogfooding" is supposedly found in eighties Microsoft, which coined the phrase from Alpo dog food commercials at the time wherein Lorne Greene assured a perhaps dubious public that he fed his own dogs Alpo. Ergo "dogfood" as the Valley term for using your own product, with the implication of its being a vote of confidence.

a marketing team actually running marketing campaigns, and then selling the prospective customers in a legal but slightly sketchy underbelly of the online world called the "lead generation" industry. Adchemy sold nothing itself, only the lists of people it had found via ads to those who actually sold something, like a mortgage refinancing or a criminology degree. It's serious business, though, and Adchemy made something like $6 million per month selling mortgage leads to QuickenLoans, and online education leads to the University of Phoenix (I want to take a shower just reading those names). In the same way that a trust fund just makes a drug addict's spiral more long lasting and painful, a cash-generating business that doesn't improve the product postpones the inevitable by floating the charade, all the while actually making failure more likely. This strategy can work as far as keeping a company afloat while it's working out the kinks in its core program, but it's tricky, and it requires absolute management discipline to not lose focus on the product the company was created to perfect. Murthy was like the one heroin-addicted lab rat who could never stop hitting the lever for more.

Third, Adchemy had no clients for the actual product. An absolutely clear sign of flailing failure is when a company's quarterly report features a new set of corporate logos, each a breathlessly awaited beta customer who's just going to blow the doors off usage or revenue in the future.* That's fine for one quarterly report, but after a year's worth of an ever-changing list of beta customers, with none morphing into

---

* More startupese for you: Products are loosely classified into two initial versions, "alpha" and "beta." "Alpha" is a very incomplete and (probably) buggy version of the product that only very daring (to not say foolish) test clients ("alpha customers") would even venture to try. "Beta" is still an initial version, but with most of the first kinks fixed. A "beta customer" is therefore an early customer, but still one using a product vaguely on this side of more or less a production, running version.

full-on clients with contracts and recurring revenue, you're chasing a mirage. All you're seeing is a logo version of the sales team's leads list as they churn through potential clients.

The last symptom of terminal illness, counterintuitively enough, is loyal employees.

Despite the mismanagement, many of Adchemy's two hundred or so employees felt a strong sense of loyalty to both Murthy and the company. Many of these were very skilled professionals who could have been employed elsewhere, who nonetheless put up not only with the poor management of the company but also with outright mistreatment. Murthy's tantrums were legendary, and he often insulted employees and in some instances fired them without cause. He once broke my finger when he flung a baseball at me with no warning (I was standing in front of floor-to-ceiling glass, and was forced to catch a fastball), and then mocked me for it publicly for months, merely for the sake of fun.* And yet many of his employees spoke well of the company and even exercised their options to buy company stock, causing them to lose large portions of their life savings when the company folded.† Even after quitting or being fired, former employees

---

* He broke my left ring finger, right across the last joint, in a common baseball injury known as "mallet finger." During the later strife with Adchemy I'll soon tell you about, I used to intentionally bend that joint with my other hand, to feel the dull ache from the poorly setting break, and remind myself of whom I was up against.

† Startup employees who leave before a "liquidity event" like an IPO or an acquisition have a set period (usually ninety days) to either exercise their options, often at considerable cost, or lose whatever equity compensation they received, no matter how long they've been at the company. The way to think about startup employment is this: you're earning the right, via your labor and time, to invest in the company, at the stock price of the last fund-raising round, just as the company's initial venture capitalists did. That's the real compensation you're earning, and many a former employee agonizes over the decision of whether to plunk down the pile of money or not. If you wouldn't invest in a company from the get-go, you're a fool

would host Adchemy alum happy hours and get back together, like some reunion tour. Here's the lesson: when the company's employee retention strategy is cultivating Stockholm syndrome, you're in the wrong company.

Saint Augustine thought the best way to heavenly salvation was to know the route to hell, but avoid it. Consider the various paths to hell I've taken for you, dear reader, and do otherwise.

If everyone believes in delusions such as democracy or religion, they sort of become true—certainly more true than when a delusion is nothing but a presumptuous neuronal spark in someone's mind. If you consider yourself a Gates or a Musk but aren't seen as one, then you enter the realm of felt injustice. You assign yourself a certain value, but society ranks you at another. That difference between society's perception and your own is the gap of injustice you feel. Multiply that gap times your ego, and you get the total balance of rage you're to expend in your startup quest.

In just such a rage-filled state I began working on our Y Combinator application.

Two other Adchemists and I had clicked socially, and for months were constantly chatting about startup ideas. One you've already met: Matthew McEachen, a.k.a. MRM, with whom I'd built the real-time bidding engine. He was the company's longest-serving and most productive engineer, and we had collaborated, he as lead engineer and I as research scientist, on a number of projects. The second was Argyris Zymnis, a recent graduate from a famous artificial intelligence lab at Stanford. He was one of the rising stars at Adchemy, due to both his high-level machine-learning brains and his coding skill.

---

to work for it, as the cash compensation in a startup is typically woefully below market.

Aside from our lunchtime conversations and odd Sunday phone call, though, we hadn't formulated any clear business idea. Procrastinating on a Monday, I decided to read an essay by Paul Graham. PG, as he's known to the cognoscenti, founded an online store builder called Viaweb in the early days of the Web, which got bought in the $40 million range in 1997, and eventually became Yahoo Shopping. In his postacquisition freedom, he created one of the more incredible institutions in Silicon Valley: Y Combinator.*

Twice a year, every year, Y Combinator accepts a few dozen startup hopefuls into what can only be described as a startup boot camp.† They are given a tiny amount of money and the goal of shipping a product by the end of three months. Some come in with nothing but a few hacked-up lines of code and an idea; some have entire going concerns that have already raised money.‡ Three months later, they all pitch at Demo Day, a major event on the Bay Area's venture capital calendar.§

---

* The name Y Combinator comes from a type of function in the wonky world of formal mathematical logic. Speaking loosely, it's a type of recursive function: in other words, a function that takes itself as an argument. What I imagine PG intended in the name was that Y Combinator was a startup that generated yet more startups, which is indeed what it became.

† This number was in the thirty-or-so range in 2010, but was pushing a hundred by 2015.

‡ Among the technical, "hacking" as it's understood among civilians—namely, illegally breaking into and messing with computer systems—is only a secondary meaning of the word. The primary meaning is the building of systems and software, with a connotation of rough tinkering rather than fine craftsmanship. "I hacked an old Windows box to run Apple OS X," a hacker might say about some particularly interesting kludge. A "kludge," of course, is an instance of hacking.

§ Venture capitalists (VCs for short) are the bettors at the startup casino, funding startups from the earliest stages, at which investments are the price of a new car or less, to the latest, in which funding rounds can be in the hundreds of millions of dollars.

PG is the leading apostle, to not say messiah, of the startup gospel, and other than maybe Marc Andreessen, possesses the only prose style among techies that doesn't trigger a literary gag reflex. His lucid essays dispense with any ego and pretense, and read like a how-to manual for the tech endeavor. Reflecting his background in philosophy and formal logic, his tightly argued disquisitions often read almost syllogistically, like a Socratic dialogue, as he dissects funding rounds, hiring, cash flow, and product development.

Having forgotten the URL to his essay library, I entered "ycombinator.com" into my browser. The minimalist website carried a picture of a geek in a weird orange-walled room, some links to press coverage, and one link that was tantalizingly titled "Apply to get funded. Deadline March 3, 2010."

Isn't that something?

Thought #1: We should apply.

Thought #2: It's March 1.

That very afternoon, I pulled the classic move you too should use to seduce a potential cofounder into leaving his or her steady-paycheck job. I gave Argyris a physical copy of "How to Start a Startup," a blog post by Paul Graham, which is the crack-like gateway drug to the startup addiction.

We spent the next two days clandestinely hammering out our pitch in the office, or playing hooky and working at a nearby Peet's Coffee. I did most of the actual writing.

What is writing?

It's me, the author, taking the state inside my mind and, via the gift of language, grafting it onto yours. But man invented language in order to better deceive, not inform. That state I'm transmitting is often a false one, but you judge it not by the depth of its emotion in my mind, but by the beauty and pungency of the thought in yours. Thus the best deceivers are called articulate, as they make listeners and readers fall in love with the thoughts projected into their heads. It's the essential step in getting men to write you large checks, women to take off their clothes, and the crowd to read and repeat what you've thought. All with mere words: memes of meaning strung together according to grammar and good taste. Astonishing when you think about it.

The boys started hacking on a basic demo we'd be able to present, assuming we managed to beat the terrible odds and get invited to pitch the YC partners.

Specialization of labor was already happening. The boys were good at making computers do hard things via code. I was good at making people do hard things via language—and good at figuring out what big bets were worth making. The boys weren't totally convinced about this YC stuff: the money was a pittance, the equity taken large, the benefit unclear (to them). But I was as convinced as a Bible-beater is about Jesus that this would be an essential step in our future, and I would be proved more than right.

So what idea were we pitching exactly?

The short answer: it didn't matter.

Like the canniest early-stage investors, YC cared a lot more about the team at this point than whatever improbable idea we might have. The latter was really there only to judge the former; it was valueless in itself.

Don't believe me? Think your idea is worth something?

Go and try to sell it, and see what sort of price you'll get for it. Ideas without implementation, or without an exceptional team to implement them, are like assholes and opinions: everyone's got one.

Incidentally, the fastest way you can indicate your level of startup naïveté to a VC (or to anybody in tech), is either by claiming you're in "stealth"—that is, with an idea so secretly valuable you can't disclose it—or by forcing someone to sign a nondisclosure agreement before you even discuss it. You may as well tattoo LOSER on your forehead instead, to save everyone the trouble. To quote one Valley sage, if your idea is any good, it won't get stolen, you'll have to jam it down people's throats instead.

For the record, though, here's what we came up with:

One of the great challenges in marketing is the divide between the online and the offline worlds. What you buy via the Internet and your digital persona is completely separate from what you buy in person, and the two data streams rarely cross. Imagine if an advertiser knew you bought SUV-sized packages of diapers at your local Walmart; how would it target different Internet ads at you? Conversely, if you were searching online for a particular gadget, how do you know if it's sitting at your local Best Buy, ready to be bought, rather than your waiting two or three days for Amazon Prime? Our idea boiled down to building an app that allowed local store owners to scan a product's bar code, which would then instantly generate an online ad campaign that advertised the fact that the product was for sale locally.

Here's some startup pedagogy for you:

When confronted with any startup idea, ask yourself one simple question: How many miracles have to happen for this to succeed?

If the answer is zero, you're not looking at a startup, you're just dealing with a regular business like a laundry or a trucking business. All you need is capital and minimal execution, and assuming a two-way market, you'll make some profit.

To be a startup, miracles need to happen. But a precise number of miracles.

Most successful startups depend on one miracle only. For Airbnb, it was getting people to let strangers into their spare bedrooms and weekend cottages. This was a user-behavior miracle. For Google, it was creating an exponentially better search service than anything that had existed to date. This was a technical miracle. For Uber or Instacart, it was getting people to book and pay for real-world services via websites or phones. This was a consumer-workflow miracle. For Slack, it was getting people to work like they formerly chatted with their girlfriends. This is a business-workflow miracle.

For the makers of most consumer apps (e.g., Instagram),

the miracle was quite simple: getting users to use your app, and then to realize the financial value of your particular twist on a human brain interacting with keyboard or touchscreen. That was Facebook's miracle, getting every college student in America to use its platform during its early years. While there was much technical know-how required in scaling it—and had they fucked that up it would have killed them—that's not *why* it succeeded. The uniqueness and complete fickleness of such a miracle are what make investing in consumer-facing apps such a lottery. It really is a user-growth roulette wheel with razor-thin odds.

The classic sign of a shitty startup idea is that it requires at least two (or more!) miracles to succeed. This was what was wrong with ours. We had a Bible's worth of miracles to perform:

Small-business owners had to use us for all their marketing.

We had to solve the scanning-a-bar-code-with-a-phone problem.*

We had to generate a comprehensive retail product database, with relevant metadata like prices, reviews, and model numbers.

We had to programmatically generate ad campaigns based on that product database.

We had to design the world's best small-biz marketing and campaign management workflow, one that allowed even unsavvy marketers to be successful.

That was five miracles, just for starters (not to even mention practical ones like raising money and getting along with cofounders). It was four miracles too far. Any single one of those could have encompassed an entire funded startup's efforts, and in fact I could tag every line above with two

* The bar-code-reading problem circa 2010 was still relatively unsolved. A company named RedLaser would soon do so, and it was almost instantly acquired by eBay.

to three startups that had attempted it. And here we were proposing taking down all five with three scared guys and no business network or money. Even in our jackass naïveté, we started realizing this soon after the YC interview, which is why we eventually did that classic startup move: a pivot.

This is absolutely canonical startupese, and worth exploring for a second. You can't read an article in *Wired* or *Fast Company*, some fawning fiction about a startup's inexorable and well-deserved charge to world domination, without reading this word at least once.

A "pivot" is supposed to recall a ballerina's *demi détourné*, a delicate change of course as graceful as it (hopefully) seems intentional. In reality, a startup's pivot is a panicked sprint comparable to that of a *Titanic* passenger who's spotted the last open life raft. It wasn't even a onetime thing: our final product would be informally titled "Plan J," given the number of turns we had taken since "Plan A." But there you have it, dear reader: we made a "pivot." *Plié!*

But we're getting ahead of ourselves. All this would become clear only after numerous strolls with Paul Graham, something we hadn't even won the right to have yet.

Back to me skulking at Adchemy while working on a Y Combinator application. If my reading of YC's and Paul Graham's essays was correct, then bomb-throwing anarchist subversive mixed with cold-blooded execution mixed with irreverent whimsy, a sort of technology-enabled twelve-year-old boy, was precisely the YC entrepreneur profile. Figure out a point of overlooked business or technical leverage, interpose some piece of cleverness, and gleefully marvel at the resulting disruption (or destruction).

In that spirit did we respond to my favorite question on the YC application:*

---

* Little-known fact: Y Combinator alums are the first readers of all Y Combinator applications, and are essentially the first filter. This is the one question I always make it a point to read when reviewing Y Combina-

What (non-computer) system have you ever hacked?

I conducted a man-in-the-middle attack on Craigslist's online dating ads. I posted an ad as a woman looking for a man, and as a man looking for a woman. I'd pass email from real man to fictional woman as the replies of fictional man to the real women, and basically crossed the email streams. At one point I shifted each real person off my fictional email addresses, and to the corresponding opposite-sex real email addresses. For all I know, it resulted in a marriage, as I never saw emails after the rewiring of the email flow.

And on it went for the rest of the questions.

The sound-bite tagline for the inchoate idea was drawn from personal history: we were building the "Goldman Sachs of advertising," a grandiloquent assertion if there ever was one. This formulation of "the X of Y," where X and Y are two easily understood things, but their intersection is novel or intriguing, was also classic Y Combinator thinking. PG had actually suggested such a trope in his essay on pitching to investors. It's now terribly cliché, but at one point, like any meme, it enjoyed a period of almost classic establishment acceptance. Even now you hear it occasionally: "the Uber of bicycles"; "the Netflix of men's underwear"; and so on. It's a one-line way to instantly make your weird techno-business pastiche understood, even if only partially.

The boys weren't totally convinced, even as we hustled to get our application in on time. They wouldn't be totally convinced until our first YC meeting, in which we were given a rousing oration by Paul Graham. Even in those tentative Adchemy days, though, I knew YC would change everything if we got in.

---

tor applications. If the answer is left blank, my cursor is already halfway to the No button. If it reads something like "I'd never hack a system or do anything illegal" I hit that No button faster than a *Jeopardy* contestant buzzes in.

Plus, it was a prize, and a difficult-to-attain one at that. Whenever membership in some exclusive club is up for grabs, I viciously fight to win it, even if only to reject membership when offered. After all, echoing the eminent philosopher G. Marx: How good can a club be if it's willing to have lowly me as a member?

If you had been standing on the corner of Broadway and MacArthur Boulevard in Oakland the night of March 7, 2010, you would have seen a curious sight. A heavily pregnant woman, bent over in pain and scarcely able to walk, was being half carried, half dragged across the street by a tall, goateed man. The woman could barely stand, and needed to pause and cling to either the man, or any fixed object, as they struggled across the last couple hundred feet. Every ten paces or so, the woman would double over and gasp in pain, bringing everything to a halt. The man was simultaneously trying to check for traffic, keep his female companion from collapsing, tow a large suitcase, and navigate the whole lurching ensemble toward the emergency room door. That goateed man, gentle reader, was me. The woman was a former City of London derivatives trader.

She was thirty-seven weeks pregnant.

We had known each other for thirty-nine weeks.

Let's rewind before we fast-forward again.

"Life is what happens when you're making other plans."

If you ever run across an online dating profile with the above as a tagline, be aware you're in for one fucking life-changing date. I had found British Trader's profile while searching for the keyword "sailing." Thematic searches (e.g., "physics," "PhD," "beer") were my way of finding some iota of common ground with which to structure an introductory message.

At the time, online dating sites distinguished themselves mostly by the demographics of their members. Craigslist was for escorts, fat chicks in Fremont, and serial killers. OkCupid was for penniless hipster chicks who lived in shared flats in the Mission. Match.com was for professional women busy with the time-honored tradition of husband shopping. Choose your audience, and write your ad copy. Mine was heavy on the sailing and outdoor adventuring. Zero mention of diaper changes and daycare drop-offs. Truth in advertising, more or less.

She had vaguely Slavic-looking cheekbones and feline eyes. Her Match profile photo featured her at the tiller of a boat, which instantly quintupled her attractiveness. Message led to dinner date. Dinner date led to an opera outing. One early Friday evening, dressed in her corporate finest, she appeared unannounced at the boatyard. My twenty-six-foot sloop *Moksha* was hauled out on land, and I was busily refitting it for serious offshore sailing. Covered in dust and grease, I welcomed her to my boat. She climbed up the precarious twelve-foot ladder to *Moksha*'s deck, which towered over the ground due to the boat's deep keel.

Then, a romantic reversal.

The following weekend, a tall, rangy guy put his boat next to mine in the yard. A strapping and strutting South African, he walked over and we started talking boats. We got along famously, and continued our unending string of boat talk with beer and pizza at the local red-and-white-tablecloth Italian place.

He was, as fate would have it, British Trader's ex-boyfriend, who had recently and unceremoniously dumped her. This business was serious. As I'd eventually learn from British Trader, they had tried having a child despite never marrying. Their inability to conceive had convinced British Trader she was barren.

He and I ended our boozing and bullshitting and got back to work on our respective boats. As I was painting the bottom, I looked over and saw some hot chick talking to my new South African friend. I saw only her jeans-clad ass. Given my as-yet noncomprehensive knowledge of her anatomy, I didn't recognize her. Of course, it was British Trader, stopping by the yard to check randomly on my progress. Given there was only one large boatyard for serious refitting in the East Bay, meeting her recent beau wasn't a completely improbable coincidence.

Weirded out by my bonding with her ex, she decided to end the budding romance. But then a week later she changed her mind. I had brunch with her and her female confidante. On my finest social behavior, I passed muster with her friend. The next invitation was dinner at her house. When I appeared on her doorstep with a bottle of wine and a smile, she opened the door conspicuously made up, perfumed, and in a fetching dress. The moment that door swung open, I knew I had her.

The contemporary honeymoon of a several-week fuck-fest, consummated at the start of a new romantic liaison, played itself out comme il faut. No surprises really, other than British Trader's taste for being physically dominated in bed, a bit of a surprise given her alpha-female exterior. To a woman, every girlfriend of mine has been intelligent, ambitious, and independent. Until very recently, all were vastly more successful and wealthier than me. And yet, come the pressing hour of physical need, so unfolded the countless boudoir scenes recalling Fragonard's *Le Verrou*: a ravished chambermaid, half resisting and half yielding, violently seized in the arms of her predatory lover, who slams shut the bolt on the bedroom door.

The backdrop to the tryst turned relationship was a modest bungalow fixer-upper that British Trader had bought, taking advantage of a corporate relocation package. She made Bob Vila of *This Old House* look like a fucking pussy. She had ripped out the ornate and custom built-in shelves and display case from one room and installed them in another. The flooring was down to the planking, to be redone in fresh hardwood (by her, with a nail gun and lots of patience). The only room that was even remotely livable was the kitchen (which featured beautiful hardwood counters that were regularly oiled). Her bed consisted of a cheap foam mattress about the width of an extra-jumbo-sized menstrual pad inside a room stripped to the wall studs. The floor was dusty with drywall powder from the demolition, and postcoitally, it was all I could do to balance myself precariously on the edge of the pad and off the drywall dust. Morning showers were in the one functioning bathroom, whose empty window frames were covered in plastic. A molded plastic shower in the corner and a lonely-looking white porcelain toilet were the only signs of civilization in what appeared to be the inside of a garden shed. The scene of conception was either the aforementioned foam pad, or the hardwood kitchen counter.

Two generations ago, her branch of the family, moneyed Jews in czarist Russia, had seen the revolutionary writing on the wall and had fled to the United Kingdom. Another branch moved to China and became an established trading family in Harbin. In Britain, the family made the unlikely transition to landed gentry, and ran a farm in Bedfordshire. A great-uncle was elevated to the peerage, and a second cousin shared the Nobel Prize with Alexander Fleming for penicillin.

When she was in her teens, her father decided to move the family to the United States, where they suffered a financial reversal she was unwilling to talk about. Suddenly not among the moneyed class, she hustled herself through the redbrick boondocks of the University of Vermont. Citibank internship led to Deutsche Bank job, and after a few years she was an equity derivatives trader at Deutsche, holding her own against the toff sharks of the City of London.

She had wild green eyes, with unnatural red spots in her irises when you pulled close, reminiscent of that Afghan girl from the *National Geographic* cover. Her personality was flinty and rough, and as leathery as her skin. She had spent years between various jobs backpacking around the rougher parts of the world. She was an imposing, broad-shouldered presence, six feet tall in bare feet, and towering over me in heels.

Most women in the Bay Area are soft and weak, cosseted and naive despite their claims of worldliness, and generally full of shit. They have their self-regarding entitlement feminism, and ceaselessly vaunt their independence, but the reality is, come the epidemic plague or foreign invasion, they'd become precisely the sort of useless baggage you'd trade for a box of shotgun shells or a jerry can of diesel.

British Trader, on the other hand, was the sort of woman who would end up a useful ally in that postapocalypse, doing whatever work—be it carpentry, animal husbandry, or a shotgun blast to someone's back—required doing. Long story short, you wanted to tie your genetic wagon to the bucking horse of her bloodline. Which is why I was less nervous than I should have been on a random Saturday in July, when I showed up for a brunch appointment and found her uncharacteristically moody. She complained of feeling nauseated and slightly out of it.

With perhaps too much offhandedness, while grabbing the local newspaper off her couch, I suggested, "Well, perhaps do a pregnancy test."

Like any male who's played it fast and loose with the safe-sex rules, I'd had my fair share of scares. I was on season four of the show whereby tear-filled woman X shows up two weeks after the shag saying she had "missed her period" (sort of in the same way I'd say I "missed my bus"). Nothing had ever come of it, and after the third showing you just wanted to say, "Look, woman, unless you've got a screaming infant in your arms *and* it looks like me, we have nothing to talk about."

She'd have both soon enough.

"Well, I did go to the doctor," she replied instantly.

Things took on a rather portentous air for a casual Saturday-morning brunch.

"Ah . . . and?"

"I am pregnant."

BAM!

A human life.

Shit, I thought.

I could hear God laughing in his vaulted hangout. Life is what happens when you're making other plans indeed.

By her account, British Trader had broken into tears on hearing the news from her doctor, whom she had gone to see on some routine visit. Yeah, that old story. One look into her hard, green eyes, and I knew this kid was seeing the light of day.

Due more to some residual Catholic guilt and Hispanic chivalry than true love for British Trader, I sublet my one-bedroom bohemian pad in the Mission, which had followed my hippie-chick household, and moved into her home turned construction site. I'd make a go of this domesticated parental life.

If you jump into the abyss, jump headlong.

Passed out on a gurney, British Trader was bleeding. I watched with increasing alarm as red streaks traced bloody spiderwebs across her thighs. The nurses milled around like bored bureaucrats at a foreign post office, and talked about paperwork and the weather.

The progress of birthing is measured in centimeters. Seven centimeters dilated: too late for anesthesia, too late for fashionable breathing exercises. It was showtime.

I invite anyone with a philosophical bent to witness a human birth and observe as unstoppable forces meet immovable objects, with neither yielding. Modern medicine does little to resolve this paradox made flesh. The only real differences between the bloody, screaming tableau before me and that of, say, my grandmother's birth a century ago in rural northern Spain by candlelight, were the little plastic packets of mineral oil, like the salad dressing at a Denny's, that nurses would regularly crack open and pour over the heaving, tumescent mass down south.

It was a sweaty, white-knuckle affair shattered by piercing shrieks of pain that resonated across the maternity ward, and which the heavy institutional doors the nurses slammed shut did little to stifle. I quietly entertained bouts of *Mad Men*–esque nostalgia for a time when men simply paced nervously and smoked in some other room while the dirty business was completed.

After two hours of battle, old flesh yielded bloodily to new, and Zoë Ayala came into the world.

As some sort of perverse parting gift, I was given the honor of cutting the umbilical cord. As thick as a man's finger, with a yellow film over a deep purple core, it yielded to my snipping with a pair of small scissors, making a satisfying *snap* as I sheared the last fleshy connection between mother and child.

Zoë wailed mightily. The nurse plopped her onto a stainless steel scale, topped by two infrared heating lamps, like the french fry station at a McDonald's. Length and weight taken, she used a thick cotton blanket like a tortilla to wrap up Zoë. She put the baby burrito in my arms.

For the first time, Zoë settled, the tight swaddling fooling her into thinking, for a few minutes, that she was back in the warm embrace of a mother's womb. She looked unbelievably small and frail and unready for a cold, hard world.

Against all odds, YC had invited us to an interview. With a brief email, and a link to a minimalist schedule-appointment tool, the adventure was really afoot.

I had snagged us the last interview spot, on the last interview day—March 29—betting on the usual election-ballot strategy of being either first or last on any list. Thus it was late Sunday afternoon when we nervously appeared at YC HQ, an industrial space in a completely unremarkable part of Mountain View.

With zero ceremony, we were told to proceed into the interview room, where the four YC partners were arranged behind a table like a military board of inquiry. Present was, of course, Paul Graham, along with his wife, Jessica Livingston, also a partner. Jessica had conducted a comprehensive series of interviews of the world's most successful entrepreneurs for her book *Founders at Work*, which was a startup anarchist's cookbook of personal memoir and advice. I had devoured it, and so should you if you want to play in this pond.

Robert Tappan Morris (referred to as RTM by PG) was also present. He was a walking bit of computer science history, having created, in 1988, the world's first computer virus, which he released and for which he was criminally prosecuted under the then-nascent computer-fraud law. Following his conviction, he joined PG in founding Viaweb, the company whose acquisition jackpot had funded the very venture fund we were pitching. Presently he was a professor of computer science at MIT, but he still participated in YC decisions. PG's one-line encomium of RTM was as absolute as it was brief: "He's never wrong."

Trevor Blackwell was the final and fourth partner, another Viaweb cofounder. He was also the founder of Anybots, a robotics company that actually leased the building we were standing in, and in which YC would become an ever-expanding subtenant. The Anybots labs around the Y Combinator space looked like scenes from the Terminator series, and housed piles of Skynet-like robotic equipment that seemed it might come to life any moment.

"So you want to create the Goldman Sachs of advertising, eh?" PG challenged the moment we walked in.

With that abrupt start, I tried to follow our plan of my speaking for the first thirty seconds to pitch the general idea, and then to proceed to a demo of the hacked-together technology on which we'd spent several sleepless nights.

I was fifteen seconds into it when the questions started.

PG: "How do you join the online click to the physical person in the store?"

Before we could finish an answer, Trevor butted in with a question:

"What do you mean it's too expensive to buy ads across the US?"

RTM: "How are you going to even scan the products and know what's for sale?"

PG: "So how do you get paid again?"

And on it went. One of us would try to answer one question, but before we had even gotten started, there came another question, and someone else dove in.

The whole thing devolved into what might have been mistaken for a heated discussion on Israel-Palestine among a bunch of drunks of mixed political persuasions. And the pace never relented. There were two or three overlapping conversations going at once.

While jumping in to answer any hanging question, or to back up one of the boys on a statement, I was keeping an eye on the clock at my left. Oversized, like something you'd see at a sporting event, it counted down relentlessly from ten minutes to zero, all the time we had. Throughout all this, Jessica didn't say a word, and merely observed us impassively from one flank.

After more wrangling, and with no demo taking place, time was up.

"We'll talk about it and get back to you today," pronounced PG finally.

And that was that.

In retrospect, those were the ten most important minutes in my life.

Standing outside, we marinated in the stomach-churning feeling of collective failure. Randomly, we ran into one of the founders of Mixpanel, one of the many successful start-ups that had graduated from YC and had gone on to great things. YC alums often come to the interviews in an attempt to calm applicants' nerves, and to provide a better signal in the interview process. The Mixpanel founder did precisely the opposite, attacking our idea, the marketing plan, and the business model.

By the end of these two bouts of abuse, a suicide pact was but a criticism away.

"Fuck it. Let's go for a beer," I proposed.

"Yeah, let's go," echoed Argyris.

MRM, who curled into a ball when he got upset, opted to go home and be with his kids.

The beer venue was the only decent beer bar in Silicon Valley at the time, a pestilential but cozy cinder block pit that fashioned itself British, with football pennants and Premier League on the screen. The Rose & Crown was popular with the few hip Stanford grad students who hung around Palo Alto, and it fortunately tended to exclude the Abercrombie & Fitch–wearing VC larvae.

Just as a Weihenstephaner hit my hand and I searched for a bench in the narrow beer garden, the phone rang. I didn't recognize the number.

"This is Paul Graham from YC. We'd like to fund you."

Shock. Disbelief.

"Ah . . . well . . . so . . . one of the cofounders isn't here. I should probably ask him first."

WRONG ANSWER!

Like idiots, we hadn't decided among ourselves whether we were committed. The boys, MRM especially, weren't sold on this YC business.

"You need to ask him first?"

"Let me call you back in five minutes."

One major unpleasantness involved in writing a memoir

is the historian's task of rereading your personal archive of texts, messages, and emails. In contemplating an earlier version of yourself, you'll realize that young and glorious you was in fact a total and complete fuckwit. An older you, going back and whispering in your young ear, would issue not praise and encouragement, but insults and dire warnings.

I told Argyris the news and cut him off when he asked a question. I had to call MRM.

"Hello?" he answered, with what sounded like a sporting match in the background. His kids were playing soccer.

"Dude, YC wants to fund us. You in?"

It actually took some convincing. If memory serves, I even packaged it as a provisional thing we could back out of, if need be.

Calling back PG, I was horrified to get his voicemail. In as unpanicked a voice as I could manage, I left a message accepting the offer, and followed up with an email to Harjeet Taggar, a former YC founder who was helping manage the interview process.

We were in.

The languorous Sunday-afternoon crowd at Rose & Crown looked on indifferently as I called British Trader to announce the news. We'd not only managed to abandon the sinking ship of Adchemy, we'd flagged down another passing vessel in our mad swim away from that soon-to-be wreck.

Abandoning the Shipwreck

> Whoever doesn't have revolutionary genes, or doesn't have revolutionary blood. Whoever doesn't have the courage, heart, or brain that adapts itself to the effort and heroism of the revolution. Let them go! We don't want them! We don't need them!
>
> —Fidel Castro, speech at Mariel, Cuba, May 1980

APRIL 23, 2010

Here's more startup advice: if the drama around your departure from a startup recalls that of a former East German trying to jump the Wall, or Cubans hijacking airliners to Miami, then you should be as ecstatic at leaving as that same East German or Cuban.

We had decided to all go in together to Murthy's office to offer our resignations, with some vague thought that this would represent a united front. Without much warning, we entered his office on some thin pretext. I can't recall who spoke first—I think it was me—but we announced our plan to leave Adchemy and start our own thing. Murthy launched into a harangue about what ingenuous rubes we were.

"What are the five things to look for in a term sheet? I

bet you don't even know that," he challenged, looking right at me.

I had read my share of business-agreement how-tos, but this wasn't the time to test that rather tenuous knowledge. Murthy was just picking up steam, though.

"You realize when you go to a venture capitalist, the first thing he's going to do is call me, and I'm going to tell him what I think of you," he said, gesturing to his phone. "You aren't the right people to build a company. You don't know what you're doing, you're not smart or tough enough." And so it went on for a good five minutes.

One of Mark Twain's more uplifting quotes maintains that small people always belittle your ambitions, while the great make you feel that you too can be great. Murthy was most assuredly a small man. By the end of his drilling, we all doubted what would eventually prove to be the best decision any of us ever made. Shoulders slumped and heads bowed, we marched out of his glass office.

What followed was a week of nonstop harassment from Adchemy. Matt and Argyris fielded most of it, and for good reason. According to our code-repository statistics, McEachen had written about half the code in the Adchemy codebase. As employee number eleven, he was that archetypal figure on every product team: the silverback, the neckbeard, the absolute expert who knew all the secret scripts that could be run, and where all the technical bodies were buried. And he was that person for just about every product the company had ever made, all the ill-conceived, disconnected, and random functionality that lay unwanted and unmonetized in hundreds of thousands of lines of code.

Like all good bullies, Murthy & Co. could smell weakness like sharks smell blood in the water. Of the three, McEachen was the most economically dependent, as he had a stay-at-home wife, two kids, and a mortgage. He also had the greatest sense of investment in the company. So they worked the uncertainty-and-fear angle, convincing him he was throwing away all he had built at Adchemy. To sweeten the deal, they threw more equity at him. None of it was convincing, and McEachen remained steadfast.

Their attempts to keep me were relatively brief, and consisted mostly of one uncomfortable conversation with the new VP of Engineering, Chander Sarna.

Chander was a recent hire from Friendster, where he claimed to have put out the technical fires that had resulted from rapid scaling. He had brought a crew of engineers with him from the dying social network, and they formed the nucleus of his personal mafia. He managed mostly through intimidation. In his ill-fitting polyester polo shirts with color palettes stolen from the late seventies, he reminded me of the bored auto-rickshaw drivers in front of Connaught Place, Delhi, who'd overcharge you a hundred rupees to go down the street to Paharganj.

Having been told to report to his office, I took a seat in front of his desk. The bright South Bay sun of a cloudless afternoon poured in through his picture window.

"So is there anything we can do compensation-wise, Antonio?" asked Chander in his thick Indian accent.

"No way."

"Why do you want to leave?" he asked, with a concerned look that feigned an almost fatherly interest.

As always with me, my principal sin was telling the unvarnished truth.

"Because we have no products. We have no clients. There's not a single paying client for anything Adchemy has ever produced on its own."

Chander shot up from his desk.

"Of course we have paying clients," he said, gesticulating wildly at a PowerPoint slide bedecked with logos on his monitor. The slides were from Murthy's most recent quarterly pep rally. "How can you say that!?" he sputtered.

I kept my mouth shut and looked past Chander at the view of Foster City and the San Mateo bridge.

"I think I'd like to try my own thing," I offered, citing a less controversial motive.

"Look, you don't know anything about doing startups," he began, and on into the spiel about how we were clueless neophytes.

He wrapped up with a gesture at reconciliation. "And as for McEachen, he's had some problems, but we've tried working with him to improve things . . ."

McEachen and Chander seriously did not get along. McEachen's good-natured earnestness and total allegiance to unbiased technical truth conflicted severely with Chander's love of power and control. McEachen treated anyone, from an intern to the CTO, with the same frank openness, where only reason or data prevailed. Chander demanded the deferential obeisance a Prussian general expected from his troops, meanwhile pledging in turn sycophantish allegiance to Murthy. Thanks to Chander, the company had already lost its very capable head of analytics. Others would soon follow.

After he was done barking discouragement, we stared at each other for an awkward few moments. His arm rose with a quick start, indicating I could leave. That jiggly little man didn't even stand up as I walked out the door.

This scene was duly reported to Murthy, and for the next several days management was very careful to keep me out of meetings and away from product teams. I imagine they were afraid I'd propagate my theory about the productlessness of the company. For once, I kept my mouth shut.

After a tense week, it was all over but the shouting. Murthy and Chander had had their go at McEachen and me, with zero result. We would be gone within days.

Argyris would unfortunately not get off so easily. Murthy, as happened at many flailing startups, was making yet another big product bet, in a string of such bets, that was sure to turn Adchemy's fortunes around ("This time, it's different"). Argyris's algorithmic work was absolutely central to this new company-saving direction, and his departure meant delaying or forgoing that bet. For this last piece of retention skulduggery Adchemy would exploit one critical point: Argyris wasn't a US citizen.

The American immigrant visa system amounts to indentured servitude, a type of peonage. This medieval institution has a long history in the United States. Before the American Revolution, half of the European immigrants to the British colonies came over as indentured servants. Poor children or young adults, with no prospects in Europe, would sell years of their labor in exchange for passage to the Americas. Across the pond, employers would purchase these individuals from the captains who had brought them over, and they were pressed into service or apprenticed to craftsmen. Servants could be bought or sold, as with slavery. Also as in slavery, servants were subject to physical punishment, including whipping, they could not marry without permission, and their contract was enforceable by the law; escaped servants were captured and returned. If female servants became pregnant, their contract was extended to compensate for the time out of work. At the end of the contract, servants were given their "freedom dues" (a small cash payment) and set free to seek their fortunes in their new homeland.

Not much has changed in Silicon Valley.

Skilled immigrant tech workers in the United States have effectively one method of entry: the famous H-1B visa. Capped at a small yearly number, it's the ticket to the American Dream for a few tens of thousands of foreigners per year. Lasting anywhere from three to six years, the H-1B allows foreigners to prove themselves and eventually apply for permanent residency, the colloquial "green card."

Like the masters of old buying servants off the ship, tech companies are required to spend nontrivial sums for foreign hires. Many companies, particularly smaller startups, don't want the hassle, and hire only American citizens, an imposed nativism nobody talks about, and which is possibly illegal. Big companies, which know they'll be around for the years it will take to recoup their investment, are the real beneficiaries of this peonage system. Large but unexciting tech outfits like Oracle, Intel, Qualcomm, and IBM that have trouble recruiting the best American talent hire foreign engineers by the boatload. Consultancy firms that bill inflated project costs by the man-hour, such as Accenture and Deloitte, shanghai their foreign laborers, who can't quit without being eventually deported. By paying them relatively slim H-1B-stipulated salaries while eating the fat consultancy fees, such companies get rich off the artificial employment monopoly created by the visa barrier. It's a shit deal for the immigrant visa holders, but they put up with the five or so years of stultifying, exploitive labor as an admissions ticket to the tech First World. After that, they're free. Everyone abandons his or her place at the oar inside the Intel war galley immediately, but there's always someone waiting to take over.

Strictly speaking, H-1B visas are nonimmigrant and temporary, and so this hazing ritual of immigrant initiation is unlawful. Yet everyone's on the take, including the government, which charges thousands in filing fees. The entire system is so riven with institutionalized lies, political intrigue, and illegal but overlooked manipulation, it's a wonder the American tech industry exists at all.

So into this bustling slave market, echoing with the clink of leg irons and the auctioneer's cry, did we ignorantly wade. If Argyris was to join our as-yet-unnamed company, he'd need a work visa. In fact, forget working: he couldn't even legally stay in the United States once Adchemy terminated him. Immigration law stipulates a former H-1 holder must leave the country within days. *Thanks for building our tech industry, you dirty foreigner, now beat it.*

Was there a way out?

Argyris, a proud Greek with an admirable display of

Southern European enterprise and skill at sniffing out legal loopholes, found a solution. His longtime Turkish girlfriend, Simla, was studying for a PhD at Stanford under an F-1 student visa. Were they to marry, Argyris would qualify for an F-2 student spouse visa. This wouldn't let him officially work in the States, but it would let him remain there.

The only hitch was, well, getting hitched.

Simla proved very accommodating and agreed, though the "wedding" at City Hall was to be officially treated as socially nonofficial. My proposal for a bachelor party was vetoed. Greek married Turk, despite millennia of geopolitical conflict going back to Herodotus, and we still had a third founder.

Except for one stupid mistake.

As our final week at Adchemy wound down, Murthy and Chander would shut Argyris in an office and try to "sweat" him, filling his mind with dark visions of the future:

You're throwing your future away on this crazy venture, Argyris.

You're abandoning Adchemy when we most need you, Argyris.

When you leave Adchemy, your H-1 visa will be canceled and you'll be forced to leave the United States, and everything you've built here, Argyris.

Argyris put up with the hazing as best he could. But at that last point, he couldn't help himself, blurting out, "The visa isn't an issue. I'll have an F-2 through my wife. So whatever!"

This perked up the ears of Chander and Murthy. They consulted their in-house legal counsel, who, like those of any tech company, knew their way around US immigration law. They informed Argyris that working under an F-2 visa was illegal.

Strictly speaking, this wasn't completely true. F-2 visa holders are allowed to remain in the United States and be investors in US companies (which Argyris was soon to be, as founders officially "invest" in a company by buying its shares at a negligible price). And given that we had almost no money, we weren't paying ourselves, and so Argyris wasn't officially "working." Like many startup founders from foreign countries, many of whom have contributed immeasurably to the economic and technical success of this country, Argyris lived in a legal gray area until we managed to get him an H-1 visa.

That was all beside the point in Adchemy's mind, however.

As upstanding corporate citizens, they felt obliged—*obliged!*—to inform the immigration service that their former employee was attempting to violate immigration law (though again, we weren't technically).

He didn't want to be reported to the immigration authorities, did he?

Think about that for a moment: a venture-backed tech company with hundreds of employees, and high hopes of going public, was threatening to report Argyris to the much-feared US Immigration and Customs Enforcement. Referred to by the appropriately chilling acronym ICE, this agency is charged with arresting aliens and jailing them or putting them on the first plane out of the United States. Adchemy was effectively coercing Argyris, as an unscrupulous foreman of a fruit-picking crew in California's Central Valley does with illegal farmworkers.

What's even more ironic: Murthy Nukala and Chander Sarna were themselves economic immigrants, having left their native India for the United States but a few years earlier. Both had been forced to navigate the US visa system, suffer the H-1 debt bondage, and live at the pleasure of some sponsoring company. And here they were, the former slaves turned slave owners, cracking the visa whip on Argyris.

Argyris, to his everlasting credit, became fed up with this demeaning treatment. Rather than knuckle under, he bolted his balls on, went into Adchemy one last time, and told them to go suck a dick, they could report him if they wanted. And that was the end of that. If Adchemy ever reported him, we'd never know, but soon enough, after we regularized Argyris's visa status at our yet-to-be-formed company, it wouldn't matter.

On the last hour of the last day, McEachen, saint that he was, went to Murthy's office to say good-bye. He had invested over four years of his life in the company, watching it grow from a small shared space to the expansive floor of a high-end office tower. I waited impatiently by the emergency exit staircase, to avoid running into any other employees.

After ten minutes or so, he emerged, looking astonished, or maybe shell-shocked.

"He barely even looked up from the screen."

His voice cracked as he said it. He looked at me imploringly. For a moment I thought he might actually cry.

"He didn't say anything, and didn't shake my hand."

Matt McEachen, Adchemy's best, most productive engineer, until the day he left the author of the biggest chunk of Adchemy's codebase, was treated worse than a contract janitor on the way out. I marveled at a world in which well-meaning, industrious, but naive engineers are routinely manipulated by the glib entrepreneurs who seduce them into joining their startups, then relinquish them when they are no longer useful. Every Jobs has his Wozniak. I couldn't exactly claim I wasn't, to some degree, doing the same to him right then. He was merely trading Murthy for me.

Engineers can be so smart about code, and yet so dense about human motivations. They'd be better served by reading less Neal Stephenson and more Shakespeare and Patricia Highsmith.

No time for philosophy now. We were committed.

"Let's get the hell out of here, man."

I flung open the emergency exit and we flew down the stairs, five flights to the ground floor, and out of that nightmare. But Adchemy would cast a long shadow on us indeed.

The business-savvy reader will at this point be giggling at our naïveté, the schoolboyish reverence with which we beheld the corporate trappings and power we felt we were rebelling against.

Our problem was that we had never known how the sausage got made. We had never gotten our hands on the levers of the world, even slightly.

The reality is, Silicon Valley capitalism is very simple:

Investors are people with more money than time.

Employees are people with more time than money.

Entrepreneurs are simply the seductive go-betweens.

Startups are business experiments performed with other people's money.

Marketing is like sex: only losers pay for it.

Company culture is what goes without saying.

There are no real rules, only laws.

Success forgives all sins.

People who leak to you, leak about you.

Meritocracy is the propaganda we use to bless the charade.

Greed and vanity are the twin engines of bourgeois society.

Most managers are incompetent and maintain their jobs via inertia and politics.

Lawsuits are merely expensive feints in a well-scripted conflict narrative between corporate entities.

> Capitalism is an amoral farce in which every player—investor, employee, entrepreneur, consumer—is complicit.

But hey, look at these shiny iPhones. Right?

At the time, we understood none of this. We'd figure it out soon enough.

Part Two

Pseudorandomness

Pseudorandomness is a process that appears to be random but is not. Pseudorandom sequences typically exhibit statistical randomness while being generated by an entirely deterministic causal process. Such a process is easier to produce than a genuinely random one, and has the benefit that it can be used again and again to produce exactly the same numbers—useful for testing and fixing software.

—"Pseudorandomness," Wikipedia

Let Me See Your War Face

> If you ladies leave my island, if you survive recruit training, you will be a weapon, you will be a minister of death, praying for war. But until that day you are pukes. You're the lowest form of life on Earth. You are not even human fucking beings. You are nothing but unorganized grabastic pieces of amphibian shit!
>
> —R. Lee Ermey as Gunnery Sergeant Hartman
> *Full Metal Jacket* (1987)

JUNE 2010

This is how Y Combinator works.

For three months, the selected startup founders meet weekly for a dinner with some eminent startup personage. The dinners are not relaxed social affairs: they're competitive demos in which founders try to one-up each other with increasingly developed products, upward-sloping user graphs, or funding news, within a context of technocamaraderie and shared suffering. The weekly cadence imposes order on the always-full-throttle startup chaos, and is a welcome respite from the grinding toil and stomach-churning stress.

I always tried to sit directly in the front row to take the speaker's measure.

Marissa Mayer's hands shook and she spoke at an anxious clip; she arrived escorted by a Google "handler," the only speaker to do so.

Reid Hoffman, a large man, thundered like an emperor at the head of this troops, and spilled wonderful stories about the PayPal saga, the founding of LinkedIn, and going to war with Microsoft. He was by far one of the best speakers; you felt like kicking your way through a brick wall when he was done.

And on it went with the creators of Gmail and Yahoo Mail, partners at Sequoia and Google Ventures, the founders of Airbnb, Eventbrite, and Groupon and the like, regaling us with war stories from the tech trenches.

The dinner food was what Paul Graham politely called "goop on rice": an occasionally foul, sporadically delicious stew of random ingredients tossed over a bowl of rice. PG or one of the other partners would dole it out themselves, the founders forming a meandering line, like a Depression-era soup kitchen. YC's main space had a full kitchen, and supposedly PG actually cooked the "goop" himself—or at least he had in the early days. The creamy stuff with peas and some mystery fish was without a doubt the worst. Those were bad weeks. Microwaved spackling paste surely tasted better. There was general agreement the meatballs on pasta were the global maximum (which was saying something).

You obviously weren't there for the food, or even the distinguished speaker's company.

The real YC selling points were the following: access to the YC partners, access to the network of YC founders, a bankable patina of prestige, and Demo Day.

The value of the partners will be made clear as this story progresses.

The value of the network of YC companies is that it essentially constitutes a private microcosm of the greater tech world. This is often derided as the "YC mafia" by outsiders.

"Mafia" is a pejorative term bringing to mind tracksuit-wearing Russians bolting vodka, shouting into burner cellphones, and whispering to each other in raspy, Slavic tones. There is a feeling of collective defense around YC, and it does know how to circle the wagons if threatened.

The real network effect, however, was this: With the pool of YC companies expanding every year, you could probably re-create 80 percent of the consumer and infrastructure technology used in our Internet-enabled age exclusively with Y Combinator companies. Whatever need you had, whether system-monitoring tools, mobile development, or even marketing tools ("Have you heard of our product, AdGrok?"), you could find a YC company to fill it. Given that you were one of the family, you could expect excellent service and a steep discount. You could also be sure that whatever you were building would receive preferential adoption by others in the YC network, providing you with an instant set of savvy and patient users, as well as impressive logos to feature in a pitch deck. This tendency to "dogfood" YC products came straight from the top. The day YC funds an airline, I suspect PG will fly that one, and no other.

As for the value of the bankable prestige, we'd see just what that was soon enough.

So what were we building in Y Combinator?

To understand that, we'll need one last lecture on online media, and then I'll step down from the pedagogical soapbox. It's pure money, sex, and death after this, I promise.

How does Google manage to generate yearly revenues of $70 billon, greater than the GDP of Luxembourg or Belarus? It invented this magical website called Google Search, where all of humanity goes and tells Google what it wants: "Nikon D300 camera." "Online nursing degree." "Divorce lawyer in Atlanta." A world of three- and four-word desires and needs, all craving to be satisfied, all backed by wallets waiting to be opened. Injecting themselves in that last moment of purchase, at the apex of desire, Google invites you to click on an ad. Its cash register rings every time you click.

It doesn't even need to figure out what a search query is worth and price it accordingly. It simply holds an auction for every search query entered, at the moment the query occurs. The net result is that billions of times a day, Google runs an auction of keywords and accompanying bids. By looking at the bid, and estimating the likelihood of a click, Google takes the product of the two (which is how much it will make per query) and picks the highest. Then it displays the associated ad that the advertiser has created and uploaded to Google for that keyword.

Actually printing physical money would be harder.

So how many such search queries, or "keywords," in Google-speak, are there?

The second edition of the *Oxford English Dictionary*, released in 1989 and since supplemented, contains 291,000 word entries. The *Woordenboek der Nederlandsche Taal*, a dictionary of the Dutch language and the largest monolingual dictionary in the world, runs to 50,000 pages and 431,000 entries. Both works are dwarfed by the size of the keyword lists maintained by those lexicographers turned word merchants, the search engine marketers. Like a stock portfolio manager, who keeps a set of assets with a theoretical and current price, the paid search manager maintains encyclopedic word lists along with dollar-sign values, and constantly adjusts bids to reflect realized performance. These lists literally number in the millions, and look something like:

KEYWORD	COST PER CLICK	REVENUE PER CLICK
"divorce lawyer in reno"	$1.45	$0.90
"nevada cheap divorce"	$0.75	$1.10
"nevada divorce lawyer"	$5.55	$2.75

Like the classic stock picker buying low and selling high, our search engine marketer curates and trims a keyword list like a bonsai tree, buying more of well-performing keywords, and fewer of bad. If the revenue generated by post-click sales outpaces cost, up go the bid and the budget, and the reverse in the opposite case. The ratio of revenue to cost is known as "return on advertising spend" (ROAS) and is the basic metric all marketers in every medium use. As an example, ROAS is $1.10 ÷ $0.75 – 1 = 47% for "nevada cheap divorce" above. This means for every dollar I put into Google for that keyword, I get $1.47 back, at least as projected based on historical data. I'm happy to do that all day. Time to up the budget.

Such is the essential busywork behind how a Google makes more than some European countries produce in a year. That's it. You now know as much as the best search engine marketers in the world.

As a piece of clickbait-y news, want to know which is the most expensive word in the English language? Around 2011 or so, and probably still to this day, the priciest word in the global auction on words was "mesothelioma." This tongue twister is a rare form of lung disease common among former asbestos-plant workers. Thanks to a series of class-action lawsuits against former factory owners, filed by plaintiffs' attorneys who make fortunes on contingency fees, the value of this word was bid up as high as $90 per click. Want to screw a slimy lawyer? Google "mesothelioma" and start randomly clicking on the ads that appear. You're costing a lawyer almost a whole benjamin every time you do that.

Lung-cancer words, despite their superlative cost, are still a pretty niche market. What are the costliest Google keywords among relatively high-volume keywords? The ranking changes, but the top ten is always composed of some combination of "insurance," "loans," "mortgage," "classes," "credit," "lawyer," and so on. These are Google's moneymakers, which pay for the Android phones, the Chrome browser, the self-driving cars, the flying Wi-Fi balloons, and whatever weird, geeky, philanthropic shit the company is up to recently.

Think about this in the context of more traditional industries for a moment. Chain restaurants like McDonald's have a best-performing outlet in a particularly busy high-rent district. Automakers have a particularly popular, bestselling model like the Ford Fusion or the Chevy Impala that makes their quarter. Google has the words "insurance" and "loans." Those are its flagship moneymakers. It is a tech empire built on snippets of words and phrases flitting through people's minds. You as a mere consumer don't see it, but how Google ranks keywords and runs the auction determines the fate of billion-dollar companies and industries. As the gatekeeper on buying interest, Google is the bouncer at the door of almost any Internet-enabled business today, and if you as the business owner don't pay your bouncer well, he'll shut you down, as Google has done more than once.

So what was our angle on this?

Very simple.

This mountain of money Google earns doesn't flow through the simple ads-buying tools it provides. Those are too rudimentary for the experienced marketer. Middlemen companies, like brokers on an exchange, offer sophisticated tools for those spending millions a year on Google keywords. Small businesses, though—the custom jewelry maker with an online store on Etsy, the local plumber—have no such tools, as Google's crude tools are also too confusing for them, and the auction in keywords too dynamic. It's as if the financial world had large investment banks like Goldman, but no Charles Schwab for the average investor to use. Since Google makes most of its money elsewhere, and in any case doesn't have the patience or internal culture to create tools for small advertisers, the tools it does offer are dauntingly complex and ineffectual. The outstanding problem here is like the last-mile problem of an Internet service provider; some piece of technology is needed in order to travel from the fat-pipe fiber-optic cable to the home user wanting to stream Netflix. We would be that last link, allowing a mom-and-pop to finally spend money on Google, rather than pissing away some experimental budget and then getting burned out due to poorly performing keywords or ill-advised bids.

We had plenty of competition.

A company named Clickable (now dead) had an all-star cast of advertising investors, and had raised over $32 million to crack this same nut. Lexity (now dead) was founded by a former Yahoo exec, and raised $6 million. Trada (now dead) had pursued the interesting approach of crowdsourcing the problem, establishing a marketplace where advertisers could easily find campaign managers to do the workaday management of Google search campaigns. It raised $19 million, including money from Google Ventures, the venture arm of the very partner company it was connecting to advertisers.

You'll notice lots of casualties here. We didn't know it at the time, but nobody would succeed in closing the last-mile gap between Google and the universe of small business; to this day, it's an unsolved problem. Despite all this techie fix-it boosterism, not every problem has an engineering solution. That doesn't mean, of course, that you can't sell one.

Following the YC playbook, we'd do boot camp close to YC headquarters, isolated from the beguiling distractions of San Francisco.

I found us a cheap one-bedroom apartment to serve as an office three blocks west of Castro Street, the main drag in Mountain View. Other than serving as Google's hometown, Mountain View is just one more in the string of towns dotting the 101 and the Caltrain line from San Francisco to San Jose. More down-market and working-class than posh Palo Alto or Menlo Park, it housed a couple of startups, as well as the law firm Fenwick & West, an entity we would, sadly, come to know well. Smack in the middle of downtown was Red Rock Coffee, about the most hacker and startup-y café on the Peninsula, whose weaponized sugar-and-caffeine mochas would keep us going through the coming weeks.*

I had just moved out of my Mission bachelor pad in SF and in with British Trader and little Zoë (at this point our relationship situation was tenuous but hopeful), and had furniture to spare. Our corporate headquarters soon had a futon, a mattress we'd toss on the ground in fine Tijuana-whorehouse style, and three desks we made out of cheap interior doors from Home Depot and sawhorses. We used the YC nickels to buy some computer hardware—monitors, new machines for the boys—and we set to work coding our fucking asses off.

In the first week in the pad while we waited for Argyris to disentangle himself from Adchemy, MRM and I sketched out the vision for what the AdGrok product, called the GrokBar, would look like on two big 4×8 sheets of markerboard ($11.99 at Home Depot!).†

Our initial discussion of the GrokBar actually dated to an email from me to the boys on April 16, while we were still at Adchemy, and was a shameless rip on the recently discontinued DiggBar. This was a special window that lived inside the user's browser, and allowed him or her to "Digg" (an

---

* The other star in the startup café firmament is Coupa Cafe in downtown Palo Alto. That's where you go to talk up investors, plot with cofounders, and scope out the female scenery in PA (which is dominated by Stanford undergrads, and is impressive by Bay Area standards).

† Of course, it wasn't even AdGrok yet at the time. The very first name, listed on our YC application, was Vendiamo ("let's sell" in Italian), followed by the short-lived AdShag. This last (horrible) name was inspired by a British Trader comment to the effect of "if you turn that startup office into a shag pad I'll kill you" (a "shag" is technically a seabird, resembling a cormorant). MRM coined "AdGrok," and it stuck. The "grok" reference is of course to Heinlein, and the resulting hacker lingo meaning "to deeply understand."

early version of a Facebook Like) a piece of content. Rather than requiring site owners to include special Digg code on their website, or requiring a user to cut and paste URLs into digg.com, a browsing user could simply comment and "Digg" stuff as part of his or her normal browsing behavior. It was as if someone surfing the Web had a heads-up display that showed the Internet's opinion of each piece of content, everywhere that person went online.

Given its parentage, the early GrokBar closely resembled the DiggBar, in that it accompanied users as they navigated their own online shop. Stuck in the upper reaches of a browser pane, it was slim and relatively unobtrusive, listing stats for the Google Ads you were running. As you browsed your online store, the stats would slice the data by the product whose page you were looking at, providing an in-context view of what ads on Google were driving sales for that product, and at what price. In the same way that Digg showed your friends' comments and likes of an article, the GrokBar showed you how Google was driving traffic to that product's page, which keywords people were searching for to get there, and how much you were paying to show ads alongside the search results. Of course, the bar would be present only when you were on your online store or company page, and not otherwise.

But how to sell it?

Most small startups decide to go after the small-to-medium-sized businesses (SMB) market because they think it's an easy mark. The enterprise sale is too hard, the sales cycle too long, and big companies too untrusting (perhaps reasonably so) of early-stage companies. So they sell to that venerable couple, that mythical bedrock of American values so loved by politicians: Mom and Pop. While it's true that Mom and Pop are likely to try anything once, and that the quality of their typical software and service would make Italian phone companies look cutting edge by comparison, it is also true that Mom and Pop are phenomenally flaky, and are likely to cancel their subscription to even a useful service, making user turnover a problem. Also, given that you're making fifty to one hundred dollars per month for every sale, those nickels and dimes mean any sort of high-touch sales process is unscalable even for underpaid startup founders. So you've got to scale the sale somehow, either by partnering with someone who already owns the SMB relationship (think Salesforce, or the advertising departments of newspapers), or by building on an existing platform with small-business clients, assuming that's possible with your technology.

In our case, we barely had any success with partnering, and had modest success with the building. But that's getting ahead of our story. Let's go back to that dumpy one-bedroom on Oak Street in Mountain View where three scared guys were bailing water to save their lives.

Like Marriage, but without the Fucking*

> You go to war with the army you have. They're not the army you might want or wish to have at a later time.
>
> —Donald Rumsfeld, on the Iraq War (2003)

MAY 2010

The most important decision in a startup, as in life, is picking a partner. It will determine everything that comes after. With the right team, no man or organization can stand against you, and you will ultimately triumph. With the wrong team, you'll produce internal problems even faster than the external world can, and your inevitable death will effectively be a suicide.

The cofounder relationship goes way beyond the typical professional collegiality one finds in blah corporate life. One can stretch these military analogies too far—nobody is taking incoming artillery fire here, who are we kidding?—but the startup experience does have a certain comrade-in-arms,

* This line is a Paul Graham quote about startup founders and is probably the most memorable take on the nature of the cofounder relationship: it's like you're married, but with none of the good and most of the bad.

foxhole quality to it. Nobody believes in what you're doing except this other poor fool sitting next to you, who's just as fucked as you are if you don't succeed. Nothing is keeping the entity going except your shared delusion. And there you sit, working, raging, doing both the best, and also the most poorly thought out, work of your life.

How well do you end up knowing your cofounders?

It got to the point that I could tell who had last used the toilet when I visited our bathroom. Floored with that classic eighties-era terrazzo and finished with chintzy tile, this bathroom was the unholy latrine where three very stressed-out men relieved themselves all day. MRM's shit smelled more grassy and barnyard, in keeping with his mostly vegetarian diet. Argyris's was less compost and more dankly pestilent and human.

You'll end up knowing more about your cofounders than their mothers and mates do, given enough time. Consider that when mulling over that work colleague you're thinking of applying to Y Combinator with.

This is all very touchy-feely, you might say. How's the money side work? How about titles?

Good question, and the first one you should answer with potential cofounders.

As per usual, we were unpracticed morons, and committed the classic error of every first-time startup crew; that is, we divided the equity equally. Fifty-fifty, or all thirds, or whatever—fair's fair, right?

Here's the situation that creates:

At AdGrok, every major decision became this group decision-making circle jerk, which was fine for minor product tweaks and day-to-day twiddles, but was absolutely fatal for larger questions of strategic vision and corporate culture. If we had had to make some later-stage product pivot—and we likely would have had to were we not sold—there's no way we'd have gotten agreement among the three of us on it. Such decisions aren't data-driven collaborative conclusions, driven by spreadsheets and pie charts. No, they're bold, intuitive, bet-the-company moves decided by one individual, similar to a ship's captain in a storm, or a Wall Street trader in the midst of a market move. You live and die by such decisions, and they may well be wrong, but it's more fatal to not make decisions than to make them.

Long story short, AdGrok was a complete basket case when it came to founder dynamics, and it was mostly because we were all equal in equity, and therefore in power as well. What's worse, since there were three of us, we'd commonly form two-person factions against one dissident. Personally, I'd go through periods where I was tight with Argyris (of course, against MRM), and then back to MRM against Argyris. It was madness.

Learn from our missteps, gentle reader!

Here's how it needs to be: either you've achieved a certain Vulcan-quality mind-meld with your founders, your brains welded together in the crucible of some formative life experience like the military or hard-won work experience, or there's one guy running the show (with at least 51 percent of the equity). End of story.

And titles?

The only title that matters in the early days is CEO. Anyone else can call themselves the Grand Poobah of the Sublime Glories of Cthulhu for all it matters. Startups are benevolent dictatorships. As with pirate ships, whose divisions of spoils were refreshingly egalitarian for the time, startups spread ownership (and responsibility) more equally than their conventional rivals. But like pirate ships, there's one captain in the startup. He rules essentially by fiat, tempered, of course, by all the superficial niceties of the modern workplace, plus the fact that any employees worth their pay can easily get a job elsewhere. But he still rules. Should confidence in him be truly undermined, the other founders (and, more important, board members) can mutiny, and conspire to have him removed. But until that happens, the CEO has the last word, despite all the fervid debate that happens in an early-stage startup. Everyone needs to accept that, or absent him- or herself from the proceedings.

In our first meeting with PG, which took the form of a walk around YC's office building in an industrial section of Mountain View, I was agitatedly sharing our confusion about what to build. In those early days, we were doing an entire ballet of product "pivots."

After ten minutes he stopped me.

"I think the real issue here is that you don't have a clear leader."

Pointing to me, he continued.

"It seems like it's you, from this conversation, but I think you should figure that out first."

I was already nominal CEO, but with only tepid support from the boys, particularly MRM, who still thought career seniority meant something in tech (he'd been in tech since I was in high school). This PG meeting would solidify my claim to that title.

We saw it countless times with other companies in our batch. I'm too conscious of YC *omertà* to call them out by name, but there were at least half a dozen out of roughly thirty companies (that I knew about, and possibly more) with hotly disputed leadership. Like some Third World country's government, they either crumbled due to infighting, or suffered internal coups, leaving some founders out on their asses. PG was prescient enough to diagnose this based merely on a few seconds of a practice demo, or in a first meeting (as he did with us). In one memorable case, I knew both founders, and when the inevitable showdown took place a year later, they had raised a bunch of money and were close to an acquisition. It was positively nasty, but it was something that they should have settled much earlier. As PG told us all: *Have a leader!*

Accept that he or she is a dictator. Don't like it? Think you can make a better captain? Then get the fuck out and find your own startup ship to run. If you think this is primitive, wait until we get to how the most successful tech companies, worth billions of dollars, choose their leadership.

What were my comrades-in-arms like, then?

A true engineer, Matthew McEachen could expound on almost any technical subject from the esoterica of some hardware driver to the minutiae of Apple's most recent OS X upgrade. He was the sort of guy who saw a street sign dangling off a post, and stopped to whip out a Leatherman and screw the sign back on, no matter what he was doing beforehand. If it could technically be done, he could technically do it. He also had considerable design chops, crafting our first logo, the website, business cards, anything that required an aesthete's touch.

On the minus side, he had an inflated view of his own importance in the AdGrok construct, thinking himself the engine of everything we did, as he was the senior technical person. There's lots more to a startup than your choice of database technology, though, and Argyris and I were certainly pulling our own weight in our respective ways (he on the technical side, me with everything else).* Worse, he was apt to get distracted by whatever shiny technobauble came his way, and, as many line engineers do, to expend all-consuming efforts on quashing some single technical bug,

* To be clear on roles, we all started more or less as equal hackers, with MRM as the clear technical leader given his long experience. With time, this morphed into MRM as CTO, Argyris as all-purpose hacker, and me as CEO/"guy who ran to Trader Joe's for our lunch wraps and made sure rent got paid." This was for less-than-flattering reasons: one day, after I broke the codebase again with some ill-advised code deployment, the boys took away my password that let me commit code. That's when I really became chief email officer (what CEO really means) and started focusing on everything outside a code-editing window.

or improving some unimportant part of our infrastructure, when those were petty in the overall scheme of things.

Despite his lifelong experience in tech, he reminded me of a college-age intern with his Boy Scout–ish worldview and jejune business and political opinions. He was also emotionally frail, and had to be kept happy to be productive, whether that meant monitoring what was going on at home with the wife and kiddies, or keeping the ever-belligerent Argyris off his back. If he was rattled or unhappy, his productivity suffered—and we were all rattled and unhappy most of the time.

Argyris was a Stanford PhD who had come out of a famous machine-learning lab. A true technorenaissance man, he was capable of doing everything from crafting algorithms to hacking configuration files on servers (and perfectly happy to do either). He was ideal for an early-stage startup, the true multipurpose hacker who was an asset in any situation. Adchemy was his first job out of school, and he hadn't even been there a year before hopping to AdGrok. He brought all the energy and life of untempered youth to AdGrok.

The flip side was that Argyris was also temperamental, moody, and pugnacious to the point of picking fights. I sympathized with his personal style, and you could level the same criticism at me as much as him. That whole dark, Latin/Mediterranean thing was my usual emotional state of being as well, but I (sort of) recognized that it just doesn't fly in the staid Anglo-Saxon world. Very often, Argyris added more heat than light to most meetings, and many a product discussion was demolished by the sudden detonation of his temper, which, like some emotional IED, left nothing but a street full of smoking debris and amputated limbs in its wake. He and I would nearly come to blows on a regular basis, but in that crazy Latin way, we'd get over it and go for a beer later. That emotional heat's more serious and lasting effect was that it bummed out MRM, who'd then stay home for a while to get over the general bad vibe (which only pissed off Argyris and me even more).

Argyris also tended to work on whatever he felt like on a given day. Matt, being the CTO and most senior technical guy, should have stepped in and managed his focus, but he didn't actually have the balls to do so, requiring me to come in and occasionally shout Argyris down. The face-offs would leave everyone sullen and did nothing for morale.

In addition, and perhaps more seriously, the boys would often quarrel between themselves. I had zero desire to play some peacemaker role, and thought two grown men should just hash out their goddamn working relationship already so we could get on with the rest of the show.

People go into startups thinking that the technical problems are the challenges. In practice, the technical stuff is easy, unless you're incompetent or really at the hairy edge of human knowledge—for example, putting a man on Mars. No, every real problem in startups is a people problem, and as such they're the hardest to solve, as they often don't have a real solution, much less a ready software fix. Startups are experiments in group psychology. As CEO, you're both the therapist leader, and the patient most in need of therapy.

As Geoff Ralston, a YC partner, told us: people don't really change, they just become better actors.

For all the existential challenges you'll watch us face in the coming pages, it was no external enemy that would eventually do in AdGrok. No. It was our very natures, the men we saw in the mirror every morning.

Speed Is a Feature

> If everything seems under control, you're just not going fast enough.
>
> —Mario Andretti, Formula One driver

JULY 2010

There was one day that made us realize exactly what flavor of shit we were in. We'd taste different varieties during our startup odyssey—a shit sundae is basically the essence of entrepreneurship—but this was the deep shit of anxious self-doubt, that gnawing rodent inside that eats your guts out with thoughts of "can I really pull this off?"

As an initial sniff test of the characters they had invested in, YC announced we were to have a "Prototype Day," a brief demo to reveal to other YC teams what we were working on, and (as always) spur us to ever-faster product development. "Prototype" would have been a generous description for AdGrok at that point. Our app barely even worked. There was no "production" version of it.* The only working version of it pointed to the URL localhost:3000, the very sign of

* "Production" is tech-speak for the out-in-the-wild, actually working version of a piece of software. It's what your users and the outside world see. "Development" is the mutable, being-worked-on version of code sitting on some coder's machine, whose last line of code was maybe written two

technical immaturity.* It was basically a pile of random code running on one machine.

Every team had ninety seconds to present its progress and introduce itself to the rest of the batch. The setting was the spot where our distinguished speakers delivered their weekly harangues, with a projector aimed at the front wall. The other teams would be sitting at the long benches usually occupied during the dinners. Some of the presentations were of finished products, some were early stage, but nobody seemed as behind as we were.

Then it was suddenly our turn. I plugged in the laptop, opened our crude tool in the browser, and stepped back to address the crowd—and immediately tripped over the power cable to the projector, yanking it forcibly out of the wall, sending the projector swerving across the table, and myself almost falling in the process. The screen went blank, plunging the room into darkness, and all of AdGrok started scrambling and cursing trying to get it back on. By the time we did, I had ten seconds left, of which maybe five seconds were a demo. It was a complete fucking fiasco of a first appearance.

The boys let me have it when the event was over, and I seriously doubted our ability (or, more precisely, my ability) to pull this thing off. We returned to the GrokPad with funerary faces.

Here's one of the lessons of the startup game for you:

Remember how in high school there was a clique of popular kids, always the center of attention, scoring the cheerleaders, and so on? And remember how five years later you came

---

seconds ago inside his text editor. Moving things from "dev" to "prod" is the very nature of shipping a new product.

* "Localhost" is the routing name for your local machine, and "3000" is the port number. In the Internet address scheme, it's the code running as a server on your machine; in "production" it would be running on a remote machine, and accessible by all.

back to your hometown, and randomly ran into one of those people with a name tag and a powder-blue oxford, working as assistant manager at the local Walmart? Or maybe he was already married to that cheerleader, who had gained sixty pounds after squeezing out three kids, and they now lived boring lives in the same sort of dumpy, suburban home you'd been ambitious enough to escape? Or perhaps the outcome wasn't grim: the valedictorian with his curated portfolio of admissions-winning extracurriculars ends up as an equal peer at your prestige company ten years down the line, just like you.

Startups are like that too.

Take one company in our batch as an example. And I should preface this by saying I liked this company, knew the founders, and still use their existing product, which is extraordinarily useful. We come here not to troll these men, but simply to cite them as an example of a common phenomenon.

The best presentation at Prototype Day, by far, was by a company named Rapportive, headed by its suave CEO, Rahul Vohra. He was a bit stuffily pretentious, in that way only Indians with British accents can be. The company had already raised a sizable amount of money, launched a successful product, and garnered an ocean of PR buzz. *What are they even doing here?* I thought, watching Rahul going through his immaculately prepared and presented pitch deck. He wasn't prototyping, he was closing a series A with this pitch for a tool that instastalked the person you were emailing by looking him or her up on every social network in the galaxy.*

* Startups raise successive funding rounds, for ever-higher amounts at higher company valuations, in a loosely defined progression of A, B, C, and so on. The size ranges (e.g., around $2 million to $6 million is a series A) that define these rounds are ever changing, and are a function of the generosity of the VC market just then. The "seed" money precedes this; it's the very first money in, and is what most of us raised after YC. Unlike bra

Similar to AdGrok, Rapportive's product would inject that information into your browser experience alongside your open email, giving you a social and sales heads-up display.

Fast-forward just two years (spoiler alert!): I was one of a handful of product managers at Facebook building the moneymaking machine there. Rapportive had run its course, and was looking for a soft landing. I introduced Rahul to Facebook's corporate-development team. Facebook decided to pass, but LinkedIn didn't. Rapportive had the same acquihire exit we had.

There's a Jewish folktale about a biblical king who dispatches one of his wise men to craft him a mantra that would both humble the proud and console the unfortunate. After searching in the market, where our wise man consults a local jeweler, he returns to the king with an engraved ring. The king holds the ring close and reads: THIS TOO SHALL PASS. So remember that, when lamenting your troubles, contemplating the perceived triumphs of peers and competitors, or rejoicing in that rare entrepreneurial triumph. It will all soon pass, and much faster than you think.

To a startup, media attention is like sex. There are only two types: good . . . and better. A founder should prefer to be arrested for public homosexual, pedophilic bestiality (*baaaaa!*) than to have his or her company ignored by the media. Thus far, our media footprint was fuck-all. Early-stage startups are as much packaging as substance. It was time to make a splash.

After the boys would exit the pad, I was left with an empty, trashed one-bedroom apartment and its soundtrack of the riotous Indians upstairs hosting yet another mystery

---

sizes, the letters don't actually double (e.g., double Es) after a certain point, though it seems they should, given some companies' bloated and diluted capitalization tables.

soirée. My pet theory was that they had porn-watching parties, as the parties would start out with lots of yelling and stamping, and suddenly go quiet, like similar parties I had had in my adolescent boyhood. I paced pensively across the scratched hardwood flooring. What's the biggest nerve I could possibly step on in a first post? What else but that gushing fountain of amour propre, New Yorkers' inflated self-regard? Oh yes, the startup gods were smiling!

Context: at dinner the night before, Ron Conway had mentioned being impressed with the startup scene in New York. PG had also made some random comment about it. Recalling my Goldman days, I imagined everything that was supremely wrong with New York startupwise: the lack of VC, the hustler rather than builder culture, Wall Street drawing away the best talent, the sniggering looks I got when I announced I was leaving Wall Street for a startup. Anyone who thought New York was fertile breeding ground for startups had never lived or worked there. PG was our genius guru, but like many brilliant minds, he occasionally got things flamingly and egregiously wrong, and this was one such instance.

The muses frenetically whispered their ideas, and I started typing. Apropos footnote followed amusing anecdote, followed libelous overgeneralization. After two nights of clacking away after the boys were gone, I had it.

A taste:

Open vs. Closed Source

New York's entire economy is based on monopolies of information. Wall Street banks make a mint trading because they have inside information on the market flows of the products they trade. Literary agents arbitrage scarce access to book publishers against a mass of hopeful authors. Real estate brokers (and these are brokers on *rental* properties, not properties for sale) routinely make a 15% commission when you sign a lease, pocketing a good two months' salary (read, upwards of $5000) for the privilege of telling you where there's an apartment free.

In New York, those monopolies go unchallenged.

In San Francisco, people don't pay two months' rent to a real estate pimp: they create Craigslist and make the pimp obsolete.

What else could I pimp out for page views? What other meme was flitting across the national zeitgeist?

Oh!

Who else but my former employer, that vampire squid with its tentacles violating virgins and robbing starving babies across the land? The great capitalist evil: Goldman Sachs. Everyone would cheer on its lynching. Imagine the lurid interest in what life was really like inside, plus the joy at its roasting. It would be a titillating spectacle of taboo revelation.

New York tech and life at Goldman Sachs, those would be our first two forays into the corporate-driven, mercenary written word—"content marketing," to use the hideous marketer's term for it.

According to the leading PR mythologies, day-of-the-week posting choice was critical. The media boom would reverberate depending on its magnitude and resonance inside whatever industry echo chamber it was launched. And so you wanted a few full-on workdays after launch to let that echo play out. Monday was too soon, as everyone was still jet-lagged, hungover, or otherwise groggy from the weekend, and too busy catching up on email and meetings. By Thursday, people were already thinking about the weekend, and likely ducking out early for their first happy hour of the week. Friday was for burying news, not announcing it. It's when people were fired and bad earnings reports came out.

We would post on Tuesday, which left the most time for a PR blowup to echo across the Internet, and across all levels of Internet connectedness, from the assimilated Internet cyborg to the grandmother in Kansas.

Around nine a.m. Pacific Standard Time I navigated to that venerable if niche corner of the Internet: Hacker News. A Reddit-like message board hosted by Y Combinator itself, it's a weird mix of supertechnical geeks, hustling YC founders, and that species of simultaneously frustrated and sanctimonious poseur called a "wantrapreneur." I posted the piece, while asking a few friends to upvote the article to give it some initial traction. Within minutes, it was the number one post on Hacker News, seen by every serious (and not serious) young techie in the world. Then Scoble tweeted it, and the shit really hit the fan.

Robert Scoble is a mysterious if potent figure on the tech scene. He is one of these old, pasty white guys who seem from a previous generation, if not from the outright technological Jurassic. But via the conferences he attends, the people he knows, and the gadgets he messes around with and reviews, as well as his constant tweeting, he is maniacally embroiled in the Valley ecosystem. Officially, he was then ambiguously employed at a hardware startup, but that is the least interesting thing about him. While a bit annoying in his cloying worship of all things tech, he seems fundamentally good-hearted, and he has an extensive Twitter following of Valley A-listers. If I can use the term without succumbing to the vapors, he is a tech influencer, a person whose mere tweet could make or break a company. And there it was, our post tweeted by Scoble. Which was great, except that now the blog wouldn't even load. Our blog server had melted under the crippling flood of thousands of clicks.

Absolute fucking panic in the GrokPad.

Argyris and I stood nervously behind McEachen as he tried to log into the blog server machine. Naively, we had leased just a single Amazon cloud machine to serve our blog, to handle the piss-squirt of daily page views so far. Now MRM couldn't even log into it, so wedged were its CPU and network connections with insane traffic. In the silence, you could almost hear the sound of three sphincters clenching simultaneously. When we refreshed Twitter, the notifications kept piling up: people were retweeting like mad, and exponentially more people were hitting adgrok.com. All of that inbound was for naught, as the server refused to return the HTML version of my magnificent writing, with none of the eyeballs spilling over to the website and the product. Mind you, we were still in closed testing, so nobody could even use our tool; this was about announcing our existence, more than driving actual adoption. Also, we had no idea the post would be this successful. If so, we'd have been more prepared. Such that maybe people could, you know, actually use our product once they'd been driven to our website.

Fuuuuuck!

Finally, MRM got a command-line prompt on the remote blog server. With a few very-slow-to-execute commands, he managed to duplicate the blog to other quick-to-deploy Amazon machines, and redirect the unfettered fire hose of network traffic to all the new machines immediately. MRM, that resourceful savior among engineers, could probably get Linux running on a toaster oven if necessary.

I verified by going to the blog on my machine. It was up . . . we were live again. Time to start politely replying to the favorable tweets, and egging on the trolls to keep the viral threads going. The post itself quickly accumulated dozens, and eventually hundreds, of comments, positive and negative, and both equally useful. By the end of it, we had thousands of sign-ups. The new clickbait-y publishers that were only then emerging, like *Business Insider*, shamelessly copied the juiciest passages and wrote entire posts about them, drafting on our PR momentum. A producer from the television show *20/20* (that still existed?) called from New York. A reporter from *Business Insider* with the porn star name of Courtney Comstock called with follow-up questions on the New York tech scene (she'd later write about my Goldman Sachs piece as well). A random tech conference in Stockholm invited me to come speak, expenses paid. People were forwarding the post to renowned New York investors like Chris Dixon and asking for commentary. The social media hills were alive with the sound of AdGrok, and I felt like Slim Pickens at the end of *Dr. Strangelove*: a-hootin' and a-hollerin' and waving my cowboy hat around, riding the atomic bomb down to the ground, eager for the great mushroom cloud.

As a strategy, this worked better than expected. Traffic to AdGrok grew exponentially, like Fibonacci's rabbits. We were hitting fifty thousand page views a day, which wouldn't be much for *The Atlantic*, but was a lot for a startup that until the day before had . . . well . . . something like a dozen page views a day. (If we had been masochists, we could have looked at the Web server logs and realized that a half dozen of those views originated from AdGrok or from our families.)

As always, when the cards are favorable, double down.

We still had the second Goldman Sachs post in the ammo bin. I had included a link to the Goldman Sachs post in the New York tech scene one, but few had bruited about it. The PR tsunami had crested nicely on Wednesday, and continued on through the rest of the week. By Monday, the hive mind would be on to its next amusing post, and we'd need to rekindle interest.

This post would be the first in a series of hyperviral blog posts that would put AdGrok on the startup map (if not quite the customer one). Every three to four weeks, another gaseous emanation from the latrine of human thought (a.k.a. me) would appear and rocket us to the top of Hacker News (the tech geek's *Cosmo*), and make another stir in the evanescent tech buzz-o-sphere. Until AdGrok's very end, search terms like "goldman sachs" and "fuck you" (I had written a post about the ever-elusive goal of "fuck-you money") would be the most popular terms that led to clicks to our site.* It irritated MRM to no end. But hey—I didn't see fifty thousand people a day lining up to use the product we had built. We'd take eyeballs wherever we could find them.

As a result of the Amazon Web Services near fiasco, plus several more outages and server meltdowns, MRM suggested we run a "chaos monkey" from time to time. This was a software tool created and open-sourced by Netflix, meant to test a product or website's resiliency against random server failures (such as we'd just witnessed with the blog).

In order to understand both the function and the name of the chaos monkey, imagine the following: a chimpanzee rampaging through a data center, one of the air-conditioned warehouses of blinking machines that power everything from Google to Facebook. He yanks cables here, smashes a box there, and generally tears up the place. The software chaos monkey does a virtual version of the same, shutting down random machines and processes at unexpected times. The challenge is to have your particular service—Facebook messaging, Google's Gmail, your startup's blog, whatever—survive the monkey's depredations.

More symbolically, technology entrepreneurs are society's chaos monkeys, pulling the plug on everything from taxi medallions (Uber) to traditional hotels (Airbnb) to dating (Tinder). One industry after another is simply knocked

* "Fuck-you money" is the amount of money you need to say fuck you to everybody, and live financially independently at a middle-class level in a livable city like San Francisco or Seattle. We'll have much more to say on this before this book is over, as it once loomed in tantalizing closeness before disappearing, possibly forever.

out via venture-backed entrepreneurial daring and hastily shipped software. Silicon Valley is the zoo where the chaos monkeys are kept, and their numbers only grow in time. With the explosion of venture capital, there is no shortage of bananas to feed them. The question for society is whether it can survive these entrepreneurial chaos monkeys intact, and at what human cost.

D-Day

> The only thing you got in this world is what you can sell.
>
> —Arthur Miller, *Death of a Salesman*

AUGUST 26, 2010

Whether justly or no, there are specific events in life during which our characters are weighed and assayed: an all-important entrance exam, the audition in front of the big-shot director, a hard-to-get job interview. Sometimes, we don't even know the moment is one of those fulcrums on which life hinges: a first date with our future mate, the moments before a debilitating accident.

Y Combinator Demo Day is just such a pivotal event.

You cast your little white ball on the roulette wheel of life, and it comes up either a winner or a loser—and so do you. The best you can hope for, if you're an underdog outsider like me (and if you're not, you'll take it merely as your entitled due), is a place at the biggest roulette table you can find. Well, that much we had achieved, but where our little white ball would stop, we had no idea.

The rules of the Demo Day game were these: Each of the thirty-odd companies in the YC batch had two and a half minutes to present or demo its product and aspiring business to the massed crowd of Silicon Valley venture capital elite.

Since Y Combinator's space was so tiny, the presentations would go in three salvos, each in decreasing order of importance of the attendees (i.e., Sequoia would appear in the first salvo, Comcast Ventures in the last).* The companies would present in a preassigned but random order, the entire demo marathon lasting some two hours, with two breaks in between sessions.

As a sort of practice run and teaser reel, there were two rehearsals of the Demo Day pitches: one to everyone else in the batch, and one to YC alumni, playing stand-ins for the VCs. Many of the alums were investors in their own right, so it was only a partial practice. This would help hammer out the significant bumps in every demo, and alleviate some of the severe stage fright of many YC founders (including this one). Brave in technology and innovation, but perhaps a bit more gun-shy in the more human arts of marketing and self-promotion, YC founders needed a shakedown pass or two before the real moneymen were in the room.

The name "Demo Day" is something of a misnomer; it's rare to have an actual demo of a product at the event. Given the tight time constraints, it would be almost impossible to walk a potential user (consumer, advertiser, whatever) through any sort of realistic product exposition. Even if you were able to pull it off, most investors were at least as interested in the business side as the tech side, so unless the tech was miraculous, demos were a waste of time.

So the first rehearsal in front of our cohort kicked off.

I had practiced the pitch to the point that I'd be repeating the script in my dreams for years, so go-time was itself uneventful. The AdGrok pitch was simple: Google AdWords represented an immense river of money, much of

---

* Beginning in 2015, YC rented out the Computer History Museum's vast amphitheater, obviating the need for several rounds of demos. A batch is also now composed of almost a hundred companies, such has the institution grown.

which was completely undammed or untouched by anybody, as it flowed in its majestic course from the world to Google. We were going to get our hands on a part of it. Even if our take was a small fraction, it would be enough to satisfy the dreams of startup avarice.

By way of entertainment or perhaps to signal quality, the YC management held an anonymous vote among the founders for the best pitch following our rehearsal. AdGrok came in second place, close behind Rapportive, whose polished Prototype Day pitch had so dismayed me. Rather different outcome from me tripping over the cable like Charlie Chaplin, while showing off a nonexistent product, wasn't it?

In the summer of 1996, I ran with the bulls in Pamplona.

Hemingway oversold the whole thing. For starters, there's no "running of the bulls." There's a citywide festival called San Fermín (after the patron saint of Pamplona), which involves a series of bullfights as an incidental part of the general merriment. In order to transport the fighting bulls from the corral on the edge of town to the bullring, the ever-impractical Spanish decided to simply run them through town. Also in typical Spanish fashion, the local *mozos* decided to run in front of the galloping bulls to prove their manhood. Fast-forward a few hundred years, and it's now the Mardi Gras of decadent European youth.

The geometry of the thing works like this: stout wooden barricades, rising higher than you are tall, line the streets of the route. Come eight o'clock that morning, the local police officers clear the route of drunks and tourists, by whack of a baton if necessary. They leave one route of ingress open, close to city hall, for all the potential runners. Then they close the barricades. Anyone left inside is there at the risk of his or her life. For the next ten minutes, nobody will attempt to save you, and in that stretch of rough, cobblestoned street, there is neither God nor law.

I stood there during those ten unforgiving minutes before the release of the bulls. The sensation was one of prickly intensity: life slowed down in that grainy, black-and-white way in which your brain mimics the JFK assassination reels when you're doing something seriously dicey. Grown men stood with gray, downcast faces, pondering their mortality, perhaps for the first time. Some looked excited for the fray. Others just busied themselves with last-minute prep like stretching that was probably more mental than physical. Soon enough, we heard the hooves clacking on cobblestones and started running for our lives.

You'll accuse me of embellishment, but waiting outside the Y Combinator space on Demo Day felt the same way. It was an unseasonably hot day, almost 100 degrees Fahrenheit, and YC had set up a makeshift tent to shield us from the sun.

At the run-through we'd made the minor mistake of tipping our hand, and had donned our custom-made ADGROK shirts. By the time the real Demo Day rolled around, *every* startup had put in rush orders and appeared in logo-branded T-shirts. Since each company chose one background color for its swag, the anxious mob was now composed of two- and three-person cliques, all with color-coded tees: a herd of microgangs composed of unhealthy-looking geeks. People languished about, waiting their demo turn, either alert and reciting their pitch lines, reclining and toying with laptops or phones, or passed out on the floor, anticipating the inevitable.

After waiting our turn, I stood in the "next up" booth, getting wired to a mike by Y Combinator's CFO, an unflappably chipper Brit named Kirsty. The polite applause for the previous pitch dying down, I took the stage. Cued by whoever was running the laptop, I lit into it like I had just mainlined a handful of cocaine. Screenshots flew by, logos of all the current customers, growth rates, $70 billion market, Google is just the first step—there was even an appropriate amount of laughter at the one half-naked woman we'd snuck in (a lingerie company was using AdGrok to sell fancy bras). It all went as practiced, even better. If the VCs were falling asleep before AdGrok, they sure were awake after. Two and a half minutes later, it was done.

Then, we waited.

These tightly choreographed demos were interspersed with bladder-saving intermissions, during which the startup teams were unleashed on the flower of Silicon Valley capital to pitch their wares. All in all, there were about 150 founders, and at least that many investors in each Demo Day bracket, so during every intermission and for hours after, the space was absolutely nut-to-butt packed.

The mob was a roiling sea of twentysomething geeks in logoed T-shirts and jeans, and rich white guys (and they were almost all rich white guys) in button-down shirts and slacks. All were mingling and talking in and listening in all directions at once, and you literally had to elbow your way past massed twosomes, threesomes, and moresomes as you circulated around. It was a mosh pit of greed and glib persuasion, ambition trading itself for money trading itself (hopefully) for more money in the future. The boys also joined the fray, collecting business cards and names with both hands. It was the most thrilling and terrifying few hours of my life, and the coming weeks and months would be filled with echoes of that chaotic traffic.

A Conclave of Angels

Yea, he wrestled with the Angel, and prevailed;
he wept, and made supplication unto Him.
—Hosea 12:4

SEPTEMBER 2010

"It's right here, man, we're supposed to be looking at it."

"I don't see it."

"We're at the pin, this is it," I repeated semidesperately.

"Call them," offered MRM.

"Shit, it's five past five. We're late."

The inescapable conclusion was that we had gotten lost on the way to our first investor meeting. Lost and late, to boot. We had agreed to meet in a Starbucks in Los Altos, one square in the patchwork quilt of South Bay suburbia surrounding well-known hubs like Palo Alto and San Jose. Each patch was a separate maze of street numbers and grid conventions, a Cartesian lattice randomly giving way to the impractically sinuous roads used by planners to make their air-conditioned stucco nightmares seem more "organic." Having agreed to meet at the "Starbucks north of the Los Altos Country Club," where the investor had his daily midafternoon workout, we had confidently headed out from AdGrok HQ without a doubt that Google Maps would guide us true.

It was MRM at the wheel of his Honda Accord family-mobile, and me riding shotgun and navigating via a soon-to-be-revealed-as-perfidious Google Maps.

With mounting panic, I called and asked if the Starbucks was on the street whose signs we were stupidly staring at.

"Oh, yeah . . . Google thinks we're over there, but really we're not. We're over on Second Street. Sorry . . ."

Fuck us.

"Tell Russ we're going to be really late and try to reschedule," I told McEachen, who'd been the original point of contact.

So began our relationship with one of the two most important investors in the AdGrok saga. Later, after he had given us a pile of money, we learned he had been more than annoyed—he was actually pissed off by our incompetence. He almost wrote us off; if he had, then this story would have ended right here.

Who was this lifesaving character?

Russell Siegelman was a perfect exemplar of the old-school class of angel investor that typified a previous era in Valley tech, and which coexisted (some would say uneasily) with the current crop of pseudoangels.

Undergrad at MIT, Harvard MBA plus the additional laurels of Baker Scholar, he had had a long career at Microsoft, where he oversaw the creation of MSN, the Yahoo-esque content portal with messaging and email features before Facebook demolished that world, and salon.com.* He then

* At Harvard it's "Baker Scholar," at Stanford it's "Arjay Miller Scholar"; this is the added frosting on the MBA cake if you graduate within the top 10 percent gradeswise. It's the people who took their MBA classes seriously and thought that the content actually meant something rather than assuming that the entire point of an elite MBA was the curated network and

spent a decade at Kleiner Perkins Caufield & Byers (KPCB, or just "Kleiner" among the cognoscenti), the other superlative VC firm alongside Sequoia. After investing in companies and serving on boards, Siegelman had turned to private angel investing as his full-time gig—other than being a serious cyclist, of course; every superaffluent Valley personage with nothing but money and time on his or her hands seemed to spend a good chunk of it perfecting some healthy but useless skill such as road biking or kiteboarding. He was fit, in that lean, sinewy way of an elite soldier in a wartime army. Argyris and I typecast him as a paratrooper in the IDF: formidable, dependable, and kind of menacing. "Israeli Paratrooper" became his office sobriquet.

Russ invested his own money, and was answerable to nothing or nobody except his own net worth. If you doubled his money, he'd be happy. If you quadrupled it, he'd be ecstatic, though more was always better. If it looked like the company was about to implode, he wanted his money back rather than to simply write it off. Russ was the type of guy who had written first checks for companies like Oracle, Sun, and eBay in the initial boom(s): an angel when angels really did resemble some supernatural, winged creature who emerged from the heavens and miraculously jump-started your business experiment. As such, they were rational, in that they merely wanted a good return on their money, rather than a hundredfold return for their fund. They were also committed; this wasn't merely one of fifty bets made with other people's money that fit into a portfolio of risk, it was their actual skin in the game, skin they had earned playing that very same game.

Given his old-school nature, we went through the long

---

jump-starting of a new career direction (which is what you're actually paying $70K/year for, in Stanford's case). Such people often end up in venture capital, the final redoubt of individuals with discipline and ambition but no actual talent.

and somewhat haphazard vetting process such angels conduct. He called in favors from friends, themselves involved in search marketing, to sniff us out and see if we knew what we were doing. He ran our proposed road map past other friends to see if it jibed with what incumbents in the space (e.g., Facebook) were doing. He and I had long chats by phone, mutually feeling each other out, to see if there was the personal chemistry required to work with each other without friction.

Fortunately, we had contacted Russ before Demo Day (our initial aborted meeting thanks to Google Maps losing track of a Starbucks), which turned into a series of meetings with him and his personal brain trust. So all this lurching due diligence transpired before we had other investors in the mix. As we'd soon find out, timing was everything, and if we hadn't been grooming Russ (and he us) for weeks before, we'd have lost what became our lead investor and company-saving cherub.

After we successfully jumped through his hastily arranged obstacle course, he finally invited me over to his home in Old Palo Alto. Even within the privileged confines of PA, there are gradations of status. Old Palo Alto is where the Valley elite live. Steve Jobs and Google cofounder Larry Page had both lived in Old PA at some point. The broad tree-lined streets conceal tasteful Tudor-style, Craftsman, or faux-Spanish mansions, often nestled in miniature compounds (Paul Graham, the YC guru, lived in such a home). The lots are surprisingly modest—Palo Alto was not always an enclave for the fabulously wealthy, far from—but if you wanted expansive estates you'd live in more rural-seeming Atherton or Woodside anyhow, as many of the elite did when they started larger families.*

* Palo Alto means "tall stick" in Spanish, and it refers to a thousand-year-old redwood tree that served as a landmark along El Camino Real, the royal road the Spanish built when colonizing Alta California, and

The house, on Santa Rita Avenue, did not disappoint. An updated Craftsman, it bristled with gables and arched windows, and was embellished with expensive stone and wood accents. Russ met me at the door wearing his usual uniform of an old T-shirt and shorts, and looking as if he had just finished a long bike ride (which he probably had). The inside was baronial, and encompassed a vaulted, lofty space that the exterior, partially shielded by a thick barrier of foliage, did not suggest.

We passed Russ's office, which was paneled in an Amazon forest of hardwoods, walked around a monumental staircase framed by swooping curving banisters, and went into the open living room space. Russ's son was playing video games in a neighboring den, and I pseudosmiled a greeting as Russ led me to a dining table. Sitting on either side of a corner with Russ at the head, we got down to the subtle business of our going deal. We were (though you're no doubt tired of the fund-raising-as-dating analogy) at the third date of the VC-entrepreneur courtship: it was time to either make a move or not.

"So what cap were you thinking of raising at, and how much are you raising?"

Ah—*the cap!* Russ and I were finally talking turkey.

This is the one number—*the* number—that matters to an early-stage company raising money for the first time. It's worth a diversion.

Startups are business experiments performed with other people's money.

Here's how you fund the experiment:

The first money in is known as the seed round, as if germinating a mighty redwood tree. Historically, this money came from the proverbial friends and family, or from angels

---

which now serves as a major artery running through all the former missions (now cities) they founded. The tree still stands a few blocks from downtown Palo Alto, and a stone's throw away from the Stanford campus.

like Russ, or from the pseudoangels (as we'll soon see) like Chris Sacca. Companies from measly AdGrok to mighty General Motors are funded via a mix of debt and equity. In the startup world the first money in is usually in debt form, which is counterintuitive, and also deceptive, as it's not really debt that is paid off.

All early-stage companies, except those that raise an exceptionally large round of funding from the get-go, raise on what's called a convertible note. Despite the fancy name, it's essentially debt with a nominal interest rate. Should the company be acquired or raise yet more money, this note converts into equity in the company, such that you became an actual owner rather than a creditor. Sounds more complicated than it is. What it boils down to is this: I "lend" you $100,000 to start a company. When you raise your next round of cash, I expect to get $100,000 in equity, at whatever the going price of equity is at that point.

Here's a simple example, with numbers chosen for ease of exposition, not business reality.

An investor writes you a check for $100,000 to get the startup going. A year later, after hitting some product or usage milestones, you raise $1 million on a $10 million valuation (your typical postseed funding round, referred to as a "series A"). That debt—the original $100,000—converts into equity in the company. Given that the valuation is $10 million, and the investor put in $100,000, he now owns 1 percent of the company.

From the point of the view of the investor, this is actually problematic. Say you're the hot startup of the moment in the midst of a bubble, and you raise on some crazy valuation, such as $100 million. Well, pity our poor angel investor; he gets only 0.1 percent of the company. In essence, the better the company does, the less of it he gets. While he's guaranteed (in theory) to get a price per share equal to follow-on investors, that's actually a gross mispricing of his risk, as he put his money in far earlier, when the company was far riskier.

Enter the investor's great friend: the cap. The cap dictates the maximum number at which the company will be valued, for the purposes of calculating the investor's stake when the company takes more investment capital. In our previous example, say the initial $100,000 investment had been done at a cap of $3 million. Then, despite the company's raising later at a valuation of $10 million, the angel's stake amounts to $100,000 ÷ $3 million = 3.3%, a much bigger slice. The angel's effective price per share is that of the cap (rather than that of the valuation), giving him a huge discount on the equity compared with investors who just put money in. As a result, this cap is perceived in essence, if not in contractual reality, to be a proxy for the valuation of the company at the time of the angel's investment. Early-stage entrepreneurs will bandy about their cap number as if it were a real company valuation, when in truth it's an input to a hypothetical calculation that may or may not play out in the future.

Funding a company via equity, rather than debt, is a different beast. With a capped note, there's no universal agreed-upon value. You can bounce from investor to investor, like a bee from flower to flower gathering pollen, getting notes signed at various caps, and no one need be the wiser. In priced-equity rounds, however, everyone has to agree on a share price and a total amount sold, and everyone must sign on the dotted line at once. Typically there's a round lead, usually the biggest investor in that round, who will help you herd the other investor cats into the deal. Also, the contractual legal work is more complex, and hence more expensive. Then the bank wires fly and you're money. To make an analogy, a capped note is like having to seduce five women one after the other, while an equity round is having to convince five women to do a sixsome with you. The latter is exponentially harder than the former.*

* The women analogy breaks down in that, unlike with women, the more investors you seduce into your moresome, the more likely others are to

Why all this obsession with either a cap or a real valuation? Does it matter more than mere phallic jockeying for a big number?

Yes, because the great enemy of every entrepreneur, the villain hiding in each cap table, is that monster of gradual, withering decay: dilution (!).* This refers to the obvious numerical fact that a company is in some ways a big, creamy cheesecake. You and your cofounders might own 90 percent of it to begin with (with 10 percent left for the eventual employee-option pool), but the more money you take in, the smaller the founders' segment becomes. The higher the valuations (or the caps), the less the investors' take, even for the same amount of money they give you. And so with each successive round of funding, the smaller your piece of cheesecake gets, no matter how the investors take their share, via debt or equity—and that's why entrepreneurs struggle to keep that cap (or valuation) as high as possible. It's effectively setting the price of that cheesecake wedge they're selling, as well as its size. The higher the price, the less cheesecake they have to sell for the same amount of funding cash in the bank.

What Russ and I were about to negotiate at that dining table of his, couched in the warm bosom of cosseted Palo Alto wealth, was precisely the price of AdGrok cheesecake, or this pseudovaluation that would determine everything. In the summer of 2010, for the prechosen YC elite, a good cap was in the $6 million range. A stellar cap was around $8 million, and only a really buzzy company like Hipmunk, a travel startup that was a Reddit founder's second act, got close to that. The middle of the YC pack (where we were) was in the

---

join. This is an expression of the lemming-like nature of tech investors, most of whom scarcely merit the title.

* The "cap table" is the capitalization table, a list detailing each owner of equity (investor, founder, or employee) and how much of the company he or she owns. It's about the most important document at any company. Every member of that table will know his or her number down to the decimal.

$3 million to $4 million range. By the time this dinner-table conversation took place, Demo Day had come and gone, and we were talking to several investors. I had felt them out and realized we were safely in $3 million cap territory, and perhaps more. So to his answer about raising money:

"Russ, we're raising five hundred to seven hundred fifty thousand at a cap of four million. I know we talked about three million, but I don't think that's where other investors are right now."

Russ, betting his own money, greeted the news with some dismay.

"That sounds really rich."

Pause.

"Let me know where you end up with the other investors . . ." Followed by a sideways shake of the head.

One of the few skills that I could bring to the startup game was my ability to detect human weakness. Like fresh dog shit on a man's shoe, it stunk from across the room, and I could smell it. Russ's hesitation and wavering headshake were a clear tell: he'd do $4 million if properly pushed; we just needed to provide a sense of urgency.

We'd have a burning sense of urgency soon enough—although it wouldn't push the cap in the direction we expected.

The other big investor in AdGrok was a case-study contrast to our Israeli Paratrooper. Chris Sacca was and is one of the most famous angel investors in Silicon Valley. A loud and opinionated social media presence, earlyish Googler, and early investor in Twitter and Uber, he was one of the half dozen or so stars in the early-stage investment firmament. His 24-karat-gold name in your cap table worked that essential but elusive miracle: convincing other weak-kneed investors to invest simply due to his presence. Unlike Russ, he did not invest his own money, at least not exclusively. At this level of the investor stratosphere, these micro-VCs raised funds of between $20 million and $40 million, taking money from other members of the tech wealthy who didn't want to bother with vetting companies and playing the funding game. For these professional investors, despite their public swagger, they had a boss, or rather a fund of bosses, who owned the money they invested. If they didn't produce a generous return for that fund, they were back to being do-it-yourself angels (assuming they had any personal money left).

Sacca had emailed me the moment I had gotten off the stage at Demo Day. "I dig it" was the subject line, and then he mentioned his Googler background and understanding of what we were doing.

Sacca will figure prominently in the story ahead; however, our sole face-to-face meeting was the one he suggested a week after Demo Day. The week's delay was caused by the fact that he lived in the lakeside ski resort town of Truckee, nestled in the alpine paradise of Lake Tahoe three hours from San Francisco, where groups of young startupistas would rent houses, or old, rich startupistas (like Sacca) would own them.

Our meeting place was Brickhouse Café, an oddly dumpy and mediocre Western-themed two-floor bar-diner in the very heart of the SoMa startup district of San Francisco, and one of the go-to meeting places (along with the Creamery) for funding and acquisition scheming. It was next door to Alexander's, the pricey, expense-account steakhouse par excellence (splurge, and get the freshly truffled filet), and a block away from that epicenter of all things startup, South Park.

Argyris insisted on coming along on this scavenging foray, despite my desire to insulate the boys from the money-grubbing bullshit. We found Sacca inside, as advertised in his prolific social media persona, in a Western-themed cowboy shirt (very apropos for the venue) sitting in one of the hard-backed wooden booths. He made a gesture of standing up and shaking our hands before we nestled in the cramped booth and got down to business.

As with the YC pitch, Argyris and I tag-teamed Sacca, preaching the (now) well-practiced AdGrok gospel. Within about a half hour, or less, he announced, "I'm in!" and the meeting was more or less over. Just like that.

Both sides of the booth got up to leave, and Sacca darted toward the door, then hung a quick left and took the stairs to the mezzanine. We sauntered out of the restaurant, both still shell-shocked at the ease of the thing. On the threshold, we ran into Solomon Hykes, a founder from our YC batch.* We exchanged rushed greetings, before somewhat stupidly announcing we were there to see Sacca. "So am I," he said, and leapt up the stairs to the mezzanine.

This would come to be a common feature of these meetings, running into YC classmates coming to or from meetings with some prominent investor. It felt like everyone was in some sort of speed-dating event held all over the Bay Area, in cafés and conference rooms from San Francisco to Menlo Park, trying to find that hurried mutual fit that would lead to another meeting (if necessary) or a check (if possible).

For us, right then, this was a victory, all the more important for being the first in the fund-raising race. Sacca was in the bag, and we had a gold-plated name in the cap table now. But we needed to go after even bigger piles of money if we were going to do this right.

---

* Solomon Hykes's company DotCloud made computer infrastructure management tools, and would eventually morph into Docker, a new paradigm in systems deployment and management. What would become its flagship product was in fact an open-source spin-off of an internal project that met sudden (and one supposes, surprising) industry-wide acceptance, while its original YC product languished. By 2015, that product had become so successful Docker achieved "unicorn" status, meaning a greater-than-billion-dollar valuation, becoming one of the most promising companies in Silicon Valley, and the unquestioned champion from our YC batch. Along the way, however, it peeled off one of the cofounders, Sebastien Pahl, in a founder shake-up. Even the best suffer startup drama.

The Hill of Sand

SHYLOCK: A pound of man's flesh taken from a man
Is not so estimable, profitable neither,
As flesh of muttons, beefs, or goats. I say,
To buy his favour, I extend this friendship:
If he will take it, so; if not, adieu;
And, for my love, I pray you wrong me not.
ANTONIO: Yes Shylock, I will seal unto this bond.
—William Shakespeare, *The Merchant of Venice*

SEPTEMBER 2010

Speaking of Venetians: most everything we know as modern banking originated in the northern Italian city-states of the early and mid-Renaissance. The bankers of the day were Jews; many were Sephardic Jews fleeing the 1492 expulsion order from Spain's *Reyes Católicos.* The church disallowed Christians from practicing usury, granting Jews an unexpected windfall in the form of a religiously ordained monopoly on moneylending. They were otherwise persecuted and oppressed, forced to wear distinguishing signs, prohibited from land ownership and most trades, and barred from living inside the city walls. By 1516 the Jews were proving themselves too useful, and Venice's doges considered the issue of allowing them residence inside the city. They were granted living rights in a dirty, gritty part of the city named the Ghetto Nuovo. (*Ghetto* means "foundry," referring to the slag heaps left by the neighborhood's previous occupants.) Locked behind the ghetto's walls at night, the Jews plied their moneylending trade during the day, with Christians traveling to the otherwise rancid part of the city to borrow cash.

The modern-day Silicon Valley ghetto, though sadly without the moneymen living behind locked gates as in erstwhile Venice, is Sand Hill Road. A meandering stretch of two-lane blacktop that wends its way from Palo Alto to Menlo Park, this uninspiring piece of suburban scenery is swarmed by aspiring entrepreneurs with a laptop in hand and a sly pitch in mind.

In New York, the old joke is that Wall Street starts in a graveyard and ends in the river. In Silicon Valley, just as symbolically, Sand Hill Road starts in a shopping mall and ends at a particle accelerator. The shopping mall is the Stanford Shopping Center, a suburban monument to upscale consumption built on land formerly occupied by Senator Leland Stanford's vineyards. After World War II and before the tech boom from which it so richly profited, Stanford University was a mediocre institution with sagging fortunes, which it tried to revive by leasing land to developers. The resulting shopping mall, standing proudly alongside the Valley's preeminent academic institution, is an excellent reminder of the values underlying Silicon Valley (not to mention Stanford students and staff).

The particle accelerator is the Stanford Linear Accelerator Center, SLAC for short. As venture capitalists and wealthy alums prefer funding Googles to winning Nobel Prizes (of which SLAC has several), the facility is funded by the US Department of Energy. The runway for its accelerated particles travels alongside Sand Hill Road, under Interstate 280, and into the foothills of the Santa Cruz Mountains, which define the western border of Silicon Valley.

Lastly, there's a high-class brothel: the Rosewood Sand

Hill, a posh restaurant and hotel complex wedged in between SLAC and the Sand Hill–Interstate 280 intersection. Thursday nights at Sand Hill are famous for serving as "cougar nights," where older, lonely women (and younger ones explicitly on the clock) congregate to ensnare Sand Hill's wealthy denizens.

So you see, there are all sorts of strivers and strumpets on Sand Hill, trying to cadge that next score from the guy in the Audi R8. I was merely one more hustler among the many.

Our first big-money institutional VC meeting was with Sequoia. Founded in 1972 by Don Valentine, himself a part of the first generation of Valley companies like Fairchild Semiconductor, Sequoia was the absolute crème de la crème, the *capo di tutti capi* of the venture capital world.*

This meeting had been the result of an initial pitch to Mark Dempster, the marketing partner at Sequoia charged with the Y Combinator relationship. YC had held a "Sequoia Day" in the first few weeks of our batch, reflecting the accelerator's growing clout with large VC firms. The day before, I had reminded the boys that we were pitching the biggest VC firm in the Valley, and to not fuck up anything in the codebase. True to form, the boys hadn't quite realized what that meant, and had shifted the codebase such that the local code

* Fairchild Semiconductor occupies a legendary place in US tech history, with its founders and employees going on to found industry stalwarts like Intel, among others. The original team that seeded Fairchild, however, met at a very different company: the equally (in)famous Shockley Semiconductor Labs. William Shockley was a Nobel laureate and the inventor of that central artifact of our electronic age, the transistor. He also contributed his seed to a sperm bank of recognized geniuses and Olympians, and ended his career embroiled in polemics about scientific racism and eugenics. By the time of his death, he was a bitter, broken man of ruined reputation. Don't come to Silicon Valley looking for sanity, dear reader.

running on my laptop wouldn't work anymore (they were hacking away on building AdGrok, after all). I discovered this one minute before my appointment with Sequoia, when I realized that the AdGrok product suddenly wouldn't load in my browser. An angry, screaming phone call to MRM later, I had an emailed screenshot off his laptop as eye candy.

The pitch, to the extent we can call my desperate salesmanship that, involved lots of clever phrasing and hand waving (for lack of anything else). But sometimes you score the pot off a pair of 2s. Dempster took a shine to our idea, and he scheduled a more formal pitch meeting at Sequoia with his venture partner Bryan Schreier, who had led Dropbox's first serious funding round the year before.

Now that the boys realized what we were dealing with, they wanted to ride along to the pitch and see what the great Sequoia was about.

This was a bad idea. In general, either the CEO or the smooth-tongued founder designated for the purpose should be involved in the fund-raising, and that person alone. Fund-raising is an operatic drama on the order of a Latin American telenovela. Avoid the company-wide noise, and contain the pointless din of the begathon to yourself (or someone) at all costs.

Sequoia was ensconced in one of the regulation two-story, poured-concrete-and-wood-trim, open-courtyard structures that dotted the manicured slopes around Sand Hill Road between Stanford and the 280. The impression was that of understated corporate efficiency, with Palo Alto's supernaturally pleasant climate lending a certain Elysian quality. If you didn't know the context, you might think it the bland corporate headquarters of some national insurance company, or perhaps the high school classrooms in a moderately affluent LA suburb.

Inside, however, the décor was sleek and California minimalist modern: dark hardwood tables, cream-colored wood floors gleaming with fresh wax, conference room chairs of contrasting exposed steel and light-colored fabric, and recessed halogen lighting everywhere. The intended effect seemed to be that of the bridge on the starship *Enterprise* in *Star Trek: The Next Generation.*

The receptionists were jaw-droppingly hot. I'm talking "got lost on the way to New York Fashion Week" hot. They took our names and escorted us into a conference room. Then I saw what was on the walls.

The real showpieces, the absolute pièces de résistance, the artworks for which this was all merely a museum, were the framed prints of corporate logos and funding-round tombstones hanging from every wall.

"Tombstones" are the chintzy engraved Lucite bricks used to commemorate a deal in high-stakes American corporate life. On Wall Street, they mark the syndication of some stock or bond deal (an IPO or a bond issue, for example) and decorate, with varying degrees of derision or seriousness, many an investment banker's desk. In Silicon Valley, the Land of No Sarcasm, they're taken seriously, and tile the walls of any über-successful VC firm. Thus did the tombstone commemorating the initial $25 million funding round for Google beam forth its rays of divine benediction, like the image of the Virgin of Guadalupe in Mexico City's basilica. Every religion requires its miracles and stories of exalted sainthood for mass veneration; capitalism's miracles simply culminate in NASDAQ ticker symbols rather than saintly relics.

Apple, Atari, Google, Oracle, Yahoo, YouTube, Zappos, PayPal, Kayak, Instagram, Airbnb, Dropbox, LinkedIn—the corporate logos hung in large framed prints, a mini-Louvre of victorious American capitalism, of corporate triumph. It was stirring stuff to be paraded past such a pantheon, presumably to see if we were equal to their legacy.

Hot Receptionist parked us inside a conference room, and the boys and I waited nervously, silent, not knowing what to expect. Bryan made his appearance shortly; beaming, good-looking, and well groomed, he had the entire

VC package. Bellarmine Prep (a Jesuit all-boys school, like mine, in San Jose), Princeton, Morgan Stanley, Google, then Sequoia. He oozed patrician ease, tinged with a hint of wolfish entrepreneurial savvy (perhaps faked, perhaps not), which seemed to be the de rigueur air of most high-end VCs. We walked him through what existed of the AdGrok product (a working demo, this time), the vision, and the opportunity. He listened politely, nodding quietly at times, and asking relevant questions. As someone who had worked in what's termed "online sales and operations" at Google, he grasped the market problem immediately.

Eventually, Sequoia would choose not to invest, purportedly due to a competing investment in Kenshoo, an Israeli company building a somewhat similar search marketing tool. Per Sequoia's email, it liked keeping "white space" between its companies. That's one of those truths that are also polite lies. Either way, Sequoia was studiously prompt and polite in communication, and even provided several introductions down the line that were helpful. In VC, as often in life, it's the incompetent and insecure who are generally the assholes; the masterful and successful—not to mention those universally perceived as the best in their field—are playing the long game. You never know where the next Airbnb is coming from.

Investment bankers have their golf, Wall Street traders have squash, and the new VC/entrepreneur tech elite has kiteboarding. An amalgam of kite flying and surfing, kiteboarding involves getting on a floating snowboard attached to a U-shaped kite the length of a small plane wing, which threatens to whisk you to Never-Never Land. Like most patrician sports, it requires lots of pricey equipment and access to select real estate. In this case, that real estate is often Crissy Field, a waterfront park in SF's douchiest neighborhood, the Marina District.

When I'd sail by the area in my forty-foot cutter, the temptation to veer into the kiteboarders' appropriated waters and take out a few VCs was almost irresistible. There they went zigzagging back and forth in front of the biggest natural wind tunnel in North America, 'twixt yacht and container ship. Occasionally one would tire, or get caught in his kite lines, and take refuge on a buoy. A passing boat would then rescue the drenched member of the tech elite from drowning or death by great white shark, which occasionally populated the entrance to the Golden Gate.

Naturally, one of the elite Valley confabs revolved exclusively around kiteboarding. A senior venture capitalist at Charles River Ventures named Bill Tai (along with professional kiteboarder Susi Mai) hosted the punnily named MaiTai kiteboarding camp in Hawaii. Like all things Valley, it mixed a certain hippie, back-to-nature transcendentalism (the organization supports several ocean charities), that American obsession with athletics, and the hard-nosed hustle of the entrepreneur.

Unlike Eastern yacht clubs, where access to the stolid establishment is gated by birth or balance sheet, access to MaiTai is bought via a mix of social capital, personal brand, and/or some ineffable flavor of cool, which often manifests itself as perceived "thought leadership" in an industry. As with so many other things there, as long as you can get someone to accept whatever alternative currency you're doling out, the Valley will always stand you another round. I knew a couple of attendees, and they were precisely the ever-present Valley players—flitting between giving and receiving venture capital; always founding one startup, advising another, or trading up between them—who were exemplars of their tight-knit world.

The Bill Tai of MaiTai fame was in our fund-raising sights. In mid–Demo Day harangue, I had noticed a dark-haired figure on the extreme right of the front row. Like politicians, who spot the one guy in the crowd who's entranced and address him specifically, both to hone the message and to focus the delivery, I had locked on him and his furious note-taking as a rhetorical crutch. He turned out to be George Zachary, a partner with Bill Tai at Charles River Ventures. After I approached him in the post–Demo Day mosh pit, he invited AdGrok to come and pitch. The boys, doing their own Demo Day hustling, also managed to wangle an invitation from Bill, his partner.

Into the pitch I went. At this point, it was like pulling the cord on the back of a vintage doll—it just rolled out like the hundredth performance of a well-practiced monologue. After I fielded the usual questions, Bill Tai, who was seated directly across from me, looked me sternly in the eye.

"But what if Microsoft comes in and offers to buy you for fifty million? Are you going to sell?"

The question tore the well-worn script from my mind, leaving me momentarily stunned. At the thought of Microsoft buying three guys and a few thousand lines of Ruby code for five followed by seven zeroes in cash, I could feel an incipient case of the giggles coming on—which, suppressed by my superego, came off as a smirk.

"Well, Bill . . . you know . . . we're really trying to go after a huge market here . . . ha! . . . and we want to solve this Google last-mile problem . . . so . . ."

The damn smirk wouldn't go away no matter how hard I tried, and the giggles simmered beneath the surface, like water on the cusp of boiling.

"So, really . . . we're in this for a much bigger outcome than just fifty million dollars . . . plus, who wants to work at Microsoft? Ha . . ."

Did any of them come from Microsoft? Shit.

I couldn't think of their CVs while suppressing giggles.

WRONG ANSWER, DICKHEAD.

A chill went through the room. I rambled on incoherently for a while with my uncooperative mug, and eventually gave up.

"Well, we like making decisions here quickly, so expect an email by tonight," Zachary uttered finally, and they handshook me out the door.

The email arrived that night, as promised, and was short and sweet: no. Tai's question about selling out, however, would prove prescient.

When I got off the stage at Y Combinator on Demo Day, two investors immediately had come after us. One was the aforementioned Chris Sacca; the other was Ben Narasin. He'd physically shot up from the massed ranks of investors and trotted after me as I ambled off the stage. Standing somewhat awkwardly just outside YC's door, I gave him an extended version of our pitch, which he consumed with that look of rapt attention, accompanied by staccato bursts of questions, which was the unmistakable sign of sincere investor interest.

Narasin was thin and small-framed, with bright blue eyes behind round wire-frame spectacles, and curly, cropped hair. He had a work uniform: button-down shirt, cotton slacks in white or khaki, a slide belt (like the sort Boy Scouts wear) with little anchors on it, and—absolutely essential—Sperry Top-Siders, blue, no socks. In all our time together over the ensuing months, I would never see him in anything else.

His intensity and fast-talking clip made you guess at New York roots, but he was actually a Southerner from Atlanta who had moved to Boston for college, and ended up in New York only later due to an interest in fashion. In the late nineties, at the beginning of the first Internet boom, he was the founder and primary shareholder of fashionmall.com, a company that produced Web storefronts for high-end clothing retailers, back when the notion of selling stuff online was an innovative breakthrough on the order of general relativity. He had taken the company public at precisely the right time before the crash and pocketed a huge sum, which meant that afterward he had embarked on that quasi-retirement of the moneyed and tasteful bon vivant: food and wine writer.

Somewhere in there he came out West and started investing in companies. His current gig was at a venture capital firm named TriplePoint Capital, where he headed its new but growing seed-stage "practice." TriplePoint was a minor oddity in the VC firmament in that it provided debt financing (money you actually had to repay!) to technology companies with real capital-expenditure needs (like a fleet of trucks). It was just getting into the equity investing game, but hey, all the cool kids were doing it and we've got a balance sheet for it, so why not? It had hired Narasin to head up its seed practice and find it deals, and so after our entrepreneur-VC impromptu first date following Demo Day, he had asked me to come in to present to his investment associate.

A word on VC titles and hierarchy.

There are various flowery titles that the VC set adorn themselves with: "associate," "principal," "analyst," "partner," "operating partner," "managing partner," "general partner," and so forth. The main distinction is whether one earns what's called "carry" or not. Simply put, carry is a piece of the financial upside in the fund whose money the firm invests.

From the point of view of the entrepreneur, this is all noise. What matters to you is whether the smiling face in front of you, wearing a crisp white collared shirt under a wool half-zip sweater, has the ability to present and defend a deal at the Monday partner meeting, and corral the other decision-making partners into agreeing to a deal. Everyone else at the VC firm is as much an accessory as the hot receptionists.

One quick way to cut through the shit: ask your pretender-to-influence, "Do you have decision-making power?" If he or she even remotely hesitates or hedges, you're speaking to a lackey (whether he or she acts like one or not). His or her only utility is to get you to the person who does have that power; everything else is so much pig swill. So route around such people if a real investment check is your goal. Arguably (and this is the canonical YC advice) don't even accept a meeting from someone who can't answer yes honestly to the above question. You're wasting your time.

Back to the drama.

I was in repeat performances of the Sand Hill VC Show when I drove up with my much-abused BMW convertible to yet another cluster of generic two-story office buildings, and parked among the Priuses, Porsches, and Teslas.

Once inside, my eyes had to adjust to the cool darkness. The receptionists were absolutely not model-esque Sequoia caliber, resembling more what you'd find in a dentist's office. I didn't know enough about the VC world to interpret that as a good or bad sign. The décor was dark by Sand Hill standards: lots of black marble tile, a gray rug, and black desks of indeterminate construction. I was left alone in a large conference room, probably where the Monday-morning partner meeting happened, to wait for Narasin's associate. The general air of the place was quiet, bordering on absolutely silent. Nary a hum from a computer fan or ventilation. That's one of the most striking things about VC offices: even in the middle of the day, they are absolutely still, like an empty museum or library.

Narasin's associate made an appearance: Indian, MBA from some American school, your standard-issue entry-level VC. Evidently we had a couple of professional relations in common, who had put in a good word. This stresses the importance of cultivating a network in Silicon Valley. Unlike on Wall Street, where a professional network is conceived more or less when you are, popping out of an affluent uterus in Rye, New York, and setting you on a track of Andover, Yale, Goldman for life (or not), in the Valley things are more fluid and impromptu. Any hustler who can make superficial friends of the California variety and publish a few blog thought pieces, while collecting the echo of confirmatory social media approval, is as much part of the elite as any member of a Harvard Final Club. Of course, you can lose your place just as easily, something an East Coast elite need never fear. But such is the greased pole of Silicon Valley fame and power; anyone can try to ascend, but nothing will arrest your fall.

Following this almost cosmetic associate pitch, plus more due diligence, Narasin agreed to float us to his Monday partner meeting. This was big. The Monday partner meeting is the cadence to which the entire venture-backed technology world dances. At that meeting, which typically lasts a good four to five hours, starting early and running to midafternoon with a break for lunch, the business of the venture partnership is done. Updates on existing portfolio companies are given by the relevant partners (who as often as not will have a board seat), invited entrepreneurs pitch at what's likely the most important hour of their life, and new potential deals are floated. Since this was a small seed deal, chump change really, I didn't need to come in and pitch to the assembled high and mighty (fortunately).

With VCs the yesses are usually immediate, while the nos are typically slow to arrive, if they arrive at all. If the partners reacted warmly at Monday's meeting, we'd get a call or email that very evening. If they didn't . . . well, he'd get to writing us an email at some point during the week, and all we could do was wait.

Turning and Turning in the Widening Gyre

> We spin in an ever-turning circle, and it is our delight to change the bottom for the top and the top for the bottom. You may climb up if you wish, but on this condition: don't think it an injustice when the rules of the game require you to go back down.
>
> —Boethius, *The Consolation of Philosophy*

SEPTEMBER 10, 2010

We were sitting in a celebratory post–Demo Day mood in the living room of Argyris's Mission apartment, the same space where we had hacked the first throwaway prototype whose non-demo had launched this whole YC adventure. The beers were out, and we were still surfing that wave of intoxicating startup high that fluctuates between elation and terror.

My phone rang.

"This is Rodger Cole."

Rodger was a partner at Fenwick & West, one of the big three Silicon Valley law firms. Via wiles we'll soon explore, we had rather improbably secured him to represent us, and then even effectively pay us for the privilege.

Unexpected phone calls from lawyers are never good. I straightened up in Argyris's Ikea chair and mentally braced myself.

"I'm sorry to inform you that today Adchemy filed suit against you in Santa Clara County Court."

As our lawyer of record, Rodger had been served the court documents. "I'm sending them now."

I checked my email, and there it was:

SUPERIOR COURT OF CALIFORNIA

COUNTY OF SANTA CLARA

ADCHEMY, INC.
Plaintiff
v.
ANDREW F. GARCIA-MARTINEZ*
MATTHEW R. McEACHEN
ARGYRIOS ZYMNIS
ELECTRON MINE d/b/a ADGROK

FOR MISAPPROPRIATION OF TRADE SECRETS; BREACH OF CONTRACT; INTENTIONAL INTERFERENCE WITH CONTRACTUAL RELATIONS; BREACH OF THE DUTY OF LOYALTY; & INJUNCTIVE RELIEF

That litany of boldfaced transgressions was our rap sheet. It covered just about every suable offense a Silicon Valley employee could commit, which mostly boiled down to stealing intellectual property. Since AdGrok was vaguely trafficking in the same area of paid search marketing as Adchemy, our

* Yes, I was transmogrified into "Andrew," perhaps the most egregious anglicization of my name ever. AZ's name was also misspelled.

former company was using that as the pretense for a lawsuit. Mostly, though, it was sheer Murthy ego.

We had been forewarned, Adchemy having sent legal hate mail weeks before, the sort of menacing recital of employment-agreement restrictions that serves as the warning shot across the bow in corporate litigation. This triggered our securing a preemptive relationship with Fenwick, and why Rodger was there to receive the lawsuit paperwork. I had hoped Adchemy would be slow to action, slow enough for us to finish the Demo Day fund-raising. The lifelong Machiavelli fan in me remembered that memorable line from *The Prince*: war is never avoided; it's only postponed to someone's advantage. I had thought it would be postponed to our advantage, but we'd clearly miscalculated Murthy's vindictiveness.

Most shockingly of all, we had been personally named. This wasn't a company thing, where we could hide behind the corporate veil. These charges were personal, and we stood to lose everything financially.

Wilson Sonsini Goodrich & Rosati, the most expensive and formidable law firm in Silicon Valley, had been contracted to murder us via litigation. We had maybe $2,000 in the bank at that point. An hour with a top-shelf Silicon Valley lawyer costs around $800. The only way out of this mess was by raising money and using that to defend ourselves. But Murthy had, with exquisite sadism, timed the lawsuit for precisely the worst time: at the very peak of our fund-raising power, right after YC Demo Day. Now that hard-won momentum was all gone.

We were well and truly fucked.

I'm a catastrophic thinker. I enjoy apocalypse films and zombie-invasion flicks. *The Road Warrior* (a.k.a. *Mad Max II*) is probably my favorite action film. *28 Days Later* is a close second. I don't know if it reflects a murderous antipathy to all humanity, or just a taste for anarchy and societal collapse. Either way, I always expect the worst.

Here's what I thought would happen to AdGrok in our impending legal meltdown:

MRM, who had a family to support and no stomach for a protracted fight, would quit and find a regular job.

Think about it: he had a little cash in the bank, but he had been spending that to get by while building AdGrok. Beyond some equity in a modest home, he had nothing at this point. If we lost the suit and were sent up the river, his whole family would pay the price. Gone were the karate lessons, the school trips, maybe even the house itself. The entire household would be ruined.

So what if he did leave?

Argyris and I would slog on, with him doing the technical side and me doing everything else. If we had no luck raising money, we'd turn my blogging and marketing skills to embarrassing Adchemy as much as possible. With my musings on New York tech, Goldman Sachs, and whatnot, we'd already garnered a sizable fan base of thousands of readers, many among them gossipy Valley insiders. Such a sordid legal altercation would surely draw that chattering and judgmental crowd. We'd publish every legal document with every ridiculous claim.

If that still went nowhere, and things looked really bad, what would happen?

Remember: we were personally named in the suit, and faced full personal liability for any awarded damages. The allegedly stolen Adchemy intellectual property in question, although in actuality completely worthless, had been developed after tens of millions of dollars in funding, and would be considered worth as much by the courts. With civil damages to pay, we'd be completely ruined. More than ruined, we'd be in hock up to our eyeballs. Our names in the Valley would be hopelessly sullied, as we'd be considered trade-secret thieves, practically the sexual predator of the tech world. With no job prospects, there'd be no way of paying any awarded damages.

In the event of the final apocalypse, Argyris would get on a plane to Greece, cursing the United States all the way, never to return. The suit wouldn't follow him there.

And me?

I'd burned my bridges on Wall Street with the Goldman post, so there was no going back there. British Trader could take care of Zoë, but I'd be destitute for the foreseeable future.

My real fear, and something I never shared with the boys, was that Murthy, in his manipulative rage, would offer them a job back on ridiculously good terms. They'd abandon me.

In fact, in one of the legal broadsides they sent our way, Murthy mentioned welcoming Matthew and Argyris back to Adchemy (and very pointedly not me), as if they were wayward sheep. But he never *really* tried to woo them back with a special job offer, or a personal appeal. Given how poorly he had treated both MRM and AZ on departure, it's not even clear that would have worked. But either way, Murthy was out for blood, and would stop at nothing short of destroying the entire AdGrok construct. And here he made a serious mistake.

As Sun Tzu informs us, no matter how cowardly by nature, anyone fights to the death when his back is against the wall. A wise combatant always allows his opponent a way out, something Murthy in his maniacal pursuit of us hadn't provided. Faced with no choice, even the skittish boys would fight to the end, particularly if the actual cost of the fighting, if not the risk of losing, had been passed on to others.

Despite my fears, MRM stuck it out. He would bet his family's future on AdGrok, staking the future of the very kids Argyris and I grumbled were distracting him. For all of his usual trepidation about everything, MRM was the actual daredevil here, playing capitalism all-in, and for keeps. As much as I'd often get annoyed with MRM, he took the biggest risk of all of us. I have never forgotten that.

Argyris also held firm. Just as when Adchemy threatened to report him to the immigration authorities, our Greco-Argentine PhD manned up and did his brave duty on the foundering AdGrok boat.

Here is a key insight for any startup: You may think yourself a puny midget among giants when you stride out into a marketplace, and suddenly confront such a giant via litigation or direct competition. But the reality is that larger companies often have much more to fear from you than you from them.

For starters, their will to fight is less than yours. Their employees are mercenaries who don't deeply care, and suffer from the diffuse responsibility and weak emotional investment of a larger organization. What's an existential struggle to you is merely one more set of tasks to a tuned-out engineer bored of his own product, or another legal hassle to an already overworked legal counsel thinking more about her next stock-vesting date than your suit.

Also, large companies have valuable public brands they must delicately preserve, and which can be assailed by even small companies such as yours, particularly in a tight-knit, appearances-conscious ecosystem like that of Silicon Valley.

America still loves an underdog, and you'll be surprised at how many allies come out of the woodwork when some obnoxious incumbent is challenged by a scrappy startup with a convincing story.

So long as you maintain unit cohesion and a shared sense of purpose, and have the basic rudiments of living, you will outlast, outfight, and out-rage any company that sets out to destroy you. Men with nothing to lose will stop at nothing to win.

Shortly before we had announced our departure, an early investor and mentor of Adchemy had somewhat improbably died.* Rajeev Motwani was a legendary Stanford computer science professor who had mentored countless students and entrepreneurs, including the Google founders. He was a showpiece adviser to the company, and Murthy made a big display of mourning his unexpected demise.

After all the threats and strong-arming to keep us from leaving, in the same way that an abusive husband brings home flowers to make it all right, Murthy gifted us an unsolicited intro to one of the big power attorneys in Silicon Valley, Ted Wang of Fenwick & West. With much to-do, Murthy declared that this going-away present was a posthumous homage to Rajeev. He might even have gotten a bit misty-eyed as he said it.

I immediately scheduled a call with Ted to relay our fears about the guy who had brought us together. I didn't trust Murthy to let us go so easily.

Ted turned out to be a savvy and knowledgeable Silicon Valley player. From the earliest days, his was a voice of wise counsel in dealing with Murthy. When that conflict escalated into a full-on lawsuit three months later, he unhesitatingly threw Fenwick into the fray, less because of the value of AdGrok as a startup, and more due to outrage at the offense against the informal Silicon Valley rules. A large company didn't sue a small company just because it could. This was bullying on the startup playground, and Ted Wang wasn't going to stand for it.

Once the legal bullets started flying in earnest, Ted intro-

---

* A smoker, Motwani had reportedly gone outside the Atherton home he shared with a wife and two kids for a late-night puff. His wife found him drowned the next morning in his small residential pool. Whether he had fallen in or decided to go for a late-night swim despite not knowing how was never known for certain. The county coroner measured an extremely elevated alcohol concentration in his blood.

duced us to another Fenwick partner, Rodger Cole. Cole was a litigator for Fenwick, the frontline soldier who'd conduct the actual war. He was not the swaggering legal gladiator you'd expect, and his absolutely calculated and frigid demeanor led to our nicknaming him "the Undertaker."

There was still the little issue of payment, though. Ted liked us, but not enough to do this for free. Ted and the Undertaker each billed out at something like $600 to $700 per hour. But the rapport we had built with Ted was worth more than money in the bank, as was our pathetic underdog role. We'd have to convincingly count on that somehow.

As matters turned out, without Fenwick, we would never have been able to mount a defense. To say Murthy was punished for his one iota of kindness would be an understatement. The lesson here is: if you're going to be an egomaniacal, sociopathic prick, then do it properly and murder your enemies outright, rather than throw them a bone and expect to kill them later if there is trouble. They might just turn that bone into a weapon.

¡No Pasarán!

> Right, as the world goes, is only in question between equals in power, while the strong do what they can, and the weak suffer what they must.
>
> —Thucydides, *History of the Peloponnesian War*

OCTOBER 2010

Raising money while having a lawsuit over your head is like walking into a singles bar with a T-shirt announcing, "I'm HIV positive. How about you?" It doesn't bode well for your prospects.

You can't not tell potential investors, although you can stave off telling them until their greedy little pens are hovering right over the dotted line—at which point you drop the bomb, and hope they don't run screaming. I took a sad roll call of all the investors we had been talking to and were inching to a close, and told them the news. Many of them bailed.

Some stayed in tenuously but wanted to know more about the suit and its potential costs. As much as we tried to downplay it—just the price of doing business!—they wanted details. So I had to put them on the phone with the Undertaker, who would give them an edited lowdown on the situation, and then I'd hope they'd return my calls.

Russ and Sacca, to their everlasting credit, did not bail at the first sign of trouble. They had the most money verbally committed; Russ was the presumptive lead of the round and the biggest check, and Sacca was our big name. But my Wall Street quant's heart knew that if we managed to raise, that risk would be priced into our funding terms, one way or the other.

In order to get a damage-control estimate I could (maybe) show to investors, I had the Undertaker prepare a detailed breakdown of every step of the litigation process, along with the respective price tag, all the way out to a full jury trial. The numbers were staggering. It would cost us a full half million just to get to the actual trial, plus another half million or more after that. All together we were looking at around $1.5 million for the full lawsuit, including judgment and final wrap-up, stretching out over the next eighteen months.

As any good aspiring CEO would do, I made an Excel spreadsheet, for in tabular data lies truth.

It listed all our realistic expenses projected for the next year, along with predicted legal costs and their probable timeline (discovery in six months, trial in twelve months, and so on). It wouldn't be a startup without some glib optimism, so I included revenue numbers based on a near-term launch and some percent growth rate in users and monetization. Finally, I plotted our running cash on hand on a line graph, with time on the lower axis, and pondered the trajectory.

The plot resembled the infographic that accompanies every newspaper article on an airline catastrophe: first a plateau, then the sudden start of a descent—was it engine failure? pilot error?—and then a precipitous drop right into the ground, a burning, fuel-soaked hole decorated with singed clothes and body parts the ultimate result.

No matter what numbers I used for revenue, costs, or legal expenses, the AdGrok airplane would not stay airborne.* Even if we didn't have the lawsuit hanging over us, it would have been dicey, but we'd have had more runway at least. Every way I tried to slice the data in the cash-burn spreadsheet, which we nicknamed the "Death Clock," I saw no way we could realistically defend ourselves in a lawsuit with as little as $400,000 to $500,000 raised. We would bleed $20,000 a month in legal fees, and between that and salary and expenses, be dead in the water after nine months to a year (at most).

I didn't show the projections to the boys; it would just depress them pointlessly. I also didn't share it with investors. AdGrok was dead on arrival if this got out.

So I lied.

I diminished the costs of the lawsuit to far below the Undertaker's projections, meanwhile moving our projected launch date forward to next month to generate revenues immediately, an impossibility given all the changes the boys were making to the product. Then I jacked up the growth rate to an unconscionable amount. It was outright chicanery, cooking the books in the worst form. But it was either that or give up now, and surrender was unthinkable.

I still can't believe the investors believed my numbers, but they did.

Russ, who had offered to lead the round and was therefore absolutely pivotal to our pulling this off, seemed particularly assuaged by the projections. He must have been willfully blind to them, or I just wore him down in phone call after phone call. To my mute surprise, he offered to continue to lead the round, but at a valuation cap of $2 million instead of the $4 million we had discussed in his breakfast

---

* There's a cliché in the Valley that doing a startup is like jumping off a cliff and building an airplane on the way down. How high the cliff is and how much time you have before death are a pure function of how much money you've raised. In our case, someone was also shooting at us with an antiaircraft battery.

nook. Also, since he didn't want to be injecting money into a corpse, he conditioned his investment on our finding at least another $200,000 in additional investor money as well—so between him and the rest we'd have at least around a half million as war chest.

Russ's counteroffer presented a sliver of hope. By halving our effective valuation, we would raise enough to at least pay ourselves and keep the machine going. We'd sell way more of the company in a seed round (about 22 percent) than was typical, and this would raise eyebrows when it came time to raise a series A. Investors don't like it when a prior round of investors has bought a huge part of the company. It means that either they have to take down less of the company in their round, or the founders have to give up a lot of their share to top up the new investors, and hence lessen their incentive to do well. Also, investors like to feel you're their bitch or their boy when they wire you a bunch of money, and some other pack of moneymen also having you by the short hairs mutes that sense of ownership.

At this point, series-A drama was safely in the "problems we'd like to have" category. We'd figure it out if we ever got there. This was like worrying about your cholesterol while you were dying of cancer. So the problems were now reduced to finding another $200,000, plus seeing if we could somehow mitigate our legal bill, either by negotiating a deal with Fenwick or by crushing Murthy.

In terms of the money, if we could convince Sacca to up his investment from $100,000 to $200,000, we'd be there. Or pile in more investors. After all was said and done, with lots of artificial urgency and investor divide-and-conquer, it was a bit of both. Sacca wrote a bigger check than planned, and we got some more hangers-on in the round.

A brief discursion here, to give you a taste of the tech lunacy:

Remember Ben Narasin, he of the sockless Top-Siders? Well, he shepherded us past TriplePoint's partner meeting, and got us a yes. As was often done in these seed situations, the VC who sourced the deal would personally participate via his own cash, as well as an investment from the fund itself. And so while TriplePoint would wire us money eventually, Ben wanted to hand us a check now. Perhaps inspired by Ben's side career in food and wine writing, I proposed meeting at Loló, one of these culinary fusion experiments that smacked of an intercultural marriage. Turkish-Mexican tapas and multicolored décor that could be best described as kaleidoscopic kitsch were the setting for the only paper check we'd ever collect. But as always with Narasin, nothing was ever simple, and after a half hour of staccato repartee, he realized he actually hadn't brought a checkbook.

"Oh, wait, hold on . . . I think I've got a spare check."

He whipped out a worn-looking leather wallet from his khakis and went fishing around inside. He came up with a faded and wrinkled loose slip of paper, that emergency check some people keep wedged into their wallets in case they find themselves cashless.

"Who do I make it out to again?"

The check was from a Schwab account, no doubt the small-beans slush fund that handled his everyday banking as well as maybe the odd public equity.

"Electron Mine Inc.," I replied, using our original incorporated name (our name for marketing purposes had changed a half-dozen times).

Ruminate for a moment on a class of people who write rumpled $50,000 checks as an afterthought.

After I finally got the money in my hot little hand, Narasin distracted himself by pointing out the photos of his children he had in his wallet, which he had spread out on the bar while digging around for his "bail me out of jail" check.

"Look . . . this is who you're working for right here."

He proceeded to give us the full proud-father walkthrough. I looked at MRM, who had come along, and hoped he wouldn't say something tactless.

Finally done, we walked out into the stink and sunlight of the Mission District.

"Well, what about my kids we're working for, huh?" MRM asked.

Of course MRM would say that. Like many hardcore engineers, the man was incapable of lying and/or reading a social situation. I'm glad he held his tongue for all of thirty seconds.

More firewood on the AdGrok bonfire.

The next chunk of change came from a more mysterious if not as amusing source.

I had spotted him during one of my wanderings around YC's Demo Day. His slim physique, fitted European-style shirt, and expensive haircut set him apart from the sartorial catastrophes surrounding him. My surmise was right: Chris Kile was Swiss and represented Ace & Company, an opaque family fund run out of *Sound of Music* land. The most I ever got out of him about the provenance of the money was that it supposedly involved an Egyptian mobile telecoms fortune. Or that was the story, at least. What I know for certain is when it came time to make the tip jar ring, our dinky business account got a wire from a Swiss private bank based in Zug. Zug is where African dictators, Latin American *narcos*, Russian oligarchs, and Lebanese arms dealers go to retire. But who was a Cuban boy raised in eighties Miami kidding? A little red never made money less green. Another log on the fire.

All told, four investors stayed in the running despite all the lawsuit drama, and the amount raised came to about half a million. Even in those prebubbly days, this was a small round. But you go to war with the army, and the war chest, that you have . . .

Remember, though, this was all based on a lie. Even with that cash in the bank, we'd never survive the lawsuit. This merely meant we wouldn't die just then.

Could we mitigate the costs some way?

I had asked high-end lawyers like Ted Wang and others

for referrals to cheaper legal options. Every leading firm has a short list of cut-rate attorneys, usually one-man shops run by some more-or-less decent lawyer who had maybe burnt out or hadn't made partner at the referring firm. Their hourlies were in the $400 per hour range, rather than the $600 to $700 per hour range of the major leagues. I spoke to these solo practitioners. Their attitude was that of the nickel-and-dime shyster who gets you out of a speeding ticket. They wouldn't consider equity as payment, and didn't give a damn about the startup ecosystem.

Cash, as always, is the poor man's credit. It would actually have been more expensive to go with the cheaper lawyer, as that bill would be paid in crisp, green benjamins, rather than equity funny money.

No, we'd need to get Ted Wang on board somehow.

There's a corny math joke about a lecherous French mathematician who both is married and keeps a mistress. How does he manage to get any work done? Well, he tells the wife he's with the mistress, tells the mistress that he's with the wife, and then goes to his office and proves theorems. Which is more or less what I did at AdGrok: I told the lawyers that we had raised money and were on the fast track to success, and wouldn't they want to participate by accepting payment in shares? Then I told the investors that they could invest without fear, as the legal costs were minimal, and in any case the lawyers were accepting shares in lieu of cash. Meanwhile, Argyris and MRM went to the office and coded.

Easier joked about than done.

Ted Wang didn't want to accept equity now that we presumably had money, and he felt that he was practically subsidizing Russ by even entertaining the thought (which, of course, he was).

It became a game of vitriolic, bipolar telephone, with phone call after phone call, alternately to either Russ or Ted, each speaker on the phone angrier than the last and refusing to yield an inch to the other.

"Hi, Ted, this is Antonio," I declared, while pacing my unofficial *via dolorosa* of anxiety, Ninth Street in Alameda, the street bordering British Trader's bungalow. "Look, the investors are in, we've got the money to keep the company going but not cover the suit."

"I am absolutely not paying for a lawsuit while some rich guy profits from it."

And so it went.

Finally, through a combination of guile, greed, and simple stubbornness, we convinced Fenwick to accept a piece of AdGrok in exchange for defending it.

They'd front us $250,000 in legal fees (essentially a loan) in exchange for a percent of equity and a handful of equity options. For us, it was a marvelous trade. If the lawsuit went south and the company was finished, we'd never repay a dime. If we won the suit, we'd pay a small fraction of equity, capture all the upside, and live to fight another day. Fuck, we'd have taken the deal even if we had to hand over half the company.

Even worse for Fenwick: if we somehow escaped the lawsuit and did have a great run of usage, revenue, or luck, we could simply pay the Fenwick bill in cash out of earnings or our next funding round. There was no prepayment penalty on the deal, as there is in some bonds or mortgages, and we could simply nullify their rights to our equity by buying it out with cash. Since the equity Fenwick got was at our current valuation, this would be no different from buying out an early investor at his or her low buy-in price.

Put another way, we had sold Fenwick a one-in-a-million lottery ticket to win $250,000 . . . for $250,000. At best they'd be even, at worst we'd owe absolutely nothing, and everything in between was a gift from Fenwick to AdGrok. My quant's mind reeled at the complete mispricing of this risk. It was like the laws of physics had been upended and I was witnessing an elephant pirouetting on the tip of a chopstick. The terms were horrible for Fenwick, our idealistic legal saviors, a complete prelubed ass fuck of a deal.

Well, you can take the man out of Goldman, but you can't take Goldman out of the man, can you?

"Ted, thanks so much for your kind offer. We'd gladly accept those terms. Please send the engagement letter immediately."

Done deal.

We had money in the bank for salaries, rent, and servers, and our legal defense was now subsidized. AdGrok had survived its first existential threat, though we weren't out of the fight yet.

It was time to take care of Murthy once and for all.

There are worse ways of monetizing sociopathy than startups. If you know better ways, I'm listening.

How did Microsoft secure a monopoly on the PC desktop, creating multiple billion-dollar fortunes, and ensuring a tech hegemony that has lasted decades?

Briefly: Bill Gates came from wealthy Seattle aristocracy. During the early eighties, his mother served on the executive committee of the United Way, along with IBM's then CEO John Opel. This allowed William Henry Gates III (her son) to score a meeting with IBM about providing a code compiler for IBM's new, epoch-making product, the IBM PC. What IBM really wanted, though, was an operating system, the core code that manages memory and runs programs. Gates, whose nascent company, Microsoft, didn't have anything like an entire operating system, honestly referred IBM to a company run by Gary Kildall, a pioneer in operating systems when the real money in computers was still in the hardware. In a story couched in legend, Kildall was off flying his personal plane when IBM representatives physically came knocking at his company's office. His wife (the company's business manager) refused to sign IBM's aggressive nondisclosure agreement and sent them packing, and so IBM grudgingly went back to Gates asking about operating systems. Gates, smelling an opportunity, offered to provide one, hiring a local Seattle programmer to clone Kildall's operating system, calling it QDOS (Quick and Dirty Operating System), and which eventually shipped in the IBM PC as DOS (Disk Operating System). Gates, correctly suspecting that other hardware companies would copy IBM's approach of bundling software separately from hardware, retained copyright over this hacked and copied DOS. As a result, the proceeds from the new computing world where hardware was interchangeable, but software was not (rather than the reverse, which was the status quo in 1980), accrued to Gates and Microsoft rather than IBM.

That licensing arrangement became what we now know as Microsoft, as it grew to provide everything from word processing (can we still use that term?) to browsers, calendars, and all the rest of the worker-bee software armamentarium. And Kildall? IBM eventually threw him a bone by offering his (original) operating system alongside Microsoft's, but it was too little, too late, and it flopped.

Fast-forward thirty-five years: Gates now tours Africa as a great philanthropist and single-handedly cures malaria. Kildall eventually succumbed to alcoholism, dying in mysterious circumstances—probably a drunken brawl—in a Monterrey biker bar at age fifty-two. To quote Balzac, "The secret of great fortunes without apparent cause is a forgotten crime, as the crime was properly done." Never was a crime better concealed.

Steve Jobs?

If I were to even attempt a brief account of Jobs's crimes, based on his well-documented biographies, it would fill the rest of the book.

A representative anecdote: In 1975 Steven Jobs was a (literally) smelly hippie, fresh from a religious pilgrimage to India, working as a low-level technician at Atari. He was an arrogant, destructive presence who pissed off everyone except Atari's CEO, Nolan Bushnell, who was impressed with Jobs's wide-ranging intellect and saved him from being fired. Bushnell wanted to turn Pong, the legendary two-player game that launched the video game revolution, into a single-player version that would eventually be called Breakout (older readers will surely remember). Back in the day, a new game required hardware as well as software, with the former being more important. Bushnell announced a $700 prize for anyone who could design a hardware-software combo that would power the game, with a $1,000 bonus for every chip that was saved in manufacturing the circuit (chips used to be expensive).

Jobs convinced his eventual Apple cofounder, Steve "Woz" Wozniak, to take on the project, stipulating it had to be done in four days to fit his social schedule (he had to go pick apples at a utopian commune). Woz worked like hell, with Jobs doing the manual labor of testing the designed circuits, and they made the deadline. Jobs, however, never told Woz about the bonuses, having mentioned only the base prize. He gave Woz $350, shortchanging his collaborator, who had made the entire thing possible, and used the stolen cash to finance his lifestyle.

Steve Jobs was all smoldering ambition, ruthless will to power, and narcissistic amour propre; by all accounts of people who actually worked with him, he was a mediocre engineer who had good taste and knew how to recognize in others talents he didn't posses, and got them to work like hell for him, while fending off competitors in the meantime. In that sense, he was the absolute exemplar of your successful startup CEO, even if not in the way people commonly think.

Oh, and Zuckerberg?

As is now public record, the Facebook idea (not that ideas alone are worth much) was stolen from a pack of entitled Ivy League brats (now notable angel investors) who had contracted him to implement it. He implemented, but then decided he rather liked the idea and ran with it. Eventually, Facebook would pay tens of millions in damages to the aforementioned Ivy Leaguers (though not without evidently shortchanging them even in the settlement).*

We can come down from the rarefied heights of Gates and Jobs now.

You'll have to trust me on this: the story of just about every early-stage startup is peppered with tales such as mine. Backroom deals negotiated via phone calls to leave no legal trace, behind-the-back betrayals of investors or cofounders, seductive duping of credulous employees so they work for essentially nothing (e.g., Adchemy itself). The picture I've painted of AdGrok—and there's more sordidness where this came from, not to worry—is not some weird exception; it is the absolute rule. The tech startup scene, for all its pretensions of transparency, principled innovation, and a counterculture renouncement of pressed shirts and staid social convention, is actually a surprisingly reactionary crowd. Its members preen and puff and protect their public image, like a Victorian lady powdering her nose, and refuse to acknowledge anything contrary to their well-marketed exteriors. Sure, it's no worse than traditional industry or politics, but certainly no better either.

In the case of AdGrok, this meant no subterfuge, no underhanded blow, would be disallowed. In the startup game, there are no real rules, only laws, and weakly enforced ones at that. In the end, success would forgive any sins, as it did for Gates and Jobs, and continues to do for countless startup entrepreneurs.

Do we begrudge David the use of his sling, after all, against the towering giant Goliath?

---

* The Winklevoss twins, progenitors of the Facebook idea, scions of Yankee wealth, and both Olympic-class rowers, seem lifted from the pages of an Ian Fleming novel. They would appeal their eventual settlement, claiming Facebook swindled them in the actual value of Facebook stock at the time of their judgment. The court disagreed.

The Dog Shit Sandwich*

> Starting a company is like eating glass and staring into the abyss of death.
>
> —Elon Musk, founder of PayPal, Tesla Motors, and SpaceX

OCTOBER 2010

Adchemy was holding a legal gun to our heads. Fenwick & West provided us with our own gun, but the reality was we couldn't afford a long-drawn-out standoff, as much because of the time as the money. The only way to win was to subtly find Murthy's balls, and hold a cold, sharp knife up against them until he saw the light of reason. Given that corporate extinction and personal financial ruin were the alternatives, any means would be acceptable.

There are two weak points for tech companies, no matter how large: their investors and their potential business partners. The former influence even obdurate company lead-

* This memorable coinage came from Ted Wang, the Silicon Valley power lawyer, who vowed there'd be "no eating of dog shit sandwiches!" when the legal saber rattling started. He'd be quite wrong.

ers both by personal sway and by the fact that they often occupy voting seats on the board. If the founders lack leverage at fund-raising time, the CEO will be outnumbered on the board, and he serves at the pleasure of voting board members. This is how CEOs get voted out of office, like prime ministers via a no-confidence vote in parliamentary democracies. If keeping your job depends on pleasing someone else, even if your business card says "CEO," you've got a collar around your neck attached to a leash, and that leash can be yanked.

The other weakness is potential business partners. Shipping new product is one thing, but deals are where the startup rubber hits the revenue road. If the product is enterprise software, as it was for Adchemy, that meant a handful of deals a year was the company's entire commercial livelihood. A few big contracts, and that's what sustained the long-term value. If these were partnerships rather than deals—that is, an almost matrimonial coupling between (usually) a larger company and a smaller—then the stakes were even higher. These partnerships, like some potential royal marriage, hinged on a delicate combination of greed, long-term strategy, and a certain mutual seduction. Ugly realities like lawsuits, no matter how petty, dissolved the magic, and would send the more powerful partner fleeing. Even large companies with billions in capital fear public shaming and legal quagmires.

So, we had our balls to go after.

Now for the knives.

One Adchemy employee, over drinks, had unknowingly leaked to me that Adchemy was working on a major deal with Microsoft. This was news. The only prior pile of big, stupid money that salesman Murthy had managed to woo into the kitty was from Accenture. Adchemy was running gigantic losses, with no chance of turning on real product revenue beyond the lead-generation business. To keep the sham alive, Murthy needed to pull in someone else. Something big. Fifty million big, or even bigger. Microsoft was an obvious choice, as its also-ran search engine, Bing, was always eager to win advertisers and users away from the Google behemoth. Given the utter disaster in display advertising we had witnessed while at Adchemy, it was clear Murthy was turning his attention to the more mature search market as his last business bet. By playing to Microsoft's inferiority complex in the search business, Murthy was wooing himself some financial oxygen. We had to find a way to get to Microsoft.

For our second knife, there were the VCs. Adchemy's venture capital patrons were two absolutely first-class, blue-chip firms: August Capital and the Mayfield Fund. The partners at those funds were John Johnston at August, whose comically WASPy name matched his appearance and pedigree. At Mayfield, it was Yogen Dalal, the usual cocktail of the Indian Institute of Technology and Stanford that populated many a Silicon Valley boardroom. We had leverage over such Silicon Valley players thanks to funding trends that were then seizing Silicon Valley, and are now so commonplace as to scarcely merit mention.

Here's why: Traditionally, early-stage startup funding was the exclusive province of either the entrepreneur's personal wealth, friends and family, or business "angels." In their original form, angel investors were wealthy individuals, often former entrepreneurs themselves, who for fun or profit punted around in embryonic companies.

Most companies simply die in this early stage. Those that succeed raise their first "real" and hefty round on the series A. There the numbers are much larger, in the millions, and beyond the range of most affluent individuals. Historically, most professional venture capitalists would not mess around at the seed stage, and some even abstained from investing in early rounds like a series A. With vast funds of outside money to invest, in the hundreds of millions, the VC masters of the universe would not waste their time writing piddly $50,000 checks.*

With the rise, in 2010 or so, of the tech bubble whose ever-more-frothy heights we're witnessing even now, that entire script changed. Google and a passel of Silicon Valley acquisitions made very rich men of many Valley players. In the self-perpetuating genius of the Valley, that wealth wanted to create more tech wealth, creating an almost embarrassing glut of early-stage angel-investor money. Not only did many of these startup pickers invest their own money, they raised small funds in the $20 million to $40 million range to scale their stakes in budding companies. Angels who used to write $20,000 checks on a deal could now easily write one for $200,000 or more (e.g., our boy Sacca). In tandem, the popularity of accelerators like Y Combinator, plus a general acceptance of entrepreneurship as a career, meant lots of very skilled engineers and product people were skipping the corporate trajectory and building exciting products. The emergence of turnkey, on-demand computation like Amazon Web Services, plus off-the-shelf Web-development frameworks like Ruby on Rails, meant that new ideas were easier than ever to test. Many entrepreneurs chose to build shovels rather than dig for gold, creating more complex software building blocks to underpin the innovation, such as back-end services like Parse, accelerating the startup explosion in an almost exponential way.

The net of all this change was that seed rounds were now

---

* The insider term for outside money is "LPs," or "limited partners." These are the enormous family funds (think the Google founders and the Walton family), investment portfolios, and pension funds that, as part of a larger, generally conservative investment strategy, allocate some of their money to speculative, high-yield investments. They're "limited" partners in that while they write the initial big checks that get the ball rolling, they have no (official) impact on the eventual investment decisions, and are contractually obliged to keep their money in the mix for years.

reaching levels of former A rounds; a two-month-old company with a persuasive CEO raising $2 million and calling it a "seed" was not shocking news. With a short time to market and rapid technical development, that company could be hitting its milestones in six months, and raising its next round. With so much money, of all sizes and levels, waiting to invest, the best entrepreneurs had the luxury of choosing investors, rather than vice versa, and many investors found themselves anxiously trying to get into rounds. Due to contracts stipulating that investors in one round had the right to invest in the next, as well as personal ties between investors and entrepreneurs, investors getting in on oversubscribed A rounds had to be there in the seed round to earn that place. And that was true going up the various funding levels. That means VCs who would formerly say "Get back to me when you're raising a series A or B, kid" were basically blocked from popular companies by investors who had nurtured and supported the company since it had been two guys in a trashy office. Heavyweight funds like Mayfield and August knew this, and started doing seed investing, not to own some little piece of a company (they could write small checks all day and still not invest their entire funds) but merely as an option on the real rounds down the road.

Which brings us (finally) to our point: in the day-to-day, the lifeblood of a VC wasn't money, it was deal flow. Getting a first look at a potential Uber or Airbnb is what distinguished a first-class VC from an also-ran. Given Y Combinator's immense success in drawing the best entrepreneurs, it had a quasi-stranglehold on the best early-stage deal flow in the Valley. And since early-stage deal flow today translated into later-stage deal flow tomorrow, via the follow-on investing phenomena described, Y Combinator was the gatekeeper to the best present and future deals in the Valley. Like control of the water supply in some arid agricultural region, whoever had the most upstream control of the water sluice controlled everything else—which is what Y Combinator's

Demo Day represented. Thus, powerful and haughty VCs who wanted to attend Y Combinator's showcase pitch event had to kneel and kowtow to a sandal-wearing bear of a man with a distaste for bullshit and a flair for the written word. That man was Paul Graham, without question the canniest tech investor in human history. And it was to Paul Graham we first turned with our existential problem in those desperate days.

Like all parents, PG pretends he loves all his startup children equally. The reality is some companies get more of his attention than others. Given the conditional nature of his love, it was somewhat in doubt if he would run to AdGrok's aid, in light of the pissy, messy nature of our conflict. After all, we were a middle-of-the-pack company from our batch, not a highflier like Hipmunk or InDinero.

We needn't have worried. Even if we were the runt bastard child of the family, Papa PG brought all his protectiveness to bear. In a world where superficial relationships and glib bullshit are the rule, there's nothing more fearsome than to see true loyalty at work. PG mustered YC's full network for our cause.

It was all the more impressive because I had miscast PG as a sort of avuncular, academic presence who dabbled in dense essays about startups, hosted founder dinners, and wrote a few checks. Nothing could be further from the truth. Y Combinator was the sort of unforgiving power player that remembered the names of investors who had crossed portfolio companies in the past, or who had disseminated unflattering portraits of YC, and blacklisted them from any YC dealings, or from the minds of YC founders. This was done with little thought of the size of their funds or their influence in the Valley, leaving more than one self-important VC sputtering at a dressing-down, or left out of a round because the company's founders had gotten a warning from PG.

The harsh reality is this: to have influence in the world, you need to be willing and able to reward your friends and punish your enemies.

So it was with some relief that we learned that Paul Graham emailed Murthy to discuss the matter. Murthy, who was as much a sycophant with outsiders when he needed something as he was a tyrant with Adchemy people, replied praising his work and declaring himself to be a YC fan of many years. A long, meandering email thread had ensued (I wasn't cc'ed, but PG forwarded me a copy).

Finally, an email to me from PG:

"Come meet me at home to discuss this on Saturday. Come alone, don't bring the others, and try to keep them out of it."

Another brief lesson in startups:

Whenever you face some stressful, time-consuming, and risky challenge, firewall the rest of the company away from the mess. They'll likely add no value, and the attendant uncertainty will corrode their productivity when you likely need it most. No matter what happens in the outside world—lawsuit, money issues, the fucking zombie apocalypse—do not let it infect the company's headspace and become the top item in the internal narrative.

So I arrived alone at the PG compound in Old Palo Alto. It was in the neo-Spanish style so beloved of California architects, Stanford University itself being a good example.

There seemed to be no front door to the compound. I rounded the corner it spanned, looking for somewhere to knock. There was a bicycle leaning against a wall, with a helmet hanging from the handlebars, thrown casually next to a small door that hung ajar. Tentatively, I wandered through.

Paul Graham, the Valley's most successful tech investor,

emerged from the compound's large kitchen in his standard, never-changing uniform of a raggedy orange polo shirt, khaki shorts, and Birkenstocks (no socks). I had never seen the man in anything else.

With little in the way of buildup or greeting, PG started in: "I went over to Wilson Sonsini . . . probably the first person to ever show up on a bicycle."

I could picture the scene of PG strolling in in his Birks, still perspiring mildly from the ride, and telling the first partner he ran into, "We need to talk about this AdGrok thing."

Before we got too deep into the conspiring, Jessica, PG's wife and YC copartner, came out to discuss lunch. What ensued was a minor squabble over some leftover pasta, and why it was gone, and who had planned on eating it that afternoon. PG looked a little miffed.

I looked away to give them at least a bit of cosmetic privacy, but I was inwardly amused. I guess even YC partners quibble over who ate the leftover spaghetti.

The lunch situation patched up, PG shared his anti-Adchemy game plan. In a nutshell: YC would anathematize Adchemy's VCs, and declare that they'd never do business with YC again unless they straightened this out. Knowing PG, not only would they be disinvited from Demo Day, but PG would probably also steer companies to take money from other funds instead. Given that many if not most YC funding rounds were oversubscribed with investors, an excommunicated investor could be excluded without damaging the fund-raising company at all. At the end of the day, who really gave a shit if the check came from August versus Sequoia? That money was just as green either way. That meant that those funds would start losing YC deals wholesale to their competitors, and, as we reviewed earlier, getting locked out in the early rounds likely meant the same in the even juicier later ones. PG was about to flush a whole chunk of their deal flow down the toilet, just like that.

I smiled, imagining the sputtering fits pitched by the partners over at Mayfield and August when PG read them the riot act. YC was actually willing to sever ties with some of the most illustrious names in Valley investing over the piss squirt that was AdGrok. It may seem like nothing to you, reader, who maybe inhabits a normal realm of twenty-first-century economic life where things like tit-for-tat reciprocity enforce social codes. But in the passive-aggressive popularity contest that is Silicon Valley, someone actually going to bat for you—really going to bat, like telling important people to go fuck themselves—that's rarer and more short-lived than a snowflake in a bonfire.

I thanked PG profusely, and then he padded back into the kitchen for his lunch.

I decided I wouldn't tell the boys anything about the meeting. If PG's push resulted in nothing, it would only disappoint them.

Knife to balls application process: commenced.

The next knife requires some explanation. Coincidentally, it also involved a (future) head of YC, but at the time he was just a startup founder like me, though an exceptional one.

YC was constantly experimenting with new events and mechanisms to tweak its founder experience and provide improved mentorship, or more aggressive networking and fund-raising. One such event was Angel Day, which had arrived around the middle of our YC experience, and was announced in an email to the entire batch. It involved pitching a mini version of our eventual Demo Day presentation to a select group of elite YC investors. As with a talent show, those investors then voted on which companies they wanted to talk to, and after computing the tally, we were given two angels to prepare us for the eventual fund-raising hootenanny. We drew two very notable Silicon Valley figures: Jean-François "Jeff" Clavier and Sam Altman.

Sam Altman is the current head of Y Combinator, and the person whom Paul Graham has entrusted with transforming his brainchild into a long-lived and scalable institution. In 2010, he was CEO and founder of Loopt, a company that had pioneered the location-check-in product that Foursquare would later eclipse (only to itself stumble), and which Facebook eventually worked into its product.

At the time, though, Loopt was still a location player, and Sam would take an hour out of his busy week, usually late afternoon on a Friday, to field whatever questions I had, no agenda required. The boys came along for the first session, and never again. I think they were scared of him, and with good reason. In one of PG's essays on desirable founder qualities, he had this to say about Sam: "You could parachute him into an island full of cannibals and come back in five years and he'd be the king."

I believed it, as did the boys. His official AdGrok nickname was "Manson Lamps," after Tony Soprano's psychotic rival, who possessed an intense and unsettling stare. This was a flip and admittedly unfair comparison; Sam never proved himself anything other than a capable operator and loyal friend to YC companies.

I'm high-strung, fast-talking, and wired on a combination of caffeine, fear, and greed at all times. But "Sama," as he is known on Hacker News and Twitter, really takes the cake. After an hour with him, I was looking for the closest beer bar. Standing maybe five-seven, lean and wiry, with perpetually hunched shoulders, he has clear blue eyes of an unusual intensity. A typical meeting would involve him conducting a conversation about A, with a side tangent on topic B, while considering C, and simultaneously texting on his phone and scanning his laptop screen. The topics veered from detailed wisdom about fund-raising to term sheet dynamics and ways of getting screwed on dilution, while he simultaneously played coy on whether he'd invest in AdGrok, and then solicitously asked about team morale issues. I always steeled myself for those Friday afternoons. It was like the last flaming hoop to jump through before the weekend, not that we had much of one those days.

By the time the Adchemy storm appeared on the horizon, I felt we had built enough of a rapport to ask him for advice on the matter. In a solicitous email, I mentioned that he seemed well connected to what we had identified as Adchemy's Achilles' heel, namely, the senior Microsoft deal-making team. In my desperation to find an in with Microsoft, I had stalked people on LinkedIn like some recruiter trying to poach a hire, searching for an intersection point with Microsoft. Sama was one of those highly connected nodes that pepper the Valley; you know him, and you're not more than two hops from anybody that matters.

Sam Altman assured me he'd try to do the best he could, and promptly cut off the call.

A week went by. Driving on the 280, I saw his number flash on my phone and pulled over; Sam Altman cannot be dealt with at eighty miles per hour.

"So I talked to {name redacted}, who is Adchemy's business-development contact at Microsoft. He assures me he brought up the AdGrok issue in one of their meetings with Adchemy. He stated it was going to be problematic if Adchemy was embroiled in litigation while discussing the Microsoft deal."

I almost dropped my phone. This was precisely the decapitated horse's head in Murthy's bed that we needed. Murthy, with his back against the wall, running short of cash and with no salable product even remotely on the horizon, needed both the accounting and the marketing win of a big infusion of Microsoft money. Weasel that he was, Murthy had an overriding sense of self-preservation, and was still rational enough to realize that destroying AdGrok was not worth destroying Adchemy in the process. If indeed Microsoft BD had raised a flag about AdGrok, there's no way Adchemy could continue the suit. It would be suicidal.

"Sam, I don't know how to thank you for this."

"No problem."

Click.

Confirmation of PG having acted on our behalf was relayed less directly. One of our investor friends had visited Mayfield Capital on unrelated business. Given the open nature of most VC offices, with all conference rooms and partner spaces facing some airy, sunny central area, he could see that Yogen Dalal, the managing partner for the Adchemy investment and Silicon Valley notable, was in a conference room having what appeared to be a strained conversation with Murthy. Board meetings or advisory sessions (not that Murthy took advice from anyone) should have taken place at Adchemy, not Mayfield, at that stage. That, plus the timing, signaled that this conversation was likely about AdGrok. It seemed that PG had delivered, and Adchemy's investors had started putting the squeeze on Murthy, using their moral (not to mention financial) suasion to get Adchemy to retire the suit.

Starting from a point of outright panic verging on imminent rout, AdGrok now had Adchemy surrounded.

On one side, a potent Valley legal player was fighting the conventional legal battle, with every indication we had the wherewithal to stick out a full suit. The Undertaker was firing sharply worded missives at Santa Clara County court, rebutting Adchemy's claims, offering to provide our externally audited code as evidence of innocence, and starting the painful process of hostile depositions (which would be soul-sucking, time-burning confrontations, in which even Murthy would be personally ensnared).

On another side, Murthy's moneymen were likely yelling at him to stop being an asshole and respect unwritten Valley rules about not frivolously picking expensive fights with nascent startups. Thanks to PG's expulsion of these money changers from the Temple of Demo Day, and what that meant for their future deal flow, the VCs' very livelihoods were now at risk due to Murthy's bullshit. And by the way, why aren't you focusing on our investment, the ailing Adchemy, anyhow?

Finally, the next big partner Murthy critically needed, the last card he had to play as entrepreneur with a troubled startup, was telling him the deal hinged on settling the AdGrok mess, or else.

I'd have paid half my stake in AdGrok to look at Murthy's face when he considered the state of AdGrok-Adchemy relations.

What's it take to do startups?

It certainly isn't intelligence.

I was in the lower third of my PhD class in physics at Berkeley, and I had to take my preliminary exams three times before I passed. Most of the founders I know are certainly crafty and quick-witted, but compared with some of the certified geniuses I met in academia, they aren't going to win any Fields Medals or Nobels.

It certainly isn't technical skill. I'm a crappy programmer, and I can hack crude prototypes of finished products at best. Some founders are technical virtuosos, but I suspect most weren't the top students in their respective computer science classes (assuming they even had a formal education).

It's not unique product or market vision. Anyone who used Google's ads-buying tool for all of five minutes, and then registered that that piece of shit was a $70 billion per year moneymaker, could see the need for AdGrok. Some startup ideas were visionary, like Airbnb, but many, like Dropbox, were merely extremely well executed versions of existing technologies.

In my limited experience, there are two traits that distinguish successful startup founders at whatever level of the game, from the forgettably minuscule (e.g., AdGrok) to the epoch changing (e.g., SpaceX).

First, the ability to monomaniacally and obsessively focus on one thing and one thing only, at the expense of everything else in life. I lived, breathed, and shat AdGrok. Thanks to focusing on AdGrok, I watched my daughter grow up through the frame of a Skype window while I was in AdGrok's Mountain View shit hole. I had no social life outside of schmooze-and-booze tech events, at which I would wear my AdGrok T-shirt and engage in techno small talk with people I didn't really care about. I had no hobbies or outside activities of any kind, except very occasional trips to the gym. My sailboat, into which I had poured two years of money and weekends to restore, slowly rotted in the sun. I never read anything except the tech press. Movies were out of the question. The ladies? While I was nominally still in a relationship with British Trader, my penis was anatomically equivalent to my coccyx: a purposeless vestige of a bygone era.

Second, the ability to take and endure endless amounts of shit. I was raised under the sadistic care of a sister ten years my senior who delighted in unleashing endless taunts and abuses. My father was a domineering man, in every way. I spent years in an all-boys Catholic school filled with brutish bullies and cold, aloof priests. We did nothing but beat each other up and jerk off. I scraped by on nothing for six years as a penniless grad student in an expensive city, and then survived three years on Wall Street's most competitive trading floor during its biggest market catastrophe. Long story short: within the limited purview of white-collar travails, there's nothing I can't take for an extended period of time.

You might be asking why I'm being such a buzzkill. There must be some fun in startups, right?

Sure, there are times when an entrepreneur's life will make you feel like you've got the world by the tail. You just talked the biggest check you've ever seen out of a respected investor, and *boom!* there the amount appears, as big as life, in your previously barren bank account. You launch a product or write some blog post that goes viral, and for one shining moment, you're the talk of the tech world. But those moments are far outnumbered by the countless moments of gnawing doubt, nauseating anxiety, and endless toil. If you've got a great relationship with your cofounders, then that camaraderie can maintain you. In fact, as in sports or war, the overpowering desire to not let down your fellows is often all that keeps you going. But if you have no cofounders, or if that band-of-brothers relationship isn't there, then the only thing keeping the whole construct going is sheer, stubborn bloody-mindedness. You get up every morning, get kicked in the face, and come back for more the next day.

Unlike maniacal focus, though, which is a personality trait too difficult to mold once in adulthood, this thing—call it grit, perseverance, or whatever—is something that can be learned. If you feel you don't possess that strength within you, then go ride a bicycle across the United States, sail a boat across an ocean, or join the Marines. Whatever it takes to build those reserves of mental endurance. Or just jump into the fray, and you might surprise yourself.

Incidentally, it helps to have enemies. While love is a beautiful emotion, far more empires have been built, books written, wrongs righted, fights won, and ambitions realized out of vengeful desire to prove some critic wrong, or existential dread of some perceived enemy, than all the love in the world. Love is grand, but hate and fear last longer.

Victory

> Nothing in life is so exhilarating as to be shot at without result.
>
> —Winston Churchill,
> *The Story of the Malakand Field Force*

FEBRUARY 2011

In late October Adchemy's tone completely changed from one of bullying menace to abrupt conciliation. Unsolicited, we received an offer to dismiss the suit immediately.

By February it was all over but the lawyers' fees. We signed some token agreements: comical, infantile reaffirmations of preexisting agreements we had signed upon getting hired at Adchemy. A copy of our codebase was to be kept by Fenwick. We sent them a zipped archive the lawyers wouldn't have even known how to open on their Windows machines. It could have been ten gigabytes of bestiality porn, for all they knew, had they bothered to check. We even encrypted it, for further amusement. Nobody would ever read the officially stored version of AdGrok's code.

I sent Murthy one last taunting email when the official

termination papers went through. I'd cross paths with him only once more professionally, and never again in person.*

I've probably never hated one man so much, other than my father. There's a saying in Spanish: live long enough, and you'll watch the funeral procession of your enemy go past your door. It would take a few years, but I'd watch Murthy's funeral, all right. In 2014, Adchemy would tank definitively, and in that whimpering way of concealed failure: after raising over $130 million in capital, the company disappeared in a fire-sale "acquisition." Many employees who purchased stock in the company lost their savings in the belief that Adchemy would ultimately succeed. Their Stockholm syndrome lasted to the very end.

Murthy passed on to the oblivion he deserved. The only chapter in Silicon Valley history he'll ever have is this one, the one I've written for him.

As for AdGrok and the boys, it was time to think about a real launch.

By the time AdGrok had managed to free itself from the existential crisis, my relationship with British Trader was suffering under stress and our mutual friction. I was done with her imperious hectoring and stiff upper lip. Living with her *en concubinage* with Zoë resembled less some bohemian family sitcom, and more a stint in the Queen's army. Her brother actually was an officer in the British Army. The Grenadier Guards, no less, the chaps in red jackets and towering bearskins who cut such a figure in front of Buckingham Palace. The household was run to the beat of Pimm's cups, Sunday

* In a wholly deserved gift of fate, Adchemy pitched Facebook shortly after I joined. Gokul, knowing I had worked there, passed me the email thread and the decision of whether Facebook should engage with Adchemy or not. On the basis of my analysis, Facebook never gave them the time of day.

roasts, Marmite in the morning, mincemeat pies for holidays, and listening to the Queen's speech whenever that old hag mouthed some patriotic drivel on "the Beeb."

British Trader's desire to be absolute captain of the ship was fine, but there's only one captain of a ship or company. If she wanted the role, she could maintain the house herself.

As if it were yesterday, I recall when the denouement to this budding family saga became clear. It was a Saturday morning, a brief respite from the startup bullshit. *Car Talk* blaring on NPR as I made either pancakes or a big omelet. That feeling in the air, so rare in my life, of a certain stability and repose, glistening like the bright morning sunlight and about as fleeting.

British Trader and Zoë were traipsing around the backyard, checking on the tomato garden, or possibly the chicken coop. Stepping out the back door, which rattled and clapped shut when you let it go, I spied British Trader coming in carrying Zoë. They had been outside since before I had gotten up (another late night in San Francisco for me), and it was my first sight of Zoë that day. Her sea-blue eyes turning slowly to brown as the end of babyhood approached, the tousled brown hair, the look of impish glee she always wore, even now in youngest childhood. Those cheeks as she grinned in my direction. Like nothing else in life, she elicited an unquestioning smile, the sort of smile nothing can wipe off your face.

"You sure don't smile like that when you see me anymore," British Trader quipped, and brushed past me through the door, Zoë bundled in her arms.

It was true. The only reason I was still hanging around Alameda was that brown-haired bundle, and soon even that wouldn't be enough.

Right around when the Adchemy drama was winding down to its victorious conclusion in late 2010, I decided I had had enough of the British barracks room I was living in, and announced I was leaving the household, and British Trader.

The announcement was met with all the drama and passion you'd imagine. After the usual fussing and fighting, more heated than usual given the year of accelerated life together (a child, a renovated house, a lawsuit, a company, mostly unplanned), I found a loft sublease in San Francisco.

I had declared my intent to abandon the home front no later than December 1, move my few belongings to Potrero Hill, and focus on our newly liberated startup. On December 3, I came back to the house to pack some last belongings, and we fell into that relationship coda of mutual indulgence, part passion, part nostalgia, of which many recent breakupees are guilty.

Fast-forward two months later, to February 2011, when AdGrok was rejoicing at the official end of the Adchemy war, mockingly going through the motions of our legal obligations under the settlement agreement. Out of nowhere British Trader informs me she is once again pregnant; the calendar math takes us right back to my move-out imbroglio in December, our last tryst after a breakup desert of nonintimacy. After a brief debate, British Trader confirms her desire to keep the child, whatever my thoughts on the matter.

It occurred to me that perhaps this most recent experiment in fertility—and the first—had been planned on British Trader's part, her back up against the menopause wall, a professional woman with every means at her disposal except a willing male partner—in which case I had been snookered into fatherhood via warm smiles and pliant thighs, the oldest tricks in the book. Whether swindler or dupe, we're all either subjects or objects of one or another conspiracy in this world. Our only hope is that the profits from authoring schemes outweigh the costs of being extras in those of others; I'd need a startup per child at this rate.

Speaking of which, how did this affect AdGrok?

My first thought was to not tell the boys; they'd get more stressed-out about it than I was, and I needed them alert and productive for our looming product launch. My second thought was, well, so what? I was already neck-deep in risk; our return profile (to use Wall Street quant-speak) was absolutely binary: either we succeeded dramatically, with a million-dollar outcome, or we ignominiously failed.

What was one more child in the mix? I'd have the heir and the spare. A little redundancy, whether in technology or heredity, never hurt.

Launching!

> I observe that some men, like bad runners in the stadium, abandon their purposes when close to the goal; while it is at that particular point, more than at any other, that others secure the victory over their rivals.
>
> —Polybius, *Histories*

MARCH 2011

It had been almost exactly a year since we had been accepted by YC, ten months since the company had been founded, seven months since we had launched a production version of AdGrok, six months since we had raised money, and one month since we had officially buried Murthy in the latrine where he belonged.

A launch in our case was more a PR event than a technical one. Our website was already accepting paying customers and our product had been out in the wild for a while. The boys were launching new features with our most recent release, but really it was no more than the update to a mobile app that you're nagged to make by your smartphone. My role was to make the routine newsworthy. The tech press, even more so than the regular press, willingly covered only births, deaths, weddings, and bloody accidents: that is, a new funding round, a startup's collapse (the messier the better), acquisitions, or a nasty scandal, like a founder conflict or a sexual harassment claim.

To paraphrase Jon Bond, an agency guy we had pitched: marketing was like sex; only the losers paid for it. Like losers, we paid for it in this case, hiring a PR agency to juice the metaphorical printing presses for us. The result was a series of endless interviews in such august publications as *Internet Retailer* and *Direct Marketing News*. Like a brainwashed Manchurian candidate, I ran through my spiel for the nth time, updated for the new features launching. This was all done under "embargo," which is not nearly as exciting as the Cuban version. It's basically the promise, often disrespected, to withhold publication until a set moment and time. Like a thunderhead unleashing its plague of rain and pent-up electricity all at once, the idea was to trigger the explosion of self-perpetuating media attention that the always self-referential Internet affords.

Given the mounting schedule of journalist interviews, plus the new features ready for production, the second week of March was the natural launch window. We wanted whatever media explosion to echo, so we'd go out Monday with the launch.

Just one problem: Monday, March 7, was Zoë's first birthday. It was almost exactly a year since we'd gotten funded, and Zoë had been born right before our epically bad YC interview. As always, when the trade-off was between the startup and anything else, the startup won. Little Zoë wouldn't even remember her first birthday, and if we pulled off this AdGrok caper correctly, it would be paying for her Harvard graduation twenty-one years hence. Zoë, if you're reading this, accept my very late apologies.

On Monday, the boys pulled the trigger, and deployed the new code. The journalists published their refactored press releases. A small wave of new users signed up, sparking a round of customer support chats that we rotated among ourselves ("I tried linking my Google account but it didn't work . . .").

AdGrok was weakly on the tech map for a few days, thanks to our essentially paid-for media coverage. Launching!

Inside the Y Combinator lair, a faded drawing on a whiteboard faced the main dining/meeting hall. It featured the simple L shape of X and Y axes, along with a squiggle running from left to right accounting for the passage of time. The height represented how well a startup was doing, and the shape started with a sharp rise from zero, cresting to an apex labeled "Launch!" The peak was followed by a sudden crash and then a low plateau that ran almost the length of the plot. After much flatlining, the curve edged up slightly, before dipping again (label: "misconfigured analytics code"), and then increased at a steady pace until "acquisition." The big, yawning space between launch peak and gradual takeoff was labeled ominously in large letters: "THE TROUGH OF SORROW."

Put yourself in the mind of a startup founder for a moment: You've managed to cobble together a product and maybe some VC money. You've launched, gotten a wave of PR, and everything is firing on all cylinders. You open the analytics dashboard that tracks usage, and you see what seems like an ocean of interested users clicking around and toying with every hard-fought feature you managed to ship.

Then a few weeks go by.

The media cycle has moved on to other new, shiny things. Your analytics graphs look like the heart-rate monitor on a heart attack victim. New user sign-ups have slowed to the trickle they were prelaunch.

If you're new at this, you'll have naive models in your head about startup success. Humans like a sense of order and meaning: what happens in act 2 of a play must have stemmed from act 1. The good guy wins in the end, and the bad guy is punished. If we see a smiling entrepreneur like Drew Houston of Dropbox on the cover of *Fortune*, then we assume (A) he deserves to be there due to merit, and (B) he got there through a series of rational acts, one triumph following another in a causal chain.

However, such fairy tales reveal themselves to be the fantasies they are following a launch. You've spent months and gambled your career on a product, and then after a bit of excitement, you realize what a misshapen and misbegotten piece of shit it really is. This is the crisis that kills 90 percent or more of startups that manage to survive the initial plagues of founder disagreements, failure to ship code, and failure to raise money. This nearly uncrossable chasm is behind all those "What happened?" posts on *TechCrunch* or other tech rags that crop up when some seemingly unstoppable startup suddenly announces it is ceasing operations and giving back what's left of the investors' money. Its founders and management could not negotiate the trough of sorrow, and like some lost British adventurer trying to cross a forbidding desert, the company basically gave up and died.

This failure is not due to a mere lack of nerve, of course. It could be a company with a freemium business model that required lots of free users upgrading to paid memberships, that couldn't figure out how to get all those users in the first place. Or it could be a services company that had plenty of users, but couldn't figure out how to scale its operations (e.g., a housecleaning service that couldn't recruit and keep quality cleaners). There are infinite reasons for not making it across the trough, but it almost always involves some impediment to paying users being scalably acquired or serviced.

What's the solution?

The trendy answer is that you need to find what's called "product-market fit," which is a fancy way of saying that you need to build a thing people are willing to pay for. It turns out that's pretty hard, because you don't know what people will pay for until you ask them to, and if what you're building is truly novel, there's no history for you to go on. Fortunately, the iteration cycle in a software business is fast (we don't need to retool milling machines here), and from some approximately correct starting point we can converge on a final product, almost like successive guesses at the solution to an equation. The quicker we iterate, the more steps we can take in the direction of this mythical point of perfect fit. Each such step costs money in wages, server costs, and lost time. When that cash balance goes to zero, the game is over and we've lost. If, however, we get close enough to that perfect product-market fit, in which users pay more money for the product than it costs to operate (and than it cost to acquire those users to begin with), we've escaped the financial free fall. Recall our cliché about startups being like building a plane after jumping off a cliff; getting to a positive "run rate," as it's called, is like finally getting the wings on, firing the engine, and watching the contraption actually maintain or gain altitude (no matter how badly built it may be).

Based on our revenue and usage numbers, AdGrok was not even remotely there. What awaited us were months and months of the trough, stretching endlessly before us.

Dates @Twitter

> The combination of these two elements, enchantment and surrender, is then essential to this love we are discussing. Their combination is not a mere co-existence; they're not two parts placed together, one next to the other, but rather one is born and nourished from the other. It's love due to surrender via enchantment.
>
> —José Ortega y Gasset, *Sobre el amor*

THURSDAY, MARCH 17, 2011

Never ignore people who can write really big checks.

One of the members of my relatively small but devoted AdGrok blog fan base was an early and influential Twitter employee named Jessica Verrilli (AKA @jess). @jess was one of the public faces of the burgeoning social media juggernaut who seemed to float among the empyrean of much-watched Twitteratti, along with the founders Jack Dorsey and Ev Williams, and their various lieutenants.

The previous November she had randomly messaged me via Twitter after a particularly successful blog post. Come March, she had heard echoes of our manufactured launch buzz and asked me in for lunch at Twitter's office.

As always before meeting absolutely anyone, even for as

little as a random coffee, I did due diligence, in this case on @jess.

Here's more startup training for you:

Walking into any meeting, you should know every goddamn thing there is to know about the other person; if you don't, you're failing. Quoth Emerson and the intro screen to *Mortal Kombat 3*: "There is no knowledge that is not power," and that's especially true in terms of people. That means a combined Facebook-Twitter-LinkedIn stalk at least. You should have done that on all the players in your space already, incidentally. Read between the lines of their idealized and cosmetically enhanced CVs: less than a year at a company means they didn't vest their first year of equity, which means either they or the company sucked, possibly both. Leaving at precisely four years means they're plodders, punching the equivalent of the white-collar Silicon Valley clock until the next shift.

Which friends or connections do you have in common? Do they know your dipshit douche friends you maintain for career reasons, or the ones you actually respect? As true now as in Machiavelli's time, men are judged by the company they keep.

Where do they hang out? Cheap tastes or expensive? Do they have that "lean and hungry look" of Cassius in *Julius Caesar*, and eat at dingy taquerias, or perhaps live off cheap staples like ramen or food substitutes? Those are the truly dangerous ones, the ones who live like organized crime trigger men, guerrilla fighters, or sailors at sea—eating shitty food and living in cheap, dumpy crash pads—and who couldn't give a damn about quality of life.* Those are the people to

---

* Sam Altman, the onetime AdGrok mentor and now president of Y Combinator, gave himself scurvy by subsisting on packaged ramen while founding Loopt, his geolocation startup. Do you realize how long you need to be malnourished to suffer from scurvy? He was and is the lean-and-dangerous type.

fear, because they don't need anything an antagonist can deprive them of. Or do they have a score of check-ins at Benu, Saison, and Quince? If they're not financially independent, then they are harmless tools; they'll do anything to keep the parade of fungi terrine monkfish and tangerine-peel abalone coming.

What do they look like in photos taken over time? Do they look fit and healthy, with shots of them in corporate-branded nut-hugger biking outfits on a group ride on scenic Skyline Boulevard? Do they keep a stable work-life balance, with regularly scheduled two-hour workouts and time for a Thursday date night? Or do they look like they got ingested by a blue whale and spent three days transiting its digestive system?

Total commitment, like unconditional love, is the only type that matters. The bike-riding, date-night-going types will never give everything to a company or an idea, and are nothing more than complacent bourgeois, whatever trappings of the "disruptive innovator" they may sport, often in the form of ponderous blog posts or a bookshelf of bound B-school-level bloviation. The ones who could pass for a homeless person, though, those are the startup kamikazes who will give everything for the entrepreneurial cause, and are stopped only by death or jail.

Are they what passes for the American ruling elite? Do they hail from the urban archipelago of American privilege: Chevy Chase, Maryland; Winnetka, Illinois; Tiburon, California; Scarsdale, New York; and so forth? Or are they from Visalia, California; or Chimacum, Washington; and did they go to a high school named after an astronaut or a president? Did they go to a high school with either "Day" or "Prep" in the name, or with the titular formula "The —— School," where the blank is something majestic and/or Anglo-Saxon sounding? Then they're playing the slow-and-steady, long game, accruing social capital and personal brand gradually, like ants storing food for the winter. How did they reach the coddled precincts of the tech elite? Did they trudge along on the upper-class tour bus from the Ivy League to consulting and/or finance and burn out, or did they fight their way out of some backwater, earning their seat at the table based only on chutzpah and/or blitzkrieg-style success? The latter are fearsome, the former . . . not so much.

Before you sit down with people on whom your entire financial future and that of your descendants will depend, you should know them better than their mothers do. Know what they want—whether money, power, social approval of various flavors, or merely a comfortable life—and you can predict 90 percent of what they eventually do.

All this snooping seems weird or unethical to you? I'll note it's all public record, and no laws were harmed in the filming of this due-diligence movie.

Back to AdGrok's first date with Twitter.

Jessica, then the one-woman army that constituted Twitter's corporate-development team, was a former Division I lacrosse player for Stanford. Her father was an internist in Seattle, where she was raised. The familial abode was a five-bedroom, three-bathroom home on the shores of Lake Washington, in a posh part of Seattle. That would also explain the "Prep" in her high school. This was West Coast gentry, all right. If you must know, she was evidently dating a Twitter engineer who would wind up (spoiler alert!) interviewing me.

At the time, Twitter was housed in a generic-looking high(ish)-rise office building on Folsom Street, between Third and Fourth Streets, a few blocks north of AdGrok. I walked, taking a scenic route that led me up a back alley, across Brannan, through a side street that featured a Filipino Masonic temple (one of those inexplicable vestiges of pre-tech SF you saw occasionally), and right to South Park's fifty-yard line.

A tranquil oasis in an urban desert, South Park was reminiscent of those small, intimate parks you find in certain London neighborhoods. This is no accident. South Park was developed in the 1850s precisely as a simulacrum of such a cozy London townhouse-and-park development.

An oval roadway enclosed a grassy park with trees, benches, and an incongruous playground (incongruous as there were likely no children within a half-mile radius). By 2011 it was the epicenter of the SF startup boom, with startup logos poking out of second-story windows and off the T-shirts of the bustling crowd of nerds that churned through it at lunchtime. A few design and architecture firms still managed to survive the escalating rents, having gentrified the area in the pre-tech nineties from the vagrants and drug addicts who once populated SoMa.*

I got to Third Street and Folsom. A block farther down was the San Francisco Museum of Modern Art (SFMOMA), which has an unexciting permanent collection, but is housed in a stunning building by the Swiss architect Mario Botta. SFMOMA is the only serious art venue in the city; beyond the museum and perhaps the symphony, the city is a cultural desert. But who needs Gauguin when you've got Google?

Facing SFMOMA was the Moscone Center, named for former San Francisco mayor George Moscone, who was famously assassinated in 1978 in his office in City Hall along with Harvey Milk, the first openly gay elected official in California. An immense complex spanning two city blocks, it houses every major tech conference you can name. Oracle, Apple, Salesforce, Google, all have their product shindigs there, as well as the various niche ones like GDC (gaming), JavaOne (the Java programming language), and RSA (cybersecurity). If you have any tech career at all, you'll one day don a corporate-branded lanyard and name tag and stroll

---

* Similar to the birth of Christ in Western history, everything in San Francisco history is classified as having happened either before or after the current tech boom. Bars and restaurants are frequented (and mourned once they inevitably feel the pinch and close), not because they're exceptional in any way, but because they predate the arrival of the hated techies.

into the tightly choreographed spectacle of capitalism that is a tech conference, complete with staged product announcements, "fireside chats," and a makeshift favela of promotional booths.

I made a left on Folsom, and halfway down the street I entered the completely generic lobby of the completely generic poured-concrete building at 795 Folsom Street. Twitter had only two of the floors, but as it would do in every building it occupied, it was gradually expanding. Uniformed guards manned the reception desk, and there were two security checks, one on the ground floor, whose passing granted you a name sticker and an assigned elevator to an assigned floor. Once there, the receptionist would take your lobby name tag and give you a Twitter one in return. On the badge was a stamp in time-delay ink: it faded as time went on, and disappeared after a couple of hours, ensuring that you couldn't keep it and reuse it. All this security, which is common in large, high-profile startups, is to prevent journalists and stalking fans from getting in and stealing screenshots or overhearing conversations. In a culture in which people show up in chicken suits to formal meetings, security is one of the few things the self-consciously irreverent tech company takes seriously.

As I was soon to find is de rigueur, I was asked to sign a nondisclosure agreement that made it illegal for me to so much as leak the wallpaper design in the kitchens or reveal any knowledge, whether carnal or technical, gleaned while inside Twitter.

Then I waited. A couple of overdressed and nervous-looking people waited with me, probably job candidates. There were large-format coffee-table books, artsy tomes about the new world of data science and landscape photography, on the coffee tables. The reception area itself was tastefully paneled with reclaimed wood, and that little Twitter bird logo was on everything, down to the elegant black coffee mugs kept in the reception's minikitchen.

Jess appeared and was exactly like her publicity photos online. With an ever-present smile, she had that energetic and effusive personality of the lifelong athlete who'd cranked her endorphin levels to the human maximum.

"Want a little tour before lunch?" she offered.

How could I say no? We divagated through the offices on the way to the café.

As a workspace, it was standard SF cool startup. Long rows of shared desks, dotted with each employee's tech-company *mise en place*: large monitor, Aeron chair, smattering of books and personal effects. Loft ceilings exposed to bare concrete, and with plumbing, both literal and Internet, shooting across in long runs, thick bunches of bright blue Ethernet cables alongside the painted cast-iron pipes. Much distressed wood and hot-rolled steel furniture. Faux stag's heads molded from synthetics, and those nightmarish flocks of birds—not the bland corporate logo, but what you see populating a truly Hunter S. Thompson–esque psychedelic freakout—on bare walls, usually in some shade of bluish pastel. The company canteen continued the preening design, but at this point I'm running out of cute ways to describe the shit you see at Restoration Hardware, so you can just imagine it instead.

I'd later learn that Sara Morishige, the wife of the founder and CEO of Twitter, Ev Williams, was behind the company's very consistent design aesthetic. The bro-y dump of many tech companies this was certainly not.

Twitter numbered something like four hundred employees at this point, so it was relatively small by "big" tech-company standards. Despite that, and the fact Twitter's revenue at this point was de minimis, the café churned out fashionably healthy food, from the "comfort" variety (house-brined pastrami sandwiches) to the fancier (seared tuna on designer greens). I grabbed whatever was closest and found a seat.

I gave Jess the soft sell on AdGrok, and described our

successful (!) launch and future product plans. We kibitzed pleasantly about my blog posts, of which she was an active reader. We had first really "met" when we mutually followed and messaged each other after one particularly popular post.

Toward the end of this polite but uneventful meal, the man who would make Twitter make money appeared: a random encounter in what would be a season of such fortuitous run-ins. Tall, well coiffed, and conspicuously well dressed, even in a company where appearances mattered more than most, Adam Bain was a much-gossiped-about recent poaching from Fox, where he had led all digital monetization efforts for the Rupert Empire. In a hipster world of fixies and intentionally distressed wood (and people), he was the adult in the room keeping an eye on the register.

Jessica introduced us.

"So what are you working on?" he asked, taking a valuable minute out of his day.

In a panic, I realized I hadn't brought my AdGrok laptop to lunch, and was therefore not ready for an impromptu demo.

FAIL!

Always be closing, motherfucker.

But we had an out.

MRM, ever the inventive engineer who knew how to extract value six different ways from the same piece of code, had coded up an AdGrok-hosted demo site for the GrokBar that allowed for a demo off any machine, including tablets or phones.

"Can I show you on your laptop?" I asked, gesturing to the half-folded machine he was porting around like a security blanket, as your typical manager-class exec does.

"Sure."

Taking over Bain's machine, I demoed enough of the GrokBar to impress him, guiding him through the slick tables of performance data and sparklines, all updating gracefully as I navigated our demo e-commerce site. I wrapped the product reality in sufficient marketing sugar to make the medicine go down. Random encounter over, he headed off to his next meeting.

Jess walked me out the door to the reception area. A security guard, posted like a bouncer at the door, pointedly took my name tag with the disappearing ink on the way out.

Back at the office, Argyris was working away alone. As was happening with unsettling frequency, MRM had decided to stay home and forgo the commute from his beachside town. There was always some excuse or another, but neither Argyris nor I was buying it (Argyris least of all). The trough of sorrow was claiming casualties.

"So how'd lunch with Jess go?" Argyris asked absently, not looking up from his screen.

I stood right next to him to get his attention.

"What do you think about selling to Twitter?"

TUESDAY, MARCH 22, 2011

After our lunch, Jess had given me a formal email intro to two key people at Twitter: Kevin Weil and Alex Roetter, both engineers on the then-nascent Ads team. The weird tingle of corporate attraction I had felt on that first date with Jess had clearly been reciprocated. I was introduced as "a badass" whom they should talk to immediately.

As I hope I've made clear in many disclaimers throughout this work, there was nothing badass about my career in technology. The scant success I had was due purely to happenstance, combined with being a ruthless little shit when it counted. No, I mention this to underline how the snowballing interest of a larger company in a smaller one resembles the intoxicating enchantment one feels for a new romantic interest, house, or car. The target of your interest lays out his or her wares and tries to beguile, but past a certain point, it's you the buyer who's seducing yourself into the acquisition.

Polite emails with Kevin turned into a proposed lunch, this time with the full team. Thus did all of AdGrok HQ hoof it over to Twitter from the GrokPad, a bit tense and not knowing what to expect. Entrance routine repeated, we found ourselves around a circular table in the middle of the lunchtime hubbub in Twitter's main dining room.

Kevin Weil was a summa cum laude graduate of Harvard College and, like me, had dropped out of a PhD program in physics (he at Stanford) before boarding the tech roller coaster. Alex Roetter was a longtime Googler who had been on the founding engineering team of AdSense.* Both were line managers on the Ads team, the lieutenants in a tech company that make the actual on-the-ground army run. Between them and the AdGrok boys, the conversation soon turned to the technology challenges AdGrok had faced: scaling our back end, and, most important, dealing with Google's at times finicky Ads API. The boys described their experience hacking through and around its undocumented idiosyncrasies.

API is "application programming interface," and it's the set of functions and subroutines that an outside party can run in order to build its own third-party services on top of a company's service.

For example, the Twitter API allows someone to build a tool that gathers all your tweets and presents their engagement data (e.g., retweets, favorites) in an elegant and useful way. Effectively, it's the way computers talk to each other when they are owned by different companies. In the case of an ads system, it's the way developers build tools for so-

* AdSense was the second-place product in the Google monetization arsenal, after AdWords. You know how you get these little text ads on the right-hand side (and now even the upper header) of Google search results? AdSense is those same ads running not on a google.com search result, but on whatever random parts of the Web include a snippet of Google code on their site. It's the poor man's ad network, in that even your knitting blog could easily participate. While the monetization was low, in aggregate it amounted to a respectable revenue stream for Google.

phisticated marketers to create and manage advertisements. Since the native interfaces that large publishers like Google and Facebook provide are often unhelpful or are designed for small advertisers, an ads API is a critical part of the monetization strategy, as it's essentially the plumbing through which a large fraction of revenue will be ingested. At this point in our story, Twitter had no ads API. It barely had ads at all, having launched "Promoted Tweets" only a year before. Suspicions were of course rife that it would open an API to developers at some point, and Kevin's focus on the topic seemed to confirm it.

Suddenly Kevin, who was seated to my right, interrupted the tech kibitzing and looked at me. "Maybe you should join us on that."

"Join you? Join you how?" I asked.

"Like in acquiring you," Kevin said with a smile.

While I had experienced a premonition after the Jess lunch, actually hearing this come out of the mouth of a Twitter engineer was a very different story.

"Well, I guess we'd have to talk about that, Kevin," I said, speaking through a rapidly tightening throat.

Back at the GrokPad, we huddled. This was the first time we'd heard the term "acquisition" in any half-serious context. Being the complete neophytes that we were, we had no clue how to parse it, so I ran the news past the people we trusted, or at least would know WTF to do here.

PG was my first email. As expected, he was bearish on the whole thing, calling it a distraction, and advising us to ignore it and to get used to saying no. He was right, in the sense that any decent startup will get a dozen acquisition offers as it rises to prominence. I use the word "offer" lightly; companies will mention the possibility, but often the entire process is just an excuse for dissecting a company on the founders' time, the market intelligence a big company does to remain relevant, as well as keep from getting blindsided by an upstart. He also advised me privately to shield the boys from any acquisition chatter.

Next, I pinged Sacca.

AdGrok-Sacca relations had cooled considerably by that point, and I couldn't figure out why. After a few email exchanges in the early days of the Adchemy war, he'd gone silent. He'd ignored any and all requests for introductions at Google, his former employer, or anything else for that matter. Unlike Russ and Ben, who involved themselves on a weekly if not daily basis, and who even came out to our first conference appearance to support the effort, Sacca was basically a nonpresence in AdGrok.

That was all about to change.

Minutes after I pinged him, he called to ask what was going on. I informed him of this out-of-nowhere buyout chatter. He then called back with an inside scoop of what had transpired in that lunch: evidently Weil was extemporizing a potential acquisition offer nobody had formally agreed to.

In the weeks that followed, Sacca called at all hours, often when he was in the back of a taxi; there were texts at two a.m. We were all kind of puzzled by the change of heart, and were to a man somewhat hesitant to entrust our fates to his imperious presence. Though welcome in our funding time of need, he now demanded a faith he hadn't quite earned in sweat equity or trust-building face time. But Sacca was the professional investor, the man who invested for investors, and he had his own priorities, which were different from those of the Russ Siegelmans, not to mention our own.

A relevant detail that I mentioned earlier but which may have passed you by: Christopher Stephen Sacca was one of the largest equity stakeholders in Twitter, dating from an early investment, and purportedly from later top-ups in his stake. The word on the street was also that he had helped JPMorgan buy 10 percent of Twitter in February 2011, buying shares in private transactions from founders and employees alike, at a (relatively) stratospheric price of $21/share. Sacca was the Twitter man, constantly touting the company publicly, and in the fuzzy background of every new piece of Twitter gossip.

If anyone could guide us through the next steps, it was Sacca. But could we trust him?

WEDNESDAY, MARCH 23, 2011

"I heard the lunch went great. Can you come in and meet with Adam Bain?" Jessica had written to me, moments after we had left the meeting with Kevin and Alex.

The invitations we can't refuse.

So the next day I repeated the Twitter check-in exercise, meeting Jess yet again amid the coffee-table books, nervous job candidates, and expensive design.

She walked me all of thirty steps, and parked me in a conference room, with instructions to wait.

Upon her prompt disappearance, it became evident this was the get-to-know you meeting with Adam.

Twenty minutes went by. I started to get mildly pissed. I didn't wait this long for a beer, much less a meeting.

"Hey!" Adam Bain said, poking his head through the door.

He walked only halfway in, holding the glass door open behind him.

"Lady Gaga is here!" he announced, with the goofy expression of a teenybopper fan. He pointed down a hallway that ended in a large amphitheater, where a mass of Twitter employees had gathered.

Who the fuck was Lady Gaga?

A proviso: I am the uncoolest person you will ever meet when it comes to pop culture. I don't watch anything resembling "TV." I don't listen to what you'd call music (and

I'd call noise). An exciting Friday night to me is a bottle of Maredsous 10 Tripel, sucked down while gloomily reading Michel Houellebecq. Hopefully, strenuous fornication makes an appearance at some point, but that's about the extent of my cultural communion with my fellow man (or woman).

Also, thanks to too much mucking about with engines and firearms, my hearing is shot and I'm afflicted with a serious case of tinnitus, a constant high-pitched whistle in my hearing, which serves as the real soundtrack to my life. Lastly, as I learned in a misguided year of lessons with my piano-teacher grand-aunt, I am absolutely tone-deaf.

Long story short: I don't know shit about whatever dancing monkey of the moment is amusing the plebes.

I smiled the polite smile of someone who doesn't get the joke.

Adam took a seat directly across the narrow table. Over the course of the next forty-five minutes, he sketched out his thinking on Twitter monetization, insofar as the company understood it at the time.

He was a good pitchman. Like the best salesmen, he was suave without being slimy.

The impression I got in that hour-long meeting—and as history has certainly gone on to prove—was that if anybody could squeeze money out of the rock of billions of tweets a week, it would be Adam Bain.

SPOILER ALERT! Do not read if you like suspense, Dostoyevsky, and/or incremental character development.

Half the friends I have on Facebook, the ones dating from some long-ago period like high school or a former employer, I keep around only in order to see if my initial suppositions about them and how their lives would develop were right. I squelch them from my feed—I don't need to see the weekly puppy or child pictures—but I tune in every couple of years when my mind trips over some stale memory. Who did that beauty you crushed on finally marry? Did the pretentious kid become the smarmy yuppie you thought he would?

With the clairvoyance of hindsight, I'll provide those answers for the Twitter cast you just met.

Kevin Weil would become the head of Product for Twitter, setting the vision and timeline for everything Twitter builds. Alex Roetter would become the head of Engineering, managing that engine room of a tech company, the row upon row of busily coding engineers.

Adam Bain would become chief operating officer (COO), running the day-to-day business affairs of the company, as well as sales. Jess Verrilli would become director of Corporate Development, the one with the big checkbook and a mandate to acquire as much talent and technology as possible.

What a company builds (SVP, Product), how it builds it (SVP, Engineering), how that eventual product is operationally run (COO), and what other companies it buys (Corp Dev): those are the core functions of any large tech company, and the people from the Ads team we met during forty-eight busy hours in 2011 would, by 2015, be that core leadership of Twitter.

This isn't as improbable as it may sound.

Often at a tech company with an advertising business model bolted on to an otherwise user-facing product, the Ads team will be the weakest team in the company. Ads is perceived as a necessary evil, and marketing ain't cool, so the hotshot twenty-two-year-old kids who are the recruiting cannon fodder don't join up. The visionary CEO doesn't care about money, only the user experience, and manages by looking at usage dashboards, not revenue ones. Bold product initiatives that will rekindle always-fickle app usage are green-lit, and their resources are allocated by CEO fiat. Meanwhile, like a nanny chasing a particularly petulant charge, the Ads team runs around reactively trying to monetize whatever comes out of the product-development process.

But Twitter was different. The Ads team was actually the most dynamic, ready-to-ship, and bustling team in the organization. While the core Twitter product hasn't changed in years, the Ads team had been crackling with new products shipped regularly, one step either behind or ahead of rivals like Facebook, but always churning and burning. They also convinced the company's management to make ambitious (and stunningly large) acquisitions in the ads-technology space.

This was Twitter Ads, and so its leadership eventually becoming company leadership, however unique among consumer Internet companies, was not a huge surprise.

FRIDAY, MARCH 25, 2011

Matters really kicked into gear when Twitter sent us that sine qua non of startup scheming, a corporate NDA. This is effectively the Snapchat messaging of the corporate world: you can take a peek, but the message needs to effectively be deleted from your brain (or at least never leave it) forever.

Shit had just gotten real, and we needed a lawyer. Not a litigator like the Undertaker or Wang, whose generosity we didn't want to test anymore, but a lawyer skilled in the polite work of corporate governance.

Conveniently, a few weeks before this, I had gotten worried about our corporate paperwork. I had done the incorporation myself, as the boys were hopeless when it came to real-world deliverables like rent, payroll, or anything involving bureaucracy. But, of course, I didn't exactly know what I was doing, and had just used Y Combinator's default incorporation forms, and faxed it all from a Kinko's. The whole thing took maybe a total of two hours, from reserving a corporate name to getting confirmation from the state of Delaware. If we ever raised a real series A or got acquired, our corporate ducks would have to be in a definitive row, or their disorder would potentially sink the deal.

Long before this moment, we had the good fortune to meet the founders of Twitter's first acquisition, a geolocation technology startup named Mixer Labs. One founder was Elad Gil, a YC investor and noted blogger, whose eloquent and knowledgeable takes on the early-stage startup game I routinely devoured. The other was Othman Laraki, a former Google product manager who was then a member of the Twitter Growth team. Both would rise to senior VP positions at Twitter, and both were savvy and seasoned operators in the M&A and startup space. They were also keen traders of startup social capital, and had offered their time to occasionally advise us with no formal compensation involved.

From them we had gotten an introduction to Mitchell Zuklie, a big fish at the big-fish Silicon Valley law firm Orrick, Herrington & Sutcliffe (just "Orrick" in Valley-speak). After an effusive phone call, he arranged for his junior partner Harold Yu to give us a legal checkup.* This was all comped, of course. Like the best Valley law firms, they played the long game, and were big believers in the "first dose is free" business model. They knew that down the line there'd be expensive legal work in the offing, and so based on nothing but an introduction, the Y Combinator badge, and a half-hour conversation with me, they politely asked us to send them our incorporation docs. The following week, I had spent hour after comped hour on the phone with Yu, going through our legal health report.

* One of the surprising in-the-living-of-it details about Valley hustling is how one can mobilize an army of lawyers, accountants, engineers, PR people, public company wheeler-dealers, partner relationship people—the whole lot of what makes the Valley money machine go 'round—without meeting any of them. Of the epic-sized cast involved with AdGrok, I might have met maybe half of them. The rest never existed to me beyond phone calls and emails.

Conveniently, Mitch Zuklie and Orrick had also been corporate counsel for Mixer Labs. As such, they knew this M&A cloak-and-dagger world well, and the Twitter playbook best of all. They were the perfect lawyers to retain. Here's another lesson for the aspiring startupista: don't skimp on lawyers. An error at the hour of signing a big contract, or negotiating an acquisition, could easily cost you millions, or be the deciding factor between summers in Ibiza with your model girlfriend or taking a consolation-prize job as product manager at Oracle instead (look, you get pretax commuter cost benefits there!). Get the best legal guns you can pay for, and if you can't pay for it, convince them to accept something other than money in exchange. Lawyers didn't get into law because they're good at business; bamboozle them however so long as they get cracking.

I sent Orrick the NDA to give it a sniff test. It was probably boilerplate, but it was the first company-level NDA we had ever seen. Trust, but verify—and keep a loaded shotgun under your bed.

Consider for a moment Eurasian politics in the sixteenth through nineteenth centuries, and how different things are today.

Western Europe had not achieved the worldwide dominance it would eventually enjoy, nor had the Islamic world begun its precipitous decline. Lest we forget, Turkish artillery was using Vienna for target practice as late as 1683, and only last-minute alliances kept the Islamic world from extending clear to Bavaria. European powers competed for favor from potential Asian allies to use against other Europeans—imagine France teaming up with Iran against the United Kingdom these days, as Napoleon did in 1807—and Middle Eastern governments meddled in European affairs in a way unthinkable now.

In such a world, European states and the great Middle

Eastern powers of the Ottoman and Persian empires dealt with each other mostly as equals, with all the diplomatic frippery and double-dealing this required. A key actor in this fascinating civilizational face-off was the dragoman (the etymological root is the Arabic world for "translator"). More than a mere interpreter, the dragoman was a cultural matchmaker who selectively (mis)translated missives in order to achieve a desired diplomatic result (often unknown to either communicating party). Thus did the Sublime Porte's imperious message to Queen Victoria greeting her as a tributary get toned down to that of an esteemed diplomatic partner. When Victoria wrote back with a stiff upper lip, the dragoman would layer on the subservience an Oriental despot expected.

Of course, matters grew complicated when it came to treaties, as it was no longer an issue of translating tone but one of actual geopolitical substance. On that front, the dragomans got themselves and their employers into all sorts of trouble. While treaties were often signed in whatever diplomatic language was chosen, native translations were made for each signing party, cleaving the agreement into two versions that were often vague at best, and inconsistent at worst.

So you see we have two types of mistranslation at work: the intentional kind that serves as diplomatic lubricant to get a deal done, and the more serious kind, which leaves each side thinking it agreed to a different thing.

The Silicon Valley world is an almost perfect analogue, and we have deal dragomans of our own.

When a deal really gets under way, things assume a certain le Carré–esque intrigue. There are always two channels of communication at work in a deal: One, a formal one, typically features email and attached documents, from founders to a company's corp dev team, as well as a possibly relevant product team. The second is the informal and clandestine. For lack of a better word, let's call it scheming.

Such scheming happens either by phone or in person,

with no emails or messaging involved. As a legal note, it's against the law to record phone calls in California, and such recordings are generally inadmissible in court, save for criminal trials with a warrant. So when the scheming begins, a startup world that does 99.9 percent of its communication via the asynchronous channels of email, messaging, and social media suddenly goes old school, and every communication is conducted via hushed phone call in a closed-door conference room. That's when you can tell you're really in some juicy shit; conversely, if you're still emailing about it, there's actually nothing real going on.

This other channel partly resembles Cold War drama, and partly resembles that time you announced to your fourth-grade class that you were going to kiss Becky Walker after sixth-period PE class, and all the resulting gossiping and cross talk. As events progress, the drama becomes more and more infantile, convincing you finally—as if you needed more proof this late in your startup trajectory—that humans, even at the rarefied heights of the economic elite, are in truth scared, needy children playing at dress-up and pretending to be grown-ups.

Now, if this had been Wall Street and had involved public companies, and people such as soon-to-be-acquired startup founders, employees, and investors were engaged in a convoluted game of highly selective telephone, shuffling around inside information with the obvious intent to privately profit (in either actual cash or just influence), we'd all have been hauled off to jail, or at least indicted. But from the get-go, it was clear this was par for the tech course, and nobody batted an eye. Either you talked and played a role in the deal, or you didn't, because you feared getting fired for breaching confidentiality, but nobody was preaching sermons here either way. And sure as shit, nobody was regulating any of it.

Given the moral chiaroscuro we're entering, it becomes necessary to birth the first and only composite character in this memoir. We've named some Twitter insiders thus far, but other unnamed insiders were also involved. If everyone is guilty, then nobody is guilty. Henceforward, any Twitter insider or otherwise interested party who dishes us information, to settle a score or to help the deal get done, or for private motives we could only guess at, will be known as the catch-all collage character of—wait for it—Deep Tweet.

Yes, Deep Tweet.

Deep Tweet gave us the inside line on Twitter's real valuation, and on what terms it had just raised a mountain of money. What fraction of the total float our shares represented, the inner workings of the board, and why Twitter would eventually seem like such an unholy cluster fuck from the outside (answer: because it was a cluster fuck on the inside). The fights between and among the board and the management, often staged at dysfunctional board meetings at which every big-name board member arrived with his or her entourage. The fact that both Ev Williams and Biz Stone were mentally checked out (in fact, both would leave Twitter within two months). That there was little product leadership after the VP of Product, Jason Goldman, left. The various internal messes that every tech company subject to sudden and unexpected meteoric growth experiences, and sedulously conceals from the outside world, presenting that flawless exterior canvas, ready for the journalists to paint their pristine narrative fallacy mural.*

But what of fair play? asks the moral reader.

Sadly, the startup game isn't played according to the Marquess of Queensberry's rules. Startup entrepreneur, you are

* For the first (and the last) time in my life, I'll quote that intellectual poseur Nassim Nicholas Taleb: "The narrative fallacy addresses our limited ability to look at sequences of facts without weaving an explanation into them, or, equivalently, forcing a logical link, an arrow of relationship upon them. Where this propensity can go wrong is when it increases our impression of understanding." This fallacy is what underpins billions of dollars in tech startup value.

David before Goliath, the nascent state of Israel during the '48 war, Crockett at the Alamo, the Spartans at Thermopylae. Choose your favorite metaphor of hopelessly mismatched odds: that's you. By any rational reckoning, startups should be dead before they even start. So if some disaffected insider at the acquiring company accosts you in a bar and starts spilling the beans, you buy him another beer and lean in close. You'll need every advantage you can get.

As a bit of local color, where did these Deep Tweet meetings actually take place? Beyond the aforementioned undocumentable phone calls, we'd occasionally meet in person. One meeting place was the Epicenter Café on Harrison, between Third and Fourth.

Comically, it was located next door to a public mental health clinic for the severely disturbed and the drug addicted. On the other side of it was the SoMa Whole Foods, where the overpaid techies (your humble correspondent included) kept themselves in foofy vittles. Whether you approached Epicenter from east or west along Harrison, you wended your way through either startup hipsters dropping six dollars for organic asparagus water, or human wrecks who thought French bulldogs were in a galactic conspiracy to kill them. Often, given the reigning shabby-chic aesthetic, you couldn't immediately distinguish between the technohipsters and the drugged-out homeless. (As the hardened SoMa veteran joke goes: the homeless have Android phones, while the techies have iPhones.)

Epicenter was good for Deep Tweet, as it was Twitter's unofficial off-site café. At the time, Twitter HQ was located directly behind the restaurant, on Folsom. The café had a back door that was directly reachable from Twitter, so your contact would be waiting for you inside when you rolled up. Order some dark-as-my-soul West Coast roast and, surrounded by the usual Asperger's populace of monomaniacal geeks clacking on MacBooks, get it on with Deep Tweet, and discuss your rumble in the tech jungle.

The entire SF startup world, in case you haven't been keeping track of the geography, lives between First and Eighth Streets, and between King and Market Streets, in SF's SoMa. A former bombed-out industrial space, dotted with a few flophouses and taken over by addicts until the late nineties, it was the eight-by-eight-block playing field of global technology.

Consider for a moment what fertile fields of globe-spanning technology these human shit-strewn streets were:

Twitter provides a broadcast platform for political disaffection and political extremism, and heads of states worldwide are unseated in scandals, and governments violently overthrown in the Middle East, destabilizing an entire region.

A local startup like Airbnb takes off, and real estate values in Barcelona and Berlin get roiled. The two-century-old bourgeois fortunes of those cities, having survived both Generalísimo Franco and the US Army Air Force Bomber Command, get kicked around by a bunch of scheming geeks and designers housed in an expensively renovated former factory.

If a local app like Uber makes it big, taxi drivers in Paris and Mexico City will be rioting and sending bricks through cars' windshields. If Uber wins, Madrid taxi drivers' wives will be weeping and wondering what's for dinner.

This was the major-league, serious shit, take-no-prisoners championship of tech entrepreneurship, and if you were going to play, you'd better show up ready to bite the ass off of a bear.*

* This of course is an homage to Michael Lewis's *Liar's Poker*, in which John Gutfreund, the villain of that work, says one had to be ready to come in every morning "willing to bite the ass off of a bear" to work at Salomon Brothers.

Acquisition Chicken

> Is it a reasonable thing, I ask you, for a grown man to run about and hit a ball? Poker's the only game fit for a grown man. Then your hand is against every man and every man's hand is against yours. Team-work? Who ever made a fortune by team-work? There's only one way to make a fortune and that's to down the fellow who's up against you.
>
> —W. Somerset Maugham, "Straight Flush"

SUNDAY, MARCH 27, 2011

"It's against my interests as a Twitter employee, but I recommend you seek to create an auction for your company." So did Deep Tweet whisper in my ear, right as this acquisition party was getting started.

As CEO, I had a fiduciary duty to capture the maximum value for my shareholders, of whom I was among the largest, naturally. Funny, that word, "fiduciary." From the Latin *fiduciarius*, meaning "binding faith." Legally, it refers to a condition of one party acting on behalf of another, with complete agency and assumed trust. In practice, whenever CEOs say it is their "fiduciary duty" to do something, it means they are granting themselves moral license to screw someone. Which, of course, is what I was about to do vis-à-vis Twitter.

What was the hurry?

As soon as matters progressed with Twitter beyond the exploratory stages, and assuming the company really wanted us, it would put a term sheet on the table. Right next to that would be a no-shop contract, which would mean any real selling of the company was done. A no-shop is either a separate contract or a clause in the term sheet stipulating that the company cannot solicit other acquirers during the period of negotiation and due diligence. Usually slotted for sixty days, they're enforceable in court, and some even carry penalties. The point is to put the company's self-pimping efforts on pause while the two parties get down to the serious business of haggling.

Deep Tweet's advice was timely and correct, and to have material offers on the table to use against Twitter, we needed to start that process ASAP. In fact, we were already late, as any other company was likely to move slower than this Twitter gift that had fallen into our laps.

I beat on every door in the Valley, anyplace I could get an intro and most places I couldn't, to shop the company out. I hounded everyone I knew at Google for an intro, even going through Russ to pitch ourselves to their M&A guy. I asked Sacca, who ignored my inquiries; as we were to learn, this was a man who only ever talked his book.* To the very end, we'd never manage to get so much as an email reply from Google, despite our entire product being built on it.

I rustled up Microsoft's startup evangelist, a minor miracle worker named Joel Franusic, to get intros to the acquisitions team in Redmond. They responded, and we found time to do a remote pitch the following week.

Then, of course, there was Facebook.

* This is Wall Street–ese for someone who publicly boosts only assets he himself currently owns, selfishly promoting his own gain, rather than providing disinterested analysis or advice. It's the withering criticism leveled at the talking heads on Bloomberg or CNBC when they promote some stock or another.

It had not escaped my attention that one of the other companies in our YC batch, named Whereoscope, had a founding CEO who was now at Facebook. The company worked on mobile apps that tracked where you were, either socially to share with your girlfriend, or for the paranoid parts of the market: for example, the parents of teenagers. The CEO was a guy named Mick Johnson, whose crowning achievement at YC was ending his Demo Day pitch with a video of himself breaking a cinder block with a karate punch. He reminded me of a young Russell Crowe in *Romper Stomper*, in both looks and attitude. (If you've seen the film, this should inspire terror.)

I recalled that one day Whereoscope had just disappeared without a trace, although there had been rumors of a stealth deal. The net of it was that Johnson somehow magically reappeared as a product manager at Facebook.

I sent him an email in which I conjured the magic formula sure to evoke any acquisitive company's interest: we were "in play," and needed to talk to someone in a relevant product team before Facebook missed out on this choice opportunity. He made an intro to that star of the advertising firmament, Gokul Rajaram, a man who'd influence my life in more ways than one.

TUESDAY, MARCH 29, 2011

The scene: a claustrophobically small conference room buried inside Twitter somewhere. Jess Verrilli and Kevin Thau, Twitter's VP of Business Development, across the table from me, looking a bit awkward. I was expecting bad news.

Where things stood was as follows:

Chris Sacca, in his infinite deal-making wisdom, had told them we had another offer in the works, which was a barefaced lie. If Twitter gave us a term sheet, though, we most certainly could conjure another offer. So you see, it wasn't really a lie, merely a truth that hadn't quite birthed itself, and needed only the recipient's credulity to make it true. "Fake it till you make it" went the oft-repeated Silicon Valley saw.

As a result, Twitter felt there was a fire under its ass to produce a deal. I had read them the memo (inspired by PG's dismissive email about potential acquisitions) that we weren't willing to even undergo the acquisition colostomy unless the terms were inviting from the very beginning. And so after my bromantic date with Adam Bain the previous Wednesday, I had stipulated the need to see a term sheet sooner rather than later. Jess had actually promised one for the previous Friday.

But Twitter hadn't delivered. All we'd gotten was the boilerplate NDA that had triggered phone calls to Orrick, and nothing beyond that. I had gone grousing to Sacca, who promised that we'd get a term sheet fast, and it wouldn't be "some bullshit number, but a great deal" to convince us to sell.

With Jess, I had maintained a tone of harried and mild exasperation, all the while trying to drum up anything like a competing offer. Despite my deception around urgency that didn't really exist, Twitter owed us an answer of some sort, either yea or nay, preferably with a dollar sign attached. And this was the meeting where they were excusing themselves.

Following a brief prelude that made it clear that things hadn't gone as swimmingly at their Monday meeting as we'd hoped, she dropped this:

"We're thinking of this deal as a five-million-dollar thing."

She looked me right in the eye. Kevin sat next to her, silent and smiling.

I thought about that for a moment. That was way away from where it needed to be. We had been raising money at just under that before the Adchemy lawsuit; it needed to be double that.

After an appropriate pause I replied, "Well, I'll have to talk this over with the other founders and the investors."

Clipped good-byes, and I was out the door. The disappearing-ink name tag hadn't been more than ten minutes around my neck. A hundred yards outside, in the alleyway that ran behind Twitter, I called Sacca. He had also failed to deliver, in a way. He had promised us that Twitter would generate a term sheet quickly. He made a big show of being pissed, and vowed to get back to me.

Dawdling in the alleyway after the Sacca call, I took a look around to make sure no Twitter employees I knew were nearby, and consulted my email and calendar.

The day before, Facebook had emailed, proposing we come in and meet some of the Ads team. It was to be a formal pitch to some of their leadership. Mick's introduction to Gokul had borne fruit. Gokul's admin had confirmed the meeting that very morning: we were on for tomorrow afternoon.

I'd make sure Twitter had to hurry for real this time. I walked back south on Third Street, on what was becoming the well-trod path between Twitter and AdGrok.

Five million dollars! Just think of it. A fantastic sum.

But was it?

Before the lawsuit, we were raising on a cap (i.e., a nominal valuation) of $4 million, and even as this deal was happening, YC companies fresh out of their batch were raising at more than $5 million. The market price for acquired engineers in the Valley then was anywhere from half a million to $2 million each. That refers to the total equity vesting (probably) over four years. The salary, which was something in the $90,000 to $150,000 range, just paid for rent and beer, and wasn't part of the total sum quoted.

So $5 million for three hires plus intellectual property Twitter might use, with a premium for YC bling and "thought leadership" evinced via our glorious blog, was way too cheap. We hadn't risked everything from our finances to our sanity for just over a million each that would take four years to earn.

I could picture each of the boys digesting the offer, though, probably with their respective mates by their side. They'd have a very different take on it.

In the case of Argyris, it meant thinking about an apartment in Athens, and the fantasy he had of opening a combined café–vinyl record store with Simla, his new wife. He already came from a wealthy family, but this meant his own financial independence, and so soon after graduating.

In the case of MRM, it meant paying off his mortgage, and no worries about paying for karate lessons for the kids, not to mention help with college down the line. It would be the most he'd ever made in a long, hardworking, but not particularly remunerative career. AdGrok's first unsalaried months had knocked out what little nest egg he had. This would change everything.

How about our investors, what were their numbers?

We had effectively sold them 22 percent of the company in our desperate, undervalued seed round. Assuming a pro rata share of the deal, they'd be seeing about a million pretax. Given they'd invested just under half a mil, it meant a full-on 100 percent return. They'd double their money in just over six months; that was decent money by any honest man's standard.

Some of our investors saw it very differently, however, and the reasons underline the distinction I drew earlier between old-school angels and more modern micro-VC versions of same. To Russ, who was investing his own money, and who was essentially playing a market in people like a savvy gambler at a poker hall, this was a fine return. He'd take his cash (or shares in Twitter, if that's what it came to), possibly sell them, and then invest in other companies, upping his returns, and suffering occasional burns as well.

Sacca had a very different attitude toward potential deals. Which is why Sacca, or any VC really, would push you to mimic his own distorted risk profile, which prefers a tenfold return, even if it marginally increases the chance of complete failure. Twofold just ain't cool enough for the limited partners, and not why they handed over their money to Sacca in the first place.

The risk expectations of founders and investors can often be severely misaligned. I hate sports analogies, but here's one to explain this vital point: most VCs are playing a version of baseball in which the only way to score is to hit a home run when you're at bat. They don't care if you disgrace or impoverish yourself and strike out, and they don't care if you get a solid line drive that lands you on second. To them, strikeouts and getting on base are equally pointless, and so they'll push to proverbially "swing for the fences" no matter the count or the team you're up against.

The reason for this all-or-nothing approach is how their funds are structured. VCs (or so-called angels like Sacca) raise a fund, out of which they'll provision some number of investments. Barring doubling down on the same company, which they might do if the fund still has money when a company raises again, those investments are effectively "fire and forget." The fund's total profit will be calculated from whatever those initial bets return. Unlike, say, a hedge fund portfolio manager, who rolls the winnings from one good bet into the next, compounding a series of returns into something truly huge, VCs do not take liquidity from one company's exit and pour it into yet another's.* This, at heart, is why the go-big-or-go-home strategy makes the Silicon Valley world turn, and why entrepreneurs push themselves to be either the next Airbnb, or nothing. The entrepreneur

* This isn't absolutely, completely true. There are some funds, in the minority, which are called "evergreen funds," and which get topped up yearly by either new investors or returns from previous investments.

who bucks this and creates a long-term business of recurring revenue but relatively slow growth is dismissed as running a mere "lifestyle business," which is a dirty word among VCs. Of course, the entrepreneurs are quite happy to run a revenue-generating concern that spits out cash as low-tax dividends, and dedicate their lives to skiing or guitar playing or whatever. But their investors will hate them for it, and the entrepreneurs will suffer a loss of social capital as a result, and perhaps find they can't raise money for their next venture.

Personally, I was ecstatic that Sacca, in his role as institutional investor, would almost inevitably oppose this deal, and be my cudgel to beat the boys into rejecting it. I probably couldn't have scared up even $5,000 of my own personal money right then, but $5 million for a nine-month-old company composed of three guys and a pile of code just wasn't enough. The market price for a company at this stage was much more than that, and this little former Goldman quant sold only at the market price or better.

Alone, I would have been outgunned against the boys *and* Russ. But Sacca—loud, opinionated Sacca—would talk them out of it.

Getting Liked

> Send thou men, that they may spy out the land of Canaan, which I give unto the children of Israel; of every tribe of their fathers shall ye send a man, every one a prince among them.
>
> —Numbers 13:2

WEDNESDAY, MARCH 30, 2011

The entrance to Facebook headquarters had the word HACK written across the sliding double doors, like a tympanum frieze on a cathedral, but instead of Christ in judgment or the Last Supper, it was an injunction to craft and build.

The building itself was a generic commercial space, indistinguishable from all the other large warehouse/office spaces that dotted South Bay and were collectively referred to as "Silicon Valley." If you saw a picture, you'd think it was the industrial research lab for some fiber-optics or satellite company, and not the social media company that had managed to globally intermediate *Homo sapiens*' insatiable urge to connect and share.

Once you were past HACK, a flat-panel screen to your right displayed a real-time animation of Facebook friending activity around the globe. Every time someone accepted a friend request on Facebook, a thin white line connected the locations of the two friends. The image of the planet looked as if a horde of exotic spiders had crafted a web all over the Earth, and the web respun itself every few seconds, continuously and forever.

We signed the de rigueur NDA at the front desk in exchange for name tags, and milled nervously around the reception area, watching the usual to-and-fro of employees, job candidates, and outside partners. Entrance to the inner sanctum was via a glass door secured by magnetic lock that opened only upon swiping a badge. A watchful security guard made sure nobody tried to draft off another entrant or catch a rapidly shutting door to gain access. As at Twitter, an army of journalists and creepers was always trying to get in, and only the chosen were permitted. Whether we were worthy enough to be among them is what we were there to decide.

Gokul's admin led us through what appeared to be the central nave of the building, a wide gallery crisscrossed with rows of desks and adjoining (what else?) Aeron chairs. To the right was "The Facebook Wall," a scrolling mural of visitors' signatures so thick it was almost a solid black. Clerestory windows set into the nave's back and side, along with universal white walls, made the space feel light and airy. Patches of rubber tile over varnished concrete made it feel like the half-finished factory space it perhaps really was.

The most important person joining us was Amin Zoufonoun, Facebook's head of corporate development. He had just been poached from Google and this was his first week at Facebook. A veteran dealmaker, he had done dozens if not hundreds of deals at Google, the most prolific company-buyer in the Valley.

Almost as important was the official host of this meeting, Kang-Xing Jin, a Facebook old-timer who had joined in 2006 along with a crop of Harvard grads who had been cajoled out of dropout Zuck's alma mater. Currently he was the engineering manager for Facebook Ads, and though we didn't quite realize it at the time, he was the key player in Facebook monetization.

"Call me KX, or 'Kon-Sin,' like 'Wisconsin,' where I'm from," he offered, flashing one of those lightning-fast smiles that erupt from an otherwise emotionless face. I guessed he was in his late twenties at most, thin with square wire-rimmed glasses and an intense stare.

The others in the room were Ambar Pansari, the product manager for the Ads API, the area of the Facebook ensemble most relevant to an ads-buying tool like ours. Also present, Nipun Mathur, the product marketing manager for Facebook's API program, whom I had tried to cadge API access out of on multiple previous occasions.

The preliminaries were brief. I dug into a recessed cubby in the center of the conference table where Mac chargers, Lenovo chargers, and cables for the projector were all snaked together in a rat's nest. The adapter for each video output plug was zip-tied to the cable, to keep them from walking off.

Teasing out the right one and plugging it into my ADGROK-sticker-covered Mac, I charged into my now well-rehearsed demo. Our beautiful line graphs loaded instantly and the Google keywords with their bids and associated ad creative rendered flawlessly, as I assuredly navigated around a live partner website that made millions selling expensive smartphone covers, and whose online catalog I had almost memorized. They seemed suitably impressed; KX in particular was very excited. Smiles all around, and the room took on that slightly festive air of a group that had just shared a good joke or favorite old story.

One of the crew asked the question of how we'd use the technology inside Facebook—at which point Amin popped the bubble on the mounting lovefest by mentioning we were there because we had outside interest. Without much ado, he came out and asked who else we were talking to, looking straight at me with what I'd realize was his game face. It was interesting. KX had a serious look of intensity that lapsed into frivolity, while Amin was the opposite: affable good cheer that yielded suddenly to inscrutable calculation.

"I think you can guess who, Amin." I gestured toward the screen, which still glowed with Google keywords inside the GrokBar.

"Ah . . ." He cocked an eyebrow.

"Like you, Amin, we want to be part of the future, not the past, though," I said, referring to his barely three-day-old departure from that little search company in Mountain View.

His expression reverted to the studied affability of the dealmaker.

He had swallowed my improvised bait. He thought we had a serious offer from Google. I'd like to claim this was some brilliantly precalculated move, but in fact, it was completely extemporaneous and based on nothing but a sneaking suspicion that, while company X might have feared Y, and Y feared Z, everybody in tech feared Google.

Amin's recent arrival at Facebook from the search giant was important for one big reason: whenever someone, particularly a senior executive like Amin who was surely poached, leaves a company for a rival, he leaves behind a stench of bad mojo. Everyone on his former team is on guard, and is unlikely, at least for the first few weeks, to engage in the sort of informal information sharing that often binds people across jobs and companies. The net of it was that Amin would have no back channel into Google, and would essentially be blind to what it was really doing (or not doing), as nobody there would be on speaking terms with him. This left him open to a barefaced bluff from a company, like us, that had built its entire product on Google. That one throwaway line of mine was probably half responsible for what followed.

Dog and pony show over, the group split, everyone heading to his or her next meeting. Amin pulled me aside on the way out and assured me he'd be in touch soon.

On California Avenue, about a hundred feet outside Facebook's HACK door, the crew reconvened in the AdGrok Mobile Conference Room (i.e., the inside of MRM's Honda Accord). We owed Sacca a call about Twitter's verbal offer. I proposed not mentioning the Facebook meeting we had had two minutes ago to Sacca.

From the looks, Sacca wasn't going to be a mere adviser in this deal, he was going to be an actual player, pushing things one way or the other (and for better or worse). From his pro-Twitter boosterism, it was clear he was working us to an outcome, and if he knew about Facebook, God only knew how he'd embroil himself. Facebook was half-populated by Googlers, and he probably knew bunches of them, having been a high-profile Googler himself. The boys agreed; despite staring at the FACEBOOK 1601 S CALIFORNIA AVE sign ten yards away that all the tourists took their picture next to, we would not mention our Facebook excursion yet.

That morning, Sacca had sent an email opening with, "No fucking way should you engage on this offer."

And which went downhill from there: "We didn't partner up on this to flip at a price lower than the pre for most investments today."*

And so I expected him to be raging on this phone call, and was somewhat preemptively wincing. Surprisingly, he mostly sounded each of us out. I gave an equivocal take on

* The "pre-money valuation," or "pre," is the stated value of a company before the investors' money is added to the company's balance sheet. "Post" is that same value after you've cashed their check(s). For example, raising $1 million on $10 million pre means you've got an $11 million ($1M + $10M) post-valuation. It's paper value, plus cash on hand. Since funding received is often such a huge chunk of the total value (you're selling something like 20 percent of the company in the early rounds), you have to distinguish between the cash and the noncash valuation.

the deal; I felt too short on sway with the boys to shoot this down. In brief, I wimped out so the boys wouldn't see me as a bad guy, allowing Sacca to piss on the parade instead.

Crafty Sacca detected the weakness. The moment the call was over, he began sending me angry text after angry text, denouncing my willingness to sell for nothing. He proposed an immediate call with Russ, suspecting he was the one pushing us down the road to this deal. Driving back to SF, I called Russ and proposed a group call to discuss the deal. (I had informed him after telling Sacca, and he indeed had welcomed the news.)

By the time we had driven up the 101 in building rush-hour traffic, we had arranged a group call among Russ, Sacca, and the whole crew. We had the meeting in the parking garage at AdGrok world headquarters, me in the passenger seat, MRM in the driver's seat, and AZ in the back, the moneymen each on their respective speakerphones.

It was Sacca's show, really. In a more moderated tone than his screaming texts and emails, he built the case for cutting off all communications with Twitter until it came back with a real offer.

Tide turned, the boys and Russ agreed, and I assented. The Twitter deal thread was to be put on pause until the company could cough up more cash.

Deal drama over, for now, we all returned to the office. That evening I wrote three emails. The first was a groveling, apologetic email to Sacca, reassuring him I was not behind this deal and that we'd surely reject it. I also defended the boys, whom I thought Sacca had unfairly criticized, pointing out that they were excellent builders but not poker players.

Secondly, I wrote a long-winded and diplomatic email to Jessica stating we were not interested in a deal at the $5 million price point. With much *voulez-vous*, I politely reminded her we had work to do, and that we couldn't afford the distractions a deal discussion involved.

Lastly, I wrote to Facebook.

That evening Amin had emailed as promised, introducing me to his dealmaking subordinate Dale Dwelle, who'd manage the logistics. We had passed the first hurdle, and Facebook was impressed by the team and product. The day had been a success. Understanding our urgency around this unnamed but hinted-at other deal—the one I had actually just rejected, to be clear—they'd work on making their acquisition process speedy. Could we possibly come in on Friday, within less than forty-eight hours, for a full day of interviews? I responded that we could, and requested more information on our interviewers. We'd have to do the full due diligence workup on them, as we did with Twitter, and once more unto the breach, dear friends, once more—this time with Facebook.

Getting Poked

> If you can only be good at one thing, be good at lying . . . because if you're good at lying, you're good at everything.
>
> —@gselevator, July 25, 2013

FRIDAY, APRIL 1, 2011

Want to know what it's like getting bought by a company like Facebook?

Here's how it works:

Since this sort of early-stage "acqui-hire" is more "hire" than "acqui," every employee Facebook cares about must go through the usual hiring screen you'd experience if you had simply applied individually. The fact that you come bundled just changes the economics. We used to have unions that would give workers a magical thing called collective bargaining. Now being part of a hot startup is your union, and the only dues required are your entire life for the time you're in the startup. Welcome to our new collectivism, tovarish. By bundling the talent, though, you command a premium due to mere leverage—don't like the price, we're all off the table.

Those of you who haven't been sleeping might ask: What if some of you do well in the interviews, but some do not? Well, you're skipping ahead. Let's see how the Groksters fare.

When you get the interview-day invite from whatever admin is managing the logistics, make sure to ask for the interviewer list the day before, so you can do the good librarian's son homework you should be doing, which is stalking each and every interviewer.*

Why is that?

As with any interview, whether it be a hardball technical/engineering interview, or the foofy product manager one, the challenge is very simple: either you're incompetent and you struggle to provide even one answer you hope is right to the interview question, or you're not, and your brain produces two or three. Each of those could be right, depending on your interviewer. Truth in the world resides only in mathematical proofs and physics labs. Everywhere else, it's really a matter of opinion, and if it manages to become group opinion, it's undeservedly crowned as capital-T Truth. And so you need to determine whatever the local version of truth is you're inhabiting. And that you do by reading body language, and understanding the intellectual sauce your opponent has been marinating in (if any). With that in mind, you choose among the three alternative answers you could spout.

One more explanatory pause, and then we'll move on.

These interviews serve another, more subtle purpose. If you're offered a job that you accept, then that day spent with a slate of tormentors is in fact an initiatory hazing ritual, like the collective beating doled out to an aspiring gang member. It's weird, but you develop a certain attachment to that experience, and it's a jump start on the team bonding you'll need to succeed on the eventual job. An interviewer will always remember that he or she helped bring in someone who eventually became a valued employee. Companies also stress about the experience, and try to find the subtle balance of challenge and courtship that will attract the best talent.

* Yes, my mother was a librarian, and the library was my babysitter until high school. Did you think those Polybius quotes came from *Bartlett's*?

Many and sundry are the postinterview blog posts dissecting one or another idiosyncrasy of flagship companies like Apple, Google, or Facebook, and whether they're fair, cruel, or just random. In many ways, the interview process is the face of the company.

On to the show.

My first interviewer was Alon Amit. He was Israeli (obviously) and had done a PhD in mathematics at Jerusalem before joining Google, and eventually Facebook. Like every thirtysomething Israeli male, he was short, bald, and stocky, with an unemotional face that looked as hard as plywood. As is typical with most sabras, though, he warmed up when I gave every hint of not being a shit-for-brains. He suggested we go outside for the interview, so we sat on a bench side by side and stared somewhat distractedly at the sad-looking volleyball court in Facebook's backyard that nobody appeared to use.

Next up was Rohit Dhawan. Another Googler, he had that very well put together and confident air of someone who felt he had mastered his field of work (he was a Penn grad, of course). His angle was analytical ability, and he asked me a variant of that legendary Enrico Fermi brainteaser about piano tuners in Chicago. His variant was to estimate the number of planes in the sky at any given moment. It required nothing more than some rough base assumptions about number of airports and flights per day, and then some dimensional analysis that got us within an order of magnitude of reality, and we were done in ten minutes.

A plug for the quantitative sciences: The reality is, most humans manage to feed, clothe, and amuse themselves, and yet are not able to formulate a rational argument that stands up to informed scrutiny, derive the conclusion of a syllogistic argument, or understand a mathematical proof. Doing advanced studies in any quantitative field is like surviving Marine boot camp while the rest of the world is channel surfing and inhaling Oreos; you don't exactly need to fear the push-up test. Even when the intellectual test is being doled out as filter to the elite ranks of a globe-spanning tech company, you won't be out of your league if you understand the problem space. So if nothing else, aspiring physicist or mathematician, rest comfortable knowing you'll come out of that long academic tunnel thinking circles around most people.

For the remaining half hour, we sat in the two easy chairs in the conference room, and talked about BMWs and the relative merits of the 3 versus the 5 series, and whether the M-class upgrade was really worth the money (my view: it was).

Next was Jared Morgenstern. This was my first brush with a true Facebook old-timer. A Harvard type, like many of the original team, he joined Facebook in 2006 following postacquisition boredom at a big company that had bought his nascent social media site. Mark had seduced him into becoming one of the first members of Facebook's design team. Rangy and fit, he rolled into the room with barely a word, and asked me to design a music app for Facebook. Despite my design sense being limited to picking two roughly matching socks in the morning, I somehow managed to muddle through.

As a random intellectual test, he next asked me to explain how pairing apps that allow two phones to talk to each other when shaken simultaneously work. He had seen physics on the résumé and wanted to kick the intellectual tires. As always, how you sell yourself is how you'll be bought. This one was easy, and as with Rohit, the interview ended early.*

* Hint in case you're thinking about this: there are too many phones being shaken at one time in the world, and the GPS coordinates aren't accurate enough for mere proximity to work as the signal. When users pair their phones, they "bump" them together against each other, almost as if they were connected by a spring. And if they really were connected by springs, almost like a harmonic oscillator, what would the accelerometers in those phones be reading?

What I realized only hazily at the time was that each interview was meant to test an archetypal skill of the ideal Facebook product manager. There were five signs in this zodiac. I had just gotten out of the "designer" one, and still had a couple left to go.

As with every interview, the recruiter appeared at the appointed time, and escorted me to yet another room. The room shuffle I chalked up to the last-minute scheduling. Between rooms I scoped out the surroundings. For such a late-stage company, it still looked and felt (and smelled) like some early-stage jerry-rigged contraption like AdGrok. Generic desks pushed together into islands pell-mell, cables running everywhere, remains of food on café plates, stained and ratty carpets, skateboards and Nerf guns and assorted boy toys scattered everywhere, clusters of liquor bottles resting on what appeared to be private team bars. The whole thing looked like a flagrant OSHA violation. Not that I had any objections.

Justin Shaffer was the next inquisitor. Taller than me at probably six four or so, with a big swirling mane of hair and a three-day stubble, he shook my hand, and before his ass hit the chair was asking me questions about AdGrok. How many users? What's revenue look like? What are you optimizing for? Next steps? And so it went. . . . It felt like I was pitching a one-man VC again, and having to resell the entire venture (which I sort of was).

As the waterboarding continued, I began to notice an air of arrogance that stank like bad aftershave. I'd later realize that it was his Friend of Zuck (FoZ) status I was smelling, and to which I evidently was genetically allergic. Some allergies, it turns out, worsen on exposure.

But he seemed mentally agile, and asked the standard questions about the Gospel of Startup, which I had memorized like a biblical scholar. Per my preinterview stalking, he himself had been acqui-hired a few years earlier, from Major League Baseball no less, and formed part of the small but growing New York contingent of Facebookers that had been recruited cross-continent. His list of questions concluded, and both of us having talked at 120 miles per hour, the whole ego pissing match was over in a half hour. "Great talking!" he announced, and bolted out the door.

In retrospect, I realize that he was sniffing out one of the squishiest, and certainly guiltiest, concepts in Silicon Valley, namely that of cultural fit. Cultural fit, like the Holy Spirit in the Catholic Trinity, is that mysterious intangible, hard enough to conceive of, much less define, but critical to a job at a tech company. In theory, it's a measure of the alignment of the candidate's values regarding collaboration, style of product development, and overarching goals ("a more open and connected world") with those of the company. Since, in the self-aggrandizing view of most tech companies, their corporate "culture" is unique, and as valuable as that of an uncontacted Amazon tribe, it is hailed as precisely what undergirds their sky-high valuation. Therefore, a candidate's alignment with that culture is overwhelmingly important. Being handy with the C++ programming language isn't good enough—you also have to be one of us in thought and spirit.

In reality, though, it usually worked like this:

A female candidate who will buzzkill your weekly happy hour?

"Cultural fit."

A soft-spoken Indian or Chinese engineer, quietly competent but incapable of the hard-charging egotism that Americans almost universally wear like they do blue jeans?

"Cultural fit."

Self-taught kid from some crappy college you've never heard of, without that glib sheen of effortless superiority you get out of Harvard or Stanford?

"Cultural fit."

And so it goes.

Shaffer's machine-gun questioning and imperiousness had

rattled me. I suspected that I had failed to pass his bar, and I needed to clear my head. The day had been nothing but a series of interrogations inside small, gray, rotten-smelling rooms. The Guantánamo vibe was fatiguing. Despite the NSA-level security on checking in and the way we were handed off like booby-trapped hot potatoes that no one could drop, nobody appeared for the next interview. Wining and dining evidently not in the offing, I wandered off and tried to find something to eat.

Walking over festering carpet that looked like it had last been cleaned during the Reagan administration, I found one of the microkitchens. The only thing in the shelves resembling real food was a can of Campbell's Chicken Soup, which I opened, poured into a coffee mug, and popped into the microwave. I bolted the lukewarm sludge and then hit the men's room, conveniently next to my soup kitchen. Beeline for the urinal and unzip; release bladder and think of Fidel Castro's face. While this was going on, I noticed the background music of laptop keys clacking. This was a microbathroom, claustrophobic in layout, with only two each of johns, sinks, and urinals. Someone inside a stall was pants around ankles, ass on toilet, pounding away on a laptop. This wasn't a chatting-with-girlfriend conversation. No. This was full-on typing for twenty seconds, followed by a two-second pause for thought, and another few lines of code written, then a onetime keyboard shortcut arpeggio to save the work in a text editor like Emacs. The cadence was unmistakable; I'd heard nothing else for the past six years. The dude was full-on coding while dropping a deuce.

My own task completed, I headed to the sinks. Two big buckets next to the faucet were packed with disposable toothbrushes and small tubes of toothpaste. I took a peek in the waste bin, and noticed several discarded toothbrush wrappers. *They actually get used regularly.* People coded while they shat and needed to be provided toothbrushes at work. They had my attention.

Minding the time, I exited back to my conference room/torture cell and waited for my last interviewer. It turned out to be Gokul himself.

At that point in time, Gokul Rajaram was a legendary éminence grise in the ad-tech world. The so-called godfather of AdSense, Google's secondary gold mine after AdWords, Gokul was a constant presence on the conference circuit, and an omnipresent adviser or investor in just about every advertising technology company worth talking about.

He too had come to Facebook via a small acqui-hire, though really that had been just a career breather between his time at Google and his hiring at Facebook. University at the Indian Institute of Technology (IIT), followed by an American MBA, he was your standard-issue Indian techie, and probably that country's most valuable export after steel and Tata Motors.

"What's the first thing you would change about Facebook Ads if we hired you?"

There was about as much polish and prologue to Gokul as that of a North Korean diplomat.

"I'd build a conversion-tracking system. It's unbelievable you don't have one yet."

A conversion-tracking system is software that tells you if an advertisement has worked in driving a conversion (or "sale" in marketing-speak), and lets you retweak your marketing campaigns based on performance. An ads system without conversion tracking is like a car without rearview mirrors; nay, it's like a car without even rear or side windows. All you can see is forward, merrily driving along, not even understanding what's behind you or what you just ran over. It's a danger to yourself and others, and it was a sign of just how out-of-touch Facebook Ads management was that this somehow never got prioritized.

From Gokul's smile the conclusion was clearly . . . right answer!

And so the conversation went, traversing various potential aspects of the Facebook Ads system, and what the company needed to build.

It was a giddy Gokul—I'd soon learn he was almost always giddy—who escorted me out the door. The boys and I had arrived separately, assuming we'd get out at different times, and separately did we go back to the GrokPad. There, we compared notes. MRM and Argyris weren't exactly rousing in their reviews of the experience. In fact, it was clear that the fascist vibe the company gave off had very much rubbed them the wrong way. They had never really liked Facebook, as either product or company, going back to our visits to their developer events. The daylong hazing had done nothing to charm them.

The Various Futures of the Forking Paths

> The kingdom of heaven is like a king who prepared a wedding banquet for his son . . . but when the king came in to see the guests, he noticed a man there who was not wearing wedding clothes. He asked, "How did you get in here without wedding clothes, friend?" The man was speechless. Then the king told the attendants, "Tie him hand and foot, and throw him outside, into the darkness, where there will be weeping and gnashing of teeth." For many are invited, but few are chosen.
>
> —Matthew 22:2, 11–14

TUESDAY, APRIL 5, 2011

Ten million dollars.

Twitter was officially back in the game. They had finally come back with a real offer. While we hadn't seen a formal term sheet—and the devil was absolutely in those details—it was clear Twitter was now in the realm of 2011 tech-bubble (in)sanity. Our stonewalling had paid off. Even Sacca and I couldn't claim this wasn't a tempting offer.

I was riding that particular high when the phone rang.

"Hello, Antonio!"

It was six thirty p.m., and this was the much-awaited phone call from Amin, reporting on our proctological day of interviews at Facebook.

"So, I talked to our engineers and we have the final feedback."

In the Aaron Sorkin cinematic adaptation of this story, this is where the violins will start scraping their tension-building wail.

"I'm sorry to say that we won't be moving forward with a deal for AdGrok. The feedback on Argyris and Matt was mixed, and I don't think it's a go right now."

Fuck!

Take another kick in your scarred mug, startup guy.

"In the interests of AdGrok, can you tell me what some of the feedback was?" I sputtered.

Amin changed to that slightly hushed and tense conspiratorial tone that people use, as if hiding in the bushes, when in fact I assumed he was in a closed-door conference room. He proceeded to do some pro bono dragoman-ing. Argyris would have been a possible hire, but Matt was a definite no. Clearly MRM was a gifted engineer, but Facebook had very specific conceptions of engineering greatness. Also, there was a bit of that nebulous "cultural fit" blocking as well.

After my day of interviews, I had imagined that MRM and Facebook would get along about as well as a Berkeley hippie and a Marine scout sniper, and I was right.

"Sorry to hear that, Amin. Thanks for your time and that of everyone at Facebook."

"Hold on. While that was the feedback for the engineers, the feedback for you was different. We want you to come and join the Facebook Ads team. Your feedback was excellent, and everyone really felt you were an extremely strong candidate."

My mind stuttered a bit on that one. When in doubt, act coy.

"Well. . . . Amin, as you can understand, I'm somewhat committed to both AdGrok and this other deal we have. I'll have to think about this."

"Think about it. But again, we really want you to come to Facebook."

I looked up suddenly toward our windowed office. I had isolated myself on our balcony in an obvious bid for privacy. Argyris was inside, looking at me with a worried frown. He wanted an answer as badly as I did. I raised two fingers and mouthed "two minutes" to indicate I'd need a bit more time. He nodded, and went back to his screen.

What the fuck should I do? I couldn't tell the boys this, at least not yet.

Stealthily, making it look like I was readjusting my phone, I hung up and dialed British Trader. While I had moved out a few months ago and we were officially apart, we were still regularly in touch. You don't just cut contact with the mother of your children, and besides, she still wanted to hear about the AdGrok saga.

"Hey, what's up?"

"So, get this. Facebook doesn't want the boys, but they want me. Argyris is right here. I don't know what to do."

As an oil woman, British Trader was completely outside the tech scene, and knew little about the intricacies. But she had a savvy read on human nature in a professional setting. Also, given that I was wholly devoid of most human boundaries or morality, she provided a mainstream sanity check on my actions.

"Don't tell the boys. It will just destroy their confidence. You've got to figure out some way to manage it."

We went back and forth, with me sketching out more details, and her sharing her take.

I looked at my watch. Almost seven p.m. In a few minutes, Argyris would be off like a shot to spend quality time with Simla, the girlfriend turned wife. If I held out for a few more minutes, he'd be out of the office, and I could ignore the boys on email and have a night to think about it.

British Trader and I kept on going, and sure as shit, Argyris got a phone call from the better half, and took off with a wave and a concerned look.

With considerable relief, I hung up with British Trader, gathered my startup kit of messenger bag and laptop, and cleared out in case Argyris came back.

Here's some capital-H History for you:

Right around 1961, when the Cuban government was televising political executions like they were the Super Bowl, with death warrants signed by that Argentine mama's boy Che, whose face graces more than one misguided hippie's T-shirt, my parents fled Cuba. Like many, they left as minors, alone, rushed onto the last flights by panicked parents who foresaw (correctly) that the Iron Curtain would take a Caribbean detour around Cuba before long.

Forty-four pounds of luggage is what they could take. That was expected to encapsulate a life.

For my grandmother, who had considerably greater difficulties than my parents in getting out, five of those pounds were consumed by one essential thing: her heavy, hard-as-diamonds domino set.* Double-nine rather than double-six (Cuba being the only country where that's the standard game), the tile backing was green, and the whole set encased in a robust but simple wooden box. The only connection with a world that

* To the average American, assuming he or she has ever played at all, dominoes is a mindless child's game played in kindergarten. That game has about as much to do with Cuban dominos as the card game Asshole has to do with contract bridge. The same pieces maybe, dominos or a standard deck of cards, but a very different game.

had been riven by revolution and then throttled in the titanic struggles of the Cold War, that domino case was the vessel of memory. It recalled the evening sunsets on the veranda, the warm conversation with friends, the inky black coffee drunk late into the night, with the click-clack of tiles as soundtrack.

And now where was that domino set?

Sitting unused in a closet. Thanks to Zynga, Facebook, and other companies, old Cubans like my mother were too busy playing social games like FarmVille to gather around the table and spin the tiles that had been so painstakingly smuggled. Too busy clicking to buy $0.99 pink tractors and $1.99 spotted digital cows.

Facebook got Cuban old ladies to play computer games! And pay for it!

Think of that miracle for a moment.

And it wasn't just Cuban old ladies.

In December 2010, Zynga launched a FarmVille clone called CityVille. That game, a moronic rip-off of the far cleverer game SimCity, had accumulated one hundred million users in a month.

One hundred million users!

If humanity had waited until 2010 to invent masturbation, it would not have caught on as fast as CityVille. That's how fast Facebook could make something happen.

Here's another data point for you: As part of our push to woo Facebook, I had been getting Google Alerts on the company for months. One in particular had caught my attention. In October 2010, a mother in Florida had shaken her baby to death, as the baby would interrupt her FarmVille games with crying. A mother destroyed with her own hands what she'd been programmed over aeons to love, just to keep on responding to Facebook notifications triggered by some idiot game. Products that cause mothers to murder their infants in order to use them more, assuming they're legal, simply cannot fail in the world. Facebook was legalized crack, and at Internet scale. Such a company could certainly figure out a way to sell shoes. Twitter was cute and all, but it didn't have a casualty rate yet, no matter how much this Lady Gaga person was tweeting.

Facebook it was.

But Twitter had come up with the solid offer for AdGrok, while Facebook hadn't come up with a solid offer for anything yet.

The shambolic hipsters with the expensively decorated offices, thousand-dollar fixies in their bike stand, and the Fail Whale?* Or the hoodie-wearing frat boys with an imperial mandate who coded while they shat? Which was it going to be? Could it possibly be both?

Here's another truth about tech life: anyone who claims the Valley is meritocratic is someone who has profited vastly from it via nonmeritocratic means like happenstance, membership in a privileged cohort, or some concealed act of absolute skulduggery. Since fortune had never been on my side, and I had no privileged cohort to fall back on, skulduggery it would have to be.

Managing a combined deal between Facebook and Twitter was like trying to engineer simultaneous orgasm between a premature ejaculator and a frigid woman: nigh impossible, fraught with danger, and requiring a very steady hand.

We've mentioned Mick Johnson before in our narrative. His company had been in my YC batch and disappeared under mysterious circumstances a few months prior, with Mick magically reappearing inside Facebook. He had made the initial introduction to Facebook Ads that had kick-started this soap opera.

We both loved hoppy beer, so over pints of Lagunitas at

* As with every statement in this book, this one was true (or seemed true) at the time it was made. Twitter now is a very, very different company from what it was in 2011.

the Creamery he shared the scoop on what had happened with his company.*

He and his Aussie cofounder, James, had a long work history together. They'd been hacking mobile for years and trying to find something that stuck. After two years of making $2K a month (or less), James was done with it. He was getting serious with his girlfriend and sick of the startup gig. They agreed the company had to be sold. So Mick mustered some courage and waded into the talent-acquisition market. They pitched themselves to one and all, going through the M&A process with Twitter, Zynga, Google, Facebook, and smaller companies.

They had gotten furthest with Zynga and Twitter, with Twitter making an outright bid on the entire company. Mick was unimpressed with Twitter and didn't want to go there. Shaking a few trees, Mick had gotten an intro at Facebook. They had run Mick and James through the M&A wringer and came back with an offer for Mick and Mick alone. Zynga had also come back with an offer, but for the entire company, bringing the number of serious suitors to three. Sound familiar?

What followed was a convoluted imbroglio of haggling that would have made a Somali pirate-ransom negotiation look orderly. The net conclusion of all this was that Mick would go to Facebook, while Zynga would get James and the company. The major problem here was that both Zynga and Facebook had to make concessions to get the deal done, but neither wanted to subsidize the other's acquisition by offering more value for the hybrid sale. They perceived themselves to be locked in a zero-sum game with a company they didn't particularly like. The final terms, which I never got

* The Creamery is the ne plus ultra of SF startup cafés. You could probably raise money from a VC, hire an engineer and businessperson, and then turn around and sell the company to a big-company exec right there, before your coffee gets too cold.

out of Mick, were some weird combo of cash up front, equity on separate vesting schedules in both companies, and a corollary deal that got the investors paid.

As I would come to learn, my situation wasn't unusual, though not generally talked about. Companies with acquisition wherewithal and the nerve to use it bid for what they wanted in deals. You came in with your team and your product; they gave it the once-over, and said, "We want person A and B, but not C, and we don't care about the tech." They then offered you a lump sum for what they wanted, and you were left to double-deal, buy out, or otherwise fuck over whoever in order to get the deal done. The company—and places like Facebook and Google did this commonly—cared only about net price per engineer (or product person), not the absolute cost. And they certainly didn't care what investors got. Many an early-stage acquisition unfolded in this vulturelike way.

I took Mick's example to heart for two reasons.

The first: he had actually done it. He had rounded up a circle of the Valley's leading companies and played them against one another until he got the deal he and his cofounder wanted. He stuck it out while Zynga was getting its act together, even at risk to himself and his Facebook deal. He had done something even Paul Graham had never seen and had advised him could not be done. Furthermore, he had played his hand with virtuosity from a place of total weakness. His company had little traction and was running out of the small money it had managed to raise. If the deal had fallen through, he would have been fucked. His only real power was the ability to get Zynga and Facebook into the same room and fight.

The second reason I took his advice-by-example is that I liked Mick, and in a city full of cranky, asocial, self-absorbed, narcissistic startup founders, he came off as a real guy, a mate one could trust. He stood to gain nothing from my deal, and was helping me only as a way to pay it forward to a fellow startup founder in a bind.

By the time we had drained our glasses, I was convinced that if Mick could hack such a deal, then so could I.

But was there a cost?

Long after this AdGrok drama, I'd hear an East Coast tech guy perfectly sum up the reigning attitude in Left Coast tech: "It's like they have no memory there. It's the Land of the Stateless Machines."

A bit of context: "State" is a technical term referring to data kept in memory that a program or function needs to operate. A "state machine" is an abstract model of computation whereby a computational process alternates among a series of states, each defined by a certain set of instructions or data, and transitioning among the various states as triggered by external stimuli. Hence, a stateless machine is a device that simply processes according to some set of instructions, without any knowledge of prior history, like an amnesiac. Our East Coaster's snide point was that Californians are incapable of rancor or grudges, no matter how outrageous the effrontery. Conversely, they're not particularly rewarding of generous behavior either.

As every new arrival in California comes to learn, that superficially sunny "Hi!" they get from everybody is really, "Fuck you, I don't care." It cuts both ways, though. They won't hold it against you if you're a no-show at their wedding, and they'll step right over a homeless person on their way to a mindfulness yoga class. It's a society in which all men and women live in their own self-contained bubble, unattached to traditional anchors like family or religion, and largely unperturbed by outside social forces like income inequality or the Syrian Civil War. "Take it light, man" elevated to life philosophy. Ultimately, the Valley attitude is an empowered anomie turbocharged by selfishness, respecting some nominal "feel-good" principals of progress or collective technological striving, but in truth pursuing a continual self-development refracted through the capitalist prism: hippies with a capitalization table and a vesting schedule.

What would the Valley make of my betrayal then? How much was I sacrificing by making it?

The capitalist hippies would take me back, I reckoned, I just had to be minimally successful. The Land of the Stateless Machines would continue crunching away, ingesting people and money, and outputting products, and they'd still be happy to grind me into the mix as well.

WEDNESDAY, APRIL 6, 2011

I had decided to deceive my cofounders for the first time in our harried time together.

As with many such lies, the rationalization was that it served the greater good. The boys were already stressed to the point of hyperventilation with all the shit we'd been through, and now we were betting it all on this very flaky acquisition process that could collapse in an instant. If they realized that this Twitter process was truly do-or-die for them, they'd choke. So what you do as a CEO is internalize that stress for the company and let it consume you instead of the rest.

How's that for a masterful rationalization?

What's more, it wasn't even clear the Facebook offer was for real. In God we trust, everyone else show me an offer letter. I had called Gokul that morning and mentioned I found Facebook's interest flattering, but I needed to see an offer before I could even begin to manipulate the other side of the deal to spring me.

Today, though, was a day for Twitter.

Part of any acquisition process is what's loosely called

"due diligence." Taking both technical and legal forms, it's the snooping around an acquiring company does to make sure it's actually getting what it thinks it is. On the technical side, it means understanding the company's "stack"; that is, the pile of interrelated user interface and back-end server technologies that power the product. It might even be as detailed as line-by-line code reviews with the startup's engineers. You can fake a lot in a startup these days, what with Amazon Web Services and all sorts of off-the-shelf back-end components that let any even minimally competent duffer set up a Web app that does something. Intelligent planning for growth is rare among early startups, but it's the name of the game at a large, rapidly scaling tech company. Waiting for a team to grow from technical adolescence to mature talent was too long even for a larger company.

As a first step, Twitter had invited us in as a group to talk technical turkey with a pack of engineers that reported to Kevin Weil. We spent a tense and wonky hour locked in a room with the senior engineers on the Twitter Ads team, walking them through our back-end stack that made AdGrok possible. I'm using the corporate "we" here, as it was completely the boys' show. It had been so long since I'd even touched AdGrok code, there was little I could have said about it. While the meeting seemed to have gone well, the fact that we were going deeper in with Twitter underscored the fact that we were approaching a point of no return in terms of AdGrok investment.

"Look, we've got to figure out if we're selling or what," I said once we were out of earshot of the Twitter offices.

We were sitting at the picnic tables in South Park, the boys across from me. This was where Twitter itself was conceived in 2006, during a brainstorming session held on one of the park's slides. The irony was striking.

After some awkward dithering, and lots of downcast study of the green tabletop, we finally got to talking. For probably the first time, I confronted the boys with the fact that we hadn't shipped anything since launch almost a month before, and that the commitment from the technical side of the team seemed to be waning. Given the occasional wall between the technical side of AdGrok and everything else (i.e., between them and me), I wanted to confirm that they also had the same vibe.

They didn't disagree with me.

MRM himself seemed checked out and hadn't delivered anything on the new code front in weeks. Argyris and I had chatted about it, but so far all we'd done was to call him the mornings he was late to tell him to get his ass to AdGrok. Argyris was holding up his end, but the two had lost that wonderful mind-meld synchrony that had powered AdGrok's development from the first days in our ratty Mountain View apartment. The dev team is the engine of a tech company. If they were done, then we were dead in the water. If that engine couldn't be fixed back into productivity, then it was time to sell the company while we even could.

I looked from one to the other: they seemed tired and worried and done with the startup game. They agreed we should pursue the acquisition process to its conclusion. We had to sell AdGrok to Twitter, or else.

Retweets Are Not Endorsements

> If you want to seduce a beautiful woman, court her ugly sister.
>
> —Spanish proverb

WEDNESDAY, APRIL 13, 2011

I wouldn't be the first person in Silicon Valley history to interview at a company at which I didn't really want a job, but these were certainly somewhat unique circumstances. I had to help the boys impress Twitter so we'd get an eager acquisition offer, which I'd immediately recuse myself from by joining Facebook.

As we did at Facebook, we'd have to run the daylong gauntlet of job interviews, the boys getting engineer interviews, and me a product manager one. I got the list of interviewers from Jess, to do our usual stalking/due diligence.

Interestingly, Twitter was leveraging its internal former startup folks to suss out new ones. A good half of my interviewers had come over in Twitter's second and very recent acquisition. DabbleDB was a database company founded by Canadians, and acquired in June 2010. I'd have two founders in my lineup, and the boys would have one founder each, along with just straight Twitter engineers.

Back we went through South Park to Twitter and the whole disappearing-ink name tag thing. As at an interrogation, we were split up immediately and taken to separate rooms.

I felt stress, but second-order stress—I felt nervous for the boys. If I didn't do well, they'd suffer, not me. Of course, realistically this was as critical to me as it was to them. There was simply no way, even in the tech mosh pit, that I could abandon AdGrok if there was no bid for their side of the company. Even in the Land of the Stateless Machines, that was one underhanded machination too far. No, I'd need to help get them across the finish line here.

I recall very little from the interviews, except a comment from one of the DabbleDB engineers. After getting through the stress questions, I asked him, "So what do you like most about Twitter?"

By this point, we'd built a decent rapport, so with a nod and a wink, he said, "Well, you know, in companies like Facebook and Google, they serve you breakfast, lunch, and dinner. Here at Twitter, they only serve you breakfast and lunch."

I cringed inwardly. So the big selling point was that nobody worked late into the night, so we could have that chimerical work-life balance?* I smiled to keep the warm vibe going. But that comment more than anything else sealed my decision. I was not going to blow the biggest career wad of my life on a company that hesitated to work past six p.m. daily.

The boys and I met back at AdGrok within a few hours. For the past few days, we'd been warming up to the whole

---

* As with everything else, this was true at the time. Currently Twitter certainly does serve dinner.

Twitter idea, and excitedly sketching out what a future Twitter ads product would need to look like to succeed. They were in relatively good cheer, and had been impressed by their meetings.

It will smack of self-serving rationalization, but I was convinced that a hybrid deal in which I went to Facebook and the boys to Twitter was absolutely the best possible outcome for AdGrok.

There was one niggly detail, though: I had to break the news about the Facebook side of the deal, and the fact that I wasn't coming along with the boys to Twitter. As mentioned, I had lied to them and told them that Facebook had rejected us in toto, them and me alike. I had done this initially out of panicky chicken-shittedness, but then, on further consideration, I realized it might stress them to the point of choking with Twitter if they knew. They absolutely had to get an offer from Twitter for the master plan to come off, so this little white lie made sure that happened. But the bill would come due on that liberty with truth I had taken, and the time to settle it was fast approaching.

THURSDAY, APRIL 14, 2011

Jess sent an email, subject line: "Call," to set up some time with her and Kevin Weil.

Bingo!

Remember: if you're having phone calls, the deal is still on. Phone calls are yesses, emails are nos.

I went outside to Townsend Street to take the call.

Jess's persuasive tone told me what I needed to know in the first two seconds. Twitter wanted to buy AdGrok, for real this time. She promised a term sheet within twenty-four hours. We'd heard this from Twitter before, but I believed them this time. One giveaway: Jess called back to ask specifics about the cap table. That meant they were already thinking about the investor versus founder split in their proposed deal, one of the more important high-level parameters.

It was time to come clean with the boys. I couldn't morally justify the deception any longer.

There's a unique style of Spanish genre painting called the *desengaño*. "*Desengaño*" means literally "un-tricking," and it is best translated as the disillusion, or the unveiling of a harsh truth, to be wordy about it. Typically depicted in the *desengaño* are the everyday reveals of sordid human deception: a young man stumbling on his beloved cooing with his best friend, a businessman catching his partner pinching from the till, and so on. They are meant to be an instructive moral lesson in everyday life, elevated to an art form. The *engañado* ("tricked one") typically wears an exaggerated expression of betrayal bordering on incipient rage. The implication is that the next frame in this drama will feature some corrective moral action, such as a duel to the death by *navaja*, or an ignominious march through the streets by the manacled thief.

I was hoping the scene about to unfold in the AdGrok office that afternoon was not worthy of a Velázquez's attention.

"Hey, so we need to have a chat," I said to their backs. They turned with quizzical looks. Given the ups and downs we'd been through, they could expect anything from another lawsuit to my coming out as an aspiring transsexual.

"So, remember when I said that Facebook rejected us? Well, that wasn't completely true."

I proceeded to sketch out the situation, where I was with Facebook, and why I had concealed this from them for the past two weeks.

Following a tomblike silence, their reaction was more understanding than I expected.

"You know, I had kind of thought that maybe the Facebook thing was more complicated than you let on," said Argyris, surprisingly calmly.

Bomb defused, or at least not yet detonated, I explained to them that I thought my future lay with Facebook, and that I had every reason to believe—here I was skating on pretty thin ice—that we could pull off a combined deal if we tried.

This did not go over so well. The boys panicked; surely I'd torpedo their deal if Twitter realized it wasn't getting me as well. While on the scale of group AdGrok freak-outs this did not take a championship trophy, it did recall some of our earlier rumbles.

Diego, get in here with your paints now!

They tried to convince me to stick with the Twitter deal, but that was like trying to convince a mule to dance reggaetón. Rather than dig in and fan the mutiny with reciprocal defiance, I simply presented Facebook as a fait accompli, and not a group decision requiring consensus. They dropped their case, and, with crestfallen looks, turned back to their code-splattered monitors.

We wouldn't discuss the matter again until right before the first real deal negotiation with Twitter, and the suspense around it kind of hung in the air until then. As always, I'd find some way to make the simple complicated, and the relatively safe, risky.

The Dotted Line

> Faster, faster, faster until the thrill of speed overcomes the fear of death.
>
> —attributed to Hunter S. Thompson

FRIDAY, APRIL 15, 2011

Among the various other startups in our shared office space, many of which went on to far greater things than AdGrok, was Getaround. To use that X of Y formulation so beloved of startup self-promotion, this was Airbnb for your car. By placing a small electronic device in your car to permit controlled access, you could list your car on a user-facing site that permitted searching and filtering. The borrower paid an hourly rate, Getaround took a cut, and you got paid for owning an often idle asset, similar to a spare bedroom on Airbnb.

In the midst of this Brazilian telenovela we called tech entrepreneurship, fellow startup traveler Matt Tillman and I were plotting a bit of fun. I had noticed that a few of Getaround's investors, no doubt as part of dogfooding solidarity, had placed their cars on Getaround's site. Temptingly, there were a Tesla Roadster and a Porsche 911 somewhat incautiously for the taking. Tillman, among his various depravities, was a seasoned track racer often invited to drive for various teams in the busy Northern California racing circuit.

I pitched Tillman on taking out the two vehicles as a diligent study in the startup status quo, and he countered with making it a race to Stinson Beach. I booked the Tesla, and was emailed an appointment time and place.

Two different Getarounders whom I recognized from the founding team were there, and they made quite a production about walking me through the car, and finally giving me the keys.

"Loser pays," Tillman announced outside, where we met up. He hadn't managed to snag the Porsche but did get a Mini Cooper S. Not a bad choice for the winding hillside roads we'd be navigating, as well as the street-traffic passing duels complete with tight squeezes in between cars. With Tillman's semipro driving skills, it would be a fair fight.

I took an early, small lead through SF and over the Golden Gate bridge, using the Tesla's rocket-like acceleration to blast through the openings in traffic. Electric cars are unlike gas-powered vehicles in that their engine's RPMs can vary so widely, and the power it transmits is so constant wherever it's revving, that they don't need a transmission. A Tesla is effectively a car version of a fixie, with a bionic, doped-up Lance Armstrong pedaling. As a result, there was no shifting, no gaps in power, or lurching as the car went from zero to 120 miles per hour. It was an endless orgasm of hurtling acceleration that seemed to violate laws of physics.

Tillman was no slouch, though, and in the crowded traffic, the obvious power mismatch was immaterial. It came down to passing, a willingness to wedge oneself between cars, and taking advantage of the tiniest break in traffic. By the time we pulled off the eight-lane 101 to get on the two-lane, curving highway 1 to Stinson, I was just ahead. Despite the monster engine dynamics, the Tesla didn't handle all that well: the batteries made the car heavy despite its being so small I could barely fit inside, and it had understeer in turns. Immersed in my mental car review, I didn't notice Tillman angling for a pass on my tail. When I saw the Cooper flash past me on the left, even the Tesla couldn't accelerate fast enough to stop it, and now I was stuck riding his tail.

Fuck!

Losing is worse than death. But there wasn't much I could do about it, as the road to Stinson is notoriously curving and narrow, with cliff-like drop-offs that make any serious error equal perdition. Forget passing, even assuming I could control the hyperaccelerating Tesla around a turn, as traffic was thick on a Friday afternoon.

Finally, approaching the tiny town of Muir Beach, and just a few miles from Stinson, I spotted an (illegal) opening. The road was straight enough to see a hundred yards or so. If any car pulled out from the left side, we'd have both died in an explosion of expensive wreckage. Making sure to not tip off Tillman, I swerved across the double yellow, jerked the Tesla's nose down the opposing lane, and hit the warp drive. Let the record show that on the afternoon of April 15 (tax day!), 2011, at approximately three p.m. local time, I irresponsibly blasted through Muir Beach on the wrong side of the road doing low triple digits. The entire town was more or less a three-second blur seen through the Roadster's tiny windows.

Tillman was fucked now. With no passing lanes, no dotted centerlines, and the road now composed of gentle swerves rather than hilly hairpins, he'd never pull off a pass against the Tesla.

Ha!

A few minutes later, I pulled up in front of the Sand Dollar in Stinson, and immediately attracted a scrum of bicycle-riding local kids who oohed and ahhed over the flaming red Roadster. The car's battery was down to what seemed one-quarter, and the dashboard was signaling various warnings I didn't understand. No matter. After enough hazing of Tillman, beer, and oysters, back we went to SF.

Not sure I'd manage to get the car back with the mostly depleted battery, I drove like a grandma until I hit Lombard

Street. There I ran into a convertible Porsche 911, the twin air scoops announcing it was one of the turbo varieties. Here was a real racing machine. SF is a city populated mostly by pussies, so finding a decent street race is difficult. The driver was older and paunchy, but expensively dressed—my guess was real estate or some form of old-boys' entrepreneurship like an ad agency. Electric cars make a revving challenge impossible, so not really expecting a reaction, I just punched it when I came alongside him.

He had seen me coming. He gunned it a split-second after me, and the race was on. Lombard was thick with traffic, but moving. Every stoplight was a drag race, and Tesla and Porsche swerved and weaved through the rush-hour worker bees slumbering through their commutes and their lives. This old fucker knew how to drive and was clearly no stranger to street duels. I was a couple of cars behind him as we reached the end of three-lane Lombard. The light went yellow, and he roared through while the plodder in front of me decided to stop. Boxed in, I was screwed. The Porsche's whooshy engine sounded a vacuum-like note as it turned and disappeared down Van Ness.

Even after winning one race, there was always another, and always somebody with a faster car, wasn't there? This old guy knew that, which is why he was racing reckless young jackasses like me. He probably had a wife, kids, property, and all that bougie shit, and yet the moment he saw a challenger in his rearview, he tossed that aside for a bit of the old screeching rubber. The fact he was risking all that he had achieved by committing felonious acts of reckless driving, reckless endangerment, and "exhibition of speed" (to use the California penal code's name for it) was immaterial. He didn't get to that Porsche by turning down all-in challenges. Neither will you, gentle reader.

Back at the parking lot underneath the Moscone Center, the Getarounders were waiting for the return of their prize rental. They seemed remarkably incurious about how I could have completely uncharged a Tesla in a three-hour rental, having traveled only fifty miles (the normal range was two-hundred-plus miles). Getaround CEO Jessica Scorpio: if you're reading this, extremely belated apologies.

When I returned to a computer and a state of sanity, I had two emails waiting for me: one from Kevin Thau of Twitter, and one from Gokul, both with attached documents.

SATURDAY, APRIL 16, 2011

"You mean to tell me you had no hand in coming up with this deal meant to screw investors!?"

I almost had to hold the phone away from my ear. Sacca had just reviewed the Twitter term sheet I had forwarded.

I was stomping my usual nervous-pacing grounds: up and down Ninth Street in Alameda, in front of British Trader's house. I had made the possibly misguided move of moving back in with her and Zoë.

"I had nothing to do with this, Chris. These are the first real terms we've seen."

Twitter had been so indifferent to Sacca it had defaulted to a term sheet heavily privileging the founders, which is why Silicon Valley's most famous investor was presently yelling at me.

How right was Sacca to be angry?

Twitter (for once) had been true to its advertised word, and our deal had come in at around $10 million. However, the amount slotted to investors was not the $2 million or so you'd have expected given the cap table, but a measly $1 million.

As I was soon to learn, this is a common tactic. You pay a pittance for the company, engineering it such that investors get little, and then pack the real value into the hiring offers for the employees. *TechCrunch* would carry the news that the company sold for X million dollars, but technically it would sell for 10 percent of X, while the rest went into fat signing bonuses and heavily laden vesting schedules for the founders. With no prompting from us, Twitter had given us a plum offer.

Sacca had a right to be angry at Twitter, but he was severely overestimating my knowledge and skills. I was so clueless, I had naively assumed that investors and founders would all participate in Twitter's final acquisition price on a purely pro rata basis; basically, whatever fraction they owned in the cap table, they got. Little did I know that in the real world of deals, what's very euphemistically called the "consideration" given to investors can vary widely per the whims and machinations of the founders and the acquiring company.

How it works is this:

The acquiring company doesn't care less how money is divided between investors and employees. As we've reviewed, what they care about is price per high-value person (that is, engineers and product managers). If that works out, and the form of payment is whatever admixture of cash versus equity they prefer (or are willing to put up with), the deal looks fine to them. Every acquiring company will have such a target price per person in mind when you seriously discuss a deal. Your job as deal negotiator is to get as close to that as humanly possible.

The founders, however, have a more subtle view. A deal this small is likely not life-changing, fuck-you money. After you've rested and vested at the acquiring company, you'll likely wade into the startup fray again, need to raise money, and again live in the startup ecosystem. Screw your investors and word will get around. Also, you may have a legitimate emotional bond with your investors. After all, they often stood by you when nobody else did and, like Sacca, potentially helped get the company sold. Thus, founders face a moral choice that's quite ticklish. They can opt to reward their investors for their investments in time and money, but they're essentially paying them out of their wallet. The deal is very much a zero-sum game between founders and investors in the final stages.

To give you an idea of just how indifferent the acquiring company is to investors, keep in mind that Sacca was reputedly Twitter's largest equity shareholder after its founders, and a vocal champion of the company. He had helped arrange its last funding round, and, somewhat notoriously, was helping insiders sell their stakes in Twitter early to Wall Street speculators. To be clear, this was a favor, as it allowed employees, many of whom had worked for years for Twitter, some liquidity before the drawn-out process of an IPO. The fact such a secondary market existed for many high-profile startups was a mark of just how much the power balance had shifted away from investors and Wall Street to founders and employees in the current tech bubble.

The AdGrok deal was pocket change to Sacca (and to Twitter), but gestures matter when ego is on the line. So Sacca was kind of right to be yelling. On the other hand, his fund had doubled its money in six months. But that wasn't good enough for Sacca (or his limited partner investors). It gets worse.

"Chris, there's one more thing. As it turns out, Facebook wants to hire me, separate from the Twitter deal. They said no to the rest, but they wanted me."

<pause>

"What!?"

"Yeah. I won't say I'm sold exactly. But they want me to go to Facebook."

Lying through my teeth, obviously.

"What do you think Twitter would make of it, and would they take AdGrok without me?"

"You're FUCKING crazy. You're going to fuck up this entire deal! Of course they won't take AdGrok without you. You're just . . . you're just . . ."

He hung up on me. We'd never speak again.

Then there was the issue of Facebook.

In finance, there's the notion of what's called a "replicating portfolio." This is a set of stocks, bonds, derivatives, and whatever else mimicks the returns—while being composed of different parts—of some other portfolio of assets. Such portfolios are often dreamed up by quants to, say, profit from the rise of a given stock without having to carry the actual shares on some company's maxed-out balance sheet (i.e., what's called an "equity swap").

For Facebook, I had attempted to get Gokul to give me a replicating portfolio of my part of the Twitter deal. In fact, I had flatly told him (a bluff really) that I wouldn't abandon Twitter for anything less. And Facebook had actually delivered. Pricing the deal at Facebook's prepublic share price of $32 or so, we were at $2.3 million, which was about what my 25 percent stake in AdGrok would look like after all of Sacca's yelling was done. The numbers looked about as good as they were going to get.

I made the final decision that had been brewing for days, right there, on the spot. I'd join the hoodie people. We'd make the Twitter side of it work somehow. From the looks, we had them over a barrel on the deal, and even without me, it would probably get done. There was no better time to strike than now.

"Gokul, this is Antonio."

With a deal in play, no worries about calling on a Saturday morning.

"Thanks for sending me the official offer. I'm pleased to see we're more or less where we need to be."

"So are you ready to join?" Gokul asked. I'd soon learn that Gokul's sense of urgency wasn't some passing deal thing, but in fact, how he managed his entire professional life.

"I'm happy to join Facebook, Gokul."

"Great, man! We're so looking forward to you joining. Make sure to send me a signed copy as soon as you can, please."

Words were grand, baby, but signatures on dotted lines make the world go round.

"Will do, Gokul."

And that was that. The AdGrok drama was coming to an end.

MONDAY, APRIL 18, 2011

At the dramatic hour of high noon, we had our first post-term sheet meeting with the Twitter deal team.

I had confirmed the news about my FB departure to the boys as soon as I had committed on Saturday. It came as no surprise. If they were unhappy, they concealed it, but I noted what seemed like fear in their voices during the phone calls.

In the walk up Third Street to Twitter, we rehearsed our game plan one last time. I was to announce the fact I wasn't part of the deal in the first few minutes of the meeting. There was no use discussing a deal that included me and that wasn't going to happen. I was not to announce where I was headed, and instead simply slip out of the room if the opportunity presented itself, while making sure to calmly pass the CEO baton to MRM by indicating he was the person to speak with from that point on.

Which is not how it happened at all.

Jess met us at the reception area again and led us to a conference room containing the ever-present Kevin Thau, and a new participant: Satya Patel, Twitter's newly hired head of product. Satya had made the friendly overture of proposing a get-to-know-you coffee or drink that very morning, which I would have to awkwardly postpone in about an hour. A former Googler and partner at one of Twitter's VCs, he was rising Silicon Valley royalty.

These "power" meetings often had a comically dramatic staging to them. All the AdGrok people lined up on one side, and the Twitter team directly across from them, as if we were the US and Vietnamese diplomatic teams in 1973 hammering out a peace plan. After everyone was settled, I proceeded straight to act 1, scene 1, of our script:

"So . . . we should talk about the deal that's going to happen, not the one we've been discussing thus far. I'm sorry to say . . . but I'm actually not coming along with AdGrok on this deal, I'll be joining another company. At this point, we should talk about Argyris and Matt, and how they're going to join Twitter."

Jess looked as though she had swallowed a wasp. Kevin was as emotionless as always. Satya was the first to speak, adopting a somewhat aggressive tone: "So you're telling us you're bailing on the deal?"

"Yes," I replied, nodding as if to emphasize what was already an emphatic point.

"OK . . ." It was Jess this time. "We have to discuss this and get back to you."

Without much ado, the Twitter team stood up, which forced us to do the same. With awkward looks and downturned eyes, the AdGrok team filed out of the office. I'm not even sure anybody in the Twitter crew walked us out.

Back on the street, from the looks on their faces, the boys would have kicked me to death had it improved their lot at all.

Endgame

> Then I looked on all the works that my hands had wrought, and on the labour that I had laboured to do: and, behold, all was vanity and vexation of spirit, and there was no profit under the sun.
>
> —Ecclesiastes 2:11

MONDAY, APRIL 18, 2011, 2:00 P.M.

Back in the office, the boys made a show of going back to work on code, but their minds were elsewhere. I had just pulled a dicey ploy that presented only downside to them, mostly because of my bloody-minded insistence on going to Facebook. The same bloody-mindedness that had raised us money and defended us from legal enemies might now blow up the entire construct we had slaved to save.

Within a half hour, Twitter called back. MRM took the call; I was no longer part of the proceedings. I drank in the moment. Both of them hovering over Matt's cellphone, which was on speaker, focused on Jess Verrilli's every word. MRM wrote down the relevant deal numbers, and then repeated them back to Jess to be sure.

Wow. The bid was at $5 million and change. Much, much higher than I had expected. It was the same deal price from just over a week ago, which Sacca and I had to talk the boys out of accepting.

Twitter was playing its monster hand very weakly. They had called back within an hour of my dropping a valuation-killing bomb that reflected debilitating internal strife. If they had any balls, they'd have left AdGrok hanging in radio silence, ignoring all calls and email for a couple of days to let the boys marinate in their fear and anxiety. After the silent treatment, they could have bought all of AdGrok for a twenty-dollar Starbucks gift card, probably. Instead they had come back, within an hour, with an offer just above the original one. Twitter was being what poker pros term a call station, and a weak one at that. The boys were getting more money than they had ever hoped for, and above the price they were already willing to sell at. This deal was getting done, despite both sides' bungling and incompetence. AdGrok was already dead: the boys and Twitter were merely haggling over the price of the funeral.

Then I felt that tingle.

All I had from Facebook was its offer letter in my inbox, and Gokul's word that the company would honor the offer. I had just shit on Twitter and then rubbed its biggest shareholder's face—namely, Chris Sacca's—in the fresh, warm pile. With the boys champing at the money bit, there'd be no holding them back now; they'd do whatever deal Twitter offered, with or without me (and probably without). I needed to accept Facebook's offer immediately, but before that, an employment lawyer needed to look it over.

Silicon Valley job offers can be so complex—each a mini-acquisition for one person, complete with cash, options, vesting schedules, intellectual property agreements, and so forth—that there was an entire class of lawyer who just helped you negotiate the sale of yourself.

I called every damn lawyer we had ever talked to—Fenwick, Orrick, our cheapie contract lawyer—for a referral.

I had my newly hired employment lawyer on the phone within a half hour. "I've got an offer letter I need to know whether to sign or not. The rest of the company is getting bought by a competitor. I'm the CEO and founder. What do you need?"

"The offer letter, your stock purchase agreement with the current employer, and your employment contract," she replied tersely.

By then, the boys were running around, shuffling company docs, and nervously taking phone calls to work their deal. I was scanning reams of documents in our slow, janky scanner, and occasionally going out for a call of my own.

Things took on a certain preapocalyptic, the-Germans-are-coming tinge to it, or perhaps the atmosphere of the last few minutes inside the safe room of the American embassy in Tehran in 1979. One group transmitting vital information to a concerned party, another group collecting, scanning, and destroying information, while planning how to evacuate.

An hour went by, and finally my lawyer emailed back. "You need to accept the Facebook offer immediately. You also need to resign beforehand, or you'll break noncompetes in both contracts."

The clock read 2:45 p.m.

I quickly called Amin's report inside Facebook corp dev to see how late he'd be there. Valley dealmakers, like small-town bankers, have cushy schedules; he was out at five o'clock.

I had to catch the 3:07 Caltrain to Palo Alto to make it on time. No way I could just let this trade ride overnight.

The boys were heads down, discussing some aspect of the deal—their deal now—and I didn't interrupt as I collected my bicycle helmet and walked out the door of the office I had worked, worried, and occasionally slept in.

On the train, which I made with a minute to spare, I started typing out a resignation email on my iPhone. An hour later, I was flying up California Avenue in Palo Alto on my creaky bicycle, back to the Facebook HACK sign. I had the email ready to go on my phone, and the moment Facebook's corporate-development person poked his head out of the glass door, I hit Send.

I was an unemployed loafer for all of five minutes. Dale Dwelle, Amin Zoufonoun's subordinate, made small talk, while internally I was thinking *Come on already, give me the damn forms!* Contracts signed, he escorted me back out again.

AdGrok, our startup baby, was effectively dead, and for the first time in a very long year, I walked out into the sunny California afternoon with nothing to do.

This deal became a minor Silicon Valley oddity that confused the tech journalists who covered it; I still get questions about it to this day. The short version is that I was a complete idiot, and the deal was a badly played hand, muddled through on bravado and blissful ignorance rather than savvy calculation.

Master play would have been this:

Continue negotiating both deals in secret to squeeze out the last of the leverage, and heavily front-load the Twitter offer to include either single-trigger acceleration or lots of upfront cash.* Then accept the Twitter deal, quit the first day of work, and walk away with the up-front part of the deal right on out to Facebook. I could even have done true arbitrage and signed both Twitter and Facebook employment agreements at once, and asked Facebook for unpaid leave while Twitter got settled. This would have been in flagrant violation of noncompete clauses in both employment con-

---

* Single-trigger acceleration means a chunk of your unvested stock suddenly vests upon some agreed-upon event, usually a merger or sale. In this case, it would have meant I would have seen some of the upside of the deal immediately, for "time served" at AdGrok so to speak, upon joining Twitter, rather than having to wait for vesting to start from zero once at Twitter.

tracts, of course. Only Twitter would have cared, but like the mark in a successful con, they'd have been too embarrassed at having been played to sue, and would simply have covered it up with employees.*

That plan, however, would have required including my cofounders in the deception, as they would not have collaborated to score me a better deal, worried as they were about their own piece of the pie. Running game on your investors or your acquirers is just life in the big city, but bluffing out your cofounders, those same guys who sweated through the lows and the highs with you, is a step too far out on the prick spectrum.

Why the need for the deception right up to the brink of being a Twitter employee, dissembling my intent to eventually join Facebook? Keep this singular fact in mind: we were only ten months into AdGrok officially, and all the founders were on a vesting clock. That's right, despite carrying the weighty title of founder, nobody at AdGrok actually owned anything yet.

Why is that? Ponder for a moment. Every founder owns something like 20 to 40 percent of the company. That's as much as or more than what would be sold in a fund-raising round. If every founder owned that stake from day one, they would all essentially hold a gun to the company's temple. If any founder decided to leave following an argument (or was forced by his cofounders to resign), he'd kill the company, as no investor would fund a company in which an equivalent stake to his or hers was held by some disgruntled outsider. And so even founders in a well-established company are on a vesting schedule, and get only a quarter of their fat equity slice after a year, just as a big-company employee does.

---

* Indeed, Twitter did just that when the news of my defection broke on *TechCrunch*, and there was an internal Twitter email papering over the awkwardness I'd created by bailing, marring the celebratory air around the company's third acquisition.

The fact was that even as the wheeler-dealer CEO, I owned no part of AdGrok. Nothing. Not one share. Neither did the boys. As is the case for every early-stage entrepreneur. So to actually see any proceeds from the AdGrok side of the deal, I'd have to have been there at least another couple of months as the deal got finished up.

At the end of the day, AdGrok was simply a long, stressful job interview for Facebook (and ditto for the boys at Twitter). We all claim we "sold" AdGrok, but in reality, AdGrok was merely leverage to score the job offers that actually made us the real financial upside, job offers we would not have been able to score otherwise. The corporate-development teams of large companies, insofar as their small-company deals are concerned, are really glorified HR recruiters with fatter checkbooks. That's another little detail the self-glorifying founders of acquired companies often fail to mention.

Had I executed the optimal strategy, my return on AdGrok would likely have been hundreds of thousands or perhaps millions of dollars more than it eventually was. Plus, the additional cash or Twitter stock would have served as a hedge to my all-in position in Facebook.

Morality, such as it exists in the tech whorehouse, is an expensive hobby indeed.

Part Three

Move Fast and Break Things

Facebook was not originally created to be a company. It was built to accomplish a social mission—to make the world more open and connected.

—Mark Zuckerberg, Facebook Inc.
IPO documents (2012)

Boot Camp

> Once having traversed the threshold, the hero moves in a dream landscape of curiously fluid, ambiguous forms, where he must survive a succession of trials. The hero is covertly aided by the advice, amulets, and secret agents of the supernatural helpers whom he met before his entrance into this region. The original departure into the land of trials represented only the beginning of the long and really perilous path of initiatory conquests and moments of illumination. Dragons have now to be slain and surprising barriers passed—again, again, and again. Meanwhile there will be a multitude of preliminary victories, unretainable ecstasies, and momentary glimpses of the wonderful land.
>
> —Joseph Campbell, *The Hero with a Thousand Faces*

APRIL 25, 2011

Before the city-within-a-city campus that Facebook would come to occupy, the company was housed in two buildings in the down-market part of Palo Alto, east of Stanford's campus. One, on California Avenue, contained Zuck, Engineering, Ads, and just about everyone involved in making actual product. The second building fronted on the next artery over, Page Mill Road, and housed sales, legal, operations, and everyone involved in the nontechnical side of the Facebook machine. A fleet of tidy white shuttle buses shuffled people between them, and the occasional Facebooker walked the half mile for exercise, or just to see the sun.

The daylong session known as on-boarding was held in the nontechnical building, so white shuttle it was to Page Mill Road. The conference room was named "Pong" (and yes, the room next to it was "Ping"), a large room meant for presentations. A raised stage lined the back wall, and long, narrow desks, like hedgerows, crossed the room from right to left. As usual, I chose to sit in the front, right under the nose of the speaker, so I could catch every twitch and take the real measure.

An HR person offered some introductory drivel or other, and then it was straight to the first speaker, my superboss, the head of product for Facebook: Chris Cox.

Cox was handsome in the way of a Gosling or Depp: a tempered masculinity encased in a cuddly package, custom-made for female desire. It was a recurring internal joke at Facebook to point out the Twitter storm of oohing and ahhing whenever he took the stage at a Facebook PR event. He had the gift of the gab, which he used to great effect, weaving a seductive narrative around Facebook and the future of media. As the first speaker, he was clearly there to instill the big-picture vision of what we had been selected to help build.

"What is Facebook? Define it for me," he asked, challenging the rows of attentive faces almost the moment he appeared.

"It's a social network."

"Wrong! It's not that at all."

He scanned the audience for another answer.

Perfectly articulated, to the point I suspected she was a shill, a young, perky intern came out with: "It's your personal newspaper."

"Exactly! It's what I should be reading and thinking about, delivered personally to me every day."

He then embarked on a common trope among Valley types, framing a product in some historical continuum of prior technologies, the product currently discussed being the ultimate and inevitable final chapter in the triumphant procession. Radio and TV were depersonalized media of mass consumption, revolutionary for their time, but ultimately lacking. Steadily more focused and fragmented media—topical magazines like *Car and Driver*, your local newspaper with pull-out sections for your neighborhood—continued this trend of increasing personalization. Facebook, however, was the true teleological end goal of modern media.

Facebook was the *New York Times of You*, Channel You, available for your reading and writing, and to everyone else in the world as well, from the Valley VC to the Wall Street banker to the Indian farmer plowing a field. Everyone would tune in to the channels of their friends, as people once clicked the knob on old cathode-ray television sets, and live in a mediated world of personalized social communication. That the news story in question was written by the *Wall Street Journal* was incidental: your friend Fred had posted it, your other friend Andy had commented on it, and your wife had shared it with her friends. Here was the first taste for the new Facebook employee of a world interpreted not through traditional institutions like newspapers, books, or even governments or religions, but through the graph of personal relations. You and your friends would redefine celebrity, social worth, and what should be churning through that restless primate brain all day.

Andy Warhol was wrong. In the future, we wouldn't all be famous for fifteen minutes; we'd be famous 24/7 to fifteen people. That was the new paradigm, even if the outside world didn't realize it yet. Facebook employees—we few, we happy few—knew what world was coming, and we'd help create it.

It was a good pitch, and the kids in the audience were enraptured. Mission accomplished, Cox flashed a matinee-idol grin and disappeared from the stage in a flash, no doubt off to the other dozen meetings he had that day. I suspected this was a recurring biweekly event for Cox, the rousing speech to the new acolytes. Just the regular speech for king and country, which he had down to the point of studied and flawless spontaneity. Facebook certainly didn't skimp on putting on a good show.

The next speaker was Pedram Keyani, an engineering manager in Site Integrity. This was Facebookese, as I'd later learn, for the security team that prevented spammers, pornographers, bots, and various flavors of malignant riffraff from destroying Facebook, or your experience of it. Pedram was one of the conduits of corporate culture that Facebook relied on to perpetuate its unique values. He would lead the bimonthly "hackathons," which had originated as all-night coding sessions where engineers came up with random ideas that often became successful products (Facebook Video being one such case).* In keeping with the engineering-first cultures of most tech companies since Google, hackathons had also come to serve as pep rally–like pageants of Facebookness, more than mere excuses to code all night and eat crappy Chinese food. As I'd later learn, weirdly pointless versions of them would be held in the regional offices where no engineers even worked, as a sort of pagan celebration of the values of do-it-yourself creation, total commitment to the company, and disruptive innovation.

Pedram was here to expound on those same values. We had gotten the prophetic vision from Cox, precisely the sort

* In a story that became FB lore, Zuckerberg had actually shot down the idea of launching the primitive Facebook Video product. The engineers involved ignored him and locked themselves into a conference room for days to finish it, launching it against Zuck's wishes. Facebook is now the second biggest video-sharing site, after Google's YouTube.

of seductive propagandizing a product person does. Now it was time to hear about the martial virtues that would make that vision a reality, which was the engineer's duty.

A tall, broad-shouldered figure in a Facebook T-shirt who looked as though he worked out, Pedram commanded us in a hectoring tone: "Whatever you learned at your previous job, whatever politics and bullshit you're bringing with you, just leave all that shit behind."

Pedram proceeded to describe, with mounting passion, this new world of Facebook, where truth was the only value, selfless collaboration was the rule ("Don't worry about who gets credit"), and everyone took ownership (technically, if not financially) of what Facebook did.

Here's where the genius in the on-boarding, and more broadly in Facebook, really lay. People joined Facebook, and like immigrants at Ellis Island, left their old, dated cultures behind, replacing them with an all-consuming new one. The on-boarding experience was designed precisely as the sort of citizenship oath that new Americans took in front of a flag and a public official. It was almost religious, and taken absolutely sincerely and at face value. Even in a culture brimming with irreverent disdain, I never heard anyone utter a word of cynical trollery about Facebook and its values, either at on-boarding or during my years of work there. As with Americans and "our troops," motherhood, and the Constitution, certain things were enshrined, and nobody dared ridicule them.

In a posthistorical developed world devoid of transcendent values, whose pantheons look like North Korean grocery stores, bare shelves empty of any gods or heroes, this corporate fascism was intoxicating. Along with the new iPhone and MacBook laptop sitting in front of us, we received a laptop bag with one thing inside: a blue T-shirt emblazoned with FACEBOOK in the trademark Klavika font. On any given day, half of Facebook's employees would be wearing theirs, and many even photographed (and posted on Facebook, of course) pictures of their children wearing a Facebook onesie as their social media debut. Brownshirts became Blueshirts, and we were all part of the new social media *Sturmabteilung*.

Cynicism is the last refuge of the shiftless. I don't cite this absolutist tendency for the cheap sardonic joke, the asshole hipster who's too cool for school, but also too cool to believe in anything. No, I cite it because I was as seduced as the next guy sitting there in Pong, perhaps even more. The human need for immortality projects—those ends that dole out meaning and purpose beyond ourselves—hasn't changed since the pyramids. The only difference now is the nature of the putative Holy Land, and the means for achieving it.

After Cox's rhetoric, and Pedram's grim injunctions, we broke for a breather.

The interns huddled in groups of what seemed like old acquaintances; I assumed they knew each other from Berkeley, Stanford, MIT, or wherever they studied. Imagine being a nineteen-year-old undergrad, your entire life mediated by some admixture of Facebook, Twitter, Instagram, et al., and suddenly living and working right in the belly of the beast. If I had been afforded such opportunities at that age, you wouldn't have been able to shut me up about it with duct tape.

Outside Pong was one of the many microkitchens that dotted campus. They were micro only in comparison with the café kitchens that churned out three meals daily; nor were they really kitchens, in that there was nothing to cook there. Mostly they offered the packaged food, either hypertension- or diabetes-causing, that formed the staple diet of a moderately self-destructive university undergraduate. As a concession to crunchy Bay Area sensibilities, there were also bowls of fruit and bins of nuts or granola. I didn't realize it at the time, but Facebook was on its way to full-on Google levels of employee pampering, and the food in the kitchens would trend more upscale as time went on, going from Snickers to Toblerone, Doritos to authentically spicy Indian *chaat* snacks. The coffee also improved, forgoing a generic corporate roast for that of Philz Coffee, the locavore's coffeehouse that had started in the trendy Mission District. By the time I left, there would be a full-on Philz retail location on campus that served as caffeine fill station, social gathering point, and informal meeting venue. But that was in the still-distant future.

Glucose levels reupped, back into Pong we went.

Calmly sitting square in a lone chair up front was an Indian-looking dude with curly hair. This man needed no introduction, being famous in a more beyond-Facebook way than Pedram or even Cox. He was Chamath Palihapitiya, one of the men most responsible for Facebook's success. As head of the Growth team, which wangled new users for Facebook by encouraging things like friending, he had taken Facebook from a small network used mostly by college students to the global online identity, numbering almost a billion people by then.

He was also a competitive poker player and hosted the most legendary home game in Silicon Valley, featuring regular appearances by an all-star cast of investors and entrepreneurs, as well as the occasional poker professional or celebrity athlete. Poker was behind the best-known Chamath story, which I'd hear recounted more than once, and which perhaps best illustrates his sharklike competitiveness.

After an all-night high-stakes game, Chamath walks out fifty thousand dollars ahead. Deciding he needs some German rolling iron stat, he goes to a BMW dealership. The salesman, spotting a badly dressed kid, gives him the cold shoulder, and refuses a test drive. So Chamath heads over to the Mercedes dealership across the street. There, they don't ignore him, and he buys a car for cash on the spot. Then he drives back to the BMW dealership with his new Benz, finds the sales guy who blew him off, and shows him the sale he lost. That's who we were dealing with here.

"Look, we're not here to fuck around. You're at Facebook now, and we've got lots to do."

His spiel was the iron hand inside the velvet glove of on-boarding. MAKE AN IMPACT, GET IN OVER YOUR HEAD, DONE IS BETTER THAN PERFECT, and various other rallying cries shouted from posters dotting every wall, and we'd soon find they were also taped to our new desk monitors, in case we had missed them. This was the tenor of Chamath's somewhat rambling harangue, punctuated with lots of f-bombs, delivered in the clipped, machine-gun cadence of the Wall Street floor trader, which he'd been early in his career.

"So just fucking do it," he concluded, after twenty minutes of hectoring.

Chamath hadn't moved during his jeremiad, sitting square-shouldered, hands gripping the rear legs of his chair tightly. When he stood to leave the stage, he did so without so much as looking at anyone.

Everyone seemed to be slightly gobsmacked, as when a film director hits the audience with a cinematic plot twist in the last few seconds of a movie, and a stunned silence washes over the crowd as the credits begin to roll.

For our next lecture, the founding legends of Facebook were replaced by the stiff and formal sheriffs of corporate propriety known as HR. Two of them took the stage, sitting side by side, a male and a female, almost as if you needed one of each gender present to discuss the sensitive stuff.

Lesson one from Officer HR was one of Facebook's everpresent obsessions: secrecy.

Like Jesus speaking to his apostles, Facebook often imparted nuggets of its culture in the form of parables. The parable here concerned a misguided Facebook employee who leaked news of a soon-to-be-launched product to the tech press. Zuck reacted via a to-all email with the subject line "Please resign," an alarming presence in anybody's inbox. The email, which was projected onto the screen in Pong and read line by line, encouraged whoever had leaked to resign immediately, and excoriated the perpetrator for his or her base moral nature, highlighting how he or she had betrayed the team. The moral to this story, a parable of the prodigal son but with an unforgiving father, was clear: fuck with Facebook and security guards would be hustling you out the door like a rowdy drunk at the late-night Taco Bell.

Lesson imparted, time for that close second in Facebook priority: discretion.

As the curator of the largest collection of personal data outside of the NSA, Facebook was ripe for unprincipled internal abuse. Not only was such abuse unethical, but the PR hit from a story getting out about a jealous employee who stalked his wife, or immature interns checking out a celebrity's messages, would be monumental and hugely embarrassing. As it was, people were wary of this druglike service called Facebook, with which they shared their most intimate human experiences, but also subconsciously resented and feared. Anything less than the strictest discretion would threaten to revoke the tenuous pass that hundreds of millions of users had granted that dark-blue box to mediate their lives.

I would personally know at least one person who'd get bitten with this, and be terminated after "the Sec," as internal Facebook security was called, found out they were looking at profiles without an official reason. It was that simple: even try, and we'll catch you, and you'll be out of here so fast we'll need to send a cleanup crew to remove the still-warm coffee mug from your desk.

The crowd took in all of this silently, with at most the occasional murmur or hint of furtive chatting between neighbors. The rousing buzz of the first speakers lingered; this HR session was like the DUI check you had to negotiate while driving home from a particularly convivial party. The cops seemed amenable, if a bit stern, as they went through their script.

Then, we came to the juicy frivolities. Here, the male (oddly) took the lead and stood up to address the new employees.

Picture the Facebook corporate scene for a moment: buildings full of young, emotionally inept male geeks, and sprinkled throughout them, maybe a 10 percent population of young women. What could possibly go wrong?

Rather than harshly regulate every step of this sexual-legal minefield, Facebook preferred to lay down basic guidelines. Delicately, but unambiguously, our HR Man stated that we could ask a coworker out once, but no meant no, and you had no more lets after that. After one ask, you were done, and anything beyond that was subject to sanction.

So you get one shot on goal, do you? I thought. Better use that one shot wisely.

Next was a warning to the womenfolk. Our male HR authority, with occasional backup from his female counterpart, launched into a speech about avoiding clothing that "distracted" coworkers. I'd later learn that managers did in fact occasionally pull aside female employees and read them the riot act. One such example happened in Ads, with an intern who looked about sixteen coming in regularly in booty shorts. It was almost laughably inappropriate, but such was our disinhibited age.

For a grand finale . . . obscenity!

Among the odder forms we had had to sign as employees was one exonerating Facebook from any liability from obscenity. Whatever we saw or overheard, while at Facebook, could not be subject to litigation. It wasn't clear to me if this was due to, say, pornography on the site that we'd run across when screening it, or the remains of the bro-y culture that echoed occasionally with a dick joke or some guy passed out from happy hour in his underwear.

"We don't want to create a culture where someone is

going to HR to complain every day. If someone says something, call them out on it. Hopefully, it stops there, and you go on with your day."

Show over. We all grabbed our swag bag, laptop, and phone, and got the hell out of there.

Back at my new desk in the Ads area, I fired up the laptop. Already, there were two emails waiting. One was pro forma and simply stated "Welcome to Facebook." The other was an email from the task-tracking system, indicating I had been assigned several bugs to fix. Like every other engineer, despite my also being a product manager, I'd need to go through the engineering boot camp, the six-week course that ingested you a n00b and output you a Facebook engineer.* It was also a weeding mechanism that provided management with the first flag on potentially bad hires. Via accelerated courses in front-end code, back-end infrastructure, and everything in between, we learned the Facebook way. The company had a seemingly genetic inclination for home-brewing almost every element of its technical stack, using open-source languages or tools occasionally, but then customizing them to the point where they were more Facebook than anything else. Since even seasoned engineers came from a completely different universe, it was necessary to indoctrinate them in the One True Way. For new grads fresh out of school, with no knowledge of how real production engineering worked, their entire technical worldview would be molded to conform with Facebook's. Forever after, even while working at other companies, they'd drag along those prejudices and attitudes as if they were God's revealed truth. The Googlers now at Facebook had surely done the same.

I had five bugs to fix. I didn't even know how to code PHP, the front-end language Facebook was written in. It was

* "N00b" is hacker-speak for newbie, or beginner. In online coding forums, it's a term of withering contempt for someone obviously out of his or her depth. At Facebook, it was used semiaffectionately for a new hire.

a famously crappy language and development environment with few users those days, chosen merely because that's what Zuck knew as a hacker at Harvard.

Following the online documentation, I successfully set up a dev server, the machine on which I'd develop code, kind of like a personal sandbox. I then pulled an entire version of Facebook's code from the main repository, browsing all of it via an editor.

So this is what all the fuss was about, huh?

For giggles, I changed the text of the Like button to an obscenity, saved the code, hit Reload in my browser, which pointed to my private version of Facebook, and indeed, I could now copulate with everything on the Web.

MAKE AN IMPACT. FORTUNE FAVORS THE BOLD.

I was well on my way.

Product Masseur

> For that reason, let a prince have the credit of conquering his State, as the means will always be considered honorable, and he will be praised by all because the vulgar masses are always seduced by the appearances of things and by the outcome of events; and in this world there are only vulgar masses.
>
> —Niccolò Machiavelli, *The Prince*

JUNE 2011*

So what had Facebook hired me to do?

My official title was "product manager," commonly abbreviated as "PM."

While the role of product manager is near universal in

* The observant reader will note we've jumped ahead two months. After signing on with Facebook, I immediately did the employee on-boarding described in the previous chapter, and then went on unpaid leave to let the boys finish the AdGrok deal. A formal acquisition, even a small one, takes weeks of legal and technical due diligence. If I had publicly started work at FB, rumor would have gotten around the Valley echo chamber that AdGrok was either falling apart or getting bought, threatening the delicate deal going on. Thus, I had to act like I was still the CEO of AdGrok socially ("So how's your startup going?" "Uhh . . ."), while mostly hiding out on my tiny boat, given I had nowhere else to live or go, a penniless millionaire-on-paper.

tech companies of any size, the de facto or de jure reality of it varies widely. What the PM does is in many ways representative of how the company itself develops product. Some companies have opted for different titles. At Microsoft, they are known as "program managers." At Palantir, the secretive defense intelligence software company founded by the billionaire investor Peter Thiel, they are known as "product navigators," which sounds terribly romantic.

Whatever the flavor of title, what does a product manager, by whatever name, actually do?

The MBA-esque job description would be "CEO of the product," because those B-school pukes like sporting acronymic titles. This is many a company's definition of the role, and it's not completely wrong, though it makes the job seem statelier than it is.

A more illustrative description is "shit umbrella." If you imagine a bursting monsoon of clumpy diarrhea pouring down like God's own biblical vengeance, that is more or less where you find yourself in either a startup or a large, high-profile, and complex organization like Facebook. You, my dear product manager, are the communal manservant to your engineering team, holding a large, cumbersome *paramerde* above their heads bent over keyboards on which they furiously type.

By definition, what you do is everything that needs to be done, other than hands-on-keyboard type code. So that means sitting in endless meetings with the privacy legal team, giving highly selective and edited versions of what your product is going to do, and explaining how it fits into some antediluvian legal rubric. It means pitching a roomful of smiling and empty-headed salespeople, so they can start priming the client pump and bring spend into your new product baby. It means wheeling and dealing with other PMs to either cajole a product change or cadge some engineering resource. It means fronting for the product in high-level meetings with senior management, and trying to place it, like a quickly falling Tetris piece, into the rudimentary blueprint of their world. It means defending your team from the depredations of other PMs when they come around asking for favors, or arguing for a deprioritization of some element of your product plan for one in theirs.

As PM, if you can convince engineers to build things you stipulate, you are golden. But if you can't, then you are like the dictator who has lost control of his army. It doesn't matter if you have the United Nations or the church on your side (i.e., if management has anointed you as leader), you're ending up in front of a firing squad sooner rather than later. The most pitiful sight in the Facebook Ads team was the PMs who had lost the confidence of their engineers. Nominally in charge of some product area, they were like the government in exile of some occupied nation: sitting there with all the pomp of their position, sending emails and road maps hither and yon, and yet producing nothing.

Internally, it was a demeaning, groveling job.

Externally, it was a different story.

As a Facebook product manager, you resembled an Afghan warlord or a pirate captain: fearsome in appearance to any outsiders, the scourge of entire companies and industries, but actually barely in control of your small band of engineer-hooligans, and always one step from mutiny. To the outside world, your job was easy: a two-line email would have the senior management of any company waiting eagerly in the Facebook reception area almost instantaneously. Many were the startups I conjured thusly, they sputtering in flattery despite my showing up late and surly, demanding and getting a full walk-through of their entire product and business model, then dismissing them after a forty-five-minute meeting.

Facebook is the eight-hundred-pound gorilla in everyone's bed. To the extent you can make the gorilla do something, you have the attention of everyone. The most craven among the Facebook PMs mistake that power for their own. Such insufferable poseurs populate the ranks of every product-management corps, but the all-powerful incumbent nature of Facebook allows them to flourish more than usual.

What was my specific product?

My newfound beat was ads targeting for the Facebook Ads system. Targeting is the set of data and tools that advertisers use to define a set of users. It can be demographic in nature (e.g., thirty-to-forty-year-old females), geographic (people within five miles of Sarasota, Florida), or even based on Facebook profile data (do you have children; i.e., are you in the mommy segment?).

Targeting is where the data rubber meets the money road, so to speak. To use a physics analogy, pressure is force per unit area, and similarly, monetization is amount of data per pixel: the more data you bring to bear for every square inch of screen real estate, then the more that ad will be worth. Targeting is how that data gets applied to the screen real estate, it's the alchemy that turns pure data into real-world cash.

Since more (good) data meant more cash, measuring Facebook's per-ad monetization would be a read on how well that data–cash conversion process was running. To that end, in my first week of real work I fired up the company's revenue dashboards. The revenue dashboards were a series of internal websites, accessible only to senior management or Ads employees. Access was gated on a need-to-know basis, as total revenue was sensitive; everyone knew Facebook would go public one day, even if not precisely when, and outsiders would have loved an illicit look at the numbers.

All the revenue dashboards were black, with either yellow or white lettering, closely resembling the Bloomberg terminal you'd find on a Wall Street trading desk. They were sliceable and diceable by parameters like geography, ads product, time of day, and any other attribute relevant to the operation of the Ads system.

I went to the top-level dashboard. As I would eventually learn, Facebook always had a high-level report for every area, whether it was ads or growth or something else, with the key number that defined success set off in large yellow letters in the upper left of the screen. Monthly active users (*the* yardstick for Facebook), daily revenue, mobile users—whatever the metric was that encapsulated the health of your part of the Facebook world—there it was with unappealable finality.

Wait! What?

I looked again to make sure I hadn't narrowed the reporting to some godforsaken country with minimal monetization. I hit Reload.

Nope. This pitiful number, which I cannot share with you thanks to Facebook Legal, was Facebook's average CPM.*

It was utter dog shit. How could Facebook monetization, the much-ballyhooed future of the Internet, be so low? This was bottom-of-the-barrel stuff, comparable to what you'd monetize your Star Wars blog at if you ran AdSense ads.

To say I was stunned was an understatement. I'd dumped my company, pawned off my cofounders on Twitter, and accepted big-company assimilation . . . for this? Like most Facebook outsiders, I hadn't understood the monetization. Wooed by the external whisper numbers that were in the $2 billion per year range, I had assumed the per-impression monetization was healthy.

The reality was otherwise. Before 2013, if you wanted to know how Facebook made money, the answer was very simple: a billion times any number is still a big fucking number. Facebook monetization was laughable compared with Google's on a purely CPM basis. But usage was ungodly. Up there with heroin, carbohydrates, or a weekly paycheck: that's how addictive and rewarding Facebook was.

---

* CPM means "cost per mille," and refers to the cost for every thousand showings (or "impressions") of an ad. It's the cost per square foot of the media world.

Here's a tangible example: the Facebook mobile app at the time was utter shite in terms of responsiveness (averaging something like ninety seconds of latency in some developing countries). Despite that, many people spent hours a day on Facebook, waiting a solid minute for the app to load after every click or comment . . . ignoring their surroundings, the imploring gaze of their wives, or their children's bid for attention. All those eyeballs, over hours, turned into cheap ads that gradually, as many raindrops make a river, amassed a torrent of revenue for Facebook. That's how Facebook paid for the free food in the summer of 2011.

My second bit of first-day revelation had to do with people rather than money.

This was the personnel state of Facebook Ads when I signed on: about thirty or so engineers and one designer, spread out over about a dozen products, grouped into broad areas nucleated by six product managers, of which I was one. The whole merry circus was run by my boss, Gokul Rajaram, who seemed to always be writing three emails at once, along with attending at least two meetings, one in person, the other via Skype or his mobile.

Gokul was the nominal product leader for Ads, meaning he was the "product masseur" who gave overall direction to what Facebook actually built in Ads, as well as managing the product managers themselves, at the time an unruly lot, each with their own miniature product fiefdom.

Rather than an overall ads strategy, what we had was a general feeling in the air, a sort of collective mood that, like a slanted floor, tended to send more people one way than the other. Insofar as Targeting and related teams like Optimization—run by the Israeli who had interviewed me—were concerned, it seemed like a catch-as-catch-can circus of random road maps and product ideas. Many of the ideas emerging from this burbling chaos were interesting and exciting; many were just plain weird and almost certainly ineffectual. Lots of local mythologies, mostly unsubstantiated by data, reigned around the magical value of sharing on Facebook, or of building an audience for your Facebook page.

Just as every product manager had a product marketing manager, who spun the marketing story around that team's creations, there was a marketing analogue to Gokul as well. Brian Boland, whom we've already met in our first Zuck meeting, sat next to Gokul, and ran the growing militia of PMMs (to use the Facebook lingo). A PMM would be paired with a PM, like a marketing Twiddledee to the product Twiddledum, for every team in Facebook Ads. Sales, its army organized into a multilevel hierarchy spread over dozens of regional offices, was held at arm's length, and reported to David Fischer, one of Sheryl's gang from Google. Other than Fischer's inputs to Sheryl, Sales was a purely downstream consumer of whatever product created, getting its predigested pitch from one of Boland's PMMs.

My only time in a big company before Facebook was spent on the Goldman Sachs trading floor, which was so outlandish and idiosyncratic, it served as poor experience for the political atmosphere I now found myself in. I'd get to know this class of Gokul/Boland person very well, given that half my job was spent attempting to manipulate (mostly ineffectually) their emotions and perceptions.

Everyone who individually contributed to Facebook product reported to a Gokul or Boland: product managers (including me) to Gokul, PMMs to Boland, and engineers to their local engineering manager, who in turn reported to KX, the Ads engineering manager (whom AdGrok first pitched on meeting Facebook). Together, that management stratum ran Ads, for better or worse.

How did this largely unchoreographed corporate dance play out in practice?

Facebook Ads product management, in the Gokul mold, meant a weekly product manager meeting. At the time, it was six to eight people around a table, recounting what they'd worked on that week. There was a certain strutting, showy quality to it, almost like a Y Combinator dinner, at which you were expected to demonstrate ever-accelerating progress on your particular piece of the Facebook Ads cake. I'd mentally rehearse my script as I walked along with whatever cluster of fellow PMs into the mini–Demo Day of another weekly Gokul meeting.

Additionally, there'd be a monthly general product manager meeting, meant to create some level of cross-company cohesion. These were run by (who else?) Chris Cox, he of on-boarding-speech fame, who was then head of Facebook product. This was the YC-Demo-Day-style meeting taken to the company level, with lots of glib salesmanship, and a different momentary favorite in the PM team taking the stage each time to much applause. Every meeting, someone would get the team award for exemplary PM-ship, recommended by other PMs.* Cox had some weird thing where he'd clap by whipping his hand around repeatedly such that fingers would snap violently with every whirl, and it would be the prompt for the whole room to clap in turn.

The Ads team's mandate was very simple: make more money, but don't piss off users while doing so. The monetization side of Facebook was still stuck in that subservient role typical of earlyish-stage startups that are mostly consumer-facing, and with a CEO who abhors grubby lucre. Kind of like a patient mother trailing her destructive toddler and picking up discarded toys along the way, Ads was expected

* I got it one month for my handling of the Irish Data Privacy Audit, which was a big deal at the time, and which we'll cover soon. As often happens with awards, it was for what I thought was pretty unexceptional conduct, while other far more meritorious behavior of mine went unrewarded. Ultimately it spurred more skepticism than pride.

to make money with whatever new features the user-facing side of the company launched. Those products were not designed with monetization in mind; in fact, they were at best the output of a studied strategy around user engagement, and at worst the most recent brain dropping of whatever "visionary" product leader Zuck had confided in, or of Zuck himself. The Ads team was then forced to turn that product, success or failure, into money. Building a viable business out of that would be like trying to build a house out of parts selected at random from a Home Depot: you might be able to pull it off if you were lucky or very resourceful, but more than likely you would end up with some misshapen hut nobody would want to live in. That's precisely what Facebook Ads was until mid-2012 or so.

That was pre-IPO Facebook product manager life for you, in all its glory.

Between the conversations I was having in Ads and the corporate convocations I was part of, I began to think I'd entered some alternate universe, an unexpected social media Twilight Zone. So I did what I always did, which was snoop on everyone's background via Facebook and LinkedIn to figure out the nature of this strange company I was keeping.

It was clear that nobody—and I do mean nobody—in the Ads team had ever worked at any sort of advertising company. The only exceptions were the Googlers who had possibly worked on some publisher-side technology.

This was distinctly weird, for a couple of reasons: Ad tech is an incestuous world, and every advertising product manager or engineer has a résumé filled with stints at one or another ads startup. It is also a fairly insular world, which outsiders seldom dare to enter, and from which insiders rarely leave, shackled via some odd industry loyalty to the business of turning pixels into money.

Everyone on the Ads team seemed to have been vetted for

Facebook acceptability and values, but nobody (other than perhaps the aforementioned former Googlers) had any notion of what the outside ads world was like. What was weirder, everyone seemed absolutely cool with that. They didn't know what they didn't know, and it was a feature rather than a bug.

On the one hand, that was good, as the ads world tended to self-organize into stale patterns and product ideas: maximize the clickthrough rate, autoplay video ads for movie trailers, target "auto intenders" (i.e., people in the market for a car). It was the same old, same old everywhere. Facebook was to be a new paradigm in paid media, breaking every rule or mold. On the other hand, Christ Jesus, had anyone heard of real ads targeting based on user actions like buying something or browsing a product catalog?

Nope.

Any culture able to shut itself off from the outside world goes insane in its own unique way, and Facebook had essentially done that with its Ads team. But as on Wall Street, where even someone who knew the correct price of a security couldn't go against the will of the market, you couldn't question the reigning insanity. And so one went along.

Eventually, this cluelessness would reach its magnificent apotheosis in the rise and fall of a bet-the-company product called Open Graph, and its monetization twin, Sponsored Stories, and in later chapters you'll hear plenty about both.

As I did with Twitter, though, I'll make an explicit proviso: the statements here, and even more damning ones later, were true (or at least true as perceived by me) at the time. Tech companies, even relatively large ones, are dynamic beasts. They change quickly. Facebook's redeeming quality—the magical tendency that has saved it in the past, and will save it in the future—is its ability to rapidly adapt to changing circumstances, or to the results of its own bold product bets. In 2011 and much of 2012, the Facebook ads product was a clunker, of unproved value to even the least discerning advertisers, and completely useless to most marketers trying to actually drive sales, other than a few annoying games companies. The monetization was pathetic, the ad units themselves grotesquely small and unattractive, and the management tools on offer buggy and painful to use.

But Facebook would get very smart, very fast.

By early 2013 the company would figure out exactly where its value lay, and it would have nothing to do with any of the Byzantine gobbledygook that was being bandied about the Ads team circa 2011, or in the public-facing marketing materials it was pushing on deep-pocketed advertisers. Facebook essentially owns the online advertising future. How it went from advertising zero to hero is the crux of this story.

Google *Delenda Est*

> By itself, genius can produce original thoughts just as little as a woman by herself can bear children. Outward circumstances must come to fructify genius, and be, as it were, a father to its progeny.
>
> —Arthur Schopenhauer,
> "On Genius," *The Art of Literature*

JUNE 2011

Mark Zuckerberg is a genius.

Not in the Asperger's, autistic way depicted in the very fictional movie *The Social Network*, the cognitive genius of exceptional ability. That's a modern definition that reduces the original meaning.

Nor would I claim he was the Steve Jobsian product genius either. Anyone claiming as much will have to explain the crowded graveyard of forgotten Facebook product failures. Remember "Home," the Facebook-enabled home screen for Android phones, launched with much fanfare in 2013, Zuck appearing alongside the CEO of the soon-to-be-disappointed smartphone maker HTC? Or Facebook's misguided bet on HTML5 in 2012, which slowed the mobile app to a frustrating crawl? How about Facebook's first version of search, available in English only, mostly useful for checking out your friends' single female friends, and since discontinued?* The stand-alone mobile app Paper, which was a shameless rip-off of Flipboard?† Some unlaunched products I can't name consumed considerable resources, dying internally after Zuck changed his mind and shut them down.

If he's a product genius, then there's lots of serendipity counterbalancing his divine madness.

No. I submit he was an old-school genius, the fiery force of nature possessed by a tutelary spirit of seemingly supernatural provenance that fuels and guides him, intoxicates his circle, and compels his retinue to be great as well. The Jefferson, the Napoleon, the Alexander . . . the Jim Jones, the L. Ron Hubbard, the Joseph Smith. Keeper of a messianic vision that, though mercurial and stinting on specifics, presents an overwhelming and all-consuming picture of a new and different world. Have a mad vision, and you're a kook. Get a crowd to believe in it as well, and you're a leader. By imprinting this vision on his disciples, he founded the church of a new religion. All the early Facebook employees have their story of the moment when they saw the light, and realized that Facebook wasn't some measly social network like MySpace, but a dream of a different human experience. With all the fervor of recent converts, newly recruited followers attracted other committed, smart, and daring engineers and designers, themselves seduced by the echoes of the Zuckian vision in others.

Then there was the culture he created.

Many cool Valley companies have engineering-first cultures, but Facebook took it to a different level. The engineers

---

* "My friends of friends who are female and live in san francisco" was the most popular query for Facebook Search shortly after launch. While this search feature has been retired, FB has made considerable improvements to its search features since then.

† The internal idea incubator behind Paper and a host of other failed apps was called Creative Labs, an attempt to recapture the creative zest of corporate youth. It was shut down altogether in December 2015.

ran the place, and so long as you shipped code and didn't break anything (too often), you were golden. The spirit of subversive hackery guided everything. In the early days, a Georgia college kid named Chris Putnam created a virus that made your Facebook profile resemble MySpace, then the social media incumbent. It went rampant and started deleting user data as well. Instead of siccing the FBI dogs on Putnam, Facebook cofounder Dustin Moskovitz invited him for an interview, and offered him a job. He went on to become one of Facebook's more famous and rage-filled engineers. That was the uniquely piratical attitude: if you could get shit done and quickly, nobody cared much about credentials or traditional legalistic morality. The hacker ethos prevailed above all.

This culture is what kept twenty-three-year-old kids who were making half a million a year, in a city where there was lots of fun on offer if you had the cash, tethered to a corporate campus for fourteen-hour days. They ate three meals a day there, sometimes slept there, and did nothing but write code, review code, or comment on new features in internal Facebook groups. On the day of the IPO—Facebook's victory rally—the Ads area was full of busily working engineers at eight p.m. on a Friday. All were at that point worth real money—even fuck-you money for some—and all were writing code on the very day their paper turned to hard cash.

At Facebook, your start date was celebrated by the company the way evangelicals celebrate the day they were baptized and found Jesus, or the way new American citizens celebrate the day they took their oath in front of the flag. This event was called (really) your Faceversary, and every colleague would rush to congratulate you on Facebook (of course), just as normal people did for one another on their birthdays. Often the company or your colleagues would order you a garish surprise bouquet for your desk, with one of those huge Mylar balloons in the shape of a 2 or whatever. When someone left Facebook (usually around when the balloons said 4 or 5), everyone would treat it as a death, as you were leaving the current plane of existence and going to another one (though it wasn't assumed this next plane was better than the current one). The tombstone of your Facebook death was a photo posted on Facebook of your weathered and worn corporate ID. It was customary to include a weepy suicide note/self-written epitaph, and the post would garner hundreds of likes and comments inside a minute.

To the deceased, it felt like a passing too. When you left Facebook, you left the employee-only Facebook network, which meant that all the posts from internal groups (with secret company stuff) were gone, your posts got less distribution among other Facebook employees (who were on it 24/7, of course), and your Facebook feed, which had become your only social view on the world, suddenly slowed to a near-empty crawl. Almost instantly, someone would add you to the ex-Facebook secret groups, which served as a sort of postemployment purgatory where former employees discussed the company.

Pause and consider all this for a lingering moment: the militant engineering culture, the all-consuming work identity, the apostolic sense of devotion to a great cause. The cynics will read statements from Zuckerberg or some other senior exec about creating "a more open and connected world" and think, "Oh, what sentimental drivel." The critics will read of a new product tweak or partnership, and think Facebook is doing it only to make more money.

They're wrong.

Facebook is full of true believers who really, really, really are not doing it for the money, and really, really will not stop until every man, woman, and child on earth is staring into a blue-framed window with a Facebook logo. Which, if you think about it, is much scarier than simple greed. The greedy man can always be bought at some price or another, and his behavior is predictable. But the true zealot?

He can't be had at any price, and there's no telling what his mad visions will have him and his followers do.

That's what we're talking about with Mark Elliot Zuckerberg and the company he created.

In June 2011, Google launched an obvious Facebook copy called Google Plus. Obnoxiously wired into other Google products like Gmail and YouTube, it was meant to join all users of Google services into one online identity, much as Facebook did for the Internet as a whole. Given you had a Google Plus sign-up button practically everywhere in your Google user experience, the possibility of its network growing exponentially was very real indeed. Also, the product itself was pretty good, in some ways better than Facebook. The photo sharing was better, and more geared to serious photographers, and much of the design cleaner and more minimalist. An additional plus for Google Plus: it had no ads, as Google could subsidize it with AdWords, its paid search gold mine. This was the classic one-hand-washing-the-other tactic of the ruthless monopolist, like Microsoft using the revenue from Windows to crush Netscape Navigator with Explorer back in the nineties. By owning search, Google would bankroll taking over social media as well.

This sudden move was somewhat surprising. For years Google had been famously dismissive of Facebook, the fortified redoubts of its search monopoly making it feel untouchable. But as the one-way parade of expensive talent from Google to Facebook continued with no end in sight, Google got nervous. Companies are like countries: the populations really vote only with their feet, either coming or going. Google instituted a policy whereby any desirable Googler who got a Facebook offer would have it beaten instantly by a heaping Google counteroffer. This, of course, caused a rush of Googlers to interview at Facebook, only to use the resulting offer as a bargaining chip to improve their Google pay.

But many were legitimately leaving. The Googlers at Facebook were a bit like the Greeks during the rise of the Roman Empire: they brought lots of civilization and tech culture with them, but it was clear who was going to run the world in the near future.

Google Plus was Google finally taking note of Facebook and confronting the company head-on, rather than via cloak-and-dagger recruitment shenanigans and catty disses at tech conferences. It hit Facebook like a bomb. Zuck took it as an existential threat comparable to the Soviets placing nukes on Cuba in 1961. This was the great enemy's sally into our own hemisphere, and it gripped Zuck like nothing else. He declared "Lockdown," the first and only one during my time there. As was duly explained to the more recent employees, Lockdown was a state of war that dated to Facebook's earliest days, when no one could leave the building while the company confronted some threat, either competitive or technical.

How, might you ask, was Lockdown officially announced? We received an email at 1:45 p.m. the day Google Plus launched, instructing us to gather around the Aquarium. Actually, it technically instructed us to gather around the Lockdown sign. This was a neon sign bolted to the upper reaches of the Aquarium, above the cube of glass, almost like the No Vacancy sign on a highway motel. By the time the company had gathered itself around, that sign was illuminated, tipping us off to what was coming.

Zuckerberg was usually a poor speaker. His speech came at the rapid clip of someone accustomed to analyzing language for content only, and at the speed of a very agile mind that didn't have time for rhetorical flourishes. It was geekspeak basically, the English language as spoken by people who had four screens of computer code open at once. His bearing was aloof and disconnected from his audience, and yet he maintained that intense stare that bordered on the psychopathic. It was an unnerving look that irrevocably rattled more than one interlocutor, typically some poor employee undergoing a withering product review, and it stared out from every *Fortune* or *Time* cover he graced. It was easy to project a creepy persona onto that gaze. That unfortunate first impression, plus the mischaracterization in the film *The Social Network*, was probably responsible for half of the ever-present suspicion and paranoia surrounding Facebook's motives. But occasionally, Zuck would have a charismatic moment of lucid greatness, and it would be stunning.

The 2011 Lockdown speech didn't promise to be one of those moments. It was delivered completely impromptu from the open space next to the stretch of desks where the executive staff sat. All of Facebook's engineers, designers, and product managers gathered around him in a rapt throng; the scene brought to mind a general addressing his troops in the field.

The contest for users, he told us, would now be direct and zero-sum. Google had launched a competing product; whatever was gained by one side would be lost by the other. It was up to all of us to up our game while the world conducted live tests of Facebook versus Google's version of Facebook, and decided which it liked more. He hinted vaguely at product changes we would consider in light of this new competitor. The real point, however, was to have everyone aspire to a higher bar of reliability, user experience, and site performance.

In a company whose overarching mantras were DONE IS BETTER THAN PERFECT and PERFECT IS THE ENEMY OF THE GOOD, this represented a course correction, a shift to the concern for quality that typically lost out to the drive to ship. It was the sort of nagging paternal reminder to keep your room clean that Zuck occasionally dished out after Facebook had suffered some embarrassing bug or outage.

Rounding off another beaded string of platitudes, he changed gears and erupted with a burst of rhetoric referencing one of the ancient classics he had studied at Harvard and before. "You know, one of my favorite Roman orators ended every speech with the phrase: *Carthago delenda est*. 'Carthage must be destroyed.' For some reason I think of that now." He paused as a wave of laughter tore through the crowd.

The aforementioned orator was, of course, Cato the Elder, a noted Roman senator and inveigher against the Carthaginians who clamored for the destruction of Rome's great challenger in what became the Third Punic War. Reputedly, he ended every speech with that phrase, no matter the topic.

Carthago delenda est. Carthage must be destroyed!

Zuckerberg's tone went from paternal lecture to martial exhortation, the drama mounting with every mention of the threat Google represented. The speech ended to a roar of cheering and applause. Everyone walked out of there ready to invade Poland if need be. It was a rousing performance. *Carthage must be destroyed!*

The Facebook Analog Research Laboratory jumped into action and produced a poster with CARTHAGO DELENDA EST splashed in imperative bold type over a stylized Roman centurion's helmet. This improvised print shop printed all manner of posters and ephemera, often distributed semi-furtively at nights and on weekends, in a fashion reminiscent of Soviet samizdat. The art itself was always exceptional, evoking both the mechanical typography of WWII-era propaganda posters and contemporary Internet design, complete with faux-vintage logos. This was Facebook's ministry of propaganda, and it was originally started with no official permission or budget, in an unused warehouse space. In many ways, it was the finest exemplar of Facebook values: irreverent yet bracing in its martial qualities.

The Carthago posters went up immediately all over the campus, and were stolen almost as fast. It was announced that the cafés would be open over the weekends, and the proposal was seriously floated to have the shuttles from Palo Alto and San Francisco run on the weekends too. This would make Facebook a fully seven-days-a-week company; by whatever means, employees were expected to be in and on duty. In what was perceived as a kindly concession to the few employees with families, it was also announced that families were welcome to visit on weekends and eat in the cafés, allowing the children to at least see daddy (and yes, it was mostly daddy) on weekend afternoons. British Trader and Zoë came by, and we weren't the only family there, by any stretch. Common was the scene of the swamped Facebook employee with logo'ed hoodie spending an hour of quality time with his wife and two kids before going back to his desk.

Internal Facebook groups sprang up to dissect every element of the Google Plus product. On the day Plus launched, I noted an Ads product manager named Paul Adams in close conversation with Zuckerberg and a couple members of the high command inside a small conference room. As was well known, before he defected to Facebook, Paul had been one of the product managers for Google Plus. Now that the product had launched, he was no longer restrained by his nondisclosure agreement with Google, and Facebook was having him walk the leadership through the public aspects of the product.

Facebook was not fucking around. This was total war.

I decided to do some reconnaissance. En route to work one Sunday morning, I skipped the Palo Alto exit on the 101, and got off in Mountain View instead. Down Shoreline I went, and into the sprawling Google campus. The multicolored Google logo was everywhere, and clunky Google-colored bikes littered the courtyards. I had visited friends here before, and knew where to find the engineering buildings. I made my way there, and contemplated the parking lot.

It was empty. Completely empty.

Interesting.

I got back on the 101 North and drove to Facebook.

At the California Avenue building, I had to hunt for a parking spot. The lot was full.

It was clear which company was fighting to the death.

Carthage must be destroyed!

Leaping Headlong

> For when I do leap into the abyss, I go headlong with my heels up, and am pleased to be falling in that degrading attitude, and consider it something beautiful.
>
> —Fyodor Dostoyevsky, *The Brothers Karamazov*

AUGUST 2011

It was time to launch my first Facebook product.

I had joined Facebook toward the beginning of a product initiative called Kitten, which was firmly within my targeting purview. Like "scuba," "radar," and "laser," "Kitten" was originally an acronym, whose origins had been more or less forgotten; the name now simply referred to the current state of Facebook's topic-extraction technology. Topic extraction is one of those critical but unsexy artificial-intelligence challenges that underlie huge pieces of Internet technology (e.g., Google Search), but never receive the attention of sexy initiatives like self-driving cars. In essence, it's a programmatic way of mapping the convoluted parlance of human texts like messages, webpages, or social media posts into a dictionary of semantic categories. For example, your status update of "Tiger really managed to hit that birdie in the US Open" would be automatically mapped to the categories "Tiger Woods," "Golf," and "US Open." In a world where human speech, rife with sarcasm, typos, slang, and double meanings, is devilishly difficult to understand, it's a sophisticated hack to quickly categorize a piece of user-generated content. In the case of Ads, the goal was to put the person who had liked the Tiger Woods page, or shared a link to a golf-related article, in the "Golf" targeting segment, reachable by golf-related advertisers.

Personal anecdote: the inaugural product decision I made at Facebook was related to Kitten. My very first week on the job, I was assigned to lead the weekly targeting team meeting, involving a dozen engineers, product marketers, and outside product managers. To say I was clueless was an understatement; fortunately, the team's inertia more or less impelled the meeting forward, covering the list of agenda topics that the product manager who was filling in on targeting had provided. All eyes suddenly turned to me when there was disagreement over an explicit product decision.

The question was this: How would these newfangled targeting topics, cleverly extracted from page names and user behavior, be denoted in the targeting user interface that advertisers used to configure their ads? Facebook already had "interests" targeting in the form of text strings like "football" and "fashion"; we needed some way to deploy these special "super" keywords that represented dozens or hundreds of other related categories of meaning.

Part of the team wanted to do away with the original keywords altogether, forcing all advertisers to adopt the new, untested technology, creating a major operational challenge as advertisers struggled to adopt the new feature. Another faction wanted to simply launch the new features in addition to existing keywords, and specially designate them somehow, either in the design of the user interface, or via other means.

As I'd soon learn, the tiebreaker role of the product manager, mediating between the internal dueling factions of a product team, or channeling the voice of the eventual user among engineers lost in low-level technical detail, was pretty much the core workaday function of the job. Snapped to attention by over a dozen pairs of eyes, and with the bittersweet memory of the Twitter deal still in mind, without any hesitation, I suggested: "Keep the old keywords. Moving over the twenty percent of Facebook's revenue that uses keywords to a whole new paradigm will be untenable. In terms of markers, use a pound sign, like Twitter hashtags. Users have already been conditioned to think of #Golf as a sort of über-symbol for the high-level abstract concept of golf; this will just draft off Twitter's work. Besides, it will be kind of funny—Twitter hashtags as buyable commodities on Facebook."

This was obviously a winking reference to the company I'd just insultingly kissed off, and would serve as a kind of gallows-humor inside joke the team could laugh at months or years from now.

The notion percolated through the room, to eventual nodding agreement. Hundreds of thousands of advertisers spending hundreds of millions in marketing dollars would now be entering "#Hip Hop Music" instead of "Eminem," "50 Cent," "Drake," and an endless list of relevant keywords they'd expensively determined, via lots of trial and error, as being relevant to their desired audience. The interface wouldn't have to change (Facebook design resources were always famously strained), meaning we could launch soon, and no abrupt adoption challenge need be contemplated. We just had to market the hell out of these new targeting hashtags, and train users to prefer them over the antiquated keywords they'd made part of their Facebook marketing workflow. That meant leaning on the product marketer to lean on our partners and biggest advertisers to make them think "#Action Movies" was the hottest thing since democracy and antibiotics.

Two days into my Facebook experience, and I'd given external form to a Facebook product.

This may sound trivial, and in the scheme of things, it

sort of was. But the mundane trade-offs of technical difficulty among various implementations, the prioritization of engineering time, the vagaries of user perception, and the demands of marketing a new product are the bread and butter of everyday product manager work. Flashy new flagship-product launches, like a new iPhone birthed on a conference room stage by a strutting Steve Jobs, are what draw mainstream headlines and the attention of nontechie normals, like swine hearing the clanging of a swill bucket. But the beat to which the Valley really marches, the actual workaday cadence of technological progress, is that line product manager in a conference room or an engineering bullpen alongside a team, like the first lieutenant leading a platoon in every great war film ever made, figuring out what to build, how to build it, and how to sell it once built. Thousands of such teams dot Silicon Valley, and it's how the work of technology development really gets done.

By early August, two months after I joined, Kitten seemed ready to launch. Like knowing when to stop editing and finally publish a book, knowing when to launch is a subtle art at best, and a drunken coin toss at worst. Sometimes you don't finish a product, you merely abandon any hope of presently improving it, and out the door it goes. Product managers must either apply the brakes to impatient engineers who want their creations to see the light of day, or conversely, whip and drive to get perfectionist engineers to stop mucking with the code and procure some real users already. In general, be it at startups or aggressive companies like Facebook, there should be a cultural bias for launching. The perfect is very often the enemy of the good, and as the Facebook poster screamed from every wall: DONE IS BETTER THAN PERFECT. Very few companies have died due to launching early; at worst, you'll have a onetime product embarrassment (as Apple did with the first version of its iPhone Maps app). However, countless companies have died by losing the nerve to ship, and freezing into a coma of second-guessing, hesitation, and internal indecision. As in life, so in business: maintain a bias for action over inaction.

With that thought, we slated a Kitten launch for August 1, 2011. The product marketers weaved their seductive tales, the PM (i.e., me) ran around and made sure everyone knew what was going on, the engineers snuck in their last changes (probably without telling the PM). Then, one fine morning, a Kitten engineer manipulated the gatekeeping logic that exposed only employees to the new ads targeting, and any of Facebook's advertisers could aim money at our new hashtagged targeting segments.* The new targeting was then aimed at all users later that same day, and Kitten was out in the product wild.

There was some minimal turbulence due to minor technical bugs, as well as to one or another team being out of the loop, but otherwise, a major new feature affecting a fifth of Facebook's revenue launched without a hitch. While the success was only marginally related to my skill, I received praise from the Ads leadership for pulling off an aggressive product launch within a few weeks of joining. In essence, I had earned my spurs: I had safely shipped new product the market seemed to want, leveraging an engineering team that respected my product guidance, and with a plan to iterate the product going forward, with metrics to mark our progress. In a nutshell, that's what Facebook expected of its product managers.

Per that last point, in order to mark progress (which in Ads always meant numbers prefixed by dollar signs) we built a dashboard showing a line graph of Facebook Ads spend by type of targeting, now including Kitten, along with keywords, "broad" targeting (e.g., mothers, or business travelers), and things like gender and geography. Effectively, it was

* Unsurprisingly for a company that was so high on its own supply, a commonly used test set for products was employees themselves, and there was an easy way to limit a product to internal use only.

the fraction of total spend we'd manage to capture via this new targeting product.

A metrics dashboard that the entire team fixates on was standard Facebook practice. Those scorecards should obsess the product manager, should be the last thing he thinks of at night and the first thing he thinks of in the morning, and should be known to him, from memory, down to the decimal. Choose well what goes in that line graph, because whatever it is, a good product manager will slave away until it's going up and to the right, whatever that figure represents.

You make what you measure, so measure carefully.

Once launched, Kitten became Facebook Ads' sausage grinder, ingesting all sorts of user actions, from messages to posts to the contents of shared links, and turning them into targeting topics of various stripes. With every new piece of Facebook user data ingested, the targeting team did a test against the previous topic-targeting ingredients, seeing if the new inputs (e.g., user check-ins) improved the ads that were served to those users in the form of increased performance (and ultimately, revenue).

In time, this effort would assume more systematic shape, taking the name Project Chorizo. I even hung a real length of Spanish chorizo from my monitor, as a rallying symbol, and the targeting team got down to the serious business of monetizing every last user action on Facebook.

Just as my first view of Facebook's high-level revenue dashboard proved a dispiriting exercise, Chorizo's final results, which took months to produce, were a similar tale of woe. No user data we had, if fed freely into the topics that Facebook's savviest marketers used to target their ads, improved any performance metric we had access to. That meant that advertisers trying to find someone who, say, wanted to buy a car, benefited not at all from all the car chatter taking place on Facebook. It was as if we had fed a mile-long trainful of meat cows into a slaughterhouse, and had come out with one measly sausage to show for it. It was incomprehensible, and it tested my faith (which, believe it or not, I certainly had at that time) in Facebook's claim to unique primacy in the realm of user data.

As with many mysteries of my newfound religion, experience would disabuse me of much dearly held belief.

One Shot, One Kill*

They couldn't hit an elephant at this distance.
—General John Sedgwick,
shortly before being shot
by a Confederate sniper,
Battle of Spotsylvania, 1864

Why was it so hard to make money off Facebook's data?

Here's the best metaphor for understanding Facebook, and its attendant data-monetization challenges. Imagine yourself in a noisy, busy bar in the lively downtown of any large city in America. People chatting with friends, perhaps making new ones, taking the odd photo, hitting on someone attractive, and so forth. Facebook is that bar, and every other bar in Europe, and every busy coffeehouse in the Middle East, and every café in Latin America. Facebook is the rowdy assemblage of humanity talking, gossiping, flirting, sharing, and creating experiences.

Now imagine you have a written transcript of every conversation taking place, as well as an anonymous ID for every individual. You know where they are and whom they're

* "One shot, one kill" is the motto of the US Marine Corps Scout Snipers, that branch's unit of elite shooters. It's also the mantra of most ethical hunters.

talking with. As the product manager for Facebook's ad targeting, that's effectively what you've got.

Sounds like a lot, doesn't it?

Well, it isn't. Ask yourself how often you mention anything of commercial import when you're with friends around a sticky table in your favorite dive bar. If you had the chief marketing officers of every big brand and every merchant in the world listening over your shoulder, how often would their collective ears perk up? Actually, I know exactly how often; it's one of the earliest studies we did when I got to Facebook.

The short version is "not terribly often at all." Nobody says things like "I really love how these Adidas Adizero Boston Boost 5 shoes felt today, and I think you should buy some as well." (*Adidas! Get in here and establish some brand value with the friend while her mind is vulnerable!*) Or some beautifully parseable phrase like "I need to fly on July thirteenth to Boston, returning on July twenty-third, and wish to spend no more than three hundred and fifty dollars." (*TripAdvisor! Get in here with a fare quote!*)

And when it does, things aren't as simple as they seem. I can almost guarantee you that when the text string "Obama" appears, in either a message or a post, in the Facebook equivalent of a bar in Alabama on a Friday night, half the time it is preceded by the word "fucking," and you probably shouldn't add that person to your "#Democratic Party" targeting cluster, unless you want him to X-out every goddamn smiling Obama photo that's going to take over his Facebook experience.* Which, incidentally, is going to make Obama ads' delivery tank due to all the negative feedback, which means their account manager will soon be emailing you wondering why they can't spend their budget, and fuck you, it's your problem, and you'll grow to hate every goddamned redneck

* Facebook Ads have clickable menu in their upper-right-hand corner, featuring an X button, which allows the user to leave negative feedback. That's used by Facebook to filter ads.

in Alabama, and the Obama campaign for monitoring its ads stats so closely.

Oh, ignore any mention of an interesting word with "fucking" preceding it? Brilliant idea. How about when a message says, "What a great president Obama turned out to be, eh?" accompanied by a smirk. You didn't see the smirk in the actual wording, of course. Damn. Last I checked, no one's written a HumanSarcasm code module that flags back-handed statements. And the Interwebs are rife with more sarcasm, lies, bad puns, and double-entendres than a high school cheerleaders' convention.

Oh, and by the way, you need to solve this problem in every language in the world, because that's how international Facebook is. How's your Tigrinya?

This last point is more than a rhetorically flip answer, and bears some scrutiny.

If you asked any Facebooker why he or she worked at the company, the first answer would be some variant of "the scale," "the magnitude"—essentially, the fact that Facebook had hundreds of millions, soon to be billions, of users. Someone on the non-ads, user-facing side of the company could launch any random feature or product, and instantly, by mere virtue of being on Facebook, you'd have hundreds of millions of users, despite its possibly being a bomb of a product (and Facebook was so boldly reckless, it launched lots of bombs). These were numbers unavailable anywhere except perhaps Google, numbers that dwarfed whatever startup you might have been at, where you were lucky if you got to a hundred thousand users.

That scale worked against you when you were on the ads side, though. It was clear from Gokul's management ethos, which was essentially "Go big or go home," that we were being tasked with finding the one breakout product, à la Google AdWords, that would completely change Facebook's fortunes. Given Facebook's revenues, which were already huge (remember: a billion times anything . . .), it was very difficult to make a dent in the income statement with any product.

Countless were the ideas suggested, either by some well-meaning engineer or salesperson, or even by members of the targeting team: mostly niche-use cases that would benefit some subspecies of advertiser, and generate all of maybe $20 million in revenue. That would be an awesome sum in a startup, as again would be fifty million users for your product right out of the gate, but it was nothing in a scheme of $2 billion in annual revenues, and not worth the effort to get it off the ground.

Bucketing users in a congressional district, and allowing political advertisers to target specific voting precincts?

Nope. Sounds good, but political budgets on Facebook were relatively small then, and materialized only every four years for an election.

Using a dictionary of Spanish names, along with the use of Spanish in messages originating in the United States, for a "Hispanic cluster," appealing to advertisers trying to cash in on that demographic segment with growing buying power?

Nope. Not that many people fall into the bucket, and, anyhow, tests didn't show much of an uptick in engagement with Hispanic ads. Users were as confused as delighted by them, and didn't click through.

Using geographic data to discern whether someone is traveling far from home, and then hitting that person with ads for the "travel-intender segment"—that is, that flavor of affluent business traveler who needs greater access to airfare and hotels?

Nope again! Geographic data is tricky for various reasons not worth exploring here, and it was clear our simple heuristics were not locating the guy with the corporate AmEx and a love of legroom and minibars.

Even if any of these had worked (and this is but a tiny sampling of the barrage of ideas discussed), the financial impact would still have been relatively small. Facebook's revenue in the early days almost doubled yearly, and even now it grows by a whopping 30 percent or more per year. To earn your beer money as product manager you had to move that revenue needle a good 5 percent or so. That was about $100 million in revenue per year you had to generate, the equivalent of two or three Wall Street traders at a bank like Goldman. Between your uptick, the 5 percent from Optimization, user growth of 20 percent, and whatever other 5 percent bumps from other new products, Facebook would have a good year.* But that meant the bar on ideas was very high indeed. Often, an unsexy idea that was programmatic and platform-wide, like the first iteration of Kitten, which merely classified your likes and interests better, had more impact than cool and whizzy ideas like political targeting. As product manager, you were like a portfolio manager, betting on sets of ideas, hoping to back a winner, often based on little more than intuition. To say I was following the Facebook dictum GET IN OVER YOUR HEAD was putting it mildly. I had no idea what I was doing, but neither did the other product managers, from what I could tell. We were all making it up as we went along, some of us more skillfully than others.

---

* Optimization was on the other side of the Ads data coin from targeting. The latter involves advertisers using their knowledge and user data to select which user sees which ad; the former involves the ad network (in this case, Facebook) using its data around user behavior to choose who sees which ad. The two exist in a frenemy relationship of both symbiosis and opposition. The network would rather control ad delivery itself via optimization; while the advertiser wants the power to control what it spends money on via targeting (as well as the ability to build a storehouse of in-house marketing knowledge). In a world of perfect optimization, targeting would be unnecessary (and vice versa).

Twice Bitten, Thrice Shy

> What man has bent o'er his son's sleep, to brood
> How that face shall watch his when cold it lies?
> Or thought, as his own mother kiss'd his eyes,
> Of what her kiss was when his father woo'd?
>
> —Dante Gabriel Rossetti, *The House of Life*

SEPTEMBER 3, 2011

A second birth is considerably less dramatic than the first. If still somewhat risky, you at least know the flavor of risk involved, and don't dupe yourself with the thought of somehow controlling the proceedings. It's a crapshoot—the umbilical cord could wrap itself around the baby's neck—and there's little you can do about it.

Since I had moved out of British Trader's to a temporary San Francisco sublet, I got news of the labor via phone, and raced back to the same maternity ward at Oakland's Kaiser Permanente hospital. This birth, unlike Zoë's, did not end in the time it took to watch an episode of *House of Cards*, but was the sort of slow slog I'd always feared.

Thirty tense and sleepy hours later, I had a son.

British Trader and I had the same deadlocked debate over names as we had with Zoë Ayala. The combined constraints of Hebrew and Hispanic cultures were impossible on the male side, so negotiations rapidly broke down into uncompromising personal favorites.

Then there was also the issue of circumcision. British Trader's Judaism demanded it, but she herself was equivocal. Taking one look at my son's little wee-wee, I suddenly reeled at the thought of circumcision.

You want to do what to it?

I traded veto rights on the first name (I still had full middle-name rights) for exclusive rights over the circumcision decision. British Trader chose her personal favorite, "Noah," which I liked both for being biblical and for the boatbuilding credentials implicit in the name.

I chose Pelayo for the middle name, after the eighth-century Visigoth nobleman who initiated the seven-century-long struggle to free Spain from Islamic rule. Thus did Noah Pelayo come into the world, and I was the father to a son as well as a daughter.

My father's advice, like perhaps the advice in this book, was typically prescriptive of precisely what *not* to do in life, and I generally ignored it. But occasionally he had moments of clear-eyed brilliance, letting instructive gems drop into the otherwise barren suburban wasteland of my childhood.

One such gem was discussing the matter of the then-burgeoning Miami drug trade. This was the go-go eighties, when wholesale drug trafficking was a semiviable career option in Miami, though a short-lived one, even for a family man. We had several in our loose social circle, including more than one neighbor, who were in that trade.

"The thing about being a *marimbero* isn't the personal

risk, it's the fact they can come after your family.* They could come after *you*," he said, pointing right at me.

It was well known that after a botched deal or missed shipment, *marimberos*, particularly those savages the Colombians, would come after your family, snatch your daughter or son, and mail you their fingers one after another until you paid up. My father stuck to the relatively low-margin business of buying and selling real estate instead, and my fingers remained safely attached.

This memory was rattling in my head when I pondered my new child and the woman who'd borne him. The British Trader romantic fire was still smoldering enough to be reignited if need be. But then, that would be doing the bourgeois family thing full-on, with combined finances, expectations of pricey schools, mortgages, the entire needy contraption of settled-down life. To me, only the man who needed nothing was truly free. Until I was financially independent (e.g., fuck-you money), or the captain of a profitable enterprise, I was merely a slave whose bondage was worth one or another price, locked in as much by diapers and tuition costs as by a vesting schedule.

Like being a Miami *marimbero*, working at Facebook and signing up for daddyhood presented a harsh trade-off, at least in my mind. Sure, it paid well, but if you cranked up your lifestyle to the level of your means, then you were beholden to your industry and the people who ran it. I was in deep

---

* *Marimbero* is Miami Cuban slang for a large-scale drug trafficker, equivalent to the more common term "narco." Of indeterminate origin, *la marimba* is slang for the drug trade as a whole (of which Miami can claim a healthy stake). Curiously, the standard Spanish (and English) meaning of "marimba" is a wooden xylophone-like instrument common in South America. It caused considerable confusion when I "moved" from Miami to the United States (i.e., moved away for college) and encountered an amateur musician who claimed to be terribly into the "muh-rim-buh." I was momentarily aghast.

reruns, dating from the Goldman days, of being surrounded by professional peers in hock to their pricey lifestyles. Facebook couldn't mail me Zoë's fingers until I came up with a new targeting idea, but they sure could pull the plug on the equity gravy train that was paying for Zoë's hypothetical $2,500/month preschool in Menlo Park. Did I really want to be the Willy Loman figure, coming home after a shitty day at work, having a beer, but thinking it all worthwhile after staring into Zoë's eyes, and then glumly taking the boss's shit (again) the next day? Because that's what it would be when we slapped the Bay Area mortgage, date night in Palo Alto, and two preschools onto the cash-flow statement.

All my Facebook colleagues in the over-thirty cohort were in that dependent boat. Facebook said jump and they could only ask "How high?" And jump they did, reciting whatever corporate script and leaping through whatever hoops their paymaster required, down to the logo-ed onesie they'd slap on their newborns, photos posted on Facebook to the online applause of their equally enslaved colleagues.

You'll no doubt find this argument self-serving, the ranting of a selfish cad trying to justify his egotism, and perhaps you're right. However, having grown to adulthood under a tyrannical father I loathed, and whose oppressive presence I never stopped dreaming of escaping, I found the thought of submitting to yet another master repugnant. Not to mention never wanting to relive any sort of family situation, as either child or parent, ever again, for the same reasons of personal history. I couldn't do it, no matter the paternal draw of vulnerable newborn Noah, nor the charms and wiles of always-clever Zoë.

Informally, British Trader and I worked out a payment schedule that complied with recommended California state child-support levels. Like the Civil War draft, in which the wealthy could pay a commoner to take their spot on the firing line, I paid my way out of fatherhood, mostly out of fear of the compromise to freedom it represented. I retained visitation rights, but those would be conditional on my always rocky relationship with British Trader. It would suck, but I was ambiguous about my suitability as a father anyhow (as was British Trader). From my own experience, better no father than a bad father.

On the domestic front, I was still living in a string of temporary sublets around San Francisco's Mission District, but matters would soon become more "anchored." I bought a thirty-seven-foot sailboat with the up-front cash component of the Facebook deal. The boat was somewhat improbably located in Baltimore, so I had it trucked across the United States to Oakland, where I rerigged and launched it, after months of working in the boatyard. Finding moorage at the southernmost marina in the San Francisco Bay Area, a few miles north of Facebook in Redwood City, I commuted to work from my *Miami Vice*-esque bohemia via bicycle. As stated, my decision to live on a sailboat was based less on a desire for eccentric living, and more on a visceral rejection of the bougie lifestyle that was otherwise my lot. If I had a boat to go back to, Facebook could dominate my life only so much (or so I thought). The open ocean always awaited beckoningly, whispering at me to undo the dock lines and go.

Also, where else could I live in the Bay Area for $700 per month?

Ads Five-Oh

> There are 3 universal symbols on this planet: the dollar sign $, tits, and the soccer ball.
>
> —Po Bronson, "Game Day at San Quentin"

NOVEMBER 1, 2011

In the waning weeks of 2011, Facebook continued to strain mightily under the specter of Google Plus. Initial usage numbers, published by Google, were eye-popping, claiming hundreds of millions of users, and embodying every Facebooker's worst nightmare of being overwhelmed by the Mountain View company's greater engineering numbers, not to mention its still-dominant position as the default website to the world.

Professionally, I had well and truly been assimilated (at least overtly). My everyday work uniform had devolved to jeans, T-shirt, and a Facebook zipped fleece, a uniform that was conspicuous even by Facebook-grunt standards.* Work-wise, I continued my Sisyphean task of somehow recycling user data to increase our low clickthrough rates. Facebook ads at that point were ugly, small, postage-stamped-sized

* One Halloween, Ben Reesman, an ads engineer we'll meet later, came dressed as me as a costume. His choice of ratty jeans and fleece was dead-on (we took a side-by-side photo and posted it to Facebook, of course).

picture-and-text combinations on the far right side of the user's screen, mostly ignored by users. The thought of commercial content inside the News Feed was still sacrilegious, and not mentioned in polite company. The mere thought of using outside data in Facebook ads delivery was similarly heretical, and not even considered.

In this chaotic period, before the imposed revenue and product discipline of the IPO period, the Facebook Ads product team continued to move to the haphazard beat of Gokul's leadership. PMs were often randomly bequeathed products after another product manager had left, been fired, or was transferred to some other project, whether or not they had any qualification to lead that team, or if that product should even exist. Via that product roulette, I came to manage the Ads Review and Quality team, in addition to the Ads Targeting team. Like the Department of Homeland Security, Ads Review and Quality had a grandiloquent title that couched a good amount of power, but also a fair amount of day-to-day slapstick incompetence. Similar to the noble souls who defend our borders, Ads Review (for short) was the guardian of the Facebook Ads team, sussing out obscene ads, click fraud, payment fraud, and every flavor of shenanigan where money was converted into blue-bannered pixels.

The team consisted of two overworked engineers, coding everything from the front-end user interfaces that fraud specialists used to patrol ads to the sophisticated machine-learning algorithms used to launch them onto a potential consumer's screen. It also involved risk and fraud teams in Austin, Texas, and Hyderabad, India. These operations "specialists," who did the actual scanning of preprocessed and prefiltered photos, were trained to spot violations of Facebook Ads policy. Some violations were tame; including text in an image, which advertisers would do to cram in more alarming ad copy, was one. Some were more universal in the Bronsonian sense. One violation we memorably failed to catch was an Israeli manicuring salon that ran a photo of a woman's very well groomed pubis. It was so sleek and almost abstract, the reviewer failed to see what it was.

In cases like this, the review function was effectively crowdsourced by the users themselves. Angry pearl-clutchers everywhere would click the X in the upper-right-hand corner of the ad, and indignantly leave feedback. The software would calculate rates of negative feedback, weighting the most egregious reasons cited most heavily—misleading, offensive, or sexually inappropriate (MOSI, for short)—and triggering a rereview of that ad. A rejection would propagate to all versions of that image inside the ads system, minimizing the amount of human intervention required, and avoiding a duplication of effort.

Unscrupulous advertisers had their wiles, however, reformatting images or changing things like colors or focus slightly, so that a bit-by-bit comparison would fail to equate an already flagged photo with a "new" image that had just been submitted. By changing the image at the bit level, they avoided the filter, even if the image looked roughly the same to the human eye. To counteract this gaming, the photo-comparison software that propagated decisions had to be made fuzzy and inexact to account for this. Machine-learning models were trained to find obvious signs of scams in ad copy ("free iPad" was one such telltale). The user interfaces were constantly improved to make the human reviewers' tasks easier and more efficient, so that we wouldn't need to hire more expensive humans.

It was a terrible assignment for anybody who wanted to make his or her mark at Facebook, and it would take me months to scheme myself out of it. But before that, I had to appear as the face of this ads police department, one of the airport security lines at Facebook.

Ads Review and Quality was officially part of Product and Engineering, but it worked for Sales and Operations, which was Sheryl's grand fiefdom. Sheryl, of course, was much more than merely Zuck's consigliera and the Ads team's intercessor within the senior management stratum of the company. She was the able leader of this vast, multitiered organization, with an ever-shifting cast of names and titles spanning the geographically fragmented organization. This world encompassed everything from senior ad executives closing deals with Coca-Cola to junior-user operations people deleting a fake account. In many ways, this was the boiler room of the Facebook money machine, or at least its human-powered factory floor, and Sheryl was its unquestioned overseer.

Every quarter Sheryl scheduled a gargantuan meeting meant to show off the wonderful tools engineering was building for Sales, and how well the hybrid engineering-operations teams were collaborating. Sheryl's managerial prowess was on full display in these powwows, as she skillfully held court among the assembled lieutenants of the various subrealms. Picking up subtle psychological cues from an off-the-cuff remark here, unearthing some lingering issue that lay dormant over there, making sure every voice was heard but no voice heard too much, tamping down some burst of irrelevant drama to keep the action moving, the woman knew how to run a roomful of big names and even bigger egos.

The meeting was held in the PC Load Letter conference room, which was one of the cavernous spaces used for only the largest or most senior meetings.* Sheryl sat at the fifty-yard line of the football-field-sized table, with Don Faul at

---

* Facebook conference room names were grouped geographically into themes, often joke mash-ups, like portmanteau malapropisms. For example, one theme combined Star Wars with alcoholic drinks, producing such gems as Jar Jar Drinks, Sith on the Beach, and (my favorite) It's a Trappe! In this case, "PC Load Letter" (which was an error message on old laser printers, and which triggered a printer-destroying mob in that comedic classic *Office Space*) stood for "paper cassette load letter," and (I presume, though can't remember) other nearby conference rooms partook of the same theme.

her right hand. Faul was a former Marine platoon leader and Googler who ran Online Operations, the busy human workflow of keeping the nontechnical side of an ads machine going. He resembled a more strapping version of Don Draper.

I sat at the twenty-five-yard line, near the screen where we'd be projecting. The room started filling quickly with pairs or triplets of product managers, eng managers, and ops managers. Mark Rabkin was there as my engineering analogue, one of the first engineering hires in Facebook Ads, and a man who'd soon assume a real importance in the organization. Also there was David Clune, the operational head of the Austin-based ads police, and the one who had done most of the work on the slides I'd be presenting.

First up in the Sheryl show was a product manager named Dan Rubinstein. Dan resembled a Woody Allen figure: short, thin, nebbish, but without the crackling anxiety. Also a former Googler, he seemed like one of those old PM hands who always made sure to take good notes and get his weekly report in on time. He fronted for User Ops, which was the user police, and the user-facing version of what I did on the ads side. Ever wonder why your feed never features any form of porn or otherwise grotesque imagery? It's because a team in User Ops has managed to sift through the billion photos uploaded a day, and pick out a pile of offensive needles in an Internet scale haystack.

On the screen now, Dan launched a demo of a tool that was essentially that: on loading the Web app, a raft of user photos appeared, which a User Ops "analyst" could easily click to eliminate, like plucking weeds from a garden. That image would be banished forever, including versions with small color changes or cropping done by veteran spammers and sketchy ad types. As he walked the room through the demo, he would click on an image of a kitten—kittens evidently represented the porny pictures they'd normally filter—and that kitten would be gone, as well as all variants of that kitten image. Click, ban, reload, click, ban, reload. A well-oiled kitten-banning machine, ladies and gentlemen.

Suddenly Sheryl interrupted: "So, what's with all the kittens?"

Dan, a bit startled, peered at Sheryl, clearly confused.

"Why are all the bad photos kittens?"

Dan flatly replied, "We use kittens as the bad photos in demos, because the real bad photos are . . . you know . . . kind of obscene."

"Right," said Sheryl, "but why kittens and not something else?"

The room was deathly silent with thirty-plus sets of twitchy eyes rising from barely concealed phones and laptops to stare at Dan and his kitten-banning machine. You could almost hear everyone mentally asking in chorus: *Yeah, what is it with the kittens?*

Dan looked up at the screen as if noticing the kitten pics for the first time, and then turned to Sheryl and answered, almost under his breath:

"Well . . . for demo purposes we don't show really bad photos . . . so the engineers use kittens instead. Because, you know . . . kittens and cats are like, pu—"

He stopped right there, but he almost said "pussy" in front of the Queen of Lean, Sheryl Sandberg.

"Got it!" she expectorated. After sucking in a lungful of air, as if loading for a verbal barrage, she continued. "If there were women on that team, they'd NEVER, EVER choose those photos as demo pics. I think you should change them immediately!"

Before the salvo had even finished Dan's head was bowed, and he was madly taking notes in a small notebook. CHANGE PUSSY PHOTOS NOW! one imagined they read. He looked like a forty-year-old scolded child.

I was dying inside. You could feel either awkwardness or

repressed laughter seething from everyone in the room at this unprecedented display of management wrath and PM folly. Demoing the pussy filter to Sheryl. *Epic!*

Dan limped along with the rest of his demo, and then it was my turn. After that high-water mark of incompetence, it was hard to fuck things up. I glided through the slides, lingering on the money shot: a plot of the number of ads reviewed versus human man-hours. The former was up and to the right (MOAR ADS!), the latter was flat (fewer expensive humans!). All was right with the Ads Review world. I drowsed through the other presentations and bolted at the first opportunity.

Ads Review was but one of the security teams at Facebook charged with the monumental task of protecting one-fourth of the Internet globally—which is what Facebook represents—from scammers, hucksters, pornographers, sexual predators, violent criminals, and every kind of human detritus. It's a noble struggle (despite my lack of enthusiasm for engaging in it myself), and one whose combatants work mostly in the shadows. As with all police or spy agencies, the failures of the Facebook security teams were widely trumpeted, but successes rarely heralded. You moan about your friend's breast-feeding photo being flagged, but fail to notice the complete lack of porn in your News Feed. It's a thankless job that appeals to those with a certain shepherd-dog mentality, or simply to people who, *Dexter*-like, are themselves rogues and black-hat hackers who'd rather use their skills for good.

Our social shadow warriors did have one showcase: there was an internal Facebook group with the provocative name of "Scalps@Facebook." It was essentially an online trophy case of taxidermied delinquents, the sexual predators, stalkers, and wife-beaters whom the FB security team, in conjunction with law enforcement, had managed to catch.

The weird thing about it was that the posts featured profile photos of the alleged criminals, along with somewhat gloating accounts of how the "perp" had been hunted down, and which local law enforcement agencies had collaborated. And so Facebook employees would randomly see in their feed the guilty face of depraved desire: some guy in the Philippines or Arkansas, and his rap sheet about trying to induce fourteen-year-old girls to meet him, along with a line or two indicating he had been summarily dispatched into the maw of the legal system.

So why doesn't Facebook make more of this safeguarding role?

I don't know the official answer, but I can speculate. If Facebook were to publicize its very real efforts at stopping crime, people might associate the blue-framed window with the thought of some predatory creeper. As is, many people have an ambiguous relationship with Facebook.

Just imagine the headline: "Facebook Catches 36 Sexual Predators This Month." Some bespectacled fortysomething mother in Wisconsin, hair in a bun and pearls tightly gripped, announces to her husband: "Honey, I just know we should get Meghan off that Facebook thing, look, it's just crawling with perverts."

This is, of course, a ridiculous view. Nobody thinks AT&T should be shut down when criminals use the phone system to commit a crime, or the US Postal Service regulated when a terrorist sends a bomb through the mail. But the average Facebook user considers the service to be some sort of frivolous toy, rather than a social utility on par with running water, and therefore thinks we can just shut it down if it seems to harbor any hint of criminality.

Like the CIA not exactly advertising the drone strike that vaporized a vehicle in some godforsaken land and prevented the next terrorist tragedy from happening, Facebook keeps quiet all it does for users to protect them from humanity's worst. Whine if you must about the odd erroneously flagged post, but spare a thought for the Facebook security team, those dedicated geeks in the watchtower. They've likely put away as many (if not more) bad guys than your local law enforcement agency, and they keep their vigilant guard with nary a thanks from users. Perhaps just once, marvel at your Facebook experience, at its almost total lack of pornography, spam, hate speech, and general human detritus, and consider what spectacular systems and expertise must exist for a few hundred people to safeguard the online experience of 1.5 billion users, fully a fifth of humanity, on a continual, 24/7 basis.

The Narcissism of Privacy

> While he [Narcissus] is drinking he beholds himself reflected in the mirrored pool—and loves; loves an imagined body which contains no substance, for he deems the mirrored shade a thing of life to love.
>
> But why, O foolish boy, so vainly catching at this flitting form? Avert your gaze and you will lose your love, for this that holds your eyes is nothing save the image of yourself reflected back to you. It comes and waits with you; it has no life; it will depart if you will only go.
>
> —Ovid, *The Metamorphoses*

DECEMBER 2011

If this stretch of Facebook life seems chaotic in its random divagations, that's because it was random and unpredictable.

Life as a Facebook product manager was less being a lieutenant in some stolid industry juggernaut, and more being buffeted by constant external and internal forces. The external forces were the ever-present machinations of Google, the general temperature of the advertising world with respect to Facebook's marketing offerings, and the fortunes of Facebook's social media vision (e.g., were teenagers still using it?).

The internal forces were the fluctuations in your standing in the impromptu hierarchy of people and products inside Gokul-land, as well as the fate of the products you managed and nursed to success (or at least to quick failure).

Particularly on my beat, we were constantly sprinting half-blind through a minefield of potential legal problems, and encouraged to do so as the risky cost of innovation. For my entire career at Facebook, I was embroiled in a rolling debate with the Facebook privacy and legal teams about what we could and couldn't get away with, chiseling away at their legal trepidation, and trying to find some legal rubric that would forgive (or at least defensibly excuse) our next depredation with user data.

One day, though, and with little prompting on our part, that all came to one of those do-or-die confrontations, of which Facebook had many in its bustling drive toward Internet domination.

One of the oddities of Wall Street trading-desk life is the rapid recalibration of monetary value. Everything—whether profit or risk—is measured in units of millions of dollars, commonly called a "buck": "We lost ten bucks on that Greece trade"; "Johnny Dickhead's bonus this year was two bucks." A sum that's twenty times the median US family income becomes the basic unit of account, beyond which (if you're being punctilious) you can use decimals.

Facebook enjoyed a similar embarrassment of riches, but in users, not dollars. I never heard the use of any bundling term like "buck," but sums of millions of users were splashed around between products and test groups like chips at a one- or two-dollar poker table. What would have been an important user milestone for any consumer startup became the most minimal unit of account inside Facebook.

As a geographic tangent: New Zealand was commonly used as a test bed for new user-facing products. It was perfect due to its English-language usage, its relative isolation in terms of the social graph (i.e., most friend links were internal to the country), and, frankly, its lack of newsworthiness, so any gossip or reporting of new Facebook features ran a low risk of leaking back to the real target markets of the United States and Europe. *Aotearoa* is the original Maori word for New Zealand, which roughly translated means "Facebook test set." Thus does that verdant island nation, graced with stunning fjords and clear alpine lakes, sample whatever random product twiddle a twenty-three-year-old Facebook engineer in Menlo Park dreams up.

Of course, in the ads world, matters were rather different. As we've discussed previously, all users are certainly not created equal from the monetization perspective. Facebook made the vast majority of its revenue in the United States and Europe; other countries represented but a trickle. Immature advertising markets, the embryonic state of their e-commerce infrastructure, and their lower general wealth meant the impact of new optimization tricks or targeting data on those countries was minimal. And so the Ads team would slice off tranches of the FB user base in rich ads markets and dose them with different versions of the ads system to measure the effect of a new feature, as you would test subjects in a clinical drug trial.* The performance metrics of interest included clickthrough rates, which are a coarse measure of user interest. More convincing is the actual downstream monetization resulting from someone clicking through and buying something—assuming Facebook got

* This sort of split testing, known as A/B testing, is common for any Internet app or website. In a careful and conscientious company, it's how any sort of change is tested, either for user engagement or for things like server load due to a code change.

the conversion data, which it often didn't, given that Facebook didn't have a conversion-tracking system.

Also important, and not related to money at all, was overall usage. As you didn't want to burn out users with excessive or distracting ads, monetization and usage often existed in a zero-sum trade-off that was difficult to juggle.

After enough time had passed, all these metrics—clickthrough, monetization, usage, and so forth—would then be compared between test and normal sets. The bigger the sliver used in the test set, the less time you had to wait, as the "data velocity" was higher. Then the product tweak would be declared a success or failure, and either expanded to 100 percent of the user base, reworked, or abandoned. Facebook Ads was spinning so many product plates at once, there was always a decent chunk of the user base unwittingly serving as test subjects, even if each individual test was small.

There was ongoing concern that so much experimentation might adversely affect Facebook's top-line revenue, by damaging the user experience somehow. Therefore, the fraction of the user base that could be tested would every so often be capped. When that happened, the engineers would horse-trade among themselves parts of the user base to test their new changes. It was quantified in terms of percentages, of course, but if you translated those percentages into numbers, you'd realize the scale of the haggling.

"Look, I'll give you my Belgium, but I need a Czech Republic or maybe a Guatemala in return."

"Nah, not good enough, man. I need like at least a Malaysia to get an answer by tomorrow."

(They wouldn't literally say this, to be clear, nor were they haggling over specific countries—merely their population magnitudes in terms of percent of users—but that was the scale involved in the ordinary, day-to-day testing of even the most trivial feature, like expanding the size of the image in an ad by five pixels.)

In the midst of all this monkeying around on the part of the Ads team, I was sucked into my first serious privacy kerfuffle. Ireland was the official European Union regulator of Facebook data and privacy policies, and its data protection agency (DPA) was conducting a thorough audit of Facebook's ads targeting. As part of my role as shit umbrella/product manager for ads targeting, I had the unwelcome duty to be in on every call and meeting with some guy named Gary, who was evidently the one-man data protection office there.

How the land of suffocating Catholicism and potato famines came to be the regulator of the biggest accumulation of personal data since DNA is a curious story. Ireland, following its rise as the "Celtic Tiger" in the mid-aughts and subsequent property crash, actively encouraged American companies to choose Dublin as their European base. Ireland offered tax incentives (the corporate tax rate was very low), an educated (and desperate for work) talent pool, and a rational legal framework. The net result was that the waterfront docks east of Dublin became colonized by US tech companies like Facebook, Google, and Airbnb, each running (mostly) its sales and operations teams out of gleaming new high-rise offices. Facebook occupied several floors, each decorated with a European flag marking the spot where that country's sales and ops team lived. The joke was that the Facebook Dublin office was the Noah's ark of the EU: if continental Europe was consumed in some cataclysm, it could be repopulated with the breeding pairs located under each flag in the office. And yes, we had breeding pairs, as the office's gender ratio was true to life, unlike that at the corporate mother ship, which was a never-ending sausage party.

Given that Facebook was an Irish entity within the EU, the deal with the Europeans was that it would be (mostly) up to the Irish to police that ever-present bugbear of underworked EU bureaucrats, our data and privacy policy. Despite the fact that the entire continent was unable to itself produce even a single consumer Internet company of global scope, Europe did reserve the right to control how those (American) companies did business.

So the Irish, 4.5 million people who wouldn't even fill a Facebook test set, had us by the databases, and we needed to placate them. In an unusual move, Ireland and Facebook decided to publish the results of the audit, so you're free to read the conclusions of the official report. The net of it was that certain types of targeting that FB had toyed with, though not fully deployed, had to be discontinued by the end of the agreed audit period, which was late December. We had a couple of weeks to sort it all out and make sure we were on the right side of the Irish.

Given the impenetrable code and data sprawl, I asked one of the grandfathers of Ads, Rong Yan, who had been at Facebook all of two years, if we were engaged in any of the type of targeting we had agreed to discontinue. Rong, whose word was law about how the Ads system worked, categorically denied we were actively doing so, saying we had at most experimented with it in the past. Satisfied, I had assured the Irish and the senior Ads team there was no need to worry about that point in the deal.

Here's the great lesson for you, aspiring product manager:

The principal reason for you to be technical is not to help technically design the system under development; if you're doing that, then you're PMing wrong. No, you're technical so you can tell when engineers are bullshitting you, which will be often. At times it's accidental (as it was with Rong), due to either miscommunication, bad memory, or wishful thinking (engineers are as inclined to it as anybody). Sometimes it's more stealthy, their passive-aggressive way to disagree with the product direction ("That'll eat up all our servers"), or laziness ("It's impossible to build that"). The PM is there to give a sniff test to any such product-killing assertion.

The final day of the Irish data agreement dawned, by which time Facebook had agreed to implement all necessary changes, and I was fairly pleased at having finally done my part to settle the Facebook corporate colostomy we'd undergone. A little paranoid itch, almost like an extrasensory tingling doubt, made me wonder if we had really covered all the bases, despite the number of engineering conversations that had transpired. After all, I had stuck my neck out to assure both the Irish data authority and Facebook management that the targeting team was completely in compliance with our binding framework, and they had accepted my word.

That tingle growing, I opened up a terminal window, the basic command-line screen (imagine what you've seen in more than one computer-hacker movie) that was still how you accessed many remote Facebook servers.

I knew enough about how the back-end Ads system worked to log in and poke around the various machines. The targeting tables defined what targeting segments the Facebook Ads system used, and formed the logical glue connecting the eyeballs to the buckets of money. If the database tables underlying the targeting logic were inconsistent (e.g., certain table rows were missing when they shouldn't have been), ads targeting would cease to function, and ads would no longer be shown with every Facebook page.

Note: the existence of this targeting was not at issue—Facebook had been completely transparent with the Irish—merely its persistence beyond the agreed-upon cutoff date and time. Which at this point was in a couple of hours, assuming I had my time zones right.

On this otherwise sleepy Christmas Eve day 2011, the new Ads team area, fresh from our move from the dingy California Avenue building—more on that later—was absolutely empty except for one engineer: Hong Ge.

Hong Ge was the best-dressed man at Facebook, the aesthetic counterpoint to the schlubby hoodie-and-jeans uniform that reigned at the company, even among women. With his fitted blazers and flamboyant collared shirts, he reminded me of the hero in a Hong Kong action film. I imagined him decimating a roomful of goons with well-placed roundhouse kicks, saving the girl and the briefcase with the secret documents, then driving out in a Ferrari to Facebook, where he sat in front of a computer and made the Ads system work.

"Hey, Hong . . . you mind looking over my shoulder for a second and making sure I don't do something stupid? It's kind of important."

It was a simple command to execute. Routine really, if it wasn't for the fact it was on a live production database, and formed the heart of $2 billion in spend. And the fact I hadn't written an SQL write command in a good couple of years. Fuck this up, and it would be a SEV1, a severity-level-one bug, meaning whoever was on call would be roused from whatever bed, toilet, vacation beach, or drunken stupor they found themselves in, and asked to scramble and save the FB ship.

You're a product manager: all of the responsibility, none of the power. Fix it.

I typed UPDATE TABLE SET . . . and so on, nuking every possible piece of forbidden targeting.

"That look good, Hong?"

Hong peered at my command line through his designer glasses.

"Yeah! Looks good . . ."

Deep breath. Raise a prayer to the Virgin Mary of ALTER, Our Lady of the MySQL Commands.

<enter>

The lights flickered in the ads space.

Actually, no, they didn't. But my heart did skip a beat. A few minutes passed. A quick look at the real-time dashboards revealed that all was right with the world. We hadn't just short-circuited the Facebook money machine.

"Great!" said Hong, and he went back to his desk.

Fuck me, and the Irish, and the Irish data protection

commissioner. I closed my laptop and left Hong to hold down the fort. Time for a beer at Rose & Crown.

"Facebook is showing me an ad for X, and what do I care about that? Look how bad their ads targeting is."

Or: "Facebook just showed me an ad for nail polish, and I had my nails done yesterday and texted my friend about it. Are they reading my texts, or are they looking at satellite photos, and tracking me?"

How many times have you heard some variant of these questions?

The reality is that Facebook isn't showing you anything.

Here's what people don't understand about advertising. Facebook is simply a routing system, almost like an old-time telephone exchange, that delivers a message for money. The address on that message can be approximate (e.g., males aged thirty-five in Ohio), or it can be specific (e.g., the person who just shopped for a specific pair of shoes on Zappos). But either way, Facebook didn't make the match of user and message, and at most decides secondary things like how often the ad is seen in general, or which of two ads addressed to you is seen that particular instant. In this sense, ads on Facebook are no different from phone calls or emails. We receive commercial versions of both in the form of spam and telemarketing calls. And yet, when we get a penis-enlargement email, nobody blames Google for providing Gmail, does he? Nor do you blame AT&T for the marketing call that distracted you from *Game of Thrones.* The only difference is that while people commonly make phone calls and write emails, few if any people address and post an ad. Like infants who haven't learned object permanence yet, the Facebook whiners see an ad, the Facebook logo, and assume it's all connected. Make the ad go away, and they don't even think about it. Of course, what they should really be thinking about is how that ad got addressed, and what the advertiser, and not Facebook, knows about them.

Facebook is actually the least of their worries, and it's about the only dog in the fight that ultimately cares about the user. Unsurprisingly, those who kvetch the most about irrelevant ads are also the same bellyachers who complain when ads are too good, and seem *creepy*. No doubt, the slightly technically savvy among them are also running ad-blocking software, and advocate against the increased data collection that would improve ads and make them more relevant. If they were to publish content themselves, or work in the business of delivering all of humanity's digitized social life 24/7 all over the world, they'd realize there's a human cost to that blue-framed browser tab, and it most certainly is not free. Ad blocking is tantamount to theft, or at the very least running a toll booth without paying.

Oh, and spare me your claims that you'd be willing to pay for Facebook instead of seeing ads. It's not even clear what Facebook should charge you. The whole point of the ad auction and the dynamic marketplace for your attention is figuring that out. Setting a usage fee would be like IBM declaring it's going to pick an individual price for every investor who wants to buy a share, rather than leaving the price discovery to the open market of a stock exchange. Advertising is the only reliable business model that's worked for all but a handful of publishers, and those only among the elite, content-producing ranks of *The Economist* and the *Wall Street Journal*, who manage to charge their users. If you want to interact with the world via the Internet, then deal with ads.

Privacy is to Facebook as nuclear weapons are to Iran: this constant cloud overhead, obsessed over by outsiders even if poorly understood, and the starting point of pretty much any conversation with an outside player. As Facebook's use of your data for moneymaking purposes appeared to have been a concern of every busybody nonprofit activist and government bureaucrat, this meant a good quarter of my time was spent thinking about legal issues, and strategizing with Facebook's privacy team. If a product changes a way Facebook uses data (and if as a product manager you're not pushing the boundaries of data usage, you're not doing your job), then you'll likely be gated by Facebook's data policy. Data policy changes are an orchestrated production on the order of the Academy Awards, and not to be taken lightly. The fact that a billion users have never even read the user agreement they've consented to is immaterial. The world's lawyers certainly have, and that's the real intended audience of that document.

Not that this mattered much. Here was the reality: there were almost no legal precedents covering any of this newfangled data-privacy stuff, and that juridical gap was filled by self-serving "standards organizations" that nominally imposed a rational order, but in reality only served some agenda. Thus, as with product itself, Facebook and every major ads player that had the leverage to define its terms (e.g., Google, Apple) were making it up as they went along.

Think that's nuts? Get this.

Thanks to a privacy brouhaha in 2009, Zuck had pledged that any future changes to the data policy would be voted—*voted!*—on by users. So when we gave up trying to squeeze money from the rock of Facebook-only data, and expanded radically the usage of data by the Ads team, it was necessary to hold a referendum. Yes, really. Digital democracy, citizens of Facebook-land!

And so in late 2011 Facebook held an election. Among the measures up for voting was . . . abolishing elections forever. Democracy could opt to commit suicide. Asking people about changes to data policy is like asking about changes to the IRS tax code: the policy in question is a big, hairy beast nobody really understands, and by default people want to keep the status quo rather than think about some uncertain future change. Fortunately for Facebook, one of the original stipulations in the offer of democracy stated that 30 percent of the user base had to participate in order for the result to be binding. By 2011, Facebook's user base was over a billion, which meant about 300 million people—almost three times the number of voters in the most recent US presidential election—needed to participate. The chances were slim, but who knew? If some cat video could go viral, or those meaningless declarations about owning your data that seemed to sweep across Facebook every year like the flu, then maybe voting could too.

We needn't have worried. The adoption of the new policy lost by a landslide: 90 percent of voters were *against* the new data policy that Facebook needed to survive. But . . . almost nobody voted. Not even close to 30 percent of users. As such, the voting result was "taken under advisement"—by which we mean "ignored." And be grateful we did; Facebook would be in trouble right now otherwise, as the company-saving products that launched later would have been impossible under the old data policy.

Despite all this drama, despite getting every legal detail correct, there was still the public-relations heat around privacy to deal with, usually of the most obtuse variety. Let me give you an example, culled from early FB memory:

I would constantly get pings from the harried Facebook PR team about targeting functionality, after the *Los Angeles Times* or whoever asked *them* about our targeting abilities. The product manager was always the last hop on the buck-passing chain, so deal with it, PM.

The story usually ran as follows: the journalist, or one of her "sources," had seen ads for the San Francisco 49ers after her husband's cousin's college roommate posted a photo of himself in a 49ers jersey. *Were we using uploaded photos in our ads targeting!!??*

This was like being accused of fathering Scarlett Johansson's love child. I wish I could even reasonably be suspected of pulling that off.

Think about it for a moment. Picking out a football

jersey on some crappy cellphone photo and determining the accurate associated and commercially interesting topic (e.g., the 49ers), and assigning it to the right member of your family/social tree who shares that interest, based on reams of random drivel you've shared on Facebook, would be an image-recognition and machine-learning feat on the order of the moon landing. Facebook ads targeting is so simple, this was a preposterous thought, but no number of denials kept the journalists with their *ah-ha!* anecdotes from pressing their case.

The real answer, of course, was that the 49ers were playing that weekend, explaining both the jersey-wearing by the cousin and the fact the 49ers' agency was running a widely targeted marketing campaign.

The major misunderstanding here is that people seem to think that data that would embarrass them or pain them to reveal, or would otherwise just be creepy to imagine in someone else's hands, possesses commercial value. Look: Facebook could have a video of you fornicating wildly with a frisky German shepherd, with your Social Security number and bank details written in lipstick on the dog's back, while some deep voice in the background read out your deepest, darkest secrets from childhood and adolescence, and you know what? No advertiser would give a shit. They would, however, love to know what movie you saw on Netflix last night, what's in your Amazon shopping cart, every item you scrutinized when you last visited Best Buy, and how long it's been since you bought a car (and which car). They also want to know what mobile devices and browsers you use and every website you visit, so they can serve and track media on each aforementioned device. Almost nothing of what you share on Facebook—sweet nothings to your mistress, photos of you passed out on a couch, your secret brownie recipe—is worth anything in commercial terms. So even assuming perfectly evil behavior on Facebook's part, the company would have no use for it.

Facebook doesn't sell your data; it buys it. It does this by providing services to advertisers that incentivize them to let Facebook ingest the data you've generated outside Facebook. In fact, as we'll soon see, Facebook is one of the most jealous guardians of user data known to man. It is a black hole of data that can never leave.

All Facebook's technology is designed thusly, and that will never change. If you stop for a moment and realize how suicidally stupid it would be for Facebook to hand over its data on users to anyone, for any amount of money, you'll realize how tired that "Facebook sells your data" meme is.

Are We Savages or What?

> He who makes a beast of himself gets rid of the pain of being a man.
>
> —Samuel Johnson

DECEMBER 15, 2011

Like hermit crabs, successful companies outgrow a series of larger and larger shells.

By late 2011, the 1601 California Avenue location was feeling tight. People were packed in nut-to-butt in the Ads area, and the whole building was looking a bit run-down. This was typical of any busy tech company too focused on the metrics that mattered to bother with what appeared to be the carpet stains from a double homicide lingering in a corner (and was really hastily cleaned happy-hour vomit). The conference rooms stunk of sweat from too many people sleeping in them (or something) and the café was overcrowded like a soup kitchen.

The Facebook *nomenklatura* decided that we should move, and the New Jerusalem of Facebook was to be the abandoned remains of that tech has-been Sun Microsystems. Given the sad state of that campus, the company would have to move in stages, with the engineering teams arriving last.

When it was finally our turn, of course, nobody had actually prepared for the move, despite the email we'd all gotten weeks before from the facilities team that was managing the pilgrimage. Come the final moment, around four thirty p.m. (we were to be out of the building by five o'clock), all hell broke loose.

People started stuffing their accumulated detritus into cardboard boxes. First it was all the shit on their desks. If you lived at Facebook, you kept lots of books, the odd girlfriend photo, stuffed animals of indeterminate origin, corporate swag like mugs or mouse pads accumulated from sales conferences, maybe random stuff you'd made in off-site corporate team-building events. Then it was the team toys like skateboards and Nerf guns. Then it was the area decorations that seemed to sprout like moss around any Facebook product team: posters from the Analog Research Laboratory, gag props like a plywood altar to your engineering manager (yes, really), or the local speakeasy liquor cabinet.

Then suddenly it was kind of everything, and it wasn't just going into moving boxes. People were prying the corporate artwork off the walls, snagging the conference room name tags, and stuffing it all into laptop bags, garbage bags, whatever else they were planning to haul home.

Things got so out of control that at one point Aileen Cureton, the one admin for Ads (back when there was one for the whole team, rather than one per executive), stood up, and in her best attempt at a Marine drill-sergeant voice, started bellowing at the rampaging vandals to put down all the shit they were hauling off. Her bellows went unheeded; within the span of a quarter hour, the office had been picked clean.

Having been in a few violent demonstrations and riots (thanks to time spent studying in the Basque country in the late nineties), I couldn't quite say this was slouching toward the real car-burning, rubber-bullets-flying mayhem of legit group violence, but it was about as close as American corporate culture surely got in its early-twenty-first-century dotage.

Then an idea occurred.

There was one series of conference rooms close to Zuck and the high command whose names were supposedly inspired by the series of countries that had "tipped" to Facebook usage during the time the building was occupied, including the *madre patria* of the misbegotten Hispanic race, the original homeland of my people. Wouldn't the area around the presidential palace fall last to the revolutionary violence? Perhaps it was still there. . . .

I threaded my way through the pillaging mayhem and ran into Mick Johnson, the original YC comrade who had kicked off my Facebook story with his official intro and unofficial advice, who was wearing a smile and carrying AUSTRALIA in his hands. Rushing down the halls to the cluster of conference rooms in question, I found hastily detached sticky tape on one door after another. Almost all of the plaques were gone.

But not the one I wanted.

Whipping out the rigging knife I always carried, I pried against the drywall, levering the sign off. Tucking it into the front of my pants and under my Facebook fleece like a shoplifter, I made my way back to Ads just under Aileen's furious radar.

When the riot finally quieted down as everyone abandoned the building, I headed back to the boat and installed SPAIN (complete with textured braille) along the series of portholes on the starboard side. Its bright yellow corporate sterility and sans serif font offset the warm, rich browns of mahogany and cedar. All that matters in the end is what we take away from an experience—even if pried off the wall with a weathered rigging knife.

For whatever reason, Facebook always had a fascination with graffiti office art. Early on, Sean Parker, an early Svengali at Facebook who had been Zuck's adviser and temporary CEO, and who was memorably played by Justin Timberlake in *The Social Network*, had asked a noted muralist, David Choe, to paint sexually themed murals at the original Facebook offices in downtown Palo Alto. They were reputedly somewhat toned down in the final implementation. Now, years later, the same artist would be hired to decorate the bare expanses of white drywall in the new campus's reception and meeting areas—in part, I imagine, as a remedy to the fiasco that was about to take place.

With no warning, a few weeks after we had settled into the new digs, Zuck announced that we ourselves would be decorating the inside of our newly conquered corporate campus.

Certainly, the campus needed a bit of personalization. The main courtyard was still under construction, and the halls and walls gleamed with rapidly applied paint. Things had that just-moved-in feeling; despite its flaws, the old office had felt lived-in and homey, like an old, beaten-down couch you can't bring yourself to toss. The indisputable upgrade in office quality, the newness and poshness of it all, threatened to congeal into corporate sterility. Zuck informed us that we'd be given all the spray cans, brushes, and paints we wanted, and be allowed to stake out any part of the campus as our own . . . and create *art*! Given our little performance of mob violence during the moving-out step, this was a considerable leap of faith.

The appointed day arrived, and a Home Depot's worth of paints and supplies were drop-shipped into the public areas of every building. The time was early evening, when people were switching gears from the meetings and coding of the day, and pondering going either to the gym or to the cafés for dinner. With nothing in the way of direction other than Zuck's mandate to produce art, people started arming themselves with the stockpile of paints and going at it.

Of course, pandemonium ensued.

Unskilled geeks, confronted with the graffiti canvas of an unblemished wall for the first time, started sketching pathetic stick figures in the halls, with large thought bubbles featuring corny jokes about Facebook culture. People drew crude flowers, or animal figures that only the parent of the three-year-old who drew them could ever think beautiful. Slogans appeared, at a top-of-urinal level of graffiti intelligence, in random places.

An older guy, no doubt some engineering manager with a lengthy LinkedIn CV and a mortgaged house in San Mateo, was leading his child by the hand while aforementioned child sprayed a continuous red line down the still-virgin white hallway, Hansel and Gretel leaving a trail of bread crumbs.

An ambitious engineer set up shop in the heavily trafficked public square between what was then Ads and Growth, and one of the busiest thoroughfares. Using a printout of a comic book scene in hand as guide, he started sketching a Superman emerging fist-first from a jumble of figures and shapes. Like a good muralist, he was busily engaged with the initial line sketch, which he'd have time only to partially fill with color before he abruptly departed. It resembled Jesus in Michelangelo's *Last Judgment*, a twisted shape flinging the universe around him.

Some teams kicked into product-development mode, dreaming up artistic visions around some central theme. The product manager handled logistical matters like masking tape, marking pens, and stencils, and the engineers did the actual work. It was a microcosm of Facebook product development itself. One of these depicted a huge unicorn head over a complicated tessellated pattern that looked algorithmically generated. These were about the only efforts that could even remotely be titled art.

This mayhem lasted for a good two days.

That weekend Zuck sent another to-all email (or maybe it was posted in the general Facebook internal group to which everyone belonged), the gist being: I trusted you to create art, and what you fuckers did was vandalize the place. This was of course true. The place looked like an alleyway in the Mission now, not the offices of the world's most promising tech startup. Worse: the Mission actually had some epic mural art; Facebook's art was comparable to that inside a blasted-out favela.

By his own report, Zuck had spent two days walking the entire FB campus, marking everything that was to be taken down. Indeed, come Monday, there was a thick band of blue masking tape marking every badly conceived attempt, or bit of joyful vandalism. Zuck must have gone through ten rolls of the stuff.

Immediately, Roddy Lindsay, one of the Facebook old-timers and keepers of the corporate culture, created a comment macro inside the code-review system. The code-review tool is how a Facebook engineer sees the world and does 90 percent of his work, submitting his code for consideration to the engineering team, where it is hotly debated almost as if it were in an online forum. The macros are geek emoticons, a witty or instructive image or GIF often reminiscent of kitschy Internet memes. There are hundreds of them, and they are like a rebus of engineering commentary, either encouraging someone to boldly ship a new feature, or pejoratively insulting some code-writer's ability. At the time, typing "bluetape" produced an image of a piece of blue masking tape on a wall, indicating that a piece of code should be removed for the sake of aesthetics and/or sanity.

This was Facebook culture for you: lots of bold, unconventional experiments, mostly failures with some notable successes, an immediate course correction to prune the failure, and then internalizing the experience via the culture. The crap murals and bluetape were as core to Facebook as the Like button (and Beacon).*

* Beacon was the emblematic Facebook product fiasco. Launched in 2007, before online (over)sharing was commonplace, Beacon posted your Web browsing activity to your feed. The oft-cited Beacon disaster was a real-life guy shopping for an engagement ring, and the putative fiancée finding out about his imminent proposal via Facebook. Awkward! Beacon resulted in a class-action suit and was soon officially shut down. On the old campus, Facebook had a series of conference rooms named after ill-conceived disasters: Land War in Southeast Asia, Knife to a Gun Fight, and . . . Beacon!

O Death

"A glorious moment, but I have a dread foreboding that some day the same doom will be pronounced on my own country." It would be difficult to mention an utterance more statesmanlike and more profound. For at the moment of our greatest triumph and of disaster to our enemies to reflect on our own situation and on the possible reversal of circumstances, and generally to bear in mind at the season of success the mutability of Fortune, is like a great and perfect man, a man in short worthy to be remembered.

—Polybius, *Histories*

JANUARY 2012

As mentioned, our new, freshly defaced campus had been formerly occupied by a bygone tech juggernaut, Sun Microsystems. It's ancient history now, but Sun once made *the* servers that powered the Internet. Whether it was the fast (and expensive) machines that sat in colocation facilities around the world serving up the Web, or powerful machines that sat on the desks of such high-end users as scientists or engineers, each with a full suite of development tools to produce yet more Internet technology, Sun was synonymous with the tech boom of the early 2000s. Yet it got complacent, and when Linux running on commodity hardware became the infrastructure of choice for most smart tech companies (including Google), Sun did nothing to stem the tide that led to its extinction.

When we moved into Menlo Park, there were Sun logos on lots of conference room doors and public spaces. Rather than remove them all, Zuck ordered that a few of them remain. Like corporate memento mori, they were to remind employees that Facebook could also go the way of extinction, and be reduced one day to logos and swag.

The biggest such fossil was to be found behind the Facebook sign with its enormous Like button, featuring the ubiquitous blue upraised thumb, host to an almost 24/7 cluster of selfie-taking tourists. On the back of Facebook's only publicly facing sign, and as big as a billiard table, was the logo that used to represent the sleek, new digital future. It was as tattered and flaking as some historical artifact. When Facebook arrived, instead of replacing the original sign, management had simply flipped it around, and intentionally neglected to paint or cover the back. It read SUN MICROSYSTEMS, along with the quadrangular logo made of S figures that used to appear at the top of every Web page you loaded.

This too shall pass. What befell Sun could befall us too, so MOVE FAST AND BREAK THINGS! Zuck was saying by implication.

Perhaps even the mighty Facebook Like button would one day be looked upon like the inscription on the fragment of Ozymandias's statue in Shelley's rumination on the transience of human ambition: an arrogant spasm of striving, forgotten and abandoned.

Every morning I bicycled the six miles from my sailboat docked in Redwood City to the new campus, which sat on an artificial spit of land poking into the tidal marshes that formed the San Francisco Bay's boggy southern tip. This wasn't as picturesque as it may sound: it was two miles of dusty pedaling next to the concrete quarries alongside the Port of Redwood City, two miles of getting buzzed by trucks through a neglected waterfront neighborhood, and then (finally) two miles of preserved marshlands (if the algae were blooming, it smelled like a camp toilet).

Hang the bicycle on the always-jammed racks inside the card-activated main door, and shower time. The bathrooms were undersized for Facebook's population, and there were no actual locker rooms. As such, the hard-core cyclists hung their ridiculous Spandex nut-huggers on the towel racks, intentionally inside out to air the sweaty crotches (blech!).

My sailboat living situation was unusual. The company was made up of about half suburban stiffs (older, married, childrened) who lived on the Peninsula, in "bedroom communities" like Menlo Park or Mountain View, depending on how early they had joined and how wealthy they were. The other half (young, hipster, fresh out of school) lived in the trendy and expensive parts of San Francisco. The latter were trucked in on company buses. That's right, Facebook ran a pool of shuttles that carted people either the thirty miles from SF to Menlo Park, or from downtown Palo Alto.*

These buses were a metaphor for what was happening in the Bay Area (and, I'd venture, the entire economy), a symbolism not lost on the antitechie protesters, given their penchant for smashing the buses' windows occasionally. One set of people got one set of goods and services, and the ones with tech company IDs clipped into their belts got very much another.

Picture the scene, Valley traveler: Twenty-Fourth Street

---

* Things have since gotten even more serious. Facebook has a navy now! There's a Facebook boat that services increasingly popular Oakland. It rips through wind and wave from Alameda in the East Bay to the marina just north of Facebook where I kept my boat, where another shuttle to campus waits. The official Facebook airline, flying in employees from LA or Seattle, can't be far behind.

and Valencia in the Mission District (hipsterville now, but historically a poor Mexican neighborhood). White charter buses, studiously unmarked by logos, compete for bus stop space with lurching, ramshackle SF Muni buses. One fleet of buses is for the alpha-plus-plus SF residents, and features comfortable seats and Wi-Fi. The other is for the proles, and features at least one incontinent homeless man raving deliriously next to the only open seat. Careful, though! Given there are at least three companies hosting corporate shuttles, you have to make sure you get on the right one (easier said than done, given the lack of signage). Get on the wrong one, and you'll find yourself headed to Google or Genentech instead. Of course, this did happen, and frequently. When infiltrated, someone would post on the Facebook Commute group indicating there was a Google spy on the bus, and to keep conversations down and screens hidden. What happened to those spies, I'm not quite sure. I wouldn't be surprised if HR kept recruiters on board, like the FAA air marshals on international flights, in order to snap them up as new hires the moment the doors closed.*

While waiting for the bus during the bouts I was living in SF (depending on whatever girlfriend drama was going on), I'd amuse myself by trying to guess which group clustered together belonged to what company. In time, you trained a mental model: the Googlers were older and nerdier looking (you could cheat by looking for the bunch of colored

---

* This joke is truer than you may think. I was nearly one of those confused bus-goers once. Getting off the Caltrain at the Palo Alto station, from where Facebook and a bunch of tech companies ran private buses, I saw a passenger sitting with a "Facebook" logo-ed bag, the shuttle doors rapidly closing. I darted for it and made it. Something about the smell of it set me off, and I asked, "This is the Facebook shuttle, right?" as I crossed the threshold. Smiling, Mr. Facebook Bag looked up and said, "Actually, it's the Tesla shuttle; I only used to work at Facebook. You're free to get on though if you'd like, and we can chat." I burst out laughing and retreated. But Tesla had just launched a new model, and it was tempting.

spheres on their infantile corporate IDs), while Facebookers were younger and a bit edgier. Once on board, you'd start the day's worth of email (or code in the case of the engineers) while bouncing around and hopefully missing the traffic snarl that congealed southbound around nine a.m.

Once inside Facebooklandia, which you wouldn't leave for the next twelve hours or so, you'd make a beeline for the café and the first of three free meals you'd have on campus. If you were a product manager, you were likely bolting it while checking email in the fifteen minutes before your first meeting, your first of anywhere from six to twelve, plus another two to three impromptu ones. Your Microsoft Calendar, which ruled your life via audio reminders from your corporate iPhone, as well as those of your colleagues, was fought over like a hundred yards of no-man's-land during World War I. The moment you would clear a meeting slot on your calendar, someone would likely send you an invite to fill it (there was an internal tool that helped with the ongoing calendar jigsaw puzzle).

The joke was that the biggest advantage of being at Facebook was not having to explain why you were on Facebook all day. Aside from putting the product through its paces, much of Facebook's collaborative work was done via Facebook itself. Every product team had an internal Facebook group for the team, perhaps several, one for each subset of "shareholders" in the product (e.g., sales, marketing, and engineering).*

Poopin'!

This was one of those culture-defining inside-Facebook jokes. If you were so foolish as to leave your laptop unlocked or unguarded among that loutish lot, then anyone had full

* There was an entire internal Facebook, in which only employees could ever see posts, likes, or comments. It functioned very much like the Facebook at Work product—basically Facebook as enterprise-collaboration software.

right to open your browser (which had at least two to three tabs open to Facebook) and post a status update involving a mundane gastrointestinal task ("Jell-O," for whatever reason, was the slightly more tasteful alternative).

Looking up from your desk, just another generic white surface exactly like Zuck's, what greets you? The product teams are clustered around their product and engineering managers; the Ads floor, which seems to be forever expanding into other floors and hallways, is a patchwork quilt of these teams. You know the route, like an ant in the pile, to the three to four with whom you collaborate. Senior management sits at one set of desks, close to whoever else was in the Ads *nomenklatura* that millisecond (it changes often). This is your native habitat as a product manager.

They say childhood ends when we first seriously realize we're going to die. For a startup, there's a similarly maturing moment, often right at the cusp of expansive success, when the founders realize their creation has left its organizational infancy.

Why do Facebook and Twitter acquire piddly little companies like AdGrok, FriendFeed, and Aardvark? We've already discussed how corporate mergers and acquisitions are basically recruitment via other means in the Valley's overheated market for technical talent. But there is another motivation: by hybridizing their corporate DNA with the pluck and daring of the startup entrepreneur, they revitalize their internal cultures and add traits not typically found among their recruitment fodder (i.e., smart but obedient engineering grads). It's like the intentional mixing of refined European breeds with wild dingoes in Australia that produced the smart and rangy Australian cattle dog.

Almost invariably (and there are exceptions) the startup product disappears into the maw of the acquiring company, and is never seen again. But those founders and early employees, skilled at creating something out of nothing when armed with very little, bring their technical flair and product chutzpah to a lumbering organization that is already forgetting its pioneering roots.

Or such was the theory.

While many such acquirees did end up having successful careers at Facebook, those who succeeded either were given incredibly wide latitude by Zuck to do what they wanted (e.g., the Instagram team), or had to adapt to their new circumstances and rein in the startup wildness a bit. Those who did neither . . . well, let's not jump ahead.

None of this was clear to me in the beginning; on the contrary, coming in as a "successful" startup entrepreneur meant you had lots of starting social capital. Everyone treated me like some champion on a victory lap. But inside, I felt like the survivor of a shipwreck: cold, wet, hands shaking, and a Red Cross blanket thrown over my shoulders, wondering just what the fuck had happened. How I'd gotten from the wild, untethered AdGrok shipwreck in the making to the corporate Elysium of free burgers and mission statements was an ontological puzzle. But the first rule of startups is also true of any fast-paced, competitive workplace like Facebook: act like you belong there, even if you don't.

One morning, all the employees arrived to find a 4×6 bound red book on their desks. The title was *Facebook Was Not Originally Created to Be a Company*, the resounding declaration that Zuck would eventually include in Facebook's IPO documents. Inside was a slickly designed rumination on corporate values, mostly tasteful juxtapositions of typically Facebook office tableaux (a passed-out engineer on a couch), inspiring artifacts from Facebook's history (a photo of early Facebook employees gathered at one modest dinner table), and somewhat kitschy stock photos of the inspirational-calendar genre (an overwhelming, wide-angle night sky). The content was either more storied Facebook lore (that time engineers convinced journalists Facebook was shipping a Fax button that would fax your photos), or tastefully typeset excerpts from the gospel according to Facebook ("The quick shall inherit the earth"; "We don't build services to make money, we make money to build services").

The penultimate page captured the spirit best. In white sans serif font, against a stark black background, it read:

> If we don't create the thing that kills Facebook, someone else will.
>
> "Embracing change" isn't enough. It has to be so hardwired into who we are that even talking about it seems redundant. The Internet is not a friendly place. Things that don't stay relevant don't even get the luxury of leaving ruins. They disappear.

Mark that well, FB soldier.

In a thousand small ways, the company was forever reminding its people of the cost of failure. Facebook had the death awareness of the person planning on living forever. Death didn't inspire fear, however; only a reminder of the discipline required to keep decay at bay. I had never seen a company before or since so maniacal in ensuring the perpetuation of its original values. It was like the United States on the Fourth of July, every day:

OUR WORK IS NEVER OVER

MAKE IT FASTER

WHAT WOULD YOU DO IF YOU WEREN'T AFRAID?

THIS JOURNEY 1% FINISHED

Like the naive new recruit, I took those values to heart. And like the new recruit, I'd realize only later that the Facebook reality was rather more complicated.

The Barbaric Yawn

To fill the hour—that is happiness; to fill the hour, and leave no crevice for a repentance or an approval.

—Ralph Waldo Emerson, *Experience*

JANUARY 2012

Track racing is an exhilarating pursuit.

You take your performance car that you irresponsibly street-race all the time through busy streets filled with potholes and around turns with bad camber, and you're suddenly on a flawless surface winding through sweeping, perfectly sloped turns with full license to go apeshit. The nature of track racing is that you're flooring either the throttle or the brake at all times, either exploding out of turns or stopping suddenly to make them. No bandwidth spent looking for cops or that slow-driving old lady in an Accord means you are exclusively focused on your vehicle, the track, and the g-forces pulling you sideways. If you hit a flow state, it's one of those transcendent unions of man, machine, and the physical world that take you outside yourself into a point-like state of consciousness. You are all tense sinew and twitching nerve, a beast strapped into a machine, with no past, no future, just that one 130-mile-per-hour moment.

Add in two dozen other gearhead degenerates going apeshit along with you on the track, and you've got yourself a ten-lap ticket straight to your own mental redline. When you finally pull off the track into the pits, your overheated car will reek of burnt brake and clutch, your damp clothes are glued with sweat to your skin, and you'll remove your driving gloves with shaking hands. The adrenaline crash will hit, and you'll be reminded of the moments after your first fight, or your first real fuck.

Then you drive home.

Your mental physics have been recalibrated, and so you floor the throttle by default and settle into what seems a comfortable cruising speed of . . . 110 miles per hour. After whooshing past the right lane for a while, you're forced to suddenly brake for some irresponsible dickhead who's doing—oh, is the speedometer lying to me?—80 miles per hour, ten over the posted speed limit. Then you look around and take stock of your new driving environment. Everything feels incredibly slow; it's like you're crawling. You can't believe this is 80 miles per hour. You're indignant.

How can anyone fucking have an accident at this speed?

I could basically duct-tape my steering wheel in place, fall asleep, and still get home.

None of these idiots know how to drive and should lose their licenses, and the speed limit needs to be at least 100 miles per hour.

You realize you've been living in a different world from most people for the past few hours, and now you're in a world that . . . moves . . . as . . . slow . . . as . . . molasses.

This is what it feels like to go from a startup to a big company.

Even Facebook, whose ability to maintain a fast-moving, always-be-shipping culture well into corporate middle age was admirable and unique, was simply a German-style autobahn, not a racetrack. The days of a few engineers going rogue and launching Facebook Video despite Zuck's wishes were long gone. Most vehicles moved at the speed limit, lots of trucks hogged the right lane, and a select few drivers traveled at full speed in the left lane (with no-speed-limit passes given out by Zuck alone, and anyone else who dared race ahead did so at peril to his or her career).

A more middling company will feel like an American highway: originally well constructed, but now beset with a slew of problems stemming from long-neglected repairs and drivers who don't understand the notion of lane discipline. The shitkicker Town Car in the left lane doing forty-five miles per hour and blocking traffic, the bro with his Supra lowrider and fart can zipping past on the right halfway into the breakdown lane, trucks using middle lanes to pass despite outpacing each other by all of two miles per hour.

When you join Apple or Google from a startup, you're literally and figuratively commuting on the 101 going southbound in the morning: more or less moving, but basically one of a pack of indistinguishable vehicles all signaling before you change lanes, respecting the HOV lane, and routing around jackasses.

In the worst case (ahem, Oracle), your big company is the Paharganj neighborhood of Delhi at rush hour: a nightmarish jumble of rickshaws, taxis, trucks, pedestrians, and cows, all trying to get somewhere, and nobody moving despite the crescendo of horns and voices.

As early as a few months into Facebook, once the novelty had worn off, I could feel myself growing bored and frustrated with the speedometer stuck in the middle double digits. Product development in Ads was sluggish and curiously hesitant. The targeting team continued trying to squeeze juice out of the dry data lemon, and Gokul kept on riding the Ads team mercilessly, while offering nothing in the way of direction. The Facebook cast was unfailingly competent but not the race car drivers of my previous startup life, and it seemed I was waiting to get somewhere. Given the nature of technology compensation, I actually was.

Here's how people get paid in Silicon Valley:

Like most employees, I had a vesting calendar that determined the speed and cadence of my equity being awarded. And as with most employees, my equity compensation vested over four years, with one-fourth coming after exactly one year, and then 1/16th coming every financial quarter after that. Your net worth (particularly if you, like me, had most of it in the stock of the company you were at) resembled a stair-step plot of gradual but swiftly accumulating value. Despite the deal drama, I had a boilerplate employment contract, except my numbers were larger due to my acqui-hire leverage and brinksmanship in playing Gokul against Twitter. Nonetheless, I'd have to patiently wait out my vesting schedule; the joke term for doing so in less spirited companies than Facebook was being a "VIP"—that is, "vesting in peace."

My one major oversight was failing to realize that the impatient startup entrepreneur, the guy addicted to the smell of burnt clutch and the engine's throaty roar, was never going to stick around for four years and vest in peace (something the corp dev people who put together my offer surely realized, those bastards). You were really going to spend at best two years there, so halve the number on your offer or term sheet, and then halve it again if it's in the form of stock rather than options (thanks to ass-backward IRS treatment of Valley compensation). Doesn't look like such a great deal now, does it?

To measure progress, I put a countdown clock app on my MacBook's dashboard, measuring the time until my first vesting, beyond which I already couldn't imagine staying. The clock counted in minutes, hours, and days, and I referred to it often, especially after a particularly challenging meeting that reeked of corporate cant and catatonia.

An idle mind is the devil's playground, as the saying goes, so in the meantime I got down to the serious business, as some product managers do, of trying to bang my product marketing manager.

PMMess, as we'll call her, was composed of alternating Bézier curves from top to bottom: convex, then concave, and then convex again, in a vertical undulation you couldn't take your eyes off of. Unlike most women at Facebook (or in the Bay Area, really) she knew how to dress; forties-style, form-fitting dresses from neck to knee were her mainstay. Her blond hair was offset by olive skin, and bright blue eyes shone like headlights from her neotenic face.

She had a charming perfectionism around email orthography and usage, despite the generally rushed illiteracy that reigned in Facebook corporate communication. We traded flirtarious barbs around whether CPM was an initialism or an abbreviation, and whether a needlessly flowery formulation of mine, written in response to some insipid corporate conversation, was a metonym or a metaphor.

Like me, PMMess would lose herself in bouts of louche, ethanolic self-destruction that typically ended in some disinhibited act of carnality. A couple of times already, such behavior had involved me, though only at a relatively PG-rated level of barside making out. It was time to close the deal.

Friday afternoons at Facebook in those days had a happy-hour feel to them. Zuck would do his company-wide Q&A, for which employees could propose or vote on questions beforehand to ask the commander in chief.* I'd occasionally attend depending on the winning questions (they were posted in an internal Facebook group), and after would rush the keg of whatever swill they were serving before the twenty-three-year-old, hoodie-clad masses got there. The Ads crew would drift through at some point, huddling at

* The company-wide "all hands" meeting on late Friday afternoons is as close as the Valley gets to a universal tradition. They're called "TGIF" at Google (though now held on Thursdays for international time zone reasons), and "Tea Time" at Twitter, where they feature on-tap kombucha (at last count, they have three different kinds). It's a chance for senior leadership to address the ranks and explain what's going on up the chain, as well as to address public rumors or news circulating in the company (which, if the company is in play at all, will be an ever-present chorus).

an outdoor picnic bench if the weather was agreeable: Mark Rabkin, Fidji Simo (then a marketer, eventually a product manager), Brian Boland, et al.—the Ads cool kids one could actually have a drink with, relatively rare in those days.

A particularly boisterous crew at these informal courtyard shenanigans was the Ads Product Marketing team. In Ads, but a separate "org" than Boland's mafia, it was headed by Mike Fox, an easygoing Midwesterner. The team's role in the Facebook construct was interesting. For all of social media's avant-garde pretensions, it still had to wade into places like Bentonville, Arkansas, or Auburn Hills, Michigan, and convince companies that sold or made actual things (like Walmart and Chrysler, respectively) to spend money on Facebook. Making the Facebook sale to the CEO of General Motors was like teaching an Amazonian tribesman how to set a clock radio: possible, so long as you couched it in their language and framed it in whatever quirky mythology they held sacred. Fox, along with his henchmen Doug Frisbie, Dan Tretola, and Galyn Burke, were the emissaries to those weary giants of flesh and steel.

The Fox crew was always out in force every happy hour. PMMess was a frequent coconspirator in the marketing bash. Well pregamed at the picnic tables around the café that hosted the Zuck Q&A, the group decamped to continue the mayhem elsewhere.

Destination: the Shady Lady Bar, one of the more epic emanations of jerry-rigged Facebook bar culture. It looked like the inside of an Elks Lodge in Des Moines, Iowa, complete with signed celebrity photos from washed-up seventies stars (e.g., Burt Reynolds) and a counter decked out in padded vinyl and Formica. The bar had been reanimated in Building 10 after the move from California Avenue. Building 10 was at the end of the curved loop of buildings that formed the campus; it served as the official entrance and reception to Facebook, as well as housing random teams like Ops or Legal. Reception lobby plus non-engineers meant that at seven p.m. on a Friday, it was more desolate than the Mojave. The Fox gang plus PMMess were nicely blitzed by this point, and we took over the space. Hoping to find something other than the mass-market beer served at Q&A, I opened the fridge and found myself staring at an unopened bottle of Thunderbird, the bum wine par excellence. By God, I'd never even seen one, just heard of it. Everything else was total rotgut as well. The one working tap seemed to pour something reminiscent of Coors Light. This bar might have been a piece of conceptual art rather than a functioning watering hole.

The real intoxicant here, though, was PMMess in a fitted dress. Through wiles I can't recall now, I somehow induced her to leave the circus for the surrounding rows of abandoned desks. Besotted prurience was easily conjured again, and suddenly privacy was at a premium. Without losing the full-body press, I reached out and swung open a mysterious door embedded in a wall a couple of yards away. It was a utility closet filled with cleaning supplies and the detritus of Facebook life: propaganda posters, geek toys, and packing boxes.

Gently hauling us both inside, I closed the door, and the combat continued.

As PMMess stood a head and a half shorter than me, this required some contortions. The fact it was pitch black meant we lost any sense of equilibrium, and I pressed an arm against the left side wall for balance.

The Battle of the Bra Clasp was going on behind her back, a vicious, winner-take-all contest, a two-person Siege of Leningrad. PMMess wasn't resisting, but Victoria's Secret was. My one-handed bra opening skills were decidedly rusty. It didn't help that I felt something wrapped around my foot, like an extension cord, or perhaps a cardboard box.

She tasted sweet, with a bit of biscuitiness from the happy-hour beer (she was a beer hound too).

One . . . more . . . wire . . . loop . . . sticking . . . get . . . off . . . now.

Something clattered as I partially lost my balance and took my weight off that foot.

Victory was mine!

The bra had given way.

Time to storm the parliament building with a face-first dive into her cleavage. The darkness and her proximity made it more of a head butt. I went forehead-first into her sternum, and we both went slightly off balance, her leaning back and against the wall, me stooping.

I was definitely stepping inside either a bucket or a cardboard box. If I tried to take a step, cartoon physics would surely take over, and I'd slip as if in a friction-free universe. I'd launch myself through the door for the entire ads marketing team to see, complete with action lines and sound effects, not to mention a partially bare-breasted product marketing manager. I held my ground rather than risking a move.

The engine of mutual lust was revving, but I didn't feel it was quite revved high enough to attempt carnal union. A Facebook broom-closet boink would have been well beyond the pale even for me.

Matters simmered rather than boiled over. Erotic brakes applied, I cracked the door ajar; the coast was clear. Being careful to put my weight on the unencumbered foot, I exited first, followed by PMMess a few seconds later.

Back at the Lady, all of ten steps away, we'd not been missed, and rejoined the fray without any visible eyebrows being raised. Just another Facebook Friday. I looked at PMMess, and her feline eyes projected warmth and conspiratorial glee.

After the happy-hour momentum at the Shady Lady wound down, we abandoned the marketing crew and headed back to the Ads area, strolling down the recently completed courtyard, and stopping at the odd bench or wall to continue our necking. This was ill advised from the professional perspective, but fortunately at ten p.m. on a Friday, even Facebook was on the empty side, and this had no repercussions (beyond some gossip on the Ads team).

Normally such a scene, at that hour and/or state of sobriety, would have taken place while stumbling down Valencia Street in the Mission, and would have had a far more kinetic conclusion. But instead, we both went back to our desks like the sane, hardworking professionals we were.

Even on the extracurricular front, Facebook was no racetrack.

Going Public

> The more powerful the class, the more it claims not to exist, and its power is employed above all to enforce this claim.
>
> —Guy Debord, *The Society of Spectacle*

FEBRUARY 1, 2012

Emails from Mark were always bracing. He preferred FB messages in general, so email meant something serious was afoot. The first lines of this morning's directive—do not share the contents of this email, or the Sec will come get you—didn't allay the momentary alarm.

The "Sec," of course, was the internal security apparatus, which caught people looking at user profiles or leaking confidential information. As with the Stasi in East Germany, all who lived under its jurisdiction knew they were being watched.

The email instructed us to assemble at four o'clock that afternoon in "the tent." As the campus's main courtyard was still under construction, Facebook had erected what resembled an expansive gospel-revival tent in one of the football-field-sized parking lots to serve as a company-wide rallying hall. And so the throngs poured out of the doors at five minutes to four to hear the news from the prophet of our religion. I arrived late as usual, and took a seat in the back row.

Mark started by announcing that the company was officially filing to go public. A spontaneous cheer erupted and he was forced to pause. Then, in one of his more rambling speeches, he warned how going public would also bring the distracting eye of public scrutiny, including no small amount of ridicule. That was something that Facebookers, in their sheltered amour propre, had never been forced to endure.

Given the potential distractions of frivolities like the stock price and whatever the *Wall Street Journal* might say about a service it surely didn't understand, Zuck had one message to impart: *Stay focused on our mission!*

As the child of Cuban exiles, I was reminded by this scene of a piece of collective cultural memory: Castro giving a photogenic victory speech on a flag-draped podium surrounded by his olive-green-clad coterie, during the early days of the revolution. The swirling immediacy of the moment, that spark of history being made before your eyes, the cheering, sea-like crowd, the charismatic contortions on Castro's face. That feeling that the universe had conspired to make something big happen right *there* in front of you, and you were a part of it by being present. That's what stared out at you from photos by Glinn and Korda in those heady days of early 1959, which is why they transfixed the world, and still decorate some confused malcontent's bedroom in Berlin or La Paz.

In Havana, my cousins were forced to listen to rambling speeches about maintaining core values inside a one-dimensional cult of personality. In Menlo Park, I was sitting in a tent full of people wearing identical uniforms of Facebook swag and doing the same.

Back in Havana, my cousins were eyeing posters of Che and Fidel on crumbling buildings and the sides of lurching, belching buses. Alongside were rousing posters, designed in that wonderfully retro socialist realism only the Cubans still embraced: *¡TODO POR LA REVOLUCIÓN! ¡HASTA LA VICTORIA SIEMPRE! ¡PATRIA O MUERTE, VENCEREMOS!*

Meanwhile, I was walking around Facebook, surrounded by stenciled portraits of Mark and equally exhortatory posters: PROCEED AND BE BOLD! GET IN OVER YOUR HEAD! MAKE AN IMPACT!

At their extremes, capitalism and communism become equivalent:

Endless toil motivated by lapidary ideals handed down by a revered and unquestioned leader, and put into practice by a leadership caste selected for its adherence to aforementioned principles, and richly rewarded for its willingness to grind whatever human grist the mill required?

Same in both.

A (mostly) pliant media that flatters the existing system of production, framing it as the only such system possible?

Check!

Foot soldiers who sacrifice their families and personal lives for the efficient running of the system, and who view their sole human value through the prism of advancement within that system?

Welcome to the People's Republic of Facebook.

But one can simply quit a job in capitalism, while from communism there is no escape, you'll protest.

As for the actual ability to opt out under capitalism: look at Seattle or SF real estate prices, and the cost of a decent US education, and consider whether Amazon or Facebook employees could really opt out of their treadmill. I've never known one who did, and I know many.

Ask your average family providers, even those in a two-income family, whether they felt they could simply quit when they liked. They could barely get a few weeks off when they had a child, much less opt out. Switching jobs would amount to nothing more than changing the color of the shackles.

As the ever-sagacious @gselevator quoted: in communism people made lines for bread, while in capitalism they make lines for iPhones. Sure, iPhones are better than bread, and the standard of living in capitalist countries is clearly higher, but the lived experiences of either, from the point of view of the working proles, bears more than a passing resemblance.

The reality is that capitalism, communism, and every other sweeping ideology feed off the same human drives—the founder's or revolutionary's narcissistic will to power, and the mass man's desire to be part of something bigger than himself—even if with very different outcomes. National Socialism, Technofuturism, Bolshevism, the Islamic State, Pan-Arabism, *la Commune*, Jonestown, the Crusades, *la mission civilisatrice*, the white man's burden, evangelical Christianity, Manifest Destiny, Spanish Falangism, the Church of Latter-day Saints, the Cuban Revolution—the villain with a thousand faces, yoking together the monomaniac's twitchy urge and the follower's hunger for a role in some captivating story.

What would our historians do without that loyal stagecoach, that motive force, of history? What would I even be writing about?

I had chosen a seat behind a detached pair, who on further inspection proved to be Chris Cox, head of FB Product, and Naomi Gleit, a Harvard grad who'd joined as employee number twenty-nine, and was now reputed to be the current longest-serving employee other than Mark.

Naomi, between hushed chats with Cox, was clicking away on her laptop, paying little attention to the Zuckian harangue. I peered over her shoulder at her screen. She was scrolling down an email with a number of links, and progressively clicking each one into existence as another tab on her browser. Clickathon finished, she began switching slowly from tab to tab, lingering on each with an appraiser's eye. They were real estate listings, each for a different San Francisco property. Catching the address of one, I opened my MacBook and used our great enemy Google to find the address. The location was a decent but not exceptionally choice part of Diamond Heights, a popular, quiet neighborhood for many nesting techies. The real estate agency had done its Google homework, and the listing was easy to find. It was one of these modernist deconstructionist takes on the Victorian paradigm the new structure had likely replaced: all black stone, stained wood, and ridged zinc, with the merest hint of some abstract notions of bay windows, but mostly an asymmetric monstrosity. List price: $2,400,000.

We need to maintain focus while we go public, uttered the social media *comandante.*

Every über-successful tech company has gone through the same struggle to keep people from being distracted by potential share price. What made companies like Facebook unique was the persistent scale of the wealth discrepancy, as early employees stayed on and the growing company hired help that was decently paid, but not due to receive anything like life-changing riches.

In a society defined wholly by consumption, the difficulty of wealthy and nonwealthy Facebookers discussing money would be comparable to a Swedish anarchist discussing political philosophies with an Islamic State militant. And so the protocol is to not talk about it at all publicly. People of course did discuss it among themselves. Among what were surely many such groups, there was one called NR250, which was more or less a collaborative how-to on being affluent. The title came from "New Rich," and the 250 from its originally involving the first 250 or so employees, or so the story goes (and at this point it's more than just early Facebookers). Yes, they were literally nouveaux riches in all senses of the term, and from all reports (more than one member has dished to me) they acted like it. How to buy land under an LLC to hide the fact you're amassing a compound, the best resort on Maui, how to book or lease private jets, the best high-end credit cards to use, and so forth. But not a word of it while on campus.

In day-to-day terms, it was something like what the famous Google masseuse Bonnie Brown wrote in her autobiography about that company's encounter with the bipartite wealth split:

> A sharp contrast developed between Googlers working side by side. While one was looking at local movie times on his monitor, the other was booking a flight to Belize for the weekend. How was the conversation Monday morning going to sound now?

The members of this ruling class furiously denied their very existence, however. Naturally, if you were to poll Southern whites about racism, they'd stubbornly maintain that the South was an exemplar of equal rights. The British upper class would declare their country to be the model of meritocracy. To the extent I can use the word "privilege" without feeling like a social justice warrior and puking in my mouth, the beneficiaries of such privilege <heave> never see it. Similar to the proverbial fish who doesn't see the water it's floating in, the FB nobility didn't grasp their pride of place in the corporate hierarchy.

At a more formal level, that attitude meant Facebook didn't have table-stakes benefits like 401(k) matching for years. As I once joked to British Trader when she asked if Facebook had a pension scheme, the IPO was the pension. Except, of course, it wasn't for many Facebookers, as later employees (including this one) were not due to receive life-changing wealth when the company went public.* Facebook

* Here's roughly what Facebook engineers made coming in right before the IPO (I know because I referred some friends to FB, and we'd discuss their offers off the record). If they had a few years of experience, but were not a "star" with unique skills, they could expect a salary in the $125K to $150K range, with about $500K in equity (at the then-current private market price for FB shares, which was around $30), vesting over four years.

eventually did commit to matching retirement contributions, but the internal debates on the topic revealed the rift between the haves and the have-mores. Some didn't understand the problem (the have-mores), and some worried about tuition at Stanford and affording a home in even relatively modest San Mateo (the haves, sort of).

What was intriguing was how the unwealthy embraced the system, even if they weren't the beneficiaries of this new social order we'd all joined. The junior hire was sucked along by enthusiasm and cluelessness, but the more senior employees at the middle-manager level knew the score. They knew that they lived one lifestyle, but their old-timer supervisor, who wasn't necessarily more talented, lived very much another.

This was a textbook case of the Marxist argument that capitalists instill the values of the property owner into their managerial classes, while still keeping most of the fruits of labor, in order to make common cause against the exploited proletariat, even though manager and worker have more in common than either does with the senior leadership. Even the most flag-waving Facebook (or Amazon or Google) middle manager, hired when the company was mature, realized he didn't make beans compared with what the early employees and founders—the true owners of the company—were worth. And yet the managers sided with their overseers against the very people they worked alongside every day. Say what you like about Marxism in practice, but it describes our contemporary technobourgeois society exactly.

If they were stars, or were PhD-level research scientists, that equity could get as high as $1 million to $1.25 million over four years. This is all in very taxable restricted stock units (RSUs), rather than options (which the old-timers had received). When you consider that FB's share price would almost quadruple in the ensuing two years, plus the performance bonuses an employee would receive along the way, even a relatively junior engineer could expect to walk away after four years with something like $1 million to $3 million in net worth, assuming he or she acted rationally.

As in companies, so in nations: the national conversation also ignored the socioeconomic rift, almost geologic in size, between how the affluent and the just-making-it lived. Facebook was merely the United States in microcosm.

Keep focused on our mission!

When the Flying Saucers Fail to Appear

> A man with a conviction is a hard man to change. Tell him you disagree and he turns away. Show him facts or figures and he questions your sources. Appeal to logic and he fails to see your point.
>
> —Leon Festinger et al., *When Prophecy Fails*

MARCH 2012

In 1956, the sociologist Leon Festinger published a landmark study of a cult formed around a Chicago housewife named Dorothy Martin. Martin channeled messages from extraterrestrial beings living on different "vibrational planes," which she recorded via automatic writing. Her messages predicted a catastrophic flood that would destroy the United States on December 21, 1954. The acolytes of the cult's prophet would be saved via alien spacecraft, which would whisk them off to the higher planes of existence they had been specially selected to experience.

The cult's membership grew in time, and as the apocalyptic date approached, the members left jobs, let properties and businesses languish, and alienated their disbelieving families in expectation of the end times. When the flying saucers and ensuing apocalypse failed to appear on the appointed date, the cult's believers did not lose faith. On the contrary, the experience bolstered their beliefs, annealing them into an intimate confederacy of false belief. Vestiges of the cult persist even to this day.

This study would lay the groundwork for Festinger's theory of "cognitive dissonance": the mental stress people suffer when presented with realities contrary to their deeply held beliefs. The key takeaway is that humans naturally avoid this discomfort, skirting situations that aggravate it, or ignoring data that make their mental contradiction more apparent.

Note: The purpose of the following exposition is not a neener-neener troll of Facebook, reveling in an embarrassing fiasco for the sadistic glee of it. It's a case study in how even very smart companies can go temporarily mad and believe in fairies or flying saucers, under the twin pressures of market expectation and blinkered arrogance. Every large company has languished in the delirious trance of some product folly, waking with an urgent start only when reality finally catches up with delusion. What follows is an account of Facebook's great monetization folly, its first great sally into the world of marketing technology, and its utter failure.

The original idea, on the face of it, was a good one.

First we have to rewind to the state of Facebook circa 2010, when the product you use to stalk your past or future boyfriend was very different. Those were simple times in Facebook-land: Mobile usage was low and the app was buggy and slow. Pages were the only sanctioned commercial expression on Facebook, each being a sort of simplified personal profile for a brand or business (remember, the data-rich and expansive Timeline we all now enjoy hadn't yet been launched). The only ways for someone else to get a piece of content into your feed were a friend posting it, a non-friend tagging you in a photo, and a page you had liked posting something popular. There was no way to pay and get into users' feeds directly. The few ads were small, postage-stamp-sized affairs in the far right-hand side of the page, usually for aggravating or irrelevant stuff like a game or a low-value product like a phone plan. The only "action" you could express on Facebook was Like; nothing about playing games or listening to music on Spotify. All that would come later. There was no Like button on the rest of the Internet, transmitting your emotions instantly to your feed (and those of your friends) as now.

Facebook—or, really, Zuck—saw News Feed as the untouchable magic real estate of the Internet, in which the dirty mitts grasping at filthy lucre had no place. How did Facebook make money then? Two ways, which each reflected the high-level bipartite split in the advertising world.

The advertising agencies, those moderators of commercial taste who lived in New York and were paid lots of money to spend lots of money, convinced prominent brands to buy Likes for their Facebook pages. Companies like Starbucks (on whose board Sheryl sat) or Burberry (they of the $4,000 cashmere coats) routinely forked over $10 million in order to gain five million Likes for their page. Facebook salespeople would preach the miraculous power of Likes the way a Catholic priest might sermonize on the eucharistic miracle, bread and wine turning into body and blood. However, it was never quite explained how Likes would transubstantiate into actual sales dollars. This was one of the mysteries of the Facebook faith that believers had to simply accept as beyond human understanding. To attempt to measure any of this, as with radiocarbon dating the Shroud of Turin, would have been spiritual buzzkill and fucking with the magic, so shush and pay.

The direct-response advertisers, who, you'll remember,

are those actively selling you a sweater or a flight to Boston right now, were barely represented on Facebook at the time. Facebook's targeting system was so weak that nobody could actually directly sell anything on Facebook (other than the aforementioned Likes). The only direct marketers who managed to make Facebook advertising work were developers on the FB gaming platform (e.g., Zynga). There was a bit of signal amid the noise in Facebook's "interests" targeting, which crafty marketers teased out over thousands of ads and millions of dollars spent. For example, a large gaming company discovered that people who had liked various energy drinks converted very well for *Mafia Wars*–style games. Basically, energy drinks like Monster were a proxy for that flavor of lunkheaded younger male who played those moronic mob assassination games that were popular in social gaming's heyday, and are now mostly forgotten. It was a Facebook version of the "beer and diapers" truism, cleverly obvious in that way marketers love.* The bump in performance was ludicrously small, though, and the engagement rate of Facebook ads was pitiable compared with properly targeted ads on the wider Web (not that anyone at Facebook recognized that, at least publicly).

Meanwhile, the core Facebook product launched bold initiatives around Search and Platform with the cavalier sign-off from Zuck that Ads could never get. Like the poor relation invited to a wealthy family's garden party, Ads hung

* "Beer and diapers" is an apocryphal piece of marketing folklore about a big-box retailer who supposedly hired statisticians to find which products' purchases were correlated. Lo and behold, the eggheads found that beer and diapers sold together in the same shopping cart, particularly on late Friday afternoons. The explanation? Husbands driving home from work, picking up Huggies for their wives, and getting some brews to deal with the bedlam of an infant household. Like most pieces of folklore, it's probably contrived, but it illustrates a general principle that's truth(y).

back from the Facebook festivities, nervous, unsure of itself, and embarrassed by the shabby jacket it was forced to wear.*

So what was it then, finally, this great corporate gamble?

It involved a nebulously titled product called Open Graph, the first version of which had launched at Facebook's developer conference F8 the year before I joined.† A later version added the verbal dictionary that accompanied "Like," expanding the Facebook vocabulary to things like "play," "listen," "watch," or "buy." It was the new subject-verb-object language of everything you did online. "*Antonio García Martínez listened to Wax Tailor's 'Only Once' on Spotify.*" Rather than merely express some vague approval via Like, Facebook users could now broadcast everything they were doing, with the aid of outside developers who built Facebook's new grammar into their products. By doing so, these developers made their products "social," and potentially viral. In exchange for pumping their data full-throttle into Facebook, those outside developers—music players like Spotify, or publishers like the *Washington Post*—got News Feed distribution, driving yet more users to their content and services.

That was the dream, anyhow.

The monetization side of this was almost certainly not what you're thinking. Mining or selling the data wasn't the point. By oblique analogy to Google's AdWords, in which promoted results appear alongside regular search results,

---

* Like every other statement in this book, this one stands as true at the point in time referenced. That poor relation, Ads, would soon win the lottery (or rather, provide the winning lottery prize) and no longer be huddling next to the punch bowl. But it would take a while to get there.

† Pronounced "eff-ait," and not "fate," the name F8 came from the eight hours that engineers spent in hackathons, the all-night company-wide coding sessions that produced some of Facebook's more random (and successful) products.

the distribution of certain Open Graph stories would be "boosted" and appear more often in a user's feed. Zynga and Eminem would in theory pay to have their stories boosted, and have you, the user, engage with their product or content more often. You never saw any story you couldn't have theoretically seen otherwise; you were just more likely to see it, and maybe you saw it more often. The advertiser was charged every time a user saw or clicked such a "Sponsored Story," which was the name of the monetization product.

Remember: back then, someone liking your page, and you posting something, was the only way for commercial content to even appear in News Feed. Sponsored Stories merely gave it a little kick, a little help in getting in front of your desired user (who had opted in by liking you to begin with). Of course, it wasn't merely Likes. It was you playing FarmVille, it was you listening to a certain song on Spotify, it was you watching a video on Socialcam (a long-forgotten social video site). It was every damn thing you did on Facebook, or even off Facebook, as ingested by a Facebook partner. Eventually, that would include every verb of every action you undertook on the Internet, from eating a pizza to making love to your wife (well, maybe). And it would all be boostable via the Ads system. What could possibly go wrong?

Sponsored Stories was the classic indefensible two-miracle startup idea. Miracle one was all the companies in the world doing work to integrate with Facebook and give away their data, at dubious benefit to themselves. Miracle two was those companies' marketers abandoning their old workflows and success myths for some newfangled paradigm, one with unproved and unprovable efficacy, just because Facebook said so. And so, like any two-miracle startup idea, it was almost certain to fail.

That didn't stop the Ads team, however.

While Facebook had held the previously mentioned F8 developer conference for years—its presence or absence a function of the health of its platform and developer ecosystem—Facebook has only ever held a proper marketing conference once. With the unimaginative acronym FMC, the first and only such conference was held in New York, the Vatican City of advertising, in February 2012, just as the Sponsored Stories drama was reaching its climax (or nadir, really).

A big, splashy show—think an Apple product launch or even a rock concert (and there'd be one at the end)—was thrown at, of all places, the American Museum of Natural History, on Manhattan's Upper West Side, next to Central Park. Weirdly enough, the core product engineers and managers like me had no real role there—that was for the marketing managers and salespeople—and we were pressed into mundane duties like helping people check in at the door.

"Yeah, come here and swipe your badge and check into Facebook, please," I'd say to the chief executive of some holding company, the joker who spent other people's money ineffectually for a living.

This was a show staged with a level of pomp unusual for Facebook.

There was a dimly lit "Timeline Hallway," in which you used your conference badge to swipe in and identify yourself. Your Facebook user ID had been associated with your conference registration; on swiping, the wall of monitors lit up with a slick demo of the recently launched Timeline. As in a near-death experience, you saw your entire life flash in front you from distant to recent past, along with pics of your friends, newborn children, wedding, and so on. People were wowed—who wouldn't love a Film Festival of You?—and shared their check-in on the Timeline whose summary they had just witnessed, raising the "meta" to the pomo power.

I peeled away from the glib pageant of bullshit—Facebook PMMs and salespeople chatting up the marketing heads of brands and the general managers of agencies—sidestepped a velvet rope, and explored the darkened museum.

The Museum of Natural History is one of these old-school

nineteenth-century monuments to didactic showcasing and taxidermy. Entire halls are dedicated to those artifacts of a pre–motion picture, not to mention pre-Internet, world: dioramas made to look like the Serengeti Plain or the Atacama Desert, filled with lynxes and wildebeests, a domestic-looking pair of rhinos. How long could the museum convince anyone living to look at the stuffed dead, I wondered. Facebook & Co., to whom the museum was pimping out its august real estate, was busily working to nuke the human mind of the necessary attention span.

The keynote to this festival of schmoozing was given by Sheryl, who delivered a forgettable string of Facebook platitudes for forty-five minutes. The point wasn't the content, but seeing The Sheryl, live and in person. It was the taste of the Oprah-like celebrity, something to justify the taxi ride to the Upper West Side from Midtown.

Sheryl was followed by the relative noncelebrity Paul Adams, a product manager on the Ads team. Adams was making a name for himself as a Malcolm Gladwell of the brave new social media world, having published a book called *Grouped: How Small Groups of Friends Are the Key to Influence on the Social Web*. Like Gladwell, he had cherry-picked a few seminovel conclusions from sociological research around relationship networks, and had woven it into a grand, overarching story about the future of media and consumption, doled out in bite-size morsels that fit inside a media buyer's brain. The net of it was that new ideas and products propagated via ever-changing social-influencer networks, and that figuring out the network, and exploiting the mutual influence of friends on one another, was the key to making your voice heard or product sold. This fit perfectly with the grand Open Graph–Sponsored Stories delusion, in that Facebook's weird little ads with your friends' faces on them were precisely what you needed to make someone aspire to a $60,000 BMW 3-series M-class coupe.

Of course, Paul, to the extent he believed the Facebook

script himself rather than exploiting it merely to plug his book and personal brand, was completely wrong, and Facebook's own research revealed as much. Right before the conference, the Facebook research team had published a paper on comparative click behavior that studied the impact of precisely this "social context" that Facebook was presently flat-out selling to the gathered agency illuminati.* Their conclusions were, strictly speaking, mildly positive, but chilling in the overall scheme of things.

According to Facebook Research, the inclusion of social context (i.e., the addition of "your friend Joe liked" to a text ad) lifted clickthrough rates something like 40 to 60 percent versus similar ads without your friend's smiling face. That sounds like a lot, and certainly it was better than the alternative of no effect. In practice, though, this was terrible news. The clickthrough rates on Facebook ads were abysmal, mostly due to their crappy targeting. A 0.05 percent clickthrough rate was average; achieve a rate of 0.11 percent and you were ordering the truffled steak at Alexander's in SoMa (on the client's dime, of course). Compared with regular display advertising, Facebook ads didn't even register; even the worst-targeted ads (e.g., those moronic "punch the monkey" pseudogame banners) got clickthrough rates of at least 0.1 percent, and well-targeted ads using first-party data and rich, dynamic creative got click rates as high as 1 percent or more. It meant Facebook ads underperformed by as much as

---

* Titled *Social Influence in Social Advertising: Evidence from Field Experiments*, the paper would eventually appear at an Association for Computing Machinery e-commerce conference, with Eytan Bakshy, Dean Eckles, Rong Yan, and Itamar Rosenn as its authors. Facebook's data-science team was absolutely top-notch and boasted both already-prominent academics and young, up-and-coming PhDs who were ecstatic to get their busy hands on Facebook's vast store of proprietary data. The team's papers, such as this one, were always carefully executed experiments that often called bullshit on some social media truism—often one that originated with Facebook itself.

twenty times, if you were actually doing the bookkeeping (which many FB advertisers were not). Thus, a 60 percent bump in performance was nice, but it was piddly-boo compared with the lift generated by real, piping-hot targeting data. Facebook had bet its entire monetization future on a scheme that modestly boosted clickthrough, and even then it wasn't clear why; the Facebook Research paper mentioned a host of possible experimental confounds. I had seen an early version of the paper and reviewed the basic results, and knew how much of this cheerleading around social context was wishful thinking.

I wasn't the only one, of course. Facebook's ads partners, independent companies that made money creating and managing ads for clients, knew the Facebook ad system better than the people who had created it. In meeting after meeting with these partners, they'd stress as diplomatically as they could that they weren't seeing any real performance difference with the new Sponsored Stories. The ads partners were receiving tremendous pressure from Facebook to push Sponsored Stories on clients; as was then typically the case, Facebook Ads products had to be forced down the throats of partners, who then forced them down the throats of advertisers. Since Facebook Ads didn't ship products that people actually asked for, launching always had a certain foie-gras-duck-undergoing-gavage quality to it: open up and pump it in.*

However, to my earlier point, the performance gains at-

* The justification for this is an attitude best expressed in an apocryphal quote usually credited to the automotive pioneer Henry Ford, and bandied about by would-be visionaries: "If I had asked what my customers wanted, they'd have said 'faster horses.'" The idea here is that the truly prophetic product leader can figure out what users want, even if users themselves can't really conceptualize it. Facebook Ads operated under this collective delusion for years, and still does to a certain extent.

tributed to Sponsored Stories (to the extent they even existed outside the perfect test conditions of the Facebook data-science team) weren't significant in the everyday noise of a live ads campaign. And so the partners were struggling to get advertisers to invest in the new, sexy hotness. Facebook's reaction was to basically tell them to grip the goose tighter and stick the tube farther down its throat.

Yet despite all these hints of failure and fundamentally wrong direction, here we were at the big FMC show, with Paul Adams standing onstage with an image of a stylized social network behind him, like George C. Scott in *Patton* holding forth before an immense American flag, lecturing the media elite about their patriotic duty in this social media war we'd all been drafted into. All I could do was look around and stare at the rapt faces, in disbelief at the fraud of it all. When it came to product marketing in tech, that old Fleet Street mantra was law: never let the facts get in the way of a good story.

The concluding gala was held in the museum's cavernous Hall of Ocean Life. Surrounded by fascinating and completely ignored displays of marine life, including a life-size blue whale model dangling from the ceiling, the Facebook marketing army was beguiling the nicely drunken New York media elite. At some point, Alicia Keys and a piano suddenly appeared, as if airlifted in, on one side of the huge gallery. The party kicked into high gear, and even the Facebookers stopped pretending to sell anything. I didn't know who this Keys person was or why every salesperson around me was squirming in excitement. Large crowds trigger my always incipient misanthropy, and when the crush of people became a mob, I booked it out of there in an Uber. By the time I got back to the Ace Hotel in the Flatiron, my feed had a hundred copies of the same image: a spotlit woman at a piano, under a whale, with hundreds of cheering people. *The best thing ever*, droned the social media masses. To the salespeople, who led shitty, underpaid lives spent rehearsing the script of a movie in which they never starred, this was one of the very reasons for working at Facebook. Everyone got his show in the end.

It's easy for us to see the madness of Sponsored Stories now. The ecstatic throes of cultish product development resemble fog in more than one way. As with fog, when you're in the middle of it, you can't really see it. The fog obscures the farthest reaches of your vision, but everything in your vicinity looks normal. The true density of a fog bank can be seen only from a distance, at a remove. Nobody inside the Ads org—from Sheryl to the top Ads leadership, freshly poached from Google, to the line product managers like me—ever called bullshit on this utterly improbable business model.

Brian Boland, then the VP of Ads Product Marketing, and the marketing analogue to Gokul, had a magnum of Veuve Clicquot on his desk tagged with a Post-it predicting "10% revenue from Sponsored Stories." As with many failed or stalled product ventures at Facebook, Boland was leading the blind charge. The goal for Sponsored Stories was to get to at least a tenth of Facebook revenue by the end of 2011. Well, the numbers never even got close. I always wondered what happened to that bottle; I'm guessing Boland quietly took it home and drank it to the thought of all those entreating emails and client pitches.

As part of the collective noodling on just what the hell to do, I participated in the first of what would be a long series of Sheryl meetings. Sheryl's role in the Ads construct was interesting. During that time, her conference room—whose name "Only Good News" soon assumed an ironic tinge—would serve as the final appellate court in any disputes on product direction inside the Ads organization (and there were many). Since Zuck had more or less completely outsourced the management of monetization to her, she was the vicar of the social media Christ, the viceroy of the Zuckian throne. She would front for his leadership, as well as strategize how to best gain his favor, a billion-dollar skill in which she excelled above all others.

On a sunny day in March 2012 the Ads high command, plus a few relevant PMs like your humble correspondent, gathered in Sheryl's lair to discuss the worsening revenue situation. The IPO was in a couple of months. Forward-looking growth was not what the market had come to expect via the leaked whisper numbers about FB revenue, which had historically almost doubled year to year. Sponsored Stories was a bust, and all Facebook had to offer was more fairy tales about Facebook pages and the magical effects of followers to one's brand. Those fairy tales had been believed for a while, with the biggest brand budgets in the world—Burberry, Ford, Starbucks, BMW—spending money on Likes they didn't know what to do with, and that at best were a license to spam users' News Feeds.

Toward the end of the meeting, Sheryl finally snapped:

"That's it! Starbucks isn't going to spend ten million dollars per year for Likes. No one will do that anymore!"

She was of course right. The Like-buying party was officially over. Revenue growth was cratering. If Facebook didn't cook up something else, we were fucked.

Monetizing the Tumor

> Growth for the sake of growth is the ideology of the cancer cell.
>
> —Edward Abbey, *The Journey Home*

MARCH 2012

The sudden revenue desperation would breed many monsters, and a few product beauties. As was often my lot with Gokul, I was handed one of the product monsters, the most egregiously grasping and ill-conceived new revenue idea in a season grown thick with them. This idea was of particular interest, since it brought me into contact and conflict with the single most important group at Facebook, the one team that above all others can be credited with Facebook's humanity-spanning success.

That team was known simply as "Growth."

There are three certainties in life: death, taxes, and Facebook user growth.

The Ads team takes users and turns them into money. The Growth team takes money and turns it into users. Together they form the counterweighted yin-yang of Facebook. Appropriately enough, after our move from California Avenue, the two teams occupied opposing wings of Building 17.

The only solid marketers in all of Facebook were to be found not in Ads, but on the Growth team. Guys like Alex

Schultz, a big, beefy, loudmouthed Brit with a shaved head and a mean glare. Or Brian Piepgrass, a soft-spoken, ever-smiling Canadian who had never graduated from college, but who managed over a hundred million in annual marketing spend. These guys knew all the tricks. Before anyone on the Ads team even knew what real-time ad exchanges were (despite their having been around for years), the Growth team used them to retarget users who had almost registered for Facebook, but then through some fluke of Internet distraction decided to click away elsewhere.

Growth exploited every piece of psychological gimcrackery, every tool of visual legerdemain, to turn a pair of eyeballs into a Facebook user ID. Like the best direct-response marketers, they calculated statistics like clickthrough and conversion rates out to three decimals, and maintained comprehensive databases of user data. Whether via Skinnerian or Pavlovian psychology, they'd figure out the optimal rate to send reminder emails about in-Facebook events (like mentions or new posts from friends) for optimal response. They'd cut deals with mobile carriers to facilitate the Facebook user experience in dodgy countries with slow data service.

It was Growth that maintained a map of the world, like the board in a very-late-stage game of Risk, which tracked Facebook's global domination. At this stage, the only countries Growth had not managed to tip were either weird, dictatorial, or corrupt (or all three): Russia, Burma, Vietnam, and Iran.* Growth people were daily involved in the feverish crusade to turn those countries Facebook blue. One by one, every country fell to their relentless ministrations, and the also-rans in the social network space (Hi5, Orkut, MySpace) disappeared like some exotic and forgotten species of seabird.

The reality is that Facebook has been so successful, it's

* China, perhaps most saliently, was also not Facebook blue. The Chinese government has an express policy of blocking Facebook, and that social media gap is filled by local copycats.

actually running out of humans on the planet. Ponder the numbers: there are about three billion people on the Internet, where the latter is broadly defined as any sort of networked data, texts, browser, social media, whatever. Of these people, six hundred million are Chinese, and therefore effectively unreachable by Facebook. In Russia, thanks to Vkontakte and other copycat social networks, Facebook's share of the country's ninety million Internet users is also small, though it may yet win that fight. That leaves about 2.35 billion people ripe for the Facebook plucking.

While Facebook seems ubiquitous to the plugged-in, chattering classes, its usage is not universal among even entrenched Internet users. In the United States, for example, by far the company's most established and sticky market, only three-quarters of Internet users are actively on FB. That ratio of FB to Internet user is worse in other countries, so even full FB saturation in a given market doesn't imply total Facebook adoption. Let's (very) optimistically assume full US-level penetration for any market. Without China and Russia, and taking a 25 percent haircut of people who'll never join or stay (as is the case in the United States), that leaves around 1.8 billion potential Facebook users globally. That's it.

In the first quarter of 2015, Facebook announced it had 1.44 billion users. Based on its public 2014 numbers, FB is growing at around 13 percent a year, and that pace is slowing. Even assuming it maintains that growth into 2016, that means it's got one year of user growth left in it, and then that's it: Facebook has run out of humans on the Internet.

The company can solve this by either making more humans (hard even for Facebook), or connecting what humans there are left on the planet. This is why Internet.org exists, a vaguely public-spirited, and somewhat controversial, campaign by Facebook to wire all of India with free Internet, with regions like Brazil and Africa soon to follow. In early 2014 Facebook acquired a British aerospace firm, Ascenta, which specialized in solar-powered unmanned aerial vehicles. Facebook plans on flying a Wi-Fi-enabled air force of such craft over the developing world, giving them Internet. Just picture ultralight carbon-fiber aircraft buzzing over African savannas constantly, while locals check their Facebook feeds as they watch over their herds.

Facebook can't wait for the developing world to get to First World standards of connectivity, so it must create it for them, using ad revenues in the developed world to subsidize this new air force's deployment. In time, monetization will follow usage, as it always does. Money follows eyeballs, even if slowly.

Eventually Russia, Iran, India, Brazil, and parts of Africa will fall to the Growth team's patient ministrations. Then, Mark Zuckerberg, like a young Alexander the Great at the Indus River, will weep for having no more world to conquer.

This all sounds very airy-fairy, so here's a real example of the Ads versus Growth dialectic to illustrate:

Among the various weird products I happened to manage while at Facebook, one is particularly relevant. Let's flash-forward for a moment. The Logout Experience (LOX) was one of Facebook's mid-2012 IPO period "completely fucking desperate let's make more money now" products.

Basically it was this: when you logged out of Facebook, instead of seeing the usual Facebook log-in/register page, you would see what amounted to the upper half of a regular Facebook page; that is, the cover photo and header that we all know from our own Facebook profiles. The idea was to sell this space to the richest and stupidest advertiser of all, the legacy-admissions student of digital media: the brand marketer. Brand marketers, like politicians, are people paid to spend other people's money. In this case, their putative goal is to raise "brand awareness," that diaphanous and quasi-intangible substance that makes you covet a $10,000 Rolex Submariner when you finally get that bonus or promotion.

The other equally trigger-happy marketer who would supposedly devour LOX was the Hollywood-centric agency that wished to trumpet the release of another cinematic crime against humanity. The Logout Experience was Facebook's attempt to present a tempting target to those marketers, the equivalent of a large banner ad or takeover.

The name "LOX," a bit of product marketing genius from Scott Shapiro, stemmed from the historical tradition of naming Facebook Ads products after either birds or fishes. Given this was a form of preserved Facebook (i.e., you saw it after having already logged out), FB salmon became FB LOX, and a product was born.

So far, so mercenary.

What was the problem?

In Ads, we had completely failed to realize the importance of the logout page on FB.

A bit of background: In most developing countries, people do not own desktop computers, and their phones are non-smartphone pieces of shit (this is, of course, gradually changing). So people do what you do as a Western backpacker in Brazil or India or whatever: they use an Internet café or other public computer. They log in, use Facebook at some rate per hour, and then log out. What they leave behind is the logout screen, which just so happens to be the most common webpage up on browsers in the world. Really. You walk into a library or café anywhere in the world, and most of the screens will be glowing Facebook blue. And that is also how most new Facebook users in these countries came into being, not to mention nudging existing users into using Facebook. A fact that we in Ads did not even begin to appreciate.

The key to understanding the somewhat tense Ads-Growth dialectic is this: What makes a user use the product does not necessarily make money, and the reverse is also true. In fact, they're anticorrelated in general, and you can drive engagement or make money, but not both at once.

With LOX, we were proposing blocking the very gateway to FB user growth, in exchange for a few hundred thousand dollars from *The Hangover Part III*. It was likely a seriously bad trade for Facebook that the Growth team had every reason to reject, and that wouldn't even be on the table were it not for the little detail of the IPO.

This obviously set the stage for several tense meetings with the Growth team: the aforementioned bullheaded Alex Schultz (whom I actually liked and got along with), and the aforementioned Naomi Gleit, who was a senior member of the team. They raged like we were proposing murdering rescue puppies and selling them as chicken wings for our next monetization model, even though they couldn't seem to quite quantify the actual cost in usage of our taking over the logout page every once in a while. To be fair, we had kind of sprung this on them, the question was a subtle and complex one, and they had other, bigger problems than helping out Ads. But still, it was impossible to gauge a definitive money versus growth trade-off, which meant that outrage and personal sway (which the Growth team had mountains of) clinched it.

In the end, the net of the Ads-Growth pissing match was that we could run LOX units only in certain countries, places where Growth had already defeated all other social media comers, but not in others, where the battle was still a bit tenuous. And so, the sales playbook, as orchestrated by Scott Shapiro of LOX-naming fame, featured this ad unit only in countries like the United States, where Facebook reigned triumphant, but not in Brazil, where the cadaver of Google's pitiable early social media effort Orkut was still warm. Such was the eternal tug-of-war between monetization and growth that I had stumbled into, and was more than happy to abandon at the first opportunity. A few weeks later, we launched LOX, the sales team ran with it, and I never paid attention to it ever again.

The Great Awakening

> And he causeth all, both small and great, rich and poor, free and slave, to receive a mark in their right hand, or in their foreheads: and that no man might buy or sell, save he that had the mark, . . . or the number of his name.
>
> —Revelation 13:16–17

MARCH 2012

What's the first thing every child learns? What's the first lesson we impart to a new pet? What makes us snap instantly out of any reverie, no matter how deep?

A name.

It's simple, but magical when you think about it: you say a special word, and the person (or dog, or infant) turns and directs his or her attention at you. Involuntary and yet so fundamental, it's practically the definition of self-awareness: I know who I am, and will respond when called. At the core of how we express ourselves lies a name; every language textbook starts with the mock dialogue *my name is . . . je m'appelle . . . ich heiße.* It's central to our identity; there's nothing more dehumanizing than losing one's name as a result of political persecution or incarceration, being reduced to an inhuman number in an assembly line of brutality. Without our names, *we* wouldn't be *us*.

Modern advertising is just selective name-calling, which is why it's so wonderfully primal. How is that? The only difference between the various marketing channels we think are so distinct is the names we use to address the target audience. How advertising works is effectively a call-and-response of names, with some mechanisms being far more efficient than others.

So what are those names?

In the direct-mail advertising world, it's the postal address we affix to a piece of third-class mail. For example, if Bed Bath & Beyond wants to get my attention with one of its wonderful 20 percent off coupons, it calls out:

> Antonio García Martínez
> 1 Clarence Place #13
> San Francisco, CA 94107

If it wants to reach me on my mobile device, my name there is:

> 38400000-8cf0-11bd-b23e-10b96e40000d

That's my quasi-immutable device ID, broadcast hundreds of times a day on mobile ad exchanges.

On my laptop, my name is this:

> 07J6yJPMB9juTowar.AWXGQnGPA1MCmThgb9wN-4vLoUpg.BUUtWg.rg.FTN.0.AWUxZtUf

This is the contents of the Facebook retargeting cookie, which is used to target ads to you based on your Web browsing.

Though it may not be obvious, each of these keys is associated with a wealth of our personal behavior data: every website we've been to, many things we've bought in physical stores, and every app we've used and what we did there.*

The longevity of these keys and their associated data is important, however. We move our physical address less often than we clear the cookies in our browser, or than McAfee does for us. Changing devices is somewhere in between, which is why data-privacy issues on mobile are so much more challenging than on desktop.†

The biggest thing going on in marketing right now, what is generating tens of billions of dollars in investment and endless scheming inside the bowels of Facebook, Google, Amazon, and Apple, is the puzzle of how to tie these different sets of names together, and who controls the links. That's it. Other than this *Game of Thrones* power struggle among the great digital powers to control identity, targeting, and attribution, everything else is a parasitic sideshow scarcely worth the hassle of following.

Mobile, desktop, and offline: every marketer is chasing

---

* A slice-of-life side note on corporate life: while the entire identity vision was a group effort, this metaphor for Facebook identity as various names for the same person, for which Facebook was global messenger, was authored by me, and first pitched in an early slide deck. In a Sheryl meeting that followed shortly after, Boland, ever the Sheryl lackey, took my slides from a group email, replaced the personal details with his own (down to his family's home address in Atherton!), and presented the vision to Sheryl. I was torn between outrage and humor as Boland walked through it right in front of me (he'd of course neglected to even mention it beforehand). Those plodding middle managers and their wiles!

† The longer data persists, the more users and politicians worry. In the case of mobile, the device ID that's used to track and target you is (mostly) permanent, and is associated with the physical device in your hand. If Facebook were to accidentally leak the fact you liked "Kanye West" or are a thirty-four-year-old male, then that data will be associated with your device ID, and reused by unscrupulous outsiders forever. Browser cookies, which tend to last a few weeks at most, don't present that threat.

after three chimerical and incomplete images of its consumer targets, like a punch-drunk boxer seeing triple and throwing wild haymakers in every direction. But behind it all there's a single person: a nervous ball of needs, wants, and anxieties, whose species evolved in a Paleolithic world of toothy predators and the hunter-gatherer feast-famine duality, and who is presently confronted, a mere blip of time later, with an endless feast of blinking lights and hyperoptimized stimuli. Can you blame the poor beasts for clicking themselves to death with Candy Crush Saga, or maniacally (and frictionlessly) squandering resources they don't have on things they don't need? The real unmet challenge here is reconciling all those various names for that one fidgety brain. This is what we figured out in 2012. This is why Facebook invested such an extraordinary amount of time, money, and people in its biggest ads-related acquisition to date, Atlas (and much more on that soon enough).

How would this work in practice?

Say you browse for something on Target's website while at work, but you don't want to buy it, because your boss is around and whipping out your credit card is awkward. Using the desktop-to-mobile identity-join provided by Facebook, Target finds you playing a mobile game on your smartphone while commuting home. It takes over your app experience for a few seconds, perhaps between levels (such a complete device takeover is known as an "interstitial"). Internalizing those calls to consume, even if subconsciously, you're eventually nudged into buying that coveted thing when finally at home on your personal machine. Using the device-joining ability of Facebook, the advertiser knows who you are on the three devices: work laptop, mobile device, and home desktop.

Or perhaps, to really strut our identity stuff here, you buy it only a week later, when you stop by the store. You pay for the item using your rewards card, for which you entered an address and phone number when you registered. Using the on-boarding technology we'll get to shortly, Target has already joined that to your browsers and mobile devices, forming a complete online and offline picture of you as a consumer.

What happens then?

The revenue from that sale (whether online or in the physical store) is credited toward the mobile media ad impression the advertiser paid for. Thanks to this identity bridge between all devices, advertisers know exactly what paid media influenced you to consume. The ad server, the company that actually showed you the ad on that mobile game you were playing, understands exactly which set of flashing pixels, the most virtual thing in the world, made you spend cold, hard cash. Suddenly, that mobile ad impression the games publisher sold you becomes that much more valuable.

Sounds Big Brother–ish, you might think.

But who really is Big Brother these days?

Facebook or Google? Nah, not even close. The NSA and the entire Snowden surveillance state? Maybe, if you frequent jihadist websites. The FBI-CIA apparatus? Yes and no. They took a decade to get Bin Laden, and shut down people selling drugs online via Silk Road only after the founder made some clumsy mistakes.

I submit that the role of modern-day Big Brother is actually played by companies you've likely never heard about. Companies with names like Acxiom, Experian, Epsilon, Merkle, and Neustar (among others). These are the companies that since the dawn of the direct-marketing age in the sixties and seventies have been tracking all of consumer America. They know your name, address, phone number, email address, education level, rough income, who else is in your household and their ages and spending patterns, and which consumer segment you fit into—and they've been accumulating this information since before the Internet even existed.

But it gets better.

They suck in what's known as customer relations management (CRM) data from most big retailers, basically the rap sheet on each and every customer—the data holy of holies for them. They supplement any incomplete data, construct ever more accurate personal profiles, craft targeting segments for use online and off, and employ them to find similar people in their endless consumer database. Unlike the Stasi's archives, now available to former East Germans, no one, with few exceptions, can access these records.

Does that all matter?

We live in a society in which your cultural, religious, or political identity has been supplanted by your consumption patterns ("soccer mom"; "iPad generation"; "Nascar dad"). In fact, companies like Nielsen have constructed detailed menageries of consumers, organized along multiple dimensions like family size, education, income, dwelling, and so forth, and with amusing monikers like "Beltway Boomers" and "Country Casuals." Marketed as the "PRIZM Segments," they form a sort of predictive zodiac of consumption, purportedly allowing marketers to tailor their inducements to demographic archetypes.

You consume; therefore, you are. These companies are the caretakers of that non-Internet commercial identity, and frankly not much else about you matters in this capitalistic world. Think about it: Which would most terrify you to have posted on a billboard in your hometown: your voting record during the last ten years of elections, or your buying history at Walmart (or on Amazon)?

Exactly.

And how did this enormous nationwide surveillance apparatus, without even the merest hint of oversight or regulation, come to exist? The mail, ladies and gentlemen. That's right, the postage-stamp people.

Get this.

By the Post Office's own figures, direct-mail advertising resulted in over $17 billion in revenue to the Post Office in postage alone, propping up what would otherwise be a bankrupt organization. The entire direct-mail industry, that crap in the mail you throw away, is surely north of a $50 billion a year industry if you consider design, printing, targeting data, and postage.

To put that in perspective, all of Google makes just over that much in a year. In 2014, online marketers spent about $19 billion on display (basically, the Internet other than Google and Facebook). So we've got almost another Google, three Internets, or three Facebooks of money waiting in the offline sidelines.

Think about that for a second, particularly if you, like me, live in the maelstrom of pixels and electrons that characterizes contemporary digital life. To do direct mail, you have to kill a tree, make it into paper, hire a designer, print something pretty on it, properly package or envelope the thing, and then pay the Post Office around $.20 in bulk to send it. Do the math. It works out to about $1,000 CPMs (cost per thousand views). Most online media sells for somewhere around $1 CPM, perhaps a bit more. That means online advertising can get away with being a thousand times less effective than mail, and still come out even in terms of your marketing return.

Ask yourself: Which have you done more recently, clicked on an ad and bought something online, as rare as that may be, or responded to a mail solicitation?

Yep.

So there's a pile of money $50 billion tall waiting to launch itself into digital media if it can just figure out how to translate all that data it has into a form of online identity.

This is already happening. Sort of.

The term of art to describe this witchcraft is "data onboarding," and it works as follows: Companies like Datalogix, Neustar, and LiveRamp buy Web real estate on second-tier social networks (Hi5 or Orkut, anyone?), email newsletters, dating sites (hint: Match.com doesn't just make money on subscriptions), or anywhere that personal information like name and address meets a browser. That means these on-boarding companies literally have a tiny image (usually just white space) on whatever your browser is loading when you're interacting with an email or with a website where you've got an account—anyplace that knows offline details about you. That's enough for them to either drop a cookie or read one that's already there. Since they know from the newsletter you're reading that your email is agm@gmail.com, or from Match.com that your name is Antonio García Martínez, they know to associate that browser cookie with various pieces of your personal information. That personal information is stored in a database, along with the browser cookie that corresponds to it, forming a bridge from real-world you to the browser version of you. It's probably in hashed form, but that's just privacy theater; if everyone agrees on the same hash function, it doesn't matter how it's stored.*

That join, between a cookie and personal information, is then sold and resold a bazillion times a day to whoever is willing to pay for it. Using our description of keys above, we've joined a physical address, phone number, or legal name to an online device: the world of atoms has become bits, and vice versa.

Why is this important?

Think about it: Media publishers like Facebook and Google are just more efficient versions of the post office. They deliver a message for money. They'll even give you a return receipt if you ask for it. What's different is the address they use to send it. In our mediated age, we've gotten to the point that a Facebook or Google user ID is a better way

---

* Hashing is a computer-science construct at the core of much we do on the Internet. In very simplified form, it's a function that maps arbitrary inputs to stable numerical outputs. It's a veiled, leakproof way of comparing data, without giving up all the goods. You get to check equality of identity, without revealing identity itself (in the case of unmatched people). Think of it as a data condom: the action still takes place, but no extraneous data is shared.

of reaching you than a name or physical address. I can scar your retinas for almost nothing (relatively) if I know your Facebook user ID; your name and address would do nothing for me—unless, of course, they provided the primary key to a database of buying behavior spanning decades. Which they do, and that's the only reason, along with the legacy inertia of big-company business relationships, that Acxiom, Epsilon, et al. are even still in business.

On-boarding in the Facebook context is even cleverer. Facebook and companies like Acxiom and Datalogix have compared personal data (with none sharing actual data with the other, again via the miracle of hashing), and joined the universal FB user ID to the analogous IDs inside Acxiom, Datalogix, and Epsilon.

The advantage that Facebook and Google have over the regular data on-boarders is twofold: they have much more of your personal data, and they see you online all the time. The match rate (i.e., the percentage of offline personas that can be found online) for Facebook's Custom Audiences product, introduced in 2012 (and more on that shortly), is as high as 90 percent. That means for every hundred people marketers target via Custom Audiences, Facebook will find ninety of them, a shockingly high fraction in the fuzzy world of advertising.

Facebook, Google, and others have achieved the holy grail of all marketers: a high-fidelity, persistent, and immutable pseudonym for every consumer online. Even better, they've joined that to your real-world persona, the one that shows up bleary-eyed at two a.m. at a Target in El Cerrito looking for tampons or a six-pack of Natural Light.

Incidentally, this is all public, and fully documented by Facebook press releases. It's just poorly understood and no one thinks about it. But people probably should.

I've delivered this now lengthy disquisition on digital marketing in a fairly straightforward and clear manner, as I hope you'll agree. There was nothing remotely straightforward or clear about the process by which Facebook arrived at these conclusions, however. In fact, this master plan, which emerged as Facebook's strategic play for digital dominance, took a good year of feverish debate, endless meetings with dozens of advertising companies, and full-throttle product development that changed direction the moment it started.

One of the more popular Facebook posters announced EVERY DAY FEELS LIKE A WEEK, which was true. Facebook was such an all-consuming mosh pit of a job, it felt you had somehow survived five days when you finally clocked out at ten p.m. (every day). Every month felt like a year. And a year? Well, you can imagine what that felt like.

The people most directly responsible for Facebook's digital marketing vision from the product perspective were Brian Boland, Mark Rabkin, Mathew Varghese, Brian Rosenthal, and me. There was also considerable assistance from Ben Reesman, Hari Manikarnika, and Gary Wu, engineers who were on a team I'd lead that pioneered a novel approach to the identity problem. It's worth pausing for a moment to describe the cast of characters.

Boland we've already met. He was at this point director of product marketing for Ads, and would soon enough be VP for Ads Technology.

Rabkin was an interesting character. The child of Soviet Jews in that bumper crop of tech talent that the US harvested from Brezhnev on, he was a rising engineering management star in Facebook Ads. We had initially worked together when he managed the ads infrastructure that was critical to targeting, and we'd grown close via many product collaborations. All ambitious men want either to please their fathers or to punch them in the goddamned face. Rabkin was the former, taking feedback on his performance seriously, going to grad school to please aforementioned father, and generally believing in the powers that be. I was the latter, and that's what ultimately would divide us (not to mention condition our respective attitudes toward Facebook's management).

Varghese was a Google product manager with a PhD in electrical engineering and a background in data. Time elsewhere had made him immune to blinkered Facebook bullshit, and he'd eventually take over the targeting team after I got swallowed by other products.

Rosenthal was an exceptionally capable and easygoing engineering manager on the targeting team who'd manage one of two engineering teams that came out of this ideation process. He represented the best in Facebook engineering: irreverence without disrespect, competence without arrogance, ambition without ego.

How did we finally get on the right track? The way Facebook sussed out anything: it mooched information from potential acquirees and business partners via meetings of dubious good faith, and then figured out how to hack the outside world to its advantage. It's what every large company with incumbent leverage does, incidentally.

Thus did some permutation of this crew, with one or another product marketer or engineer in tow, visit or meet with every company in this space, and I do mean every. Companies called Turn and MediaMath, which had each built the leading programmatic ads-buying technologies for ad agencies—the product interfaces looked like the cockpit of an F-16—patiently walked us through every technical and business aspect of their world. The market leader in third-party targeting data, a data broker named BlueKai, schematically guided us along every piece of its data plumbing. Meetings with Acxiom and Epsilon yielded explanations of how they warehoused all the world's consumer information, and used it with pinpoint targeting accuracy.

The tech companies in this world were extraordinarily savvy, and understood better than we did how Facebook could monetize its data. During these initial meetings, in which we delicately (or so we thought) asked leading and instructive questions, these companies very patiently answered them all. On more than one occasion, I caught a look or overheard a slipped comment that revealed just how incredulous they were at our cluelessness. I'm sure they went back to their offices and had a good laugh at our stupid questions. But we were Facebook, so they had to smile to our faces and appear promptly at every meeting in a giving mood.

The old-school companies that came out of the direct-mail world were less technically savvy. I still remember our first meeting with Experian.* They didn't know what the hell was up, and I'm sure whoever Boland or Rob Daniel (our business-development guy) first contacted was probably the wrong entry point to the company, but the net of it was they sent out a relatively junior B team. Given the epic data join Facebook was contemplating, this was a time-wasting mistake on their part, but we went with the meeting we had. This sharp point of the intimidating direct-mail spear was composed of two people: a nice, matronly woman named Carmen, and a kind of rumpled, wrinkled dude whose name I forget. Carmen held a large box in her arms.

It should be noted that Experian was based in Schaumberg, Illinois (a distant suburb of Chicago; I had to look it up), and they had flown out from the heartland for this meeting.

"I brought you these. Enjoy!" Carmen thrust the box into my arms, and the emetic smell of vegetable shortening hit my nostrils.

---

* You might know Experian as one of the Big Three credit bureaus that determine your financial reliability. That's but one side of their business, and a relatively small one at that. The other business is tracking everything you buy with that credit they helped you get.

"Ah . . . and these are?" I asked, with a smile plastered on my face.

"Cookies!" said Carmen. She looked like a woman who enjoyed baked goods.

"Ah-ha . . ." I said, and looked down.

It was a red-and-white striped box with the name of a local bakery plastered on it. Looked like the small-town institution that produced the Proustian madeleines of a Midwestern childhood. "Schultz's Bakery. Est. 1929." That sort of thing.

Trying to make light of this awkwardness, I ventured some humor:

"But I thought we were bringing the cookies to this deal . . ."

Carmen and Rumpled Guy looked at me, smiling in that polite way you do when you've missed a beat. The entire proposed relationship was of course a huge trade of Experian's personal data for Facebook's cookie data (since Facebook knew every browser you were on). Experian brought to the table everything you bought in the physical world along with your name, email, and address, and Facebook was to tell it where you were online; ergo, the browser cookies. But they didn't get that . . . or much of anything in the meeting that followed.

We were clueless relative to the wizened ad-tech pros who had built an edifice we didn't understand outside our walled Facebook garden. Yet we lived in a different world from these direct-mail people. Facebook was kind of stuck in the middle, and trying to move in both directions at once.

Barbarians at the Gates

And the LORD said unto Joshua: . . . "Ye shall compass the city, all the men of war, going about the city once. Thus shalt thou do six days. . . . And the seventh day ye shall compass the city seven times, and the priests shall blow with the horns.

"And it shall be, that when they make a long blast with the ram's horn, and when ye hear the sound of the horn, all the people shall shout with a great shout; *and the wall of the city shall fall down flat*, and the people shall go up every man straight before him."

—Joshua 6:2–5

MARCH 13, 2012

I had my own ideas about how Facebook could finally join the outside world of real ads targeting, and stave off the coming revenue catastrophe.

Here was the reality: the Facebook Ads system was backward, clunky, buggy, and slow. If you were to date it by what previous ads-technology incarnation it resembled, you'd say it was like Yahoo circa 2007, in terms of actual value of data and targeting ability. If Zuck knew anything about ads (and he largely didn't) he'd likely have been embarrassed by the rudimentary state of Facebook's ads system, from the purely technical if not the monetary level. As I've said before, a billion times anything is still a big number, so Facebook was still making respectable revenue, but if you had asked any advertising-technology entrepreneur about the status of Facebook in the middle of 2012, he or she likely would have replied with an indiscreet chuckle.

This was a state of affairs not even remotely acknowledged internally, of course. Facebook Ads didn't know what it didn't know. The company was like the rich moneybags' son: short on skill, but long on an inheritance, and everyone had to deal with him to be part of the action, no matter how cockeyed his ideas.

Seen from the jaundiced eye of the outside advertising world, Facebook had for years been completely unconnected to any outside data source, with no real tracking or attribution to figure out which Facebook ads were working (and where). Now we were proposing rendering a quarter of the Internet targetable via all the online data in existence. Every product you'd looked at or bought, everything known about your online reading or browsing habits—it was all going to be inside your Facebook experience now.

There were two ways to do this.

The first would end up being called Custom Audiences (CA), and was an extension of the existing ads system. Like the data "on-boarding" we talked about earlier, it would be a way to join offline data like names, addresses, and emails to Facebook users. That was its original and sole intent, though it soon grew into much more.

The second, more interesting approach, Facebook Exchange, or FBX, would form the final chapter in the programmatic takeover of digital media: a real-time exchange connecting the world's advertising data, user by user, and ad impression by ad impression, to the Facebook experience.*

How did it all work?

In the CA case, advertisers had to upload lists of email addresses, phone numbers, names, or other personally identifiable information (PII), and manually craft some targeting cluster ("people who bought something last month"). The Facebook technology, drafting as it was off recycled targeting technology, was creaky and slow, and often broke down.

In the FBX case, it would be the New York Stock Exchange of eyeballs, human desire traded for money billions of times a day in real time. With this real-time pipe from the outside world to all of Facebook, the company would go from targeting someone who had accidentally liked Jay-Z two years ago to targeting someone who had just chosen between three different shoes at Zappos, or read an article on the new Mazda Miata, or bought something on eBay, just like *that*!

Facebook needed—*needed!*—a real-time ad exchange.

A move of this magnitude could be approved only by the topmost level of the Facebook Ads high command. As such, it was necessary to sell the Ads high command on a technology most had never heard of, much less understood. Rank ignorance was an unsteady base for a decision, so the leadership had to have the perception of understanding conveyed to them somehow. Hard to believe now, but at the time nobody at Facebook knew anything about retargeting, with the exception of the Growth team, and they lived in their own world.

---

* I'd coin the name and acronym FBX at two a.m. some night in the hell-for-leather blur that was the month of FBX conception and gestation. I recalled some marketing nostrum or another about how brand names with an X stand out. Plus, it was a trolling reference to AdX, the Google exchange.

I would be the product's internal champion, and navigate Facebook's internal turmoil to conjure resources and consensus. I'd also make sure all the proper people were in meetings and pitch sessions. But someone from outside had to serve as the voice of the market. Someone who knew the world of programmatic advertising inside and out, and yet had the nonsleazy salesmanship and technical chops it would take to convince Facebook engineering and product managers. Finding a knowledgeable yet trustworthy player in the advertising space was like finding a snowball in hell. But then, someone came to mind.

Zach Coelius was one of the more colorful figures in the Valley advertising world. A Midwestern boy from Minnesota, he had appeared in San Francisco out of nowhere in 2005, and had made himself a figure in the VC landscape by playing in the high-stakes poker games put on by wealthy angel investors. After taking their money at the poker table, he'd take even larger sums from them in the form of investments. He formed a company with his sister doing some trendy and pointless idea, but in 2006 he sensed the way the advertising winds were blowing. Along with several other companies who became competitors, he started a "demand-side platform" (DSP): the sophisticated ads-buying technology that, like a stockbroker, interfaced with exchanges in the service of ads buyers.

I barely knew Zach at the time and had interacted with him precisely once, but that once had made an impression. During the AdGrok days, I'd played in a biweekly low-stakes poker game that rotated among the various early-stage startups in SoMa. The variant of poker we played was called Hold 'Em, and it was the poker flavor of the moment, played in most tournaments. Two cards were dealt per player, and a set of communal table cards completed the usual five-card poker hands.

Two tables, featuring about a dozen tech geeks, were going when a brown-haired guy in a scarlet T-shirt that screamed TRIGGIT appeared. He seated himself between the tables, with nary a hello, and started playing a hand at each table. He played hyperaggressively—what poker wonks call "loose aggressive"—and transformed what was a fairly social, sluggish game into a street fight. I managed to avoid the runaway aggression truck, until I was dealt two aces. Sneaking a look at them, I decided to "slowplay" them, betting less aggressively than I should, merely to keep players in the game and ponying up money I'd soon win. Feeling the general table weakness, the guy in the red shirt plunked down a pile of chips, betting in aggressively as usual. I called and raised a largish amount, inducing him to follow and snapping the slowplay trap. Zach took one look at me and folded. Everyone else did the same. I collected the (small) bets I had managed to capture thanks to underplaying a monster hand, then half-jokingly asked him why he had backed down so abruptly.

"Because you had a monster hand. I could tell the moment you looked at your cards," he replied.

I flipped over the two aces and showed the table. "Indeed," I said, impressed and embarrassed by his ability to read me.

Of course, I had connected the shirt with the name at this point, and knew whom I was dealing with. In that moment, I recalled an offhand comment AdGrok's lead investor, Russell Siegelman, had made: he had invested in Triggit, but had been pushed out of later rounds by its aggressive CEO. Using that bridge, I mentioned to Zach that he and I shared a common investor, glossing over the fact of Zach's little putsch.* He casually corrected me—Russ was a *former* investor—but with that we started talking about advertising.

Fast-forward two years, and he was about the only person

---

* To startup founders, sharing a common investor is like being from two families joined by marriage. It isn't quite blood family, but it is a common bond that can result in investor intros and maybe mutual aid.

I knew inside the real-time advertising world. If he could see through me, then he could see through the fish who would be sitting at the Facebook conference table.* I carefully navigated the packed schedules and prickly admins of Facebook Ads executives, and found one one-hour slot where everyone who mattered in Ads was free, and invited Zach to come in and pitch to the assembled Facebook notables.

Five minutes before the meeting, I personally rounded up the distinguished attendees: KX, Hegeman (the legendary head of Ads optimization), Boland, Rabkin, a dozen engineers. Meeting attendance at Facebook was about as flaky as a meth head's promises to quit, so sometimes tugging at the leash was required.

Zach pulled off a bravura performance. For one hour, he held the Ads management team spellbound at the sweep and scope of programmatic ads buying, for both direct-marketing and brand advertisers. It was the shiny bauble that Facebook needed in its public-company future. We skipped the slick sales pitch, and focused on the gee-whiz coolness of all that real-time data and decisioning made possible (which is how you sold the engineering-heavy management), along with lots of whiteboard schematics mapping out the business case, and the meeting ended in a rare lovefest. An entire management stratum that was usually completely uninterested in the ads world outside Facebook was suddenly fired up and excited.

I'd make sure to exploit the burst of enthusiasm fully in the coming days, following up with an entire product and business case that reiterated the need for Facebook's entry (finally) into the real ads-targeting space. It felt like Y Combinator Demo Day all over again, but with an audience of Facebook product and engineering leaders, and with an even more successful result.

---

* A "fish" is the chump or the sucker at the table, who's taken advantage of by practiced players. As the saying goes, if you look around the table and can't tell who the sucker is, then you're the sucker.

MAY 4, 2012

Five weeks.

Five weeks was what we had to ship a real-time ads exchange for Facebook.

If we shipped by June 15, it would be the end of the second quarter (Q2), and we'd be ready to book revenue in Q3, the first full quarter after the IPO. If we had advertiser adoption dialed in, then we could stand to profit from the always huge Q4, when every retailer was incinerating mountains of money on advertising to make its numbers in the Christmas shopping season. It was an insane timeline, but there was no choice.

Since the Zach pitch, Sponsored Stories had well and truly died, and the company was under no more illusions about Facebook fairy dust.

I was given all of three engineers for the ambitious task.

Ben Reesman looked like a guy who did multimillion-dollar real estate deals in Los Angeles, not someone who slung sophisticated back-end code for Facebook's ever-expanding and needy ads infrastructure. He made the very first code change for FBX, allowing Facebook's data store to accept the targeting pseudonyms—the nicknames for you, the Facebook user—we'd soon start shooting around billions of times a day. He was a brogrammer, a title he wore with pride. This was a species of educated, well-socialized frat boy who coded PHP or C++, all the while maintaining the dress and hygiene of a college junior at the Alpha Tau Omega house at UVA.* He was, in many ways, the antithesis of the unkempt basement dweller people call to mind when think-

* To be fair to Reesman, despite fitting the fashion bill, he was far from being a frat boy, actually having left college under unusual circumstances (and after never formally going to high school). His exceptional programming skills were self-taught, and his talent absolutely innate. Like a Melville character, part of his story was both recorded and concealed in tattoos

ing about programmers. Think instead of Bluto (played by John Belushi) in *Animal House*, but slimmed down, and with a computer science education (and perhaps even $200 sunglasses). Code, curls, and girls, those were the priorities of the day, and in that order.* It reflected the reality that coding, far from being the loserly redoubt of the socially isolated loner, was now the avenue for social mobility and elitism of even the football captain. Whenever real money and status were on the line, as they were now, the status-craving males were never far behind, whatever the task.

Facebook played a significant role in the coining of the meme. A senior Facebook engineer named Nick Schrock had started a "Brogramming" Facebook page that achieved cult status, even outside Facebook. As a measure of its bro-y cheek, it once parodied Facebook's own terms of service (a fairly serious legal document subject to constant debate and rewriting) by rephrasing it in brogrammerese and posting it publicly. (Sample line: "We give lots of fucks about your privacy, so we wrote this. Read it, so you know what the fuck we're going to do with the shit you post.") The tech ecosystem and its chroniclers like *TechCrunch*, forever agonizing about the deplorable state of women in tech, started howling about the corrosive effects of such a culture. (Some internal wags helpfully suggested starting a page for the female version of a brogrammer, "hogrammers" as they were known, or, more politely, "brogrammettes.")

One of the signs of Facebook's maturing and becoming "serious" was that the CTO forced Schrock to delete the page, lest it be perceived as sexist and unwelcoming. Great was the disappointment (at least between Reesman and me) that Facebook would nix one of its curious cultural artifacts.

---

he had on his arm, a series of bits, literal 1s and 0s, representing in binary various events in his life.

* To be clear, "curls" refers to biceps curls, the signature exercise of the iron-pumping gym rats, which many brogrammers are.

The next FBX guerrilla fighter was Hari.

Shreehari "Hari" Manikarnika was the only engineer at Facebook whom I had known and worked with before my arrival there. An engineer at Yahoo before joining the hated Adchemy, he had worked briefly with me on some search technology before I bailed for AdGrok. When he too had realized Adchemy was a sinking ship, my former AdGrok cofounders and I had tried recruiting him: AZ and MRM to Twitter, and me to Facebook. During a sixteen-hour drinking bout with Hari and his wife that started at Zeitgeist and ended with me dressed as a policeman at a Mission District costume party at four a.m., I convinced him to join Facebook. Food tastes even better when stolen off someone else's plate, and I took considerable joy in besting my former cofounders at the recruitment game.

Lastly, there was Gary.

Gary Wu and I had worked together since my first days at Facebook on the targeting team. He was slight of build and usually quiet, but intense and opinionated when discussing matters technical. The only across-the-room screaming match I ever witnessed at Facebook was between Gary and a Russian engineer who had somehow pissed him off. Gary took his work very seriously, and any technical or product proposal floated by me or other members of the team had to pass Gary's review. Usually in such situations, often at our daily stand-up, when we went over everyone's tasks and progress to date, Gary's eyes grew narrow and focused, and he fired out a torrent of heavily accented commentary, usually before a speaker had finished. It was a harsh but necessary reality check, particularly given Gary's comprehensive knowledge of the Ads system.

This was the army I had. It felt like being back in Y Combinator, except with the suffocating presence of Facebook hanging over us. The code name for the FBX project would be "Owl." Since this would be the first time Facebook advertisers could actually stealthily target this or that user, as though they were barn owls finding a mouse in the dark, I dedicated it to the order Strigiformes, that noble hunter.

As a side note, I'd also code-named the original Custom Audiences, since I was its first product manager. Perhaps revealing a nascent antipathy, I called it "Vulture," as it seemed to live off the carrion of offline email lists, that bottom-feeder of the marketing space. Brian Rosenthal, the engineering manager for Custom Audiences, eventually upgraded it to "Eagle." Owl and Eagle: Facebook's first two forays into real ads targeting, the moneymaking Big Brothers.

For the sake of morale—I was a full-service product manager after all—I ordered a full-size owl model, actually a scarecrow for pigeons, from Amazon. Reesman nicknamed it "Trackie the Owl," and it sat next to the window at the edge of the FBX area. A solar panel powered a small electric motor that turned its head, ostensibly to scare away birds. Since the tinted glass and narrow courtyard conspired to keep the office shady, the motor had enough juice to move the head only occasionally, causing the figure to suddenly come alive at odd moments, and scaring the bejeezus out of any unwary neighbor.

The real requirements for FBX were far less comical than the absurdist team-building scarecrow swag.

FBX wasn't merely a new ads feature. It was an entirely new ads system parallel to the existing Facebook one. The exchange would have separate data stores with billions of lines of data, reflecting the various data joins to the outside world we had made. The FBX code itself, unlike anything inside Facebook Ads, would have to contact machines all over the world for bids and ads in real time, and react to bids just as quickly, all of this tens of billions of times per day, hundreds of thousands of times per second. How ads themselves were created and uploaded would be different, allowing advertisers that much-coveted (and before FBX impossible) ability to dynamically fine-tune ads for every user and every ad experience. Ads statistics, the boring bean-counting task critical to keep the budgets flowing, would have to exist separately and work for advertisers and their accounting departments. Not to mention a whole suite of internal tools and dashboards to monitor the health of this beast we had created, making sure bids weren't getting dropped, or we weren't slamming our partners with too many requests for bids.

On the business side, we (by which I mean the royal PM "we") would have to find advertising software companies as partners, and on-board them with a list of documents, specifications, and integrations tests. We'd have to program them with a sales spiel for their advertisers, so they could in turn pitch their clients and convince them that this newfangled exchange was worth spending money on. All the while, we'd need to build a product that eased the adoption hurdle for advertisers as much as possible, no small task. Facebook, for reasons I won't belabor here, had a completely different ads environment from the standard-issue programmatic exchange. The ads themselves were different, Facebook restrictions around data leakage were different, and how the exchange worked was different from your regular ad exchange. In the span of a couple of months, we'd have to ramp up an entirely separate revenue channel for Facebook, with effectively zero support from Facebook management, all the while cajoling the FBX partners to induce their advertisers to spend money, under the misleading premise that FBX would be a long-term play for the company.

The problem boiled down to this: I had promised the Ads leadership $100 million in revenue in 2012, to juice the post-IPO quarters. That was the trade that had bought even these meager resources. It was game time.

IPA > IPO

> The more one limits oneself, the closer one is to the infinite; these people, as unworldly as they seem, burrow like termites into their own particular material to construct, in miniature, a strange and utterly individual image of the world.
>
> —Stefan Zweig, *Chess Story*

MAY 17, 2012

Time to call Jimmy.

Jimmy was my exotic beer dealer at Willows, the local family-owned grocery store in Menlo Park, which had survived the chain-store assault of Whole Foods by developing a thriving sideline in craft beer. The market was on Willow Road, which started just outside 24-karat Palo Alto, then wended its way through equally gold-plated Menlo Park and past the VA hospital that Ken Kesey once worked in and that inspired *One Flew Over the Cuckoo's Nest.* Almost as if on an exotic safari, Willow Road then traversed East Palo Alto, the local slum that once had the highest murder rate in the Bay Area (two of the local schools are named after César Chávez and Ron McNair, an African American astronaut), before ending at Facebook's entrance gate, complete with Like sign ringed by an ever-present scrum of tourists.

Like a true dealer, Jimmy took calls at any hour. And when

called on a random (to him) Friday at twelve thirty a.m., it was no biggie. Payment? Don't worry about it . . . just get the keg and pay me when you come in.

The situation was this: Facebook was finally going public. This meant Facebook stock would be traded on the NASDAQ for the first time. In order to duplicate all the old-timey capitalist theatrics, back when an exchange was a physical space full of traders whose day would start with an opening bell, NASDAQ marked the occasion with its own purely cosmetic bell that was rung with great fanfare in New York's Times Square, and the apotheotic scene was projected onto a billboard screen overlooking that crucible of tourist kitsch.

Zuck had other ideas, though.

Appearing besuited in New York would be a step down for such a history-warping company. No, the IPO proceedings would take place at Facebook.

That's right. Zuck and the FB high command wanted to stage their assumption into the technological heavens from Facebook's own courtyard. This was like Napoleon and his coronation, which he insisted take place in his Paris backyard rather than in Reims Cathedral, where they'd been held since the tenth century. Furthermore, similar to Napoleon snatching Charlemagne's crown out of Pope Pius's hands and crowning himself and Josephine, no outside blessing was required from NASDAQ or Wall Street. Zuck would stage the production, pushing the bell button himself right next to his beloved Aquarium.

From that moment on, Facebook would have a public-facing share price, and employees who either were less fired with zealotry than Zuck or simply didn't have three commas in their net worth like he did were apt to get soft and worry about that volatile number. In order to make sure nobody fixated on the IPO stock price, the high command declared a hackathon the night before. The theory was that if everyone stayed up the entire night hacking, then they'd be conked out the next day, sleeping through the first day of trading. As with many neat Facebook theories, reality would prove to be rather more complicated. But this was the plan.

As a useless, email-writing product manager, I had few options to contribute to this IPO pregame beyond urging it along in the bacchanal direction. I had once, memorably, brewed beer at the office, and decided to recruit a crew to make a batch for the IPO festivities.* My home-brewing setup was still intact, and under the FBX desks. We had upgraded our Ads drinking facilities, and I had bought the team a real tap and kegerator, which I filled with a locally brewed IPA and an arsenal of bottled Belgians. The first rule of brewing: you must be drinking beer while making it.

Come the big night, I set up shop right in the middle of the courtyard, in front of the one café that stayed open all night. The huge, steaming brew kettle and flaming burner certainly got attention. The beer tap alongside helped too. Zuck sauntered by, took one look at the scene, and shook

---

* This is a true story: When I moved onto the boat, I had to put my home-brewing apparatus somewhere, so I stored it on Facebook's campus. Come some hackathon, aided by some of the other craft-beer degenerates, I deployed the five-gallon brew setup, all the while draining a respectable stockpile of Belgian ales. When it came time to chill the boiled protobeer, we connected the large coil of copper tubing to the faucet in the second-floor kitchen of Building 16. We were apprised of the fact it was raining on Zuck's desk (and that of every other member of senior management), which was directly underneath the kitchen, when security rushed in with panicked faces. Evidently we had burst the plumbing in the kitchen with our high-pressure cooling. Undaunted, our brave beer crew (who were in a state of considerable inebriation) finished the brew, and left the large carboy to ferment in the Ads area. Toward four o'clock that morning, upon reaching quasisobriety and recalling my duties as product manager of this venture, I sent an apologetic email to Zuck, promising a bottle of the brew as recompense. There were no repercussions from our lark, and I still owe Zuck a bottle, as we kegged the beer instead (which was excellent; we killed it inside of an hour). *Move fast and break things*—including the plumbing.

his head before walking on to the cafeteria. Boland and I were in the throes of a short-lived bout of friendliness given our close work on Custom Audiences, and he hung around and helped out. PMMess was also flitting around, although it seemed that dish had definitely cooled. The presence of her boss, Boland, with whom she had an always ambiguous relationship, didn't help matters.

I poured beers for the ever-changing scrum of Ads peeps who would swing by, or even random Facebookers. There was that carnivalesque feeling in the air when humanity achieved, for one fleeting moment, a state of generous fellowship with its fellow man, a festive celebration of the universe being so kind as to favor us, a communion among fellow bipedal primates.

Then the beer gave out.

The brew still had some time to go (we wouldn't even try to cool it using Facebook's crappy plumbing again), and a beer shortage was a cardinal sin. That's when I called Jimmy. Source secured, I asked Boland if he could maybe drive, as I was starting to see double from the liquid tour through Belgium we'd just taken.

I climbed into in his beater Volvo station wagon, with its worn tan leather interior abused by too many kids and trips to weekend soccer games. The car looked as though lots of people and their hurried meals had ridden in it. To break up the awkward intimacy of sitting next to each other in a confined space, I asked somewhat absently where he lived. "Atherton" came the reply, the exclusive neighborhood where Sheryl, among other truly elite tech tycoons, lived. "We rent," he was quick to add, perhaps reacting to my impressed look.

When confronted with an unwelcome social situation (which is most of them), I default to a Terry Gross pose of interviewing journalist.

"So how'd you end up at Facebook from Microsoft?"

"Sheryl recruited and convinced me."

Ah. That might explain why his lips were hermetically sealed to her ass.

"How'd that go?"

"Well, she basically convinced me by saying: 'Look, I either hire you now and you come work for Facebook, or a year from now I'll hire you to work for the guy whose job I'm offering you right now.' And that's what convinced me."

Oh, Sheryl Sandberg and her wiles. So that's how you seduced the Bolands of the world: you offered them a rung up on the ladder they thought they'd miss out on otherwise.

By the time I had gotten Boland's informal CV, we'd arrived at Willows. In a second, I understood the charm of owning your own bar or restaurant, as the idle wealthy often did. You simply walked in and took what you wanted. Which is more or less what Boland and I did, swaggering into the Willows at one a.m. along with the last-minute tampon-and-diaper buyers, mentioning Jimmy's name. We scooped up a keg of their best IPA like we owned the place, threw it into the back of his Volvo, and off we barreled back to the compound.

Fast-forward another two hours.

The second keg was now officially dead as well. The initial rush of the turbo alcohol-and-greed drunk had worn off. The pretense of this actually being a hackathon with productive work going on was wearing thin. One of the strange hypocrisies around the "hacker way" was that the company was so big most employees didn't have the ability to hack on anything at all, engineers being vastly outnumbered by every flavor of corporate camp follower. Typically these nonhackers would just absent themselves from the geeky nocturnal ritual, but you couldn't miss out on the pre-IPO party, so there was every salesperson, admin, operations specialist, and IT help-desk attendant well into the wee hours, milling around without much to do. Certainly the company had neglected to schedule anything remotely festive or musical. Facebook's Spartan virtues contraindicated celebration, even at the moment of their corporate apotheosis. Many of these people would be worth real, liquid money come the next day.* In any normal company, people would be doing lines of cocaine off desks and getting it on in conference rooms. Not so at Facebook. Corporate discipline was maintained.

Fast-forward another two hours. Five a.m. now, the wee hours.

I considered going to the boat and sleeping, but feared missing the big moment. Doing laps around campus to keep myself awake, I ran into Boland again, who this time had a bottle of twelve-year single-malt. He and PMMess were hanging out at one of the tables in the open space between Ads and Growth, which still featured the half-finished Superman mural that had appeared on the Night of the Spray Paint.

They invited me to join, and while never a whisky guy, it would have been rude to refuse. So did this improbable trio kill the last hour before the big event. A passing former Ads engineer posted a photo of me: I looked delirious and unkempt, with rings under my eyes and a paper cup in my hand. I was wearing the Facebook uniform of a logo-ed zipped fleece, and had trotted out an old AdGrok T-shirt underneath for the occasion.

I was only semiconscious at this point. We had started pulling insane hours trying to ship FBX on time, and my deficit on the sleep front was truly Greek in scale. But the crepuscular redness of a new California day was breaking! The moment drew near!

We all wandered outside, where a crowd was gathering.

---

* Technically, that isn't quite true. There is a "lockout" period after an IPO (typically 180 days, though it can be shorter) when insiders like employees cannot legally sell their shares. This means employees must impatiently sit and watch their company's share price fluctuate—and their net worth along with it—all the while completely unable to transact anything.

Overnight, Facilities had erected what looked like a rock-concert stage, with a football-stadium-sized screen framed by scaffolding and lights. At the base of it stood a towerlike podium with a glass lectern. Embedded in that glass was the button that Zuck would push to trigger the public company genesis. Behind and above the podium was an image of those three icons whose nagging notifications had created this multibillion dollar empire: two human figures, representing friend requests; dialogue bubbles for messages; and a globe for likes and comments. This trinity, internally known as "the jewels," appeared in every manifestation of Facebook, whether mobile or desktop, and the red notifications that popped up on them were now the world's operant conditioning candy. The effect onstage was to make the scene itself seem like a Facebook page.

As dawn grew brighter the courtyard filled, and soon it was packed elbow to elbow. The postive mood had revived, and the crowd was noisy with gossiping expectation and the occasional whoop. A commotion could be noticed around the podium, and soon Facebook's leadership started appearing one by one: Zuck, Sheryl, David Fischer, Elliot Schrage, Pedram Keyani, Chris Cox (both Keyani and Cox had addressed my on-boarding), Javier Olivan (head of Growth), Greg Badros (then running Ads), and so on.

It was 6:25 a.m., and history was about to be made.

The scene was projected, political-rally style, onto the large screen, allowing everyone in the courtyard to follow along. One of the NASDAQ emissaries (someone had stuck Facebook shirts on them) introduced Zuck as the company's "visionary," as if he needed an intro.

Out of nowhere a booming female voice announced that the scene was also playing in "Times Square New York!" Evidently, the whole scene would be broadcast above Chinese tourists taking photos with the Naked Cowboy.

Silence regained, Zuck took the mike: "So in a few minutes I'm going to ring this bell and we're all going to get back to work."

Stay focused on our mission!

Zuck gave a few celebratory remarks that you almost couldn't hear over the cheering. The countdown to opening without a visible clock increased the suspense, as you didn't quite know when it would come. Finally, the magic time somehow signaled, everyone at the podium started counting down in unison: 5 . . . 4 . . . 3 . . . 2 . . . 1!

Zuck smacked his hand down on the glass facing him, almost knocking over the entire assembly. A recording played the quaint sound of an old school fire alarm. Everyone started cheering like it was New Year's. The assembled grandees started a group hug. Everyone in the crowd took the same photo at once. History being made! Facebook IPO! We were living and watching it; our friends can only envy, our grandkids can only imagine when we tell them the story! Feel that temporary pause in baseline human existential angst by being part of something bigger than yourself, usually ignoble like a lynch mob, sometimes heroic like D-Day, rarely profitable like an IPO.

People had looks of delirious joy on their faces as they found their friends or teammates to take a group photo with and record the moment. Employees bestowed on the experience the highest praise possible: they posted it as an MLE ("Major Life Event") on their Timelines, a rank usually enjoyed by only births and marriage. It was a big block of white space with a single headline and photo, like newspapers when the Apollo astronauts walked on the Moon. "Facebook Goes Public" was the headline, with details like "once in a lifetime" and "once-in-a-generation company."

Churchill once noted in a parliamentary speech, "It has been said that democracy is the worst form of government except for all those other forms that have been tried from time to time."

Similarly, capitalism is the worst form of managing the means of production, except for yet worse ways. We should treat it as such rather than turning it into the Blue State secular religion, alongside yoga and John Oliver.

What's my big beef with capitalism? That it desacralizes everything, robs the world of wonder, and leaves it as nothing more than a vulgar market. The fastest way to cheapen anything—be it a woman, a favor, or a work of art—is to put a price tag on it. And that's what capitalism is, a busy greengrocer going through his store with a price-sticker machine—*ka-CHUNK! ka-CHUNK!*—$4.10 for eggs, $5 for coffee at Sightglass, $5,000 per month for a run-down one-bedroom in the Mission.

Think I'm exaggerating?

Stop and think for a moment what this whole IPO ritual was about. For the first time, Facebook shares would have a public price. For all the pageantry and cheering, this was Mr. Market coming along with his price-sticker machine and—*ka-CHUNK!*—putting one on Facebook for $38 per share. And everyone was ecstatic about it. It was one of the highlights of the technology industry, and one of the "once in a lifetime" moments of our age. In pre-postmodern times, only a divine ritual of ancient origin, victory in war, or the direct experience of meaningful culture via shared songs, dances, or art would cause anybody such revelry. Now we're driven to ecstasies of delirium because we have a price tag, and our life's labors are validated by the fact it does. That's the smoldering ambition of every entrepreneur: to one day create an organization that society deems worthy of a price tag.

These are the only real values we have left in the twilight of history, the tired dead end of liberal democratic capitalism, at least here in the California fringes of Western civilization. Clap at the clever people getting rich, and hope you're among them.

Is it a wonder that the inhabitants of such a world clamor for contrived rituals of artificial significance like Burning Man, given the utter bankruptcy of meaning in their corporatized culture? Should we be surprised that they cling to identities, clusters of consumption patterns, that seem lifted from the ads-targeting system at Facebook: "hipster millennials," "urban mommies," "affluent suburbanites"?

Ortega y Gasset wrote: "Men play at tragedy because they do not believe in the reality of the tragedy which is actually being staged in the civilized world." Tragedy plays like the IPO were bound to pale for those who felt the call of real tragedy, the tragedy that poets once captured in verse, and that fathers once passed on to sons. Would the inevitable descendants of that cheering courtyard crowd one day gather with their forebears, perhaps in front of a fireplace, and ask, "Hey, Grandpa, what was it like to be at the Facebook IPO?" the way previous generations asked about Normandy or the settling of the Western frontier?

I doubt it. Even as a participant in this false Mass, the temporary thrill giving way quickly to fatigue and a budding hangover, I wondered what would happen to the culture when it couldn't even produce spectacles like this anymore.

When I returned to work that afternoon after a nap on the boat, I was expecting to find an empty campus. On the Ads floor, however, I found everyone diligently at his desk as if nothing had happened that morning. The Zuckian injunction to get back to work had been followed.

Just to stick my finger symbolically in Zuck's eye, I fired up Google Finance and checked the stock price. NASDAQ had evidently screwed up the market open (despite the pyrotechnics in the courtyard), and the stock hadn't started trading until eleven a.m. Eastern time. It had started around $42 officially, and had closed around $38. A flat day, which is counterintuitively great news.

Even though I wouldn't be able to sell stock for a good several months thanks to the lockout, I did now have a real, ticking market price for the pieces of paper that constituted my real compensation.

So what was I making?

Facebook's original offer was 75,000 shares, vesting over four years, in addition to a $175,000 salary. I had managed to wangle the equivalent of 5,000 shares up front in cash to pay for credit cards, a new car (with the license plate ADGROK, of course), and the sailboat I was then living on—about $200,000 in cash all together.

That left 70,000 shares.

Assuming nominal performance, from both me and the company (our bonuses were a product of individual performance reviews and a company-wide multiplier more or less arbitrarily chosen by Zuck), I'd get get a cash bonus in the 7 to 15 percent range (Wall Street this wasn't). There would be equity top-ups as well: assuming OK reviews, it would likely be in the low single-digit thousand-share range. If I had some big promotion or started climbing the corporate ladder for real, it would be considerably more than that.

Here's what it came to, assuming shares valued at the IPO price:

$38 per share

×

(70,000 shares ÷ 4 years + 3,000 shares annual bonus) +

($175,000 base salary + $17,500 rough annual bonus)

= $971,500 per year

Not quite a million.

Seem like much? It wasn't.

Remember, this was taxed as common income, even the shares I'd waited a year for, given the IRS's incomprehension of tech compensation. So it was really about $550,000 take-home per year, or about twelve times the median US family income, for a guy whose biggest line-item expenditures were fancy Belgian beer and marine hardware.

This was about San Francisco middle class, or barely, really. Coupled with another tech salary from a spouse, it would be the high-six-figure take-home that would permit a normal, though not posh, life in what was becoming the country's priciest city. It meant that I and my hypothetical spouse could afford a house, though we'd need a mortgage, as average apartment prices in Noe Valley were $1.5 million or so. (Want a proper house? You're talking $3 million and up.) It meant the kids could attend private school and avoid the public school savages. It meant occasional weekends in Tahoe, Christmas somewhere exotic, and Hawaii a couple of times a year, maybe. It meant a new BMW X5 for the missus every three years, and maybe splurging on a Tesla S for me.

But that's about it. And if I lost the Facebook teat, kiss it all good-bye; already-public companies weren't comping at these rates, and earlier-stage companies were paying piles of risky paper.

There are only two inflection points in personal wealth, two points where your life really changes. One is the aforementioned fuck-you money, the other is the even loftier fuck-the-world money.

Before that first rung of fuck-you money, when you're counting your nickels and dimes and shares and bonuses and what all to get to a few hundred K of dosh, all that changes is what I'll call your indifference threshold to expense. If before you didn't think about dropping $6 for another pint of beer with your friends (and believe me, I've lived through times when I had to think about even that), now you don't think about the pricey $60 salmon lunch at Anchor & Hope.

If previously you thought before indulging yourself with some questionably useful $50 gadget, now you'll drop $500 on a new phone or ultracompact projector without thinking about it. As if you lived in some dodgy country undergoing a period of hyperinflation, what used to be worth $10 in mental decision cost now takes $100 to trigger. It's like your mental decimal point of concern has moved over a zero (or perhaps more than one). You're not even really thinking about costs until you've broken $1,000.

This sliding around of an indifference threshold is peanuts in the scheme of things. Real transformation happens at the first real rung on the wealth ladder. Fuck-you money is like reaching the break-even point in the startup of you, and it means you are no longer beholden to outside forces. Imagine that inflection point for a moment.

I didn't quite realize all this, sitting there on the first day the company was public, looking at a stock price, but I would soon enough. I'd see not just my fortunes change (even if not in a fully "fuck you" sort of way) very quickly; those of everyone around would change as well. From the slightly ridiculous nights out (I recall a double steak dinner and four-figure restaurant bills in there somewhere), to the rather rapid accumulation of Porsches, Corvettes, and even the odd Ferrari in the parking lot, things did assume a certain debauched air at Facebook, despite all the corporate clamor for austere discipline.

That was all in the future. Right then, it just seemed I was finally going to live at something above a subsistence level, and have more than peanuts in the bank. I quickly flipped to the countdown timer on my Mac, the one I had set to count down to my first year of vesting when I joined. I'd make a quarter of my nut on July 15, in about two months. It couldn't arrive fast enough.

Oh, and the beer we brewed the night before? I'd title it the "IPO IPA." Like the IPO itself, it was a bit of a disappointment, nowhere near as good as Zuck's Wet Desk IPA.

Two weeks later, we finished the keg all the same, but it felt more like duty than anything else. Somehow, brewing in a spirit of good fellowship, and the hilarity of drenching the CEO's desk, had produced a better product than the strained group celebration of the IPO.

Initial Public Offering: A Reevaluation

> Prices, like everything else, move along the line of least resistance. They will do whatever comes easiest.
>
> —Edwin Lefèvre, *Reminiscences of a Stock Operator*

MAY 18, 2012

The news coverage surrounding the IPO, even from the supposedly savvy tech and financial press, was a reminder of that harsh lesson of life: there are those who write headlines about money for a living, and then there are those who make money. "Facebook IPO Blunder" announced *Fortune*; "Mark Zuckerberg's Big Facebook Mistake," thundered *Forbes*; "Facebook Disappoints on Its Opening Day" intoned *VentureBeat*, a Valley insider rag that should have known better.

Despite such headlines, Facebook's IPO was not a fiasco; it was without question the most successful tech IPO in financial history. If you don't understand why, then you don't understand how IPOs work, and you should read on.

What's an IPO, exactly? A company decides it wants to "float" part of its equity on the public markets, allowing employees and founders to sell private shares to pay them off for years of service, as well as sell shares out of the corporate treasury to have some money in the bank. Large investment banks (such as my former employer Goldman Sachs) form what's called a "syndicate" ("mafia" might be a better term) wherein they offer to effectively buy those shares from Facebook, and then sell them into the capital markets, usually by pushing it via their sales force onto wealthy clients or institutional investors. That syndicate either guarantees a price ("firm commitment") or promises to get the best price it can ("best effort"). In the former case, the bank is taking real execution risk, and stands to lose money if it doesn't engineer a "pop" in the stock on opening day. To mitigate the risk, the bank convinces the offering company to expect a lower price, while simultaneously jacking up what real price the market will bear with a zealous sales pitch to the market's deepest pockets. Thus, it is absolutely jejune to think that a stock's rise on opening day is due to clamoring and unexpected interest. Similar to Captain Renault in *Casablanca*, Wall Street bankers are shocked—*shocked!*—that there should be such a large and positive price dislocation in the market they just rigged.

As proof of the complete charlatanism at work in most IPOs, let's ask ourselves a question: Are there other situations in the financial world in which the banks are responsible for setting, ab initio so to speak, a fair market price, and in which that routinely works out?

Why, yes, in fact. It happens every morning when thousands of stocks start trading on the public exchanges. How does the first price of the day in IBM get set? Back in the days of floor traders, the "specialists" responsible for trading that stock weighed the amount of buying versus selling interest, and calculated a reasonable "midmarket" price. They then offered to buy at slightly less, and sell at slightly more, than that price when the market opened, supplying the liquidity they're paid to provide via the narrow bid-ask spread they pocket on every trade. Modern electronic exchanges have replaced the manual process with an algorithmic one, but it's essentially the same. On opening, trading initiates smoothly from a stew of overnight speculation and imaginary price movements into real trades and shares changing hands. How often does one see 20 to 30 percent price changes on opening in US exchanges? Never, basically, other than after catastrophic events like market meltdowns or 9/11.

Given Wall Street banks' consummate skill in (usually) running orderly markets when their money and reputations are on the line, isn't it a wonder that they should suddenly find it impossible to engineer an IPO in which the price doesn't pop 20 percent on open? Even assuming there were some ever-present estimation error, isn't it striking too how they always manage to underestimate the price on the first day, making themselves a fortune, rather than overestimating and causing themselves a loss?

Facebook shredded the usual IPO script.

The stock opened at $42, and closed at $38.37, which put the financial press in a howling tizzy of complaint, and which nicely screwed the bankers.

The negotiations were way, way, way above my pay grade, so I have no idea how David Ebersman, Facebook's then CFO, managed to coerce or cajole the bankers into offering a high and fair price, essentially screwing themselves in the process. But he and whoever else on the Facebook side deserve the Nobel Prize in economics for doing so. They even squeezed the bankers on fees. Oh, yes: in addition to fleecing you with overt price manipulation, bankers are paid a flat fee for their exertions. Facebook's syndicate accepted a modest fee of just over 1 percent, rather than a more typical fee that sometimes runs as high as 7 percent.

While the press jeered about the "disastrous IPO," the feeling inside the company was one of utter triumph. Facebook had gone public without getting skinned alive, and it now had a mountain of money to recruit the best engineers, acquire budding competitors, and outspend rivals on product development, all with minimal dilution of the shareholders (i.e., of us, the employees).

Here is your lesson from the Facebook IPO: whenever you see the headline "Stock X Pops on First Day of Trading and Declared a Success," instead think "Founders and employees just got completely screwed, and the bankers and their wealthy clients made fortunes." Because that's what happened, and *didn't* happen, in the case of Facebook.

Flash Boys

> I have never yet been afraid of men who set up marketplaces in the middle of their city, where they lie and cheat one another.
>
> —Herodotus, *Histories*

JUNE 15, 2012

120 milliseconds is about one-third of the time it takes a human to blink an eye.

That's what we had to play with. That's how much time an FBX partner had to return a bid and an ad when requested to by the exchange, an auction process that would take place fifty billion times a day, or about half a million times per second. Any longer than that, and it threatened to delay the Facebook page load. If you should ever be standing in a postlaunch Zuck demo, and the FBX ads load a tick slower than the rest of the page—or, worse, make the entire page load slowly—then you are on the fast train to a job at Dropbox, and don't let the Facebook door hit your ass on the way out.

Those 120 milliseconds included the network latency, meaning the time elapsed when the bits flowed out of the Facebook pipe to the outside Internet, and to wherever the FBX partner's machine was located, and back again.

This presented a serious and seemingly insurmountable technical challenge. Because Facebook was then being served for the entire world out of data centers in North Carolina, California, and Oregon, European marketers and their mountains of data had to talk to machines in the United States, often on both coasts. In order to comprehend the feasibility, I calculated the spherical distance between North Carolina and Amsterdam (where much of European tech is hosted on server farms), to see if it was even theoretically possible to respond to ad auction requests. Light travels fast (299,792,458 meters per second), but not fast enough. It was 23 milliseconds one way, and that was assuming lossless fiber-optic cable running directly on a great circle route from Facebook's machines to the advertiser, a ridiculous simplification of the reality. Pinging the distance from an East Coast machine revealed a more realistic 60-millisecond one-way travel time. There was no way to beat the relativistic bound, and for as long as I was at the company, we lost money in Europe as many of those requests simply timed out, and FBX did not participate in the auction.

If you've read Michael Lewis's *Flash Boys*, which details the ultrafast, high-frequency trading that takes place on the stock exchange, you'll recall his prefatory riff on a hedge fund that ran a fiber-optic cable from New York to Chicago. The goal was to shave a few milliseconds off the regular Internet route between the two financial hubs, and gain a split-second advantage over other high-frequency shops. The cost was reputedly $300 million, which indicated the stakes involved.

You'll see that my analogy to Wall Street for programmatic media wasn't merely historical; it was an exact comparison reflecting both business and technical realities. FBX was the Flash Boys of media, trading quanta of human attention at the speed of light. Every time you load a new page in Facebook, not to mention most of the Internet, optical signals crisscross the globe to hundreds of waiting machines, all announcing, like some phalanx of royal trumpeters, your impending arrival.

So what happens to those globe-spanning bid requests, assuming they don't drown in their trans-Atlantic undersea cable? The people listening for your presence in billions of such requests per day are known as "demand-side platforms" (DSPs), and they're the stockbrokers of this real-time media world, working in the employ of the advertiser or agency who wants to sell you something.* The DSP quickly unpacks the bid request, and queries its data for anything it knows about you: sites you've browsed, shopping carts you've abandoned, that airfare quote you got and never acted upon. They're all there and returned within milliseconds via state-of-the-art databases hyperoptimized for the purpose. Much of that data isn't even directly observed by the advertisers in question. Companies have done deals for the right to rent a little piece of the webpage on sites of commercial interest, just enough to touch your browser and see who you are. These data brokers put you in some targeting segment—for example, "travel intenders" (i.e., people about to spend money on hotels)—and then resell you as "third-party data." Since everyone has a pseudonym for you via your Web browser, and that browser is known to Facebook, Google, and everyone else, that data can be used to target you. This is all anonymous (in the sense of Facebook data never leaking out), but it's everything you do online. All of it is more spice in the targeting sausage going through the advertising

* In case you're wondering, yes, there is such a thing as a "supply-side platform" (SSP). It's the sell-side technology that DSPs and other buyers plug into, and it helps publishers monetize their sites and apps. Often that technology is a real-time exchange. In many ways, FBX is an SSP, except that unlike most SSPs, which try to sign as many publishers as possible, this one has only one big client: Facebook itself.

meat grinder, and is trafficked millions of times per second (whether you know or like it or not).

The real-time, millisecond bids from Facebook Exchange then fed into the regular ads auction that Facebook was holding on behalf of non-FBX advertisers. At which point Facebook, with all of its vaunted data, became merely one more DSP in the auction, just one more broker doing its business. The difference was, the rest of the Facebook Ads system had Facebook's set of data, while the FBX advertisers, however many there were in that auction, had their own data from the non-Facebook world. Since both the Facebook Ads system and the outside world now received a request for an ad via FBX, we had put outside advertisers on an equal footing with Facebook itself, and may the best man (or bid) win.

I saw it as a feature. Facebook saw it as a bug.

This was FBX's unforgivable sin: it allowed outsiders the same ability to optimize and target ads alongside the Facebook Ads machinery, choosing whom to target, on which page, and at whatever frequency, just as Facebook did. That equality of outside parties and Facebook was something Ads management could not abide. For all the bluster about Facebook's wonderful data, management was unwilling to go head-to-head with outside data, because the managers suspected they'd lose. Which they mostly did: the bids of FBX advertisers were typically way higher than bids brought in by the rest of the Ads system, meaning FBX advertisers tended to win the auction for users' attention more often. Of course their bids were higher: FBX bidders knew you had just spec'ed out a Jack Spade handbag or had bought diapers last week; Facebook by contrast knew you had liked Jim Carrey's fan page a year ago. Whose bid for an ad was going to come in at $30 CPM?*

---

* That didn't mean FBX's marginal contribution to FB revenue was as dramatic as the difference in bid. Like most online ad auctions, Facebook

Note: There was nothing magical about FBX. It was merely sophisticated plumbing. The point was that joining Facebook Ads, via a real-time exchange, to a world of data it didn't previously have access to was the fastest and most sophisticated way to get that data into Facebook. Custom Audiences could also bring the exact same data into Facebook, but nobody who dealt in sophisticated targeting for a living wanted to use Facebook's clunky infrastructure to facilitate it. To cite loose technical analogies, CA versus FBX was like faxes versus email. Surely Silicon Valley's most aggressive company would see the historical inevitability of programmatic exchanges and their technical superiority.

MOVE FAST AND BREAK THINGS! they told us.

FORTUNE FAVORS THE BOLD! the poster said.

But here is where I shamefully displayed my naïveté. For someone who had spotted the resemblance between Goldman Sachs and Facebook within an hour of meeting the latter, I had forgotten my lessons learned at the former. When it came to monetization, Facebook had no interest in real innovation. It liked its faxes. Like any large company, Facebook would always aim to create monopoly pricing power and maintain information asymmetry, rather than drive true innovation. If Facebook played with the outside world, it always played with loaded dice.

Recall the depths of the credit crash at Goldman back in 2008. Goldman could have pushed for the obvious technical step of trading credit derivatives on exchanges, which

---

ran a "second price" auction. The economic specifics are PhD level, but essentially it meant you paid the amount of the next-highest bid, rather than what *you* bid. If one did the math, it meant a much better price-discovery mechanism overall. To truly increase total revenue, you needed a density of bids at the "clearing price" the ad impression had sold for, pushing the aggregate prices paid upward. No density, and all those high bids did nothing for the bottom line. So our goal was to increase the overlap between outside FBX bidding interest and the ads volume FB brought to market. That's what obsessed us on the FBX team.

would have resulted in greater volume and greater transparency, and taken the regulatory heat off. But would Goldman cede its information asymmetry in the form of the trading flows that it, and only it, saw? Would it cede the ability to more or less arbitrarily set prices for credit risk, alongside a tightly knit network of brokers, effectively manipulating the market to its own benefit, rather than offering an open one?

Of course not. And neither would Facebook, when it came down to it.

I wasn't thinking about that on June 15, though. Because that was the day the first successful bid on FBX finally was made, with one of FBX's better partner companies, TellApart.* We had pulled it off—we'd built an ads exchange and a parallel ads system to Facebook in about five weeks of engineering work, and maybe two months total of product ideation. The mood was high at the FBX table. Trackie the Owl would finally be able to eat his long-sought mouse. Initial volume was of course light, and what would preoccupy us all for the next six months was increasing the volume of bids and money as quickly as possible and making FBX the centerpiece of an entire vision of how Facebook should monetize. Eventually, though, the race became simply to make FBX too big for even Facebook's murderous management to kill. FBX was fighting for its life almost from the moment it was born.

---

* One of the more impressive companies in the original FBX partner list, TellApart would curiously enough sell to Twitter in 2015.

Full Frontal Facebook

In time, the savage bull doth bear the yoke.
—William Shakespeare, *Much Ado about Nothing*

OCTOBER 9, 2012

For Facebook, circa late 2012 was a moment worth savoring. Caught between startup infancy and big-company adulthood, Facebook in the year of the IPO gleamed in a brief adolescence, never to be repeated.

What was it like?

<beep!>

Microsoft Calendar, that cruel taskmaster, reminding me of a meeting.

Since launching FBX in June with a limited set of partners, we had begun admitting as many as possible. Every additional partner was an additional set of advertisers, which was more money and budget and internal leverage for me to use in FBX's favor.

Every meeting with a potential FBX partner essentially boiled down to me taking a meeting with their product team and dictating just what the hell they were going to do—and motherfuckers, you'd better tell me what I want to hear or you're off Facebook Island, not that you were even invited in the first place. That approach had more or less worked, particularly in the early days, as every outside partner jockeyed for the prestige of a place among the first or second wave.

Except for Amazon.

There, the always tenuous and yet strategic relationship overrode my PM droit du seigneur over FBX. That was the meeting my phone was reminding me of, and with a groan of exasperation I dropped everything for it.

To paraphrase Lord Palmerston about great nations, companies like Facebook had no eternal allies and no perpetual enemies, they merely had eternal and perpetual interests. Despite the various "partner programs" it ran, Facebook didn't really have partner companies, much less real friends. It perceived the world as populated by either fearsome enemies that presented existential threats—and there were only a few of these—or companies that presented convenient temporary alliances. Facebook's good graces were always conditional, and it was a foolish company indeed that took them for granted.

Amazon clearly fell into the former category.

Jeff Bezos was a maniacal leader who would stop at nothing until his vision of the world was realized, and who had inspired, cajoled, or intimidated an army to implement that vision. Zuck looked over at Bezos in Seattle, or Larry Page from Google in Mountain View, or (in the past) Steve Jobs from Apple in Cupertino, and he saw more than just a tech company and a chief executive. He saw a reflection of himself among those men, and that was terrifying. Other players in the tech or media worlds could be outwitted, out-engineered, or otherwise co-opted or bought off, but not these alpha companies. With Amazon or Google, the Facebook army had to close ranks and present a phalanx, and possibly battle an equal foe whose CEO was just as much of a kamikaze as Zuck was (*Carthage must be destroyed!*).

(Twitter didn't even enter this worldview, and was merely

a distraction. Zuck had once famously derided the company as "a clown car that drove into a gold mine," and that's possibly the last time anyone at Facebook had thought about it.)

And so any business-development process with those Great Power companies was always a grinding negotiation on the order of an arms-reduction treaty: lots of internal pomp and circumstance; interminable meetings held at long, crowded conference tables; and very little incremental progress. When a contract was finally produced, it was batted back and forth by the lawyers, and covered in red lines rejecting one or another clause.

With good reason too. These companies without question were smart, thought in decades rather than the years (maximum) of most tech companies, and had the wherewithal to project their own agenda despite Facebook's wishes. Oh, and while we all pretended to be friends, nobody was even remotely stupid enough to believe that.

The meeting with Amazon went well, at least at the engineering and product level. The specific team involved was called A9, which was the Amazon subsidiary wholly responsible for that behemoth's search and advertising technologies.* Effectively, it was the private, in-house technology shop that built Amazon's own DSP, the brokerage house that let Amazon buy ads anywhere on the Internet to drive you back to your Amazon shopping cart. The company spent hundreds of millions of dollars on advertising, and it could turn on FBX revenue in a huge way for us. Naturally, A9 would be the group that would develop any FBX technology, as it had already done on Google's exchange.

---

* A9 is a numeronym, a common trope in Valley naming aesthetics. It stood for "Algorithms" (the letter "A" plus nine other letters), since sophisticated computer instructions were how Amazon was to succeed in this new world of quantitative marketing. The top-tier venture capital firm a16z, for "A(ndreessen Horowit)z," followed similar logic. Such wonky abbreviation must scratch some deep OCD itch in the geek psyche.

Amazon's engineers were sharp, knowledgeable, and knew the programmatic ads-buying world inside and out. They got it, instantly, and I was looking forward to having them build their sophisticated tools on our newborn platform, and Facebook competing with Google for their inexhaustible ad budgets.

Then the business guys got involved.

A9 was run by Matt Battles, who through the course of this three-hour meeting (and others yet to come) revealed himself as a sort of Svengali character, grasping all the important technical and product details of our proposed collaboration, and adopting a pose of aloof and calculating skepticism about the whole thing. He seemed willfully tenuous about the proposed calculation, almost as if to reinforce that it meant more to Facebook than to Amazon to get this deal done (which it probably did).

Our Facebook business-development person, as well as the Amazon partner manager, reflected that poker-playing pose, each adopting his own corporate stance of scrutiny and skepticism.* There were lots of hard questions from both sides on how data would get used, and potentially recycled inside the obscure inner workings of the other company. Would Facebook record what Amazon ads were shown to which person, and use that data? Even in a distant, second-order way, would Amazon ad performance be used in some Facebook model around clickthrough rates? Facebook in turn wondered how

---

* Important Facebook partners (Apple, Amazon, Zynga, etc.) had permanent liaison staff assigned to them, almost like how the US State Department appoints ambassadors to foreign nations. Their role in life was not only representing Facebook's views to (often) antagonistic outside powers, but also stumping for an outside company's interests to an often oblivious Facebook. They also helped the other company navigate Facebook's Byzantine internal politics to achieve some mutually beneficial goal. These ambassadors got to know their foreign powers very well, some even going a bit native (as diplomats too long in a foreign country do), empathizing with their charges' agenda as much as with Facebook's.

far into the Amazon machine all this user-level impression data would flow, and if the product recommendations on amazon.com would suddenly reflect your interaction with ads on facebook.com. The two giants circled each other warily, neither willing to take its hand off its concealed weapon and shake hands instead.

And so the corporate standoff went . . . for months. Amazon would eventually join FBX, and its ad spend would benefit the always-demanding FBX revenue dashboard, but not until many meetings and contract negotiations later.

And what of that other stalwart Facebook competitor, Google?

The initial noises around Google Plus had been more than alarming, as it became increasingly clear that their foray into social media wasn't some halfhearted effort to knock off a pesky upstart. As had slowly leaked out over the past year, either via the press or current Google employees, all of Google's internal product teams were being reoriented in favor of Google Plus. Even Search, then and now the most frequented destination on the Web, was being dragged into the fray, and would supposedly sport social features. Search results would vary based on your connections via Google Plus, and anything you shared—photos, posts, even chats with Friends—would be used as part of Google's ever-powerful and mysterious search algorithm.

This was shocking news, even more so to Googlers. Search was the company's tabernacular product, the holy of holies, the one-line oracle of human knowledge that had replaced libraries and encyclopedias.

By all accounts (and Google information security was clearly not as good as Facebook's) this caused a considerable stir internally. In January 2012, at a company-wide Q&A, Google's founder Larry Page addressed this new direction forcefully, quelling the internal dissent and issuing a Googler ultimatum.

"This is the path we're headed down—a single, unified, 'beautiful' product across everything. If you don't get that, then you should probably work somewhere else."

With the gauntlet thrown down, Google products were soon ranked via one unique metric—how much did they contribute to Google's social vision?—and either consolidated or discarded appropriately.

As part of the budding media seduction around this new product, Google posted whopping usage numbers. By September 2012, Google announced the service had 400 million registered users and 100 million active ones. Facebook hadn't even quite reached a billion users yet, and it had taken the company four years to reach the milestone—100 million users—that Google had reached in one. This caused something close to panic inside Facebook, but the reality on the battlefield was rather different from what Google was letting on.

This contest had so rattled the search giant, intoxicated as they were with unfamiliar existential anxiety about the threat that Facebook posed, that they abandoned their usual sober objectivity around engineering staples like data and began faking their usage numbers to impress the outside world, and (no doubt) to intimidate Facebook.

This was the classic new-product sham, the "fake it till you make it" of the unscrupulous startupista, meant to flatter both ego and chances of future (real) success by projecting an image of present (imagined) success.

The numbers were taken seriously initially—after all, it wasn't absurd to think Google could drive usage quickly—but after a while, even the paranoid likes of FB insiders (not to mention the outside world) realized Google was juicing the numbers, like an Enron accountant would do a revenue report. Usage is always somewhat in the eye of the beholder, and Google was considering anyone a "user" who had ever so much as clicked on a Google Plus button as part of their usual Google experience. Given the overnight proliferation of Google Plus buttons all over the Google-user experience, like mushrooms on a shady knoll, one could claim "usage" when a Google user so much as checked email or uploaded a private photo. The reality was Google Plus users were rarely posting or engaging with posted content, and they certainly weren't returning repeatedly, like the proverbial lab rat in the drug experiment hitting the lever for another drop of cocaine water (as they did on Facebook).

To further stoke the fighting spirit (as well as internal trollery), the face of Google Plus was a perfect target of Facebook-ian contempt. Vic Gundotra was a former Microsoft exec who'd climbed the treacherous corporate ladder there before jumping to Google. It was he who had whispered a litany of fear into Larry Page's ear, who had greenlit the project, and it was he who headed the rushed and top-down effort (unusual for Google) to ship a product within an ambitious one hundred days.

The man oozed an off-putting smarminess as he stumped loudly for Google Plus in countless media interviews and Google-sponsored events. What was most insulting to a Facebooker was his studious omission of any mention of the social media behemoth in any public statement, as if the very raison d'être for his now-towering presence at Google didn't even exist. Like some Orwellian copywriter, engineering language and perception to suit a nonexistent fictional reality, Google would never explicitly mention the Facebook elephant in the room in any public statement. "Networks are for networking," intoned Gundotra. "Circles are for the right people," he continued, referring to Google Circles, a way of organizing social contacts shamelessly copied from Facebook's long-ignored Lists feature.

Within Facebook, Vic assumed the role of Emmanuel Goldstein from Orwell's *1984*, and many were the rips and jibes that he suffered in internal Facebook groups, a socially mediated Two Minutes' Hate, whenever someone posted a link to one of his pro-Google bloviations. This had gone beyond mere corporate rivalry and had become a personal struggle to many Facebookers who saw their identities wrapped up in the company, Facebook as an expression of themselves (or was it vice versa?).

"Gokul, I've only got three people to create an entire platform and business, and produce tens of millions in revenue in a few months."*

The scene was the final minutes of my more or less weekly one-on-one with Gokul, my official manager, although his management was largely symbolic in those chaotic days.†

"Three, Antonio! It's like the movie *300*. You're Spartans, man. Spartans! You can do it."

Gokul was referring to the cinema version of the Frank Miller comic, which had come out a couple of years earlier,

* Most products in tech, at least on the Internet side, launch half-baked, as what's called an MVP, or "minimum viable product." This is the minimum level of functionality you can provide and still sanely call your creation a product. In FBX's case, this meant the real-time auction worked with the basic ads-buying protocol we had designed, but we had none of the monitoring tools, debugging tools, or error notifications we'd need to properly manage this beast, nor the more advanced functionality, such as cross-browser identity matching, that we'd dreamed up. That would all be built in the nine months after launch, with one very overworked engineer (Hari) and one intern.

† "One-on-one" was Facebookese for the meeting between employee and manager that represented the bulk of the "management" that transpired at the company. These meetings were usually taken seriously, and if you happened to walk into one taking place at a café table or in a conference room, it was protocol to give the manager-managee duo space. Of course, these meetings were jokes with Gokul, who mostly asked when promised revenue was materializing.

and had been a hit among the geek set. It depicted the early days of the Greco-Persian Wars of the fourth century BC, as filtered through modern superhero aesthetics.

"You realize, Gokul, that the Spartans lost at Thermopylae, right?"

He shook his head, looked away, and said nothing, as he always did when confronted with an awkward reality. We had reached his stand-up desk, on which stood an unused monitor (Gokul didn't have the patience to plug in the cable). It was clear our weekly one-on-one was over.

I walked back to the FBX hooch with nothing to offer the team in terms of increased resources. Despite an auspicious beginning to FBX, and strong public and media interest in the product, Facebook was unwilling to invest anything beyond a couple of engineers and a handful of part-time support staff. This may seem incongruous, but it was in keeping with the Facebook zeitgeist. FBX, despite its initial promise and my vision of it as the centerpiece of Facebook's future ads-targeting product, was still considered a rushed revenue stopgap, puking out cash the company needed to make post-IPO numbers. Never in over a year of lobbying did anyone one level above me in management truly understand, much less actively support, the real-time programmatic ads-buying technology that was then taking over so much of the advertising world. To the extent it could produce revenue *right now!* it received the lukewarm support of Gokul and Rabkin, and the tolerance of the sales side, which took its cues from product anyhow. My naive assumption was that if I could only make FBX into a billion-dollar business, I'd convince the recalcitrant (to not say willfully ignorant) Facebook management of the size of the overlooked opportunity, and the tide of opinion would shift.*

---

* I spent about two months convincing Gokul and Boland that FBX, as designed, did not "leak" any Facebook data, assuaging their unjustified concerns around data privacy. I don't think anyone at Facebook, other than

This was, of course, madness. Money talks, but inside Facebook at least, it spoke only if what it said was part of the bigger, accepted narrative.

As with the lawsuit during the AdGrok days, I shielded the engineers from all this political brouhaha, and acted as if it was a given that all these wonderful features we'd dreamed up—many of which we'd implemented by this point, resulting in a slew of patents—would one day see the light of day.

But in fact it was us against the world, and Facebook management.

To be someone or to do something, which would I choose?*

A man occasionally reaches a fork in life's path.

One road leads to doing something, to making an impact on his organization and his world. To being true to his values and vision, and standing with the other men who've helped build that vision. He will have to trust himself when all men doubt him, and as a reward, he will have the scorn of his professional circle heaped on his head. He will not be favored by his superiors, nor win the polite praise of his conformist peers. But maybe, just maybe, he has the chance to be right, and create something of lasting value that will transcend the consensus mediocrity inherent in any organization, even supposedly disruptive ones.

---

the FBX team itself, even at an abstract level, ever understood how Facebook's ad exchange really worked.

* Students of US military history will recognize these as the words of Col. John Boyd, a noted military aviator and conflict theorist. His pugnacious, maverick personality earned him the visceral wrath of the military's senior brass, and he never rose above the rank of colonel, despite his contributions to US military strategy, still taught to this day, and his hand in the design of such legendary aircraft as the F-15, F-16, and A-10. The Air Force never formally disavowed him, however, and he had a twenty-four-year career as a pilot and an officer.

The other road leads to being someone. He will receive the plum products, the facile praise afforded to the organization man who checks off the canonical list of petty virtues that define moral worth in his world. He will receive the applause of his peers, though it will be striking how rarely that traffic in official praise leads to actual products anybody remembers, much less advances the overall cause of the organization.

I certainly had options. I can't say I didn't.

I had outs, and could have walked away from FBX.

All I had to do was shut up, keep my head down, go through the motions with whatever shitty product was handed to me after FBX, and read along from the Facebook script about how to be a proper product manager. I might even resurrect my career if one of those products was "successful." In the rapidly ossifying Facebook culture, one could get along simply by going along.

Plus, there were real stakes on the line.

Consider the number of shares and the fact that at the time of this writing, in December 2015, Facebook is worth almost four times what it was when I struck my AdGrok deal. I had two children, whose mother's nine-to-five corporate job provided for them, though just barely. Her London trader heyday was long gone, and now her salary was that of your standard-issue MBA inside the corporate machine. I contributed a slab of cash every month, per California support guidelines, but it would be my Facebook stock vesting yet to come that would pay for private high schools and Stanford, so Zoë and Noah wouldn't have to sneak into this country's elite through the back door from cattle class, as I had to do.

Short of me pulling another startup out of my hat, any windfall would come only from the Facebook shares I was so cavalierly risking in my mad pursuit of FBX. But the ego drives, and honor compels, and stubbornness steels the will that moderation and judgment might sap. Faced as I was with an array of opponents, my reflex was the same as always: double down and dig in.

Like Col. Boyd, I'd choose to do something, rather than be somebody, and tie myself to the mast of the FBX ship, wherever it took me and whatever the future cost.

JANUARY 16, 2013

This was an embarrassment.

The senior leadership of Omnicom, one of the largest ad agencies in the world, was sitting on the other side of a long conference-room table in Building 17.

My side of the conference table was populated by the Ads senior leadership, who came out en masse only for such big-ticket guests, and the line PMs and engineers involved in the newfangled FBX and Custom Audiences stuff that had gotten so much outside attention (Mathew Varghese, me, the odd engineer).

There were four ad agencies, so-called holding companies, which served as umbrella organizations for the hundreds of smaller agencies that ruled the media world. Collectively, their revenues were in the tens of billions, and the total media spend they controlled or influenced was many times that. These motherfuckers were the real deal, the absolute A-plus, Big Swinging Media Dicks. Sitting like Zeus on Olympus, they could fire lightning bolts of media spend hither and yon, activating any publisher or media channel instantly. Facebook had been patiently seducing the agencies for years, with entire teams in its New York office dedicated to teasing spend into our new, unproved medium.

For years, that pitch had focused on the ephemeral promise of Facebook pages and Likes. But with Custom Audiences and Facebook Exchange, the agencies' ears had perked up. Suddenly, they could actually use their data and targeting on Facebook in ways they could account for, proving worth to their clients, which would generate more spend, and set the media wheel giddily turning.

At the head of the table was Josh Jacobs, the head of Accuen, Omnicom's "trading desk." That's right, with the rise of programmatic media and its exchange-like real-time markets, even the stodgy old agencies were opening business units that operated like those on Wall Street. These were the brains of the agency world—to the extent that world possessed any—and they were very savvy and bullshit immune.

"So when can we get the identity-matching stuff in via FBX?" asked one of Jacobs's lieutenants to his right.

This guy was actually in a suit, about as rare as a wallaby on Facebook's campus. He was the head of some subbranch of the Omnicom empire that ran retargeting for the holding company's clients.

I sure wasn't going to answer for the current internal shit show that had haunted the Facebook side of the table for months now. Gokul, as the senior product person present, took the question.

"We're having lots of internal discussions about that right now, but we basically haven't quite come down to a company-wide decision on our future direction."

Ugh.

What a cop-out. Burn my Facebook fleece now.

An awkward pause followed the obviously unsatisfactory answer. They sat there with their tailored shirts, good shoes, and chunky power watches, looking the very picture of East Coast Media Douchebags. They stared at our side of the table, where we slouched in our hoodies and sneakers, and waited for answers.

But there were no answers to be had.

For the past six months a vicious debate had taken place internally at Facebook about the directions of CA versus FBX. The crux of that debate, which I touched upon earlier, boiled down to the following: As Facebook waded into the world of outside data—desktop browsing, mobile app installs, offline purchases in stores, and so forth—would it build an open system that allowed advertisers to bring their data to Facebook, while preserving Facebook's user privacy and preventing data leakage to the outside world? Or, as it had in the past, would it attempt to capture as much of the ads management stack as it could, even if it meant shipping inferior product, shunting out any and all companies other than the end advertiser?* The implications for revenue, arguably the most important issue in the debate, were severe.

The completely "closed" stack that Boland was backing, which would involve an expanded version of the Custom Audiences product, would take years to build. Also, it would take years to convince advertisers to use it, as they generally preferred independent tools for ads serving and delivery that weren't so reliant on a single publisher like Facebook. Also, inertia alone would disincline them from using it, as the real-time technology that was then taking over online media, and of which FBX was an expression, was fast becoming the dominant paradigm for how sophisticated ads targeting was done.

What Omnicom and its deep-pocketed advertisers wanted was what they called "data portability"; that is, the ability to use their valuable first-party data, or expensively acquired third-party data, wherever it wanted to, whether on Facebook or in the *New York Times*. By building some

* "Stack" is a bit of techie-ese. It refers to the set of associated technologies that form the entire basis for a product. The verticality of the name is meant to capture the "stacked" nature of much of software; that is, the code driving the user interface you see, the technical glue that connects that code to a database, and the database technology itself. Another commonly referenced stack is the network stack: a browser rendering HTML it gets over HTTP, on top of TCP (transmission control protocol), which is routed over IP (Internet protocol), which it sends locally via your Wi-Fi router and a cable connection. The advertising stack is an even more convoluted clockwork assembly of ad exchange, optimization, targeting, ad server, and tracking. A whiteboard schematic would resemble a Rube Goldberg device.

tottering edifice of technology, and then limiting access to Facebook's inventory through that technology, Facebook was effectively maintaining the walled garden it had tended for years. It would brick over the narrow opening in that wall we had created with Facebook Exchange in the first place, and which had created the excitement that had led to this meeting.

The only way Facebook would convince the Omnicoms of the world—and by extension, every sophisticated advertiser—to adopt Boland's closed-stack direction was by driving so much more value via the use of Facebook's identity and cross-device data that the advertisers would swallow the bitter pill of Facebook's hard-to-use technology. As the value of that unique Facebook identity was still not completely known, this represented a risk.

The alternative was the "open" stack that the FBX team (by which I mean me, and just about only me) was loudly advocating. By building technology consistent with the growing standard, we would make adoption by advertisers quasi-instantaneous. The FBX team had already semisecretly built (but not shipped) the basic technologies that would have safely exposed Facebook identity across browsers and mobile devices. It was merely a matter of turning it on, something I had been harassing Facebook management to do for months.

To cite our perhaps overused financial analogy, imagine Facebook was a large financial-services company like Fidelity. What Facebook was proposing in the "closed" plan was this: Facebook didn't just want to offer its unique mutual fund, stock, and bond investments; it also wanted to run the exchange where those investments were traded, the brokers buying and selling on that exchange, and the stock-trading tool used to log in and trade, as well as the entire financial system around the investment platform—namely, banks, checking accounts, credit cards, the works. If you wanted to buy into the Facebook investment fund, everything from your debit card to your 401(k) retirement account would be labeled "Facebook," and work only with other Facebook-labeled products. Facebook would exist as its own financial world, completely cut off from whatever Schwab or Bank of America world you came from.

What if you wanted to buy something other than a Facebook mutual fund in this Facebook-owned and -operated financial empire? Facebook would eventually allow you to do that as well, but only through its exchange and buying tools. So you could buy a few shares of Google or General Motors, but you'd still log into the Facebook buying platform.

Would this work?

Well, maybe. If Facebook's investment offerings were so uniquely high-performing, and if your ability to buy outside stocks and bonds was actually *amplified* by doing it via Facebook's platform (versus via all the other means for buying those commodity products), then yes, people would put up with the hassle of moving their entire financial lives into Facebook-land. Not to mention, they'd put up with the very real risk of lock-in such a move represented. (Once all your financial details and data were inside Facebook, your ability to unplug from the beast and take your business elsewhere would be severely limited.)

On the technical side, the decision had major implications as well. Continuing our analogy, Facebook was technologically like some local credit union in Omaha, Nebraska, though with the deposit balances to rival Bank of America. It would have to offer every banking service known to man if it wanted to compete with the entire financial world, and that would take time, even with Facebook's inhumanly fast engineering.

Revenuewise, that meant the monetary value of this whole identity vision wouldn't be realized for years either. Such a construct, given that it was much more than the sum of its parts, would assume its real value only when it all existed. What value did Custom Audiences have if you could use its wonderful, person-centric targeting only on Facebook and not on the rest of the Internet too? If Facebook had an ad server (and we'll get into what that means in a moment) and it worked only on Facebook, who cared? An advertiser still needed its old ad server to show ads on Google-controlled Web properties and everywhere else. This glittering vision in Facebook Blue of everything running on Facebook would take years to realize.

By comparison, the value of the open plan would be realized instantaneously. If FBX had access to the identity matching we'd built on the Custom Audiences side, not to mention ads inventory on mobile, then the exchange could serve as a central clearinghouse for online identity everywhere. Everything we were ideating around identity, that entire spiel I regaled you with about names, both online and off, could be realized in a few weeks, all due to the open and standardized nature of FBX. And all of it implemented with three engineers and one cocky product manager, and not the roomful of bickering, big-company clowns that every meeting on the matter tended to feature.

Of course, to be fair to the closed plan, if it succeeded and Facebook somehow convinced the world to leave the outside Internet behind and jump headfirst into FB land, it would leave Facebook in a magnificently dominant position overall. That was the real question behind this debate: Was the performance of Facebook's ads and identity data enough to convince the world to abandon everything else for Facebook? If not, then the closed plan was Sponsored Stories Part II, and the flying saucers would again fail to appear.

This closed-versus-open debate would consume rivers of electrons in acrimonious email debates, during which your humble correspondent used potentially offensive language to describe otherwise respected members of the Ads leadership, sowing seeds that he would exponentially reap in the sweet by and by.* But right then, those email debates were being batted brusquely back and forth, and sitting in the very inboxes we all discreetly checked as the Omnicom meeting droned ever on.

Though not in that room with Omnicom, a new presence was making itself felt on the Ads team right then, a presence that would change everything for Facebook Ads. Before I introduce that transformative character, there's something critical about Facebook's culture, which we've only brushed against thus far, that you need to understand:

Facebook was an empire Napoleonic in both tenor and flavor, and like any hive of palace politics, one's proximity to the emperor around which the pageant swirled was a direct function of his or her institutional stature. Get pulled into the orbit of the Boy Dynast of Facebook, and your product got a kick of institutional momentum via the implied royal blessing: engineers would be allocated, other products canceled or pushed out of the way, and, most important, you became a fixture in the courtly firmament of the empire. Even if your product failed (and many were the stillborn or grotesquely misshapen offspring of Facebook's anointed inner circle), you lived to ship and influence another day, star undiminished, reputation unmarred. Several were the princes of Zuck's court: Blake Ross, Justin Shaffer, Sam Lessin, and many more whom a commoner such as I, rusticating in the Ads wilderness, could observe only from afar.

Fortunately, Facebook itself served as the society pages

---

* In an example of the marketing duplicity this sort of thing required, Boland, the very champion of the closed vision, has since gone on record with official Facebook PR–approved posts about how it "wasn't about closed versus open, but integration instead." There are hundreds of old emails in his inbox (many authored by me) with "closed" and "open" in their subject lines.

to its own courtly intrigue: the quasimaniacal Facebook usage among employees meant every debutante's coming out with Zuck, or every kingly banquet at In-N-Out Burger, was there for all to see. Like a Brit on a bar stool scanning tabloids for news of the royal family, the Facebook hoi polloi friended or followed whomever they could among the Facebook nobility, and watched, nose pressed against the glass, the regal extravaganza unfold.

One of those princes, first among equals, was Andrew "Boz" Bosworth, Zuck's former teaching assistant at Harvard. Purportedly raised on a horse ranch in Northern California, he was a big, bald bully with tattoos on both arms, a former member of the Harvard tae kwon do team grown thick with age. Prior to his involvement in Ads, he was the engineering brains behind the initial versions of News Feed, a fact he'd never fail to mention on a first meeting. He was the first Friend of Zuck to work in Ads, and it was understood he had been dispatched to unfuck the Ads team from the maelstrom of directionless chaos under Badros and Gokul.

In that sense, Boz was an absolute godsend, and the Ads team, not to mention Facebook's finances, has reaped the benefit of his decisive authority ever since he assumed the reins. As I hope I've managed to detail, from 2011 until early 2013, the Facebook monetization strategy distinguished itself mostly by its complete absence (other than the failed Sponsored Stories experiment). As with the British schoolchildren in William Golding's *Lord of the Flies*, when product managers and engineers were left to fend for themselves in a state of anarchy, it wasn't long before a boulder got dropped on the fat weakling, and there was a rotting pig's head on gleeful display. Boz was like the British naval officer appearing in the book's murderous climax: the feral boys, on the cusp of truly losing it, awaken, and decide to take up civilization again.

Which is more or less what happened in early 2013 when Boz started appearing in Ads meetings, and eventually took over. Suddenly, Ads could make decisions without resorting to Sheriff Sheryl, since we had our own viceroy, our own official Vicar of Zuck, running the Ads show.

But there was downside to aristocracy.

Almost comically, and against all Facebook tradition, Boz named his personal conference room after himself: LiveBoz. Decked out like a personal man cave with couches and low-slung coffee tables, rather than the upright Aeron chairs and long tables of most conference rooms, it was where we had the penultimate and testiest debate about product direction. He also seemed to have a team of professional photographers following him around in his personal life, the resulting flurry of paparazzi photos peppering his Facebook Timeline, which resembled something between an ever-present wedding album and a running Hollywood movie premiere (but with few celebrities other than himself).

In Katherine Losse's so-so firsthand account of life at early Facebook, *The Boy Kings*, she describes a mafia of Harvard recruits. They were core hires, and would go on to form the backbone of future Facebook. By all reports, the atmosphere at early Facebook was bro-y and redolent with the joshing violence typical of young, hormonal males. One of the Harvard mafiosi got into the habit of threatening other engineers that he'd "punch them in the face" if they messed up. That person was Boz, as I was able to guess while discussing the matter with a Facebook old-timer who dished details.

Quod licet Bozi, non licet bovi. Gods may do what cattle may not.

Boz might have been a god at Facebook, but what he wasn't was an ads man, as he knew nothing about the monetization space. This was no ding; most of Facebook, outside of the Ads team, had no clue how Facebook made money and the free food and shuttles got paid for. Most were quite content to stay that way, and blissfully outsourced this concern to the Ads teams and Sheryl and kept on working on whatever piece of the user-facing product was theirs.

As a form of rapid on-boarding, Boz was invited along to client meetings with the product marketers and managers. On the one hand, this was slightly preposterous. He had zero qualifications, other than Zuck's confidence, for the job.

On the other hand, who are we kidding? It was advertising technology, not orbital mechanics; a mentally agile techie, having spent an action-packed career learning (if not creating) new technologies and business models, could learn enough high-level basics to make (mostly) intelligent decisions—particularly if the entire team bent over backward to train you in a hurry. That's effectively what happened, and from late 2012 on, Boz was increasingly involved in Ads strategizing and general mass-email-thread politicking. While silent at first, getting his bearings in the new subject matter and political landscape, he'd soon grow very vocal indeed.

But before that happened, Facebook Ads, thanks to Boland no less, had one of those sudden, out-of-left-field, WTF moments that changed everything.

Microsoft Shrugged

> Atlas, with all his bulk, was changed into stone. His beard and hair became forests, his arms and shoulders cliffs, his head a summit, and his bones rocks. Each part increased in bulk till he became a mountain, and heaven with all its stars rests upon his shoulders.
>
> —Thomas Bulfinch, *Bulfinch's Mythology*

FEBRUARY 28, 2013

Any idea who Malcom McLean was?

I bet not. But that one man changed our economy more than practically anyone else in the twentieth century.

McLean was the inventor of the intermodal container, those metal boxes piled into immense heaps on the cargo ships coming from China. The genius of the container is that the entire workflow around transporting physical goods is standardized on the same 8×8×40 box. Manufacturers load goods onto eight-foot-wide palettes straight into the box. The box becomes a freight car when loaded onto railroad wheels, and once it arrives at a ship, it is directly hefted aboard via those immense cranes that dot every modern port. Piled like Legos on the ship, the boxes arrive at another port and are loaded onto a truck frame, and are driven to their destinations. It's universal: whether the ship docks in Singapore or

Oakland, its cargo will be swiftly loaded and unloaded via the magic of containerization. Intermodal containers make our global supply chain possible.

What's that got to do with ads?

Modern digital advertising has also settled on a containerized box—or, rather, a set of them. They're known as Internet Advertising Bureau (IAB) ad units for desktop ads, and Mobile Marketing Association (MMA) ad units for mobile. They come in the standard sizes, measured in pixels—728×90, 300×250, and so forth—of every banner ad on the Web, with other sizes for mobile.

As in freight, the standard sizing means the ad that runs today on time.com can also run on Yahoo Finance or the *New York Times* site tomorrow. It also means that much of the technical plumbing around advertising works efficiently as well: the ad servers that feed you the flashing pixels in the ad all work with the standardized sizes. The analytics software that slices and dices your data by publisher, ad size, and placement on the page also assumes the standard sizes. It's containerization applied to paid media, and in general, it works.

But there are some ships that consider themselves either too big or too important to accept containers—either because they don't like the look of them on the deck, or because they claim that moving freight is really a side business and not their mission in life. So if you want to move anything through them, you suddenly have to repack everything in whatever arbitrary, random containers these ships accept.

This situation is what we politely call "native ad formats" in the ads business. Those ships are products like Google Search, Facebook, and Twitter. Either because they started as user-focused viral plays unconcerned with monetization (Facebook, Twitter), or because they very intentionally bucked a going standard, basically because they could (Google Search), the net result is that standard ad formats get no play.

Opting for native formats creates two immense frictions for those platforms, particularly for anyone trying to bolt a traditional ad exchange onto his inventory (as we did at Facebook via FBX, and Twitter is attempting to do now with MoPub). Those two frictions are the obvious one of creative difference (i.e., the ads themselves must be graphically different from their standardized counterparts), and a subtler one that concerns how ads are delivered and counted in the ads world. The battles surrounding this latter point, I believe, will determine the ad empires of the future.

Why do ad servers matter?

At first glance, they seem inconsequential. To continue my (now perhaps stretched) nautical analogy, they're merely the container cranes that shuffle boxes around. But in fact they play a much more important role.

Look: the advertiser doesn't trust its agency, the agency doesn't trust its trading desk, the trading desk doesn't trust the ads-buying software it's using, and the ads-buying technology company doesn't trust the exchanges. The only thing that keeps this dishonest world honest is the existence of an agreed-upon source of truth. That oracle is the ad server. If a marketer wants to reach a million people in the eastern United States, showing each person no more than four ad impressions between the hours of four and ten p.m. on Thursday (a common buy for movies, incidentally, which always launch on a Friday), then that marketer will be satisfied only if the ad server report says that's what he got. The ad server isn't merely a data server spewing forth pixels on demand; it's also the accounting system that decides what gets delivered when, to whom, how often, and where on the Internet.

And that's just for fairly brainless brand marketing buys that want to make a big, broad splash. For marketers who track their performance (such as online retailers), the tyranny of the ad server yardstick is even greater, since it defines the units, in addition to the accounting, of marketing dollars.

Here's a technical parable to make it simpler:

Have you ever driven on a highway and seen those roadside billboards? You know: MCDONALD'S, FOUR MILES ON RIGHT! Even if we don't consciously process the image assaulting our retinas, our subconscious, that cradle of desires both holy and unholy, has registered it. And four miles down the road, when those golden arches appear, you will be more inclined to pull over for that prefab greasepuck. That road sign contributed an infinitesimal probability to your acting on the prompt. What if you removed it? How many burgers would go unbought as compared with when the sign was there? It's a small number, but measurable.

In the online world, seeing that advance sign is known as a viewthrough: the physical viewing of an ad, but with no resulting immediate action. Turning off the highway when you see the golden arches is known as a clickthrough: an immediate action following a marketing prompt. The relative value of viewthroughs versus clickthroughs is a subtle measurement question that needn't slow us down here. But appreciate for a moment what privileging one or the other means for someone trying to decide whether to buy more billboards or spend more on venues and storefront bling.

In a world where we know people are hungry and we have our choice of venues for locating a McDonald's, we'll invest in rent and storefront bling, as we already know we're catching somebody at a weak, hungry moment (say, at a baseball stadium or a mall's food court). We don't need signs all over the stadium or mall. We know people are hungry and where they congregate; we just need to pay the price of being there.

In a world where we're not sure if people are hungry and advertising is as much a matter of inducement as information, we'll plaster the world with billboards in the hope of getting consumers to a store, and not worry so much about happening to catch someone hungry. We're manufacturing necessity, rather than exploiting it, which is the situation on most highways. Ergo, we have billboards every other mile but stores thirty miles apart.

Why does that matter?

Google comes from the search world, in which a person simply types in a request for something. All Google has to do is get that person to the storefront. The value of a Google click is immense and expensive (which is why Google prints money). The value of a viewthrough to them is nil. In fact, it's so nil that Google opts not to even show you an ad if your query doesn't seem commercial, choosing to show you a blank billboard much of the time. Roughly half of Google queries don't generate ads in the space next to them; test it yourself. To Google, the claims of viewthrough value seem bogus, an attempt to justify wasteful media spending. As a result, its ad server counts only clickthroughs. Its manual explicitly states, "Clicks trump impressions," and Google drives that point home in every demo.

Facebook, on the other hand, worships viewthrough value. Since Facebook has no real data about your intent (i.e., it has no idea what you want), it has to manufacture desire rather than exploit it. So in Facebook's accounting, viewthrough is valuable indeed, and it would very much like credit for that splashy image (or soon, video) it inserted into your feed, even if you didn't click on it.

Let's go further. What's a Facebook Like really worth? Sharing a page post? Commenting on something? Those all have value. Like the viewthrough impressions we mentioned earlier, these things have maybe incremental value, but value nonetheless. And if your site generates a mountain of likes (rather than clicks), you need an ad server whose accounting reflects that. This is what we were missing in early 2013.

At the time, the FBX debate was still raging, and I was increasingly thinking that the fight was entering its circle-the-wagons, fight-to-the-last-man finale. I had doubled down on FBX, willingly ceding responsibilities of the ever-pointless targeting team (still trying futilely to find some data worth mining and exposing to advertisers) to another product manager.

I also lost Custom Audiences as a product I managed.

That one smarted a bit, and in retrospect, losing it was shortsighted of me. I was so wrapped up in making a success of FBX, so completely convinced that if we only scaled FBX faster than Custom Audiences, I could arm-twist Facebook management into seeing the rightness of our inevitable programmatic future.

By late 2012, though, Gokul had realized that keeping me as Custom Audiences product manager was like contracting the fox to build the new henhouse. At worst I'd ignore the task (which I occasionally did), and at best I'd build technology with back doors and escape hatches I'd exploit and recycle later in the FBX product, the real way forward. The only thing worthwhile about Custom Audiences to me was its unique ability to join online to offline via personally identifiable information like names, phone numbers, and mailing addresses, a data-joining ability I fought futilely to enable on FBX as well.*

Boland was surely behind the stripping of duties as well. He and I had already become bitter antagonists over the role of Custom Audiences in our respective targeting visions, exchanging long, acrimonious emails involving the entire senior Ads staff, from Sheryl on down. I was the lone re-

---

* In case this is confusing, a brief aside on data matching. On Custom Audiences, an advertiser uploads a list of names (potentially in the millions), and gets a large targeting segment it can run ads against in return. In FBX data matching, for each name, Facebook returns a pseudonym, and that pseudonym is used to identify you each and every time an ad appears on Facebook, via the real-time exchange mechanism we've discussed before. In Custom Audiences, it's like addressing the entire population of a city with one general message; in FBX, it's like addressing every individual in the city by name with a catered message. Put another way, it's the difference between a guillotine and a scalpel, with about the differing results you'd expect when, say, trying to excise a tumor.

fusenik attacking Boland's vision. Since Custom Audience was his proposed baby, designed to do what FBX clearly did better—namely, joining outside targeting data to Facebook Ads—my days as product manager for it were inevitably numbered. Don't underestimate those middle managers with their gluteally superglued lips too much.

Then Boland threw all of Facebook a curveball. He had made several mysterious trips to Seattle. Facebook's office in Seattle at the time was minuscule, and was mostly engineering. Since Boland never actually spoke to engineers, this was a puzzle.

But one day it was announced we were in heated negotiations to buy Atlas, Microsoft's ads server, and the also-ran to Google's incumbent ad server, DoubleClick for Publishers.

When the news propagated through the Ads team, several of the product managers involved in the outside ads world, however obliquely, ran to the IT help desk to beg or borrow a Windows laptop to check out this thing we were supposedly buying. Believe it or not, Microsoft's Atlas ran only on specific versions of Internet Explorer (in case you're too young to remember, that's a browser). Unfortunately, unlike vintage clothing, user interfaces never get so old that they're fashionable again. It was creaky and ancient and possessed a flow so convoluted that even professional ads people got lost in the mess. But thanks to an early start and years of existence, it had 20 percent market share and thousands of outside publishers, which was the real draw.

This whole deal had been cooked up by (surprise!) Boland and his former colleagues at Microsoft. For the reasons described earlier in this chapter, an ad server was a cornerstone of this all-consuming Facebook Ads stack, and his engineering a deal right then, and getting Facebook to commit to it, was another stone thrown on the balance scale of closed versus open.

Since Atlas was reputedly in acquisition talks with another big ad tech company in the programmatic space, the deal was rushed, a fait accompli before most people had even realized we were buying it. As a sort of to-all announcement, plus a forum for "speak now or forever hold your peace" on the corporate marriage, Greg Badros (who still officially ran Ads) called a meeting of all the senior staff and product managers when the Atlas negotiations had reached their head in late February.

Everyone who mattered in Ads gathered in one of the bigger conference rooms. It was a sign of how much the Ads team had grown that there were maybe forty to fifty people, and standing room only. This same meeting two years earlier wouldn't have filled the seats at a medium-sized conference table, much less a large room.

Whoever was running point on the contract details read out the high-level terms, which I'll omit due to their being mostly irrelevant and my limited love for Facebook legal hate mail. Then Badros chimed in with the short history of Atlas, mentioning how Microsoft had acquired it as part of a huge $6.2 billion acquisition in 2007 of a company called aQuantive, which was then an amalgam of advertising technologies. In true Microsoft style, it had failed to capitalize on its mammoth investment, letting one part of aQuantive after another rot on the vine, with only Atlas, which had secured for itself a stable role in the ads space, ultimately surviving. But now Microsoft wanted out of even that.

As Badros then summarized the sordid tale in one accounting fact: "So Microsoft bought them for $6.2 billion in 2007, and then wrote down $6.1 billion in value, and here we are."

Someone shouted out the obvious question: "But wait . . . where's Atlas's value in all this then?"

Badros shot back, "That's it. Point-one billion . . . that's Atlas. That's what we're buying."

Uneasy laughter made its way through the room as the

Facebook Ads management team digested the fact it was picking up Microsoft's scraps. It was a harsh reminder as well of who the big boys really were in terms of writing checks. Facebook's biggest ad tech acquisition to date was Microsoft's accounting rounding error.

Nobody raised any significant objections in that meeting, and in very short order indeed, Facebook outbid whoever else was in the running, and the deal was announced (or selectively leaked).

Many non-Facebook people discreetly expressed disbelief about the acquisition among themselves, questioning how we could buy such a neglected piece of legacy technology. Despite the deal's having originated with Boland and his old Microsoft chums, I didn't think it was such a bad move, necessarily. For a modest sum, Facebook had jump-started a presence in the display ads world in which it hitherto had been an afterthought.

Of course, with acquisitions, it's not what you pay, it's what they cost you that matters. Facebook would have to feed and maintain a mountain of crap code (and the crappy coders who created it) for a long time to come. The amount of technical debt it had to pay down was evidently huge; the "new" Atlas would be dogged by delays and wouldn't launch for over two years.*

But hey, Facebook now had a new media yardstick. It just had to convince everyone to use it.

* "Technical debt" is an oft-used concept in software development. Imagine that every time an engineer makes some quick-and-dirty fix to a piece of code—the sort of hack that will likely blow up one day and need to be fixed (again)—there's an invisible ledger in which a loan is taken out against future engineering time. That engineer can borrow now to get the trains running again, but the bill will come due later, usually with interest.

Ad Majorem Facebook *Gloriam**

There is a tide in the affairs of men,
Which, taken at the flood, leads on to fortune;
Omitted, all the voyage of their life
Is bound in shallows and in miseries.
On such a full sea are we now afloat,
And we must take the current when it serves,
Or lose our ventures.

—William Shakespeare, *Julius Caesar*

* *Ad majorem Dei gloriam* ("For the greater glory of God") is the motto of the Jesuit order of the Catholic Church. The intellectual storm troopers of that faith, the Jesuits were behind everything from wars to defend their missions in Paraguay during the seventeenth century (memorably recorded in the Robert De Niro film *The Mission*) to the education of such luminaries and rogues as Descartes and Subcomandante Marcos. To this day, they run a global network of universities, including Georgetown, Boston College, and Fordham, and countless high schools throughout Europe, Latin America, and the United States, educating elites from Silicon Valley to Santiago de Chile. Fidel Castro and I graduated from the same Jesuit school (Castro shut down the school after seizing power, and it decamped to Miami in the sixties), and I had to write "AMDG" on top of many a homework assignment in my day.

MARCH 18, 2013

Boz was no longer the dilettante guest of the Ads team, sitting in like a tourist on meetings, but the officially installed leader, Badros having been given the bump. He carried himself like he owned the place (which, of course, he kind of did). Boz's takeover of Ads represented more than a cosmetic shift in the organizational chart; we were witnessing a complete reconfiguration of the Ads space-time continuum along a single dimension from "Boz likes you" to "fired." Where you were on that continuum was yet to be determined for most Ads folks, and I had no idea where I fell.

Presumably to figure this out, Boz requested we have a one-on-one, even though I didn't report to him officially. In short order, I found myself sitting across from him at a small table in a small conference room, staring at the tattoos gracing his forearms. On his right there was a figurative map of California, on his left the word "*veritas*" encircled his wrist ("truth" in Latin, also Harvard's motto).

I had, of course, done a complete Facebook stalk going back through his time at Harvard and clear into babyhood. Thanks to the FB hashtag #tbt, I had seen his idealized and mediated autobiography from rural Northern California to Harvard to Facebook.* I had also scoped out his management philosophy, or really, his public conception of it. He clearly was one of those tough but fair types who pride themselves on directness and honesty. Truth was written on his very body, after all.

For my part, outside of physics textbooks, I found Truth to be a rather rare commodity, particularly in the tech world. I had also noticed that those who most made a big show

* #tbt (i.e., "throwback Thursday") is a common Facebook practice wherein users post photos from long ago in their lives, often from before Facebook even existed.

of believing in Truth were unusually attached to whatever well-groomed pack of lies they held dear.

The conversation proceeded quickly to my role in the Ads team. At Facebook, the performance review cycle was semi-annual, with every February and August bringing the usual political jockeying to make sure your biggest fans reviewed you, and your biggest detractors didn't quite manage to.

"You're a very divisive figure, Antonio. I read the reviews of your team members, and then that of management. They're completely opposed. One loves you, and the other hates you."

Yeah, no shit.

I could imagine the feedback, without having been told the specific authors: Reesman, Hari, and Gary and others on the FBX team all gushing praise for my dedication and product leadership. And then Gokul and Boland decrying my uncouth insubordination, smart-alecky arrogance, and corrosive criticism of current Facebook strategy.

"That's true, Boz. I've certainly made friends and enemies here. But my goal has always been to give Facebook the best ads system possible."

This was, in all seriousness, true. I could barely remember what my life was like before Facebook, and there was a trail of destruction I had caused by spending my entire life there: two children neglected, two different women whose worthy love I'd spurned, two boats rotting in neglect, and anything like an intellect or a life outside campus nonexistent due to indifference and my dedication to the Facebook cause.* Don't

* Aside from British Trader, who well and truly did love me, there was the matter of Israeli Psychologist. I've mostly omitted the tale here due to discretion, but during my time at Facebook I had a passionate romance with a former professional photographer and IDF soldier turned shrink. My last year at Facebook was spent living in her tiny Palo Alto studio. The relationship buckled under the strain of work, and came to a slow, agonizing end after I left, but not before numerous melodramatic breakups, relapses, and re-relapses.

be deceived by my withering treatment of Facebook in this book; inside every cynic lives a heartbroken idealist. If I'm now a mordant critic, it's because at one point, like Lucifer once being the proudest angel before the fall, I too lived and breathed for Facebook, perhaps even more than most.

We moved on to the topic of the open versus closed debate that was roiling all of us. While he was equivocal on the matter, he expressed his firm intent to come to a conclusion quickly and end the uncertainty that plagued every forward-looking decision Ads was making. This was one of those Delphic portents of old, which could be read either somewhat positively or negatively, depending.

Afterward, we stood up and shook hands over the small desk. The meeting had had the smell of a last meeting with the mafia capo before things turned ugly, and he started either unleashing hitmen or making offers that couldn't be refused. I didn't like the smell of it, not one bit.

APRIL 4, 2013

Boz, live. Again. This time in LiveBoz.

Gathered was everyone with a speaking part in the Great Facebook Debate of 2013: Boland, Gokul, Varghese, Boz, Scott Shapiro, and me. The stated purpose was to finally (finally!) hash out a final recommendation from Boz to Sheryl. Despite all the ballyhooed "final" meetings with Sheryl we'd had over the previous few months, we hadn't reached a conclusion.

Given the bro-y décor of the Boz man cave, it was hardly surprising the meeting soon devolved into a male pissing match.

"Custom Audiences is way ahead of FBX these days," Boland began.

Yeah, no shit, jackass. It's me and Scott and Hari against you and the entire Facebook sales and operations organization you manage or influence, as well as the engineering teams running the targeting system and the API, all of which support Custom Audiences, while I have one engineer. It's a miracle FBX is still even in the running.

My resentment at the unfair match aside, Boland was actually wrong, and for subtle reasons that he likely didn't understand.

"That's only if you count Custom Audience dollars as actually incremental. I think that's a stretch to say the least. What's in your Custom Audience revenue dashboard isn't real revenue. They should probably be discounted by half, if we're doing comparisons," I countered.

Boland and I locked hostile eyes, and Boz interrupted in his managerial, peacekeeper role with conciliatory remarks.

Here's where we really were:

For the past few months, since their respective launches in midsummer, FBX's and CA's revenues had both increased apace and were initially neck and neck. Since about December, though, and on paper (or in Facebook's revenue dashboards, which were what mattered) CA's revenue had edged out FBX's revenue significantly. The reasons for that were telling.

As mentioned earlier, FBX's technical challenges were far, far greater than CA's. We were creating an entirely new ads infrastructure, while CA was merely coasting on existing Facebook targeting technology, recycling much of the targeting logic that already existed. I would know; it's what I'd spent the previous year building. Clunky though its technology was, it marked an expansion of basic functionality already inside Facebook's API and interfaces, which meant existing Facebook advertisers could easily start spending money on it. They could do so directly via Facebook's ads-buying interfaces (for which there was no FBX equivalent) or via the third-party ads-buying tools of Facebook's advertising partners whom Facebook had pressured into supporting CA features.

FBX was designed to work seamlessly with the outside ads world more accustomed to real-time exchanges, but it wasn't without its technical and adoption issues. As I've explained, FBX required deviations from the standard programmatic playbook, such as different ad formats. This required many epic hacks by the FBX team to try to wedge an entire ads system that had evolved separately into the industry standard of online retargeting. Several aggravating months and a few patents filed later, we had largely succeeded, but that convergent iteration around market needs was something for which Facebook culture had very little patience.

Also, you had to understand the psychology of the advertisers and their simplistic categorizations of the world. Then, and even now, advertising budgets were allocated by channel—TV, radio, Facebook, Google, billboards, whatever—almost like earmarked government handouts for one or another constituency. While the type of advertising—that is, retargeting people shopping online—was precisely the same (at the abstract level) via CA or FBX, spending on CA still fell under the "Facebook" budget; hence, whatever agency was handling the budget could easily steer spend toward it without much fuss, both businesswise and technically.

In FBX land, it was a different story: we were competing for spend with budgets that had been earmarked mostly for Google and its real-time ad exchange AdX, which was how most retargeting was actually being done. This was good, in that FBX spend was truly "incremental" (to use Facebookese); that is, FBX revenue was new dollars that were not otherwise being spent on Facebook. The fact these dollars were formerly being spent on much-hated Google made them even yummier, of course. Incremental spend—new money!—was the holy grail for Facebook at that point. Incrementality was, in fact, the challenge of any new ads product at Facebook. Sure, your dashboard showed $X million in spend, but how did you know that money wouldn't have been spent on Facebook anyhow? There was no point in launching new products only to divvy up the same spend among a new set of buckets. This is why Boland's numbers were mostly bogus revenue. At most fifty cents on the dollar was actually new money, the rest coming from budgets that would have been spent on Facebook in any case.

The 100 percent incremental nature of FBX spend was a selling point to management, but, as mentioned previously, it also meant we had to convince Zappos or whomever, either directly or via our proxies the FBX partners, to explicitly allocate spend on Facebook instead of on other real-time channels. Then there was the additional fact that the advertiser had to design new ad creative to run those campaigns, which meant extra work for an as yet unproved channel. All retailers in existence had been burned spending money on Facebook before, and had fresh memories of their respective Facebook fiascoes. Since most retailers lived and died by their fourth-quarter performance around the Christmas shopping season, they were disinclined to experiment with anything truly new. Accordingly, CA felt more of the big Q4 spending bump than FBX did, with the net result that FBX had fallen behind. This weakened my hand in the ongoing poker game taking place in LiveBoz.

If I only had $1 million in spend per day to shut Boland up with, this meeting would be over very quickly, I thought.

But I didn't. There was hope, though. FBX had recovered quickly given new features we'd shipped in 2013 to further ease adoption, and strong growth was back for Q1. CA, meanwhile, had started to languish again after the strong Q4. Boland's team hadn't shipped much of anything new beyond back-end tweaks that made the system less slow. Merely not totally sucking was not a very convincing sales pitch.

After the initial mutual broadsides, the meeting quickly devolved into the usual inconclusive corporate ritual, with Boz reiterating his mantra that we'd come to a conclusion soon. He vowed to consult each and every one of us sitting here, and then to formulate a formal recommendation to Sheryl. Sheryl would either make a decision or let him make it.

Pause and think for a moment.

What's it like to be a Gokul or a Boland or a Fischer?

You've seen excellent engineers and product people come and go, as your recruiters land the best new grads from every leading school. Your privileged position inside a powerful and market-leading organization exposes you to every industry trend and player, and pads your network with a roster of power and influence. Your ability to make any company's senior management appear and deliver fawning and revealing product demos means you know everything that's going on in your industry, down to the color of the clickable buttons in the products.

And yet there you are, lips bolted like pipe flanges onto some bigwig's ass, plodding along like an ox yoked to a grain mill, grinding the grist the big-company machine requires.

Why is that?

I'll tell you why.

It's because you are without a doubt the least daring and least innovative person at your organization, because in the opportunity-rich environment in which you live, the ambitious and capable have left to pursue it. There's a negative selection in which the cream (or whatever it is that initially rises) gets constantly skimmed off, and you are what's left after years of continual skimming. Changing from big company A to big company B is cosmetic, as it's of course at least a lateral move if not a step up. You learn that what matters in a big company is to avoid falling victim to firing or layoffs, and to appear important and critical to the company's mission. You have mastered the art of "managing up": namely, controlling the feelings and perceptions of the management layer above you. You take feedback well, and make sure to be seen speedily acting on that feedback. If you have reports, you champion their careers internally (make sure they know you're doing that), and try to mold them into people like yourself, who are organizationally effective and recognized as such. In all but the most pathological organizations, your reports' success will reflect well on you and create your own success. You make sure to form allegiances and friendships with your peer managers, particularly in organizations like sales or business development that you'll need to push your business agenda forward. When there's an ineffective and incompetent member in the organization, rather than calling them an idiot to their face and firing them if possible, you channel feedback to their manager and learn to work around their incompetence. If the incompetence does not directly affect you or your team, you look the other way and focus on the levers you do control.

You're middle management: you're the necessary layer between the visionaries and risk-takers who created the organization, and the new acolytes of your religion for whom this is a job, and you are their first whiff of corporate culture and authority.

If you're cleverer than most middle managers (e.g., Gokul), you'll work at building your personal brand in a way that both augments your prestige and reflects well on the organization, all in a studiously self-effacing way that allays any concerns around thinking yourself a "star." Failing that, the logo on your business card is your strongest asset, and you need to bank as much on that as you can, right up to the moment you trade it for another (hopefully better) one.*

These were the ingredients of the toxic meeting cocktail

* Gokul is currently the head of product and engineering at Square, a trendy and fast-growing payments company started and led by Twitter founder Jack Dorsey. In November 2015, Square went public. Gokul had traded his logo wisely.

that was being poured right there in LiveBoz: the corporate aristocrat of Boz, the middle management lifer of Boland, and the obnoxious, shit-stirring self-assurance of the acqui-hired startup founder. It went down about as well as it sounds.

APRIL 12, 2013

The scene was the Only Good News conference room.

We've returned to our starting point, but under very different circumstances. The cast was almost exactly the same: Gokul, Boland, Rabkin, Sheryl, and now Boz. I had played every last card. FBX development had been pushed to its absolute max, despite what little resources we had. Using either flattery or deception, we'd gotten FBX partners to spend as much money as possible on the new platform. I had tried to charm and persuade, with whatever persuasive charisma had worked on investors and cofounders in the past, the other members of the Ads team to support a vision most of them barely understood.

That was the good.

On the bad side, I had been insubordinate to Gokul, more or less refusing to work on the bullshit make-work projects he'd assigned to distract me from FBX. I had been an insufferably obnoxious punk on the Ads team, pushing for a contrarian agenda in a culture rapidly losing its supposed tolerance for heterodoxy.

While FBX had been a qualified success, and I had received praise for doing much with very little, none of the erstwhile FBX fans in that room were now willing to stake any of their internal social capital on its future, much less on the overarching programmatic direction it represented. If Sheryl agreed to extend to FBX the data joining that was currently limited to Custom Audiences, or even to put mobile ads inventory (a product that would later dominate

Facebook monetization) on FBX, there was a chance of pulling this off. Assuming FBX continued to grow at its current healthy rate, it would eventually dwarf Custom Audiences spend, in both incremental reality and what appeared in the dashboards. If Sheryl didn't agree, then it would mean the death of FBX and everything around it: the technology itself, the innovative IP we had patented, the budgets we'd secured, the work the FBX partners had done to integrate, the bigger vision of it all. Gone. We were all-in and betting on just one card being drawn.

"You want to go ahead, Boz?" Sheryl gestured to Boz, who was sitting across from me.

"After talking to everyone concerned, including the Custom Audience and FBX teams, I think we shouldn't ship identity matching on FBX, and continue with it in Custom Audiences only. That's my recommendation."

This was going to be a short meeting.

"Everyone here has contributed to this discussion, right?" Sheryl looked around the table. We all nodded.

"Well, if that's what you think, Boz, then that's what we'll do."

I caught Boz's eye; he looked away.

Nobody moved or spoke. After so many months of discussion, it was hard to believe that a decision had actually been made.

Sheryl added finally, as if trying to snap us out of a stupor: "So that's it. Nothing of Custom Audiences on FBX. No mobile inventory on FBX either. We'll leave it as is, and keep pressing on with identity on Custom Audiences alone."

I looked out the window at an alleyway that led to the main courtyard, and the huge HACK sign pointing skyward, like a divine commandment.

Well, I had certainly HACKed.

After some closing formalities that I was too distracted to register, everyone got up to leave. There was nothing left to discuss. Gokul glanced in my direction, but looked away the moment our eyes met, and darted out of the room. He was out of the building before I could even attempt to catch up.

I wandered into the FBX area, or what was left of it.

The product I had gambled my entire Facebook career on was now effectively on life support.

For the second time in two years, I walked out of the office in the middle of the afternoon with nothing to do.

Adiós, Facebook

> For every beautiful woman, there's a man tired of screwing her.
>
> —Latin American proverb

APRIL 12, 2013—LATER THAT SAME DAY

Vesting at Facebook was quarterly, which meant that I received one-twelfth of my total equity package the fifteenth of every January, April, July, and October. Quit a day before a vesting date, and you missed out on a quarter-year of value. Join a day after a vesting date, and you also missed out. It was an odd system of lumpy payment that by and large sucked, particularly when one payment was the equivalent of three years of US median household income. Let a day slip, and there went a down payment on a house in a normal city (though not in San Francisco, of course).

The countdown timer on my Mac's dashboard had registered exactly two years since I had joined. My next (and presumably final) vesting date was April 15 (tax day!). As of today, however, I had overstayed Facebook's welcome, and as of months ago, I had overstayed my patience. It was time to go.

One had to tread very carefully in these pullout moments, and make sure to mop up those last few crumbs tossed off the great Facebook table. I didn't trust Gokul further than I could throw him, and so I needed to guard against any last-minute shenanigans. Gokul had been a lukewarm supporter of FBX and me, but like every middle manager, his loyalties lay with the powers that be. Also, for all his goofy enthusiasm, he was a schemer in the end. The devil recognized his own, and there was no reason he might not try to pull the rug out from under my feet now that he didn't need me.

I had left the office the moment the Sheryl meeting ended, and emailed Gokul to tell him I was taking Monday off. He couldn't fire me when I was on vacation. I wasn't sure if you vested at the start of day on a vesting date, or end of day. Monday was the fifteenth, but twenty-four hours can make all the difference in the world. Best to wait until the sixteenth, and see those shares resting quietly in my Schwab account before quitting.

If I quit, it wasn't clear it would be on good terms, so it made sense to clean out the desk and accumulated detritus over the weekend. More than one Facebook employee had been ushered right on out the door as soon as they had crossed the company. No need for that sad scene of the departing employee packing his corporate coffee mug, like a relic of a suddenly former life. I put everything into two large plastic bags, leaving nothing behind but my laptop.

The kegerator, veteran of two on-site homebrews and countless purchased kegs, was coming with me. I backed up my lifted Toyota Tacoma off-road truck—beaten to hell, it looked like something the Taliban would use to storm Kabul—to the front door. I wheeled out the kegerator to no discernible alarm from security, and wrestled it onto the truck's bed. So far, so good.

Come Tuesday, the shares were in my Schwab account. There was nothing else to wait for, so I went into Facebook's HQ ("MPK" to use the corporate lingo for the Menlo Park office) one last time.

There was still the issue of laptop data hygiene.

Facebook IT policy was surprisingly lax. Despite prohibitions on using insecure apps like Dropbox, Evernote, or even Google Apps, everyone did, including senior management. Still, such use was officially a foot fault. Time to delete evidence.

I started by placing every personal file and then some in Secure Empty Trash. Rather than simply unlinking the file from the file directory, it overwrote the files with random data, making resurrection quasi-impossible.

Why the paranoia? There was nothing even remotely incriminating on my machine. But as I had already found out, you didn't need to be at fault to be sued. For all of the pretty posters, this company didn't give a shit about me, and would attempt to crush me like a bug if it saw fit.

While the delete process was running, I looked at the FBX revenue dashboard one last time. The revenue dashboard, that little bitch! The collection of numbers that had ruled my life for the past year. I smiled, though. We were about to hit our second big revenue milestone, right on time.

Can't say I didn't make you any money!

<beep!>

It was Gokul on FB Messenger. Our one-on-one was scheduled for 4:00 p.m., and it was exactly 4:02.

"Are you coming to our one-on-one?"

This was strange. Not only was Gokul famously late to every meeting, he was typically pretty indifferent about his one-on-one meetings with subordinates. I had missed loads of them due to some pressing matter or another, and he had never reminded me of them.

I switched back to the disk overwrite. 70 percent . . . 80 percent . . . 90 percent . . . done.

I slammed the laptop shut and headed downstairs.

There's a great scene in Martin Scorsese's *Goodfellas* in

which Tommy, played by Joe Pesci, is about to get made. "Getting made" meant being promoted to the pantheon of mobsters who are essentially untouchable by anyone else in the criminal underworld. It was a rare honor, one accorded only to full-blooded Italians who had worked themselves up through the mob ranks.

Tommy gets to the boss's house, and there's backslapping all around, and that sort of nervous patter that precedes graduations or award ceremonies. Tommy is led into the ceremony . . . and finds an empty room. Just as it hits him that this is a setup, a bullet explodes through his forehead and he falls into a bloody heap on the floor. He had committed too many sins in the past to be made, but also knew too much to be let go.

I had never been fired in my life, but I always suspected that in extreme cases, it would kind of resemble that scene. I wasn't too far off.

The Tommy moment hit when I noticed some hot chick in the room with Gokul. Then it hit me. *Oh shit. Gokul, you steaming little cunt. You won't even let me quit.*

There were few women one would call conventionally attractive at Facebook. The few there were rarely if ever dressed for work with their femininity on display in the form of dresses and heels. A fully turned out member of the *deuxième sexe* in a conference room was as clear an angel of death as a short-barreled .38 Special revolver.

Gokul gave an awkward smile, and bolted out the door the moment I sat down.

I looked across the table. If her look was supposed to disarm me, she needed either more cleavage or more charm. I glared at her as she read through her script.

"We are offering a severance package . . ."

Here she switched into the false sotto voce that professional manipulators, like salesmen or politicians, use to make a cheap bid for personal intimacy. "We offer this to very few employees . . ."

She slipped a contractual-looking document across the table.

Non Disparagement Clause. . . . $30,000. . . . For one year from the date of this document you will not . . .

Ha!

I saw the game. This had a unique Gokul stench all over it, like that of roadkill skunk. Knowing my penchant for hyperbolic criticism, and my flair for garnering attention with a well-worded Facebook post, Gokul had decided to bribe me into silence. This additional shut-up clause would strengthen Facebook's ability to sue me should it choose to.

Just because I'm paranoid doesn't mean they're not out to get me. Good thing I had run the disk overwrite.

I pondered telling Miss HR to roll the bribe into a nice little tube and stick it up her ass. Sanity prevailed. "I'll think about it," I said, and slid that paper trap back to her side of the table.

The rest was HR boilerplate: *return all Facebook hardware . . . nonsolicitation of Facebook employees . . . assignment of all Facebook intellectual property . . .*

Yeah, yeah. The ideas I dreamed up for you, and the engineers I had working for me. They're yours. For now.

Walking out of the conference room, as luck would have it, the HR rep and I crossed an employee from an FBX partner company. I had indicated to Facebook Ads management that we should poach her, and then had personally convinced her of the glowing opportunities at Facebook. She glanced at me nervously, and I said "Hi," and smiled, as another HR girl escorted her to an interview room.

"You know, you shouldn't say good-bye to Facebook employees. That's a bad idea," said Miss HR.

"That's a Facebook partner employee we're poaching thanks to me," I replied sharply.

Not too bright, this one: FB employees don't walk in with visitor badges and an escort.

We reached my desk, which was impeccable for once, positively shining from my weekend ministrations. There was nothing on it except my laptop.

"Where's your laptop?"

"Right there," I said, pointing.

"Where's your phone?"

"I forgot it at home."

"Hm, where's your badge?"

"I also forgot it at home."

I, of course, hadn't forgotten anything. The badge would get me discounts at the Apple store forever. And the phone I hadn't wiped yet.

She hobbyhorsed nervously on her heels for a moment. The whole desk-side scene had lasted maybe thirty seconds. It felt as though she had run out of script and was waiting for a director's cue.

"Shall we just go then?" I offered helpfully.

Weirdness spell broken, we headed back down the stairs. I think she even shook my hand on the way out.

I had wanted a quick getaway, so I'd parked my redneck Porsche, a Ford Mustang GT, in the visitor's spot right outside the door, next to the "Expectant Mother" spots that Sheryl had put in, and which always sat empty. Sitting, literally, about a hundred feet away from the conference room where our little Scorsese scene had unfolded, I chatted up Gokul on Facebook.

> **ANTONIO GARCIA-MARTINEZ (4:25 P.M.):** Beat me to the punch, Gokul. I was going in there to quit.
>
> **GOKUL RAJARAM:** Are you joining another company?
>
> **ANTONIO GARCIA-MARTINEZ (4:32 P.M.):** At this point, I don't join companies, I start them. Interested in investing? :)
>
> **GOKUL RAJARAM (5:11 P.M.):** Conflict. :)*

---

* This was possibly bullshit. Gokul had more ad tech investments than all the VCs in the Valley put together. As if in a recurring sitcom gag, I'd find

ANTONIO GARCIA-MARTINEZ (5:12 P.M.): It won't be in ads, almost certainly.

GOKUL RAJARAM: I am excited you are starting a company. You are going to be a great entrepreneur.

ANTONIO GARCIA-MARTINEZ: Trust me, I'm done with getting people to click on ads.

GOKUL RAJARAM (5:13 P.M.): Ah in that case lets chat more once things are finalized.

ANTONIO GARCIA-MARTINEZ: Sure. You don't mind if I borrow some of your engineers, right?

GOKUL RAJARAM (5:29 P.M.): Remember the non-solicit! (seriously)

As I was having one last banter with Gokul, Boz messaged me. He'd been informed of the doing of the deed, to which he had to have consented, of course (if he hadn't outright instigated it). I evidently hadn't charmed someone when I needed to, given the conversation during our one-on-one. For once, the same tongue that had gotten me into trouble was unable to get me out of it. The Facebook chat with Boz was bland and stupid and not worth repeating. I'm not even sure why he bothered.

I wouldn't be the only wheat stalk that fell to the Boz scythe. Gokul himself would leave within two months, as would several of the remaining product managers.

I fired up the car's V8, enjoyed the low growl for a moment, and peeled out of the parking lot one last time.

Gokul's signed adviser agreements carelessly left on the communal Ads printer-scanner. He had more crossed allegiances and conflicts of interest than Metternich at the Congress of Vienna. It was true that every such investment had to be passed by the Facebook conflicts committee, and they had total veto power. It was also possible they'd grown much more conservative and prohibitive when the company went public. Or maybe he was just flattering me. Gokul did plenty of that too.

Hanging a right leaving campus, I aimed the car's bulging nose down Bayfront Expressway. The uninhibited quarter-mile view down the highway was as irresistible as always. I floored it, cycling quickly up the gearbox, and enjoyed the ridiculously underengineered and overpowered ride as the nose lifted and the back end started sliding. The whole bucking, shaking ensemble roared past the yuppies in their sensible Priuses and Audis, down the highway and away—finally away—from Facebook.

Pandemonium Lost

What though the field be lost?
All is not Lost; the unconquerable will,
And study of revenge, immortal hate,
And the courage never to submit or yield.
—John Milton, *Paradise Lost*

SEPTEMBER 9, 2013

Evenings with Reesman, my former FBX engineer and comrade-in-arms, were typically complete alcohol- and rage-fueled blowouts: you ended up in either the emergency room, jail, or a Hummer limo with a platoon of sleazy chicks.

The pregame was at his yuppie upscale apartment at the Paramount, which along with NEMA (where he'd also eventually live) and One Rincon Hill formed the constellation of high-rise luxury living in SoMa. The towers stood out conspicuously from the surrounding cityscape of low-slung warehouses and the occasional Victorian. Entrepreneurs lived to work, and it was every startup CEO's luxury to place the office within easy walking distance of home, or vice versa. Commuting was for the little people.

The anarchy pump had been well primed when the budding circus decided it was time to hit the streets and find a lounge, where all the expensive theatrics of private tables and bottle service would be performed.

Alex Gartrell and I linked arms and began skipping down the street like little girls, singing some ditty I can't recall. Gartrell was a big Midwesterner who'd gone to Carnegie Mellon, one of the best computer science departments in the country, on a football scholarship. He was an infrastructure engineer at Facebook, and a regular accomplice in these urban drinking sprees.

A bouncing, two-man serenade on high volume when suddenly:

Pop!

My foot made a sound like a rope snapping under tension, and suddenly I couldn't walk. The group continued on without me, and I hobbled to a fire hydrant, where I sat my ass on the uncomfortable pointy top and waited for Israeli Psychologist, who'd been lagging behind the pack, to come by and rescue me.

The next day's ER visit revealed one of those depressing diagnoses of senescence: I had ruptured my plantar fascia, the connective tissue that holds your arch together, the shocks and springs of human locomotion. Sentence: eight weeks on my ass.

I was two weeks into this forced, sofa-ridden stasis when some big news hit the tech world. Twitter was buying the biggest and most sophisticated real-time mobile ad exchange in the world, MoPub.

I had run across MoPub before: Facebook, in that noncommittal way it looked at any successful early-stage company, had kicked the tires on it two years before. I had interviewed its CEO, Jim Payne, for a product manager role. Facebook passed on MoPub, but I had been impressed. A year after that first meeting, when FBX was in high gear, I had knocked on MoPub's door more than once to talk product with Jim and his product lead, Herman Yang, back when I was still stupidly trying to convince Facebook to put its mobile inventory on FBX. MoPub knew how to run an exchange, as well as the abstruse quirks of mobile data and targeting, better than anyone else.

What Twitter was up to with the MoPub acquisition was absolutely clear: it was doing what I had tried to convince Facebook to do. Coupling its social media network to a real-time exchange, this was Twitter's version of FBX. Given the jaw-dropping size of the acquisition (the leaked number was $350 million at Twitter's then stock price), this decision had to have had major management buy-in. The entire vision the FBX team and I had cooked up for how to safely expose targeting data in a real-time way, solving the entire online identity problem in one technical step, allowing advertisers unprecedented control and flexibility in ads delivery and targeting, all the while protecting Facebook's long-term strategic assets like user data and the advertiser relationship . . . someone was going to actually do that.

With nothing to do but sit on my ass and whine about my foot, I spent two days hammering out my thoughts on the acquisition. If I hadn't become a casualty of Reesman, the God of the Chaos Monkeys, and his ever-present circus of hooligans, I doubt I would have had the focus.

The post itself, published on Medium, that new and fashionable channel for techie "thought leadership," was a smashing success. It evidently circulated internally at both Twitter and MoPub, and the heavies in the deal, like Adam Bain and Jim Payne, were retweeting it, which meant everyone down to the junior salesperson was as well.

Clearly, I had gotten it right: Twitter was building the super-FBX with MoPub's technology. Given the sensitivity around acquisitions, plus the possibility of a Federal Trade Commission investigation around monopoly-building, execs at companies in play can't comment publicly on their reasons or plans. However, they can certainly point to an effusive and insightful blog post written by an outsider. Which is what they did. I spent three days on the couch giddily dealing with the social mayhem—retweets, comments, clarifications, new follows—all the bustle and din of being a new dot on humanity's mental radar, the bright speck that always died too soon.

Given this unexpected opening, it was time for a ploy. I still had Kevin Weil's and Adam Bain's email addresses from the AdGrok machinations. We hadn't spoken since I had walked out on the AdGrok deal; I assumed I was dead to everyone at Twitter. Deep Tweet had told me that Dick Costolo, Twitter's CEO, had even sent a company-wide email at the time of the AdGrok deal, explaining away my defection as a craven character flaw.

It was with some trepidation that I wrote Adam and Kevin a conciliatory email, congratulating them on the genius deal. At worst, it would be ignored. At best, it might be something else altogether. Adam responded suggesting a meeting at Twitter.

And so there I was just two years after the AdGrok drama, checking into Twitter's new offices at Ninth and Market. The company had outgrown the office on Folsom and, after much bickering with SF's always schizophrenically inept city management, had opted to stay inside SF city limits, despite the city's threat to tax the stock options given out as compensation like candy on Halloween. The new office was just south of that crusty asshole of the SF cityscape, the Tenderloin. With Twitter setting up shop there, and the entire attendant economy of yuppie/hipster services like $5 coffee, craft beer, and expensive lofts that would no doubt arise to service it and its employees, local wags had renamed that part of the slum "the Twitterloin." Who needed urban renewal or half-competent city planning when SF had IPOs?

Name tag back around neck, I greeted Adam Bain's admin in the reception area and was walked to a conference room. Through the conference room window, I spied the two men I'd last spoken to when I was wooing them and their company, and was then wooed in return, only to ultimately spurn.

This will be very interesting.

Polite handshakes and smiles all around. Adam and Kevin sat on the other side of a round table, statutory whiteboard behind me, and floor-to-ceiling glass behind them, looking out into the engineering bullpens.

In one hour, I explained every technical, legal, and business problem Twitter was going to have with their MoPub acquisition. Through very little merit of my own, I was at that moment the world's expert in bolting a real-time ad exchange onto a social media platform with bajillions of users. Nobody knew that little niche better than me, as I had been the leader of the only team to ever attempt it.

Oh, I could tell Twitter how to do this . . . I could recite this script from recent memory.

I leapt up, took over the whiteboard, and explained the data flows from Twitter's ads system into MoPub, which were similar to the data flows from the Facebook Ads system to FBX. De-duplicating human identity across devices, ads targeting without data leakage, the whole sophisticated shebang we'd created and planned while at Facebook. Clear as black marker ink on a whiteboard, everything Twitter would be betting its monetization future on, in data-flow arrows and unique user IDs splayed all over a wall-sized board. I may not have been very good at politically maneuvering the scheming flunkeys of Boland and Fischer, but I sure could tell you how to build ads product. By the end of my presentation, Kevin and Adam sat quietly on their side of the table taking it all in.

Always show enough skin to get a second date. If in doubt, show more.

We shook hands and I was walked out to the reception area. The same pushy guard at the door made it a point to take my name tag.

A few days later Kevin emailed to propose my joining Twitter as an adviser. This was all to be sub rosa, with no public mention. If asked by the press, Twitter would have to admit I was an adviser, but otherwise, nary a word to the outside world. All it required was biweekly meetings with the various product managers who would be building the Twitter-MoPub integration, done discreetly. While on the payroll, I was not to have a corporate ID or email address, or any other official Twitter connection. I'd still be coming in the front door as a guest every time, causing a minor headache with the inefficient guards at the building's reception.

Tempting. But as always, show me numbers, baby.

Twitter provided them very quickly. This was not the company of two years ago that required a month to produce a term sheet. The pay was a thousand shares a quarter, or about $160,000 per year (at the going prepublic $40/share Twitter valuation). All for merely appearing at Twitter's offices every so often, and conveying my thoughts on the nature of real-time ads buying.

You resent that guy, and one day, you are that guy, and you wonder how you got there. I had passed, in a small way, into that advisory sphere of people who were paid serious sums of money for merely showing up. There was an entire class of Silicon Valley personage who was just that, and lived off nothing else. Can't beat meritocracies for the pay.

There were a couple of minor hitches, though.

But a few months ago, I had been a Facebook employee building exactly the same product at Twitter's biggest competitor. I was still under a nondisclosure agreement from Facebook, prohibiting the spilling of anything I had done there.

Furthermore, I was an adviser and soon to be VP of Product at Nanigans, Facebook's largest monetization partner. Nanigans was one of the big pipes that ran money into the ravenous Facebook machine, working closely with Facebook both to create new Facebook Ads features and to make them available via Nanigans's sophisticated buying tools for big-budget advertisers. To the extent Facebook partnered with anyone, the relationship with Nanigans was about as close as it got.

In case you're wondering, yes, this was a complete grudge job, wherein the goal was to move as much spend as possible from Facebook to other channels, a petty vindictiveness rivaling even Murthy's. My contribution at Nanigans was leading the product team that built the real-time buying tools to buy on Google and Twitter-MoPub, and diversify the company's offerings beyond merely Facebook. Intellectually, it was fascinating being on the other side of the buy-sell equation, actually building buying technology to talk to the real-time selling technology I had built. The real motivation, though, was returning those dollars I had originally moved from Google to Facebook, thanks to FBX, right back to Google thanks to Nanigans (and its roster of deep-pocketed advertisers) now being able to buy ads anywhere. *On ne détruit que réellement que ce qu'on remplace.**

Given all the crossed allegiances, going from the Facebook family to the Twitter one (while nominally staying inside the Facebook one at Nanigans) was no small step, and nobody in this picture, neither Facebook nor Nanigans, was bound to be very happy about it. What Twitter was asking was just shy of a breach of confidentiality, and absolute corporate treason. *Just* shy, which was how Silicon Valley worked.

I signed the offer without negotiation, and emailed Kevin Weil to convey my eagerness to get started with Twitter. He reciprocated that excitement, and suggested a time to meet with the Twitter Ads product team.

---

* "One really destroys only what one replaces." The author is Napoleon III, on overthrowing the Second French Republic and replacing it with the Second French Empire.

I was working for Twitter now, against Facebook's interests, two years after very insultingly doing the opposite. At the same time I was also working for Facebook's largest ads partner and biggest single pipe of cash.

The Land of the Stateless Machines, indeed.

Epilogue: Man Plans and God Laughs

Oft expectation fails and most oft there
Where most it promises.
—William Shakespeare, *All's Well That Ends Well*

JANUARY 2016

So what became of it all?

The Great Facebook Ads Debate of 2013 ended up being moot, or at least, a debate whose import would be more strategic and long-term than tactical and immediate.

For all the Sturm and Drang, Facebook's quarter-saving gold mine, the thing that catalyzed the stock out of the post-IPO doldrums, wasn't Custom Audiences or FBX. A third product, the only other novel ads product Facebook launched during its harried IPO period, code-named "Neko," was that savior. The product itself, like so many, was simply the combination of two otherwise disparate domains: Facebook's ever-addictive News Feed and ads inventory on the Facebook mobile app, instead of the desktop site. That's it: ads in News Feed, while the user was on his or her mobile device—that's what saved Facebook.

The person most responsible for this coup was a product manager with the improbable name of Fidji Simo. She was one of two office wives of mine (yes, I was an office Mormon), who had started her career in Facebook Ads as a lowly product marketer.* She had very quickly and skillfully navigated herself up the Facebook corporate ladder, landing herself the product manager job where Ads and the rest of the company overlapped, placing herself in the larger Facebook (and Zuck) spotlight. She was half Sicilian, half French: the latter meant black, tailored dresses and heels as high as bar stools; the former meant a formidable political ability, evolved through centuries of clannish Sicilian feuding, perfectly adapted for Facebook's management culture.

Like many successful products, News Feed Ads rode to success atop a tsunami-esque wave nobody had predicted, or at least hadn't predicted to arrive right then and so quickly. In this case, that wave was mobile usage, which in the span of a few months in 2013 suddenly constituted the majority of Facebook usage. This was a turn of events that completely upended Facebook's monetization strategy, making everything that came before mostly irrelevant, or at least secondary.

In retrospect, it's clear to see why Facebook succeeded on mobile.

For starters, data.

On desktop, the browser and its cookie pool (that even third parties like data brokers and even Facebook can read

---

* Fidji Simo also practiced office polyandry. Rather notoriously, she'd befriend whoever was on the political ascendant inside Facebook, very publicly spending time with that person socially (all documented on Facebook, of course). Like some sort of social canary in a coal mine, her momentary social circle always revealed who was important inside Ads right then.

from and write to) mean there's a lot of data sloshing around for every Web browser. The fact you're pricing your car on the Kelley Blue Book site, or searching movie times on Fandango, is something that's known not just to Fandango or Kelley, but to an entire world of data brokers and targeters.

In mobile, Web browsers generally don't accept third-party cookies, which means that someone other than the *New York Times* can't read or write data about you when you're on nytimes.com on your mobile browser. Contrast that to the data mayhem that reigns on a desktop browser. Also, that mobile browser typically does not have access to your unique device ID, which, as we'll see, is the real identifier that matters in the mobile advertising world.

Second, the triumph of apps as the core mobile experience.

Think of it this way: from the data perspective (if not the technical one), an app is like a unique browser for a specific company, which that company has built so you can experience its very particular website. You effectively have hundreds of unique browsers on your phone, with which you read content and buy goods or services. Again, compare that with desktop, where you have Chrome or Safari (or one of a handful of browsers), with which you browse thousands of sites, and all the data sloshes together across your browser's cookie pool, getting siphoned off and resold in a bajillion ways. In mobile apps, that data mosh pit doesn't exist, as all the data is siloed within the app that generated it. If you've gotten to level 47 in Candy Crush Saga, searched for a house on the Redfin real estate app, or bought something on Amazon's mobile commerce app, that data lives and dies inside those apps, and never leaves. This means that on mobile, at least datawise, you have a first-party relationship with a few apps, and that's it—there are no data middlemen.

This is actually counterintuitive if you know how mobile data is stored: on mobile, every device has a unique ID that's associated with the physical hardware you're holding in your hand.* In theory, marketers could sell all that data, associating it with your device ID, and then use it to target you on Facebook or on mobile ad exchanges.

That doesn't happen, for two reasons: First, companies like Apple have monopolistic control of their platforms, and as part of the app-approval process that allows a new app into Apple's App Store, Apple can limit the use of this magical device ID.† In general, Apple has shown itself very protective of users (Steve Jobs was famously indifferent, to not say antagonistic, to advertising), and very keen on foiling any secondary market in targeting data.

Second, app developers themselves jealously guard their data as their own, are reluctant to share it, and would rather monetize its power themselves than pursue the short-term upside of selling it, potentially to competitors.

The net of all this detailed data discussion is this: while my statements about the questionable value of Facebook data held true on desktop, which already had a mature and mostly respectable data marketplace by the time Facebook

* Since purists will no doubt squirm at this simplification, a clarification: strictly speaking, the device ID (called an IDFA, or ID for Advertising, in the Apple world), is actually a software-generated string of letters and numbers (e.g., "236A005B-700F-4889-B9CE-999EAB2B605D") that's associated with your phone, and common across all apps you run. Historically, it was an immutable physical parameter, but that changed in 2012 when privacy concerns mounted. It is now software-generated in order to allow you to opt out of advertising by changing it. For all intents and purposes, though, it's almost a serial number stamped on the circuit board of your phone.

† On submission, Apple reviews what the app actually does and what functions it calls, including the one that gets the device's IDFA. If you seem to be using it in unacceptable ways (Apple's rules are intentionally vague and their interpretation a subject of almost Talmudic debate), then your app is rejected, often for unclear reasons. This is one of those rare choke points in modern technology where one player simply rules by erratic diktat.

showed up peddling Likes, that was emphatically not the case on mobile. On mobile, targeting data was sparse, and bad when it did exist, such that even basic targeting like age and gender was a godsend to data-starved mobile marketers who'd been mostly shooting in the dark. This was confirmed in a big way when Facebook Ads launched the only truly novel thing it's launched since the IPO: the Facebook Audience Network.

AN, as it's known, is easy to understand: it's simply Facebook Ads, powered by Facebook data, running on apps other than Facebook. As such, it's the cleanest test of the value of Facebook's data.

The performance of those campaigns, in terms of both clickthrough rates for advertisers and actual monetized CPM for publishers, was very good, indicating that in the land of the mobile data blind, the one-eyed Facebook man was indeed king.

Here's the second macro reason why Facebook has triumphed on mobile, which once again highlights the deep, structural differences between the desktop and mobile worlds: On desktop, even leading publishers like the *New York Times* had trouble monetizing their Web presence, and constantly experimented with various paywall schemes in order to stem their hemorrhaging bottom lines by monetizing the sudden rush from print to digital. As a result, top-quality publishers often used advertising as a crutch to help monetize the digital presence whose business model they hadn't figured out. For advertisers, that meant ads inventory on even prestige publishers like *Vanity Fair* and the *New York Times* was readily available.

In mobile, leading app publishers—mostly games companies and a few mobile commerce companies—were adept at monetizing their users, by banking both on the gatekeeping and on the ease of payment the App Store represented (e.g., "$3.99 to download," beat it if you don't like it), as well as a general culture of savvy monetization. The newspaper people turned digital publishers were still rubbing the newsprint off their hands as they tried to figure out "this Internet thing," while the marketers inside leading games companies knew their CACs and LTVs out to three decimals.* As a result, the only mobile apps that used advertising to monetize were the long tail of free, crappy games that couldn't convince users to pay up, or second-tier social media networks that outsourced their monetization to existing networks and exchanges. As an example, for a long while (and probably still) the biggest source of ads inventory on the most respectable mobile ad exchanges was Grindr, the gay hookup app that features endless selfies of half-naked men mugging for casual sex. Want to run your ad for a new tooth whitener underneath the image of a steroid-abusing meathead tugging at his semitumescent phallus? I thought not.

Also, as you've likely noticed, the ad formats on mobile are either tiny and subtly invasive (e.g., those small blinking bars bordering the lower edge of the screen, impeding your scrolling) or large and annoying (e.g., the whole-screen takeovers called "interstitials").

All this meant that while on desktop high-quality publishers with engaging formats competed with Facebook, on mobile the pickings were very slim indeed. Nonintrusive but stylish ads, which paired well with organic content from your friends, on an app experience like Facebook, which featured supremely focused attention and a crazy-high engagement rate (clickthrough rates on Facebook's News Feed reached easily into the single-digit percentages), were very competi-

---

* CAC is "customer acquisition cost" and LTV is "lifetime value." The former is the marketing cost of getting a user to download and log into your app. The latter is the amount of revenue you'll make on a given user over the lifetime of his or her usage. If the ratio of LTV to CAC is greater than one, you're succeeding as an app publisher, since the money coming in is greater than the money going out (ignoring development and server costs for a moment, and assuming this "lifetime" isn't too long). Any app marketer should know these two numbers better than their kids' names.

tive with the mobile alternatives. This meant Facebook had the mobile advantage from the get-go.

Those two things, data and high-quality formats and placements, meant that Facebook dominated mobile like few other incumbents had managed to, and would dominate for the foreseeable future.

Of course, it's easy to say all this now, retrospectively. It certainly was not clear in the spring of 2013, when the open versus closed debate was reaching its clamorous apex and all avenues for future revenue growth were being heatedly debated. It wasn't clear even after the mobile tsunami started.

When Facebook reported its second-quarter results in June 2013, two facts triggered a market rally in FB shares. First, the number of active users on mobile had increased by more than 50 percent from the previous year. Second, and more important, revenues from mobile had roughly doubled from the previous year. This indicated that Facebook was not only successfully making the much-presaged leap to mobile (whereby all online activity was thought to be moving to devices); it was also managing to monetize there, meaning the leap wouldn't damage revenues.

What was really going on?

Facebook was slowly opening up its mobile News Feed to ads, putting on the auction block what was a formerly untouched piece of Facebook property. As 2013 ground on, Facebook turned its monetization knob gradually, opening more and more inventory for Ads, and bringing in steadily more revenue, beating expectations at every earnings call, and guiding the stock price ever higher.

Ad inventory is like real estate, and what Facebook was doing was akin to the westward expansion of the United States following the Louisiana Purchase, a onetime land-rush bonanza that featured hardy pioneers racing into the sunset, under the nominal control of an organizing government.

Multiple insiders at the time leaked to me the concern around the strategy: pimping out News Feed had to end at some point, and then what would Facebook do? There were even internal projections guesstimating when the moment would arrive, when the ads pioneers would reach the Pacific Ocean on the westward fringe of this new ads continent, and realize that the land rush and the revenue boom were over.

But again, the unexpected happened.

Facebook revenue didn't stop growing even after ads had well and truly penetrated the average user's mobile experience. Given the excellent performance, increasing advertiser budgets drove demand for what was now a relatively limited commodity. Facebook, with constant engineering advances on the Optimization team, and new data from products like News Feed Ads, was getting better at ads delivery on mobile, driving revenue gains based on pure mathematics alone. Sensing which way its future was trending, Facebook regeared the entire Ads team to focus on mobile, squeezing every advertiser, big and small, to spend as much as possible on Facebook mobile ads. It was one of those instantaneous pivots that were breathtaking in their speed and focus, with an agility that had saved Facebook more than once in the past, and of which the company could be justly proud. Not many public companies of that size, if any, could have pulled off such a sudden course change.

Even after the sudden rise of an almost pure-mobile Facebook, and even after that new continent of pixel real estate was sold to the highest bidder, Facebook revenue continued growing, pleasing investors and driving the stock ever higher. None of this, of course, was even remotely apparent in early 2013 (despite whatever Facebook claims now), when the ego pissing matches in Sheryl's conference room depicted in this book were raging.

That's the nature of Valley success, however: you try ten things, based mostly on random hunches, a few key product insights, and whatever internal mythologies your culture reveres. Seven of them fail miserably, are discontinued, and are soon quietly swept under the rug of "forever today" forgetfulness. Two do OK, for more or less the reasons you thought, but they don't blow the doors off your success metric. And one, for reasons you discover only after the fact, becomes a huge, transformational success. The amnesiac tech press weaves the narrative fallacy around the proceedings, fabricating a make-believe dramatic arc from steely-eyed product ideation to flawless and unhesitating technical execution. What was an improbable bonanza at the hands of the flailing half-blind becomes the inevitable coup of the assured visionary. The world crowns you a genius, and you start acting like one. When the next usage or revenue crisis hits, you repeat the experiment, rolling your set of product dice on the big Valley table. At some point, you don't find the crisis-solving winner, the dealer sweeps up your remaining chips, and you're busted. The company fails and your logo is recycled as a reminder of corporate mortality. Then everyone wonders how such a confirmed genius could have possibly failed, and ruminates on the transience of talent.

That day will arrive for Facebook too. It some ways, it already has; Facebook just bought its way out of it.

In 2012, a photo-sharing app called Instagram was able to show Zuckerberg something he'd never seen before: a user growth curve—relentlessly up and to the right—that resembled Facebook's own meteoric early growth. After negotiations spanning all of a weekend, Facebook snapped it up for $1 billion, thwarting Twitter's own Jack Dorsey, who had reputedly been wooing Instagram's CEO, Kevin Systrom, for months.

In 2014, another app could boast a similarly fear-inducing growth curve, and with an even higher number of users. WhatsApp, little known in the United States but practically synonymous with texting and SMS overseas, had made an international empire out of a relatively small team and a very basic app whose unique offering was making your phone number your user identity.* As with Instagram, Zuck put on his game face and wooed WhatsApp's founding CEO, Jan Koum, acquiring the company for the eye-popping amount of $19 billion in October 2014.†

The two apps—one for hipsterish, color-filtered photo sharing, the other for mundane texting in price-sensitive markets where SMS was expensive—were the sort of altogether new market directions that big companies tended to miss. WhatsApp and Instagram sold out, but the day will arrive when the leader of a globe-spanning app, the new paradigm in how *Homo sapiens sapiens* communicates via electrons and radio waves, proves as obdurate and proud as Zuckerberg himself. Then Facebook won't be able to buy its way out of trouble, and it will have to build its way out instead, a far riskier proposition.

What about FBX, our baby in this drama?

FBX's revenue, which was just starting to show signs of

---

* This was a twofold act of semiaccidental genius. First, it completely outsourced the issue of security and user operations (e.g., flagging fake users who send spam, getting authentic users their forgotten passwords) to the carriers (e.g., AT&T), who establish and maintain the human-to-phone-number mapping as part of their business. Second, it meant the Growth team's ever-present task of getting users to connect to other users was rendered trivial: simply hoover in the contact list on a user's phone, and that person has instantly "friended" everyone he or she knows (none of this Facebook business of prodding you via pseudo-ads to friend your long-lost classmate). Reportedly, the reason for spurning the usual made-up app identity of a user name–password combo for WhatsApp was due to its founder and CEO, Jan Koum, constantly losing his Skype password, and wanting to do away with a log-in process altogether.

† In a bit of feel-good Valley news that soon became folklore, Jan Koum signed the multibillion-dollar deal's documents on the door of the welfare office his family would frequent for food stamps, after they immigrated from the Ukraine. It's these anecdotal stories that warm the technolibertarian's heart, and anoint their brand of tooth-and-nail capitalism (almost de rigueur in the Valley) with the mark of a righteous meritocracy.

explosive growth toward the end of my Facebook tenure, hit its stride in the months after I departed, reaching about a half billion in revenue by early 2014, all of that absolutely new.* That means FBX was one of the fastest-growing new-revenue products in Facebook history, second only to the billion-dollar News Feed bonanza described above. And it was built with a handful of people at peak development, while News Feed ads required a small army to create and maintain.

Aside from generating a mountain of revenue with (now) zero engineering investment, a perpetual motion machine of cash, FBX also serves as Facebook's view into the growing programmatic world. With that one hole in the Facebook wall, like Goldman Sachs observing all the buy and sell orders, the Ads team can decipher its competition and build products that replace them. By selectively exposing cross-device identity and mobile inventory (the jewels of the Facebook Ads world) on its own products alone, however, Facebook induces advertisers to use its clunky substitutes rather than the much-preferred real-time FBX technology. Despite that everlasting antagonism, FBX stubbornly holds on, too profitable and too strategic to shut down (for now at least), much to the chagrin of the Bolands and the Bozes of Ads.

I'll say this now only to throw it in their faces later: eventually Facebook will have to fully support a programmatic exchange for all Facebook inventory. They are on the wrong side of technological history; the real-time interaction of human desire with online capitalism is here to stay.

Heck, even Wall Street has seen the light. Remember how we described a postcrisis Goldman considering but

---

* Or so it was leaked to me. Modeling FBX's size based on the growth of Facebook's ads system, where client budgets were going, sampling what fraction of feed posts were FBX-related, and so forth, one arrives at about the same number.

rejecting the notion of trading credit default swaps on exchanges, the inevitable evolution of that derivatives market? In 2013, Goldman finally partnered with the InterContinental Exchange (ICE), a pioneering electronic exchange trading everything from jet fuel to orange juice, to clear trades on European credit default swaps via ICE for Goldman's clients. Perhaps Facebook will one day show itself to be as much of a leader and innovator as Goldman Sachs.

What of Facebook's great enemy, Google, and its encroaching social network copy Google Plus; *Carthage must be destroyed!* and all the rest of it?

By April 2014, the Google/Facebook Punic War was over.

Zuck wouldn't burn Google to the ground, take the wives and children of Google employees as slaves, and salt the grounds of the former Google headquarters so that nothing grew there for generations, as Rome did Carthage, but it was about as ignominious a defeat as one got in the tech world.

Google signaled its capitulation when the face of Google Plus, Vic Gundotra, suddenly announced he was leaving the company. There was a "ding dong the witch is dead" note of triumph inside Facebook, and everyone breathed a sigh of relief at the passing threat.

Vic's departure was as clear a sign as any that Google had given up on social, accepting defeat at the hands of a company it had previously ignored, if not held in outright contempt. This was only confirmed when it was simultaneously announced that many Google Plus product teams, such as the chat app Hangouts or the photo-sharing app Photos, would be rolled into the Android team, Google's mobile operating system. Google spun it as Google Plus becoming not a "product" but a "platform," a sort of general-use tool that would enhance the user experience across Google's wide array of products.

This was like a general declaring that their army wasn't in retreat, but merely advancing in reverse instead. Everyone at Facebook saw through the face-saving PR wordplay.

Google Plus was over; Facebook had won. The lockdown circling of the wagons had triumphed.

Enough of the blue hoodie people. What about the Twitter flock?

In January 2016, as this book was being finished, Twitter had another of the high-level management shake-ups, like palace putsches of some Eastern despotism, for which it's somewhat famous. Kevin Weil and Alex Roetter, our initial contacts in the AdGrok deal who rose to run those twin company engines of Engineering and Product, left Twitter at once, along with some other senior executives. Somewhat shockingly, Weil left to head Product at Instagram, a Facebook company in clear competition with Twitter, whose usage numbers were dangerously plateauing by then. Adam Bain remains as COO at Twitter, and Jess, the woman who started the whole AdGrok drama, continues to run corporate development at Twitter, buying companies and people like so many canned tomatoes. The Stateless Machines of Silicon Valley keep on turning.

What of the former AdGrok crew?

As of March 2016, the boys were still engineers at Twitter, having more than vested their four-year offer. Given the offer numbers, the fact that it was in favorably taxed options, the fact that Twitter reached over $50/share well after the IPO lockout period, and bonus equity top-ups they'd have received as high-performing employees, their final score was very rich indeed.

MRM would have no trouble paying off his mortgage, no longer worry about his kids' college, and finally live the life of ease his previous two decades in tech had not afforded him.

Argyris, for his part, could have that café-and-record-store fantasy in Athens if he wanted it, and much more. Simla and he would soon have a child, buy apartments in both San Francisco and Athens, and generally live the life of the San Francisco techie privileged.

We're still on speaking terms, more or less; Argyris and

I more than MRM, but that's hardly surprising from what you've read. They've managed to forgive whatever slight they felt at the deal drama I created. After all, it worked out very well for them in the end.

And my outcome?

Practically nothing by comparison.

Recall, the Facebook offer was in restricted stock, which is taxed as common income.

Also recall, Facebook's IPO, unlike Twitter's, came out at a high price of $38, and then languished for a year around $30, occasionally going so low as $18. That IPO was great for employees and insiders worried about dilution, but not for people wanting to cash out (like me), and walk away from the Silicon Valley casino. With the lockout, insiders weren't able to sell the stock until months after the IPO, when FB was at $20. Thus I owed taxes at the maximum marginal tax rate (plus whopping California state income tax) assuming a cost basis of $38, when I had really sold at lower, effectively paying taxes on money I hadn't made. In a smaller way, mine was the plight of the first tech-boom bankruptcies, who paid taxes when prices were dear, but sold stock when prices were cheap.

I saw relatively little of my ersatz AdGrok proceeds in the form of Facebook stock. All of that three-year struggle of endless sixteen-hour days, whether for AdGrok or for Facebook (and hating most of it, as if you couldn't tell), was mostly for nothing. So you see, the boys and I have very different financial futures awaiting us.

Some of it was due to the detailed vagaries of tech compensation and the random walks of public stock prices. Mostly, though, it was due to my getting chewed up and spit out by the Facebook machine within two years, while the boys gamboled in the bucolic hipster pastures of Twitter for four years and counting—the very pastures I struggled and plotted mightily to avoid, and which I traded for the horror show that would thanklessly reject me despite the moneymaker I built them. Who says karma doesn't exist?

Speaking of unjust karma, life soon took a turn, without which you wouldn't be reading this book. In the summer of 2014, my mother was unexpectedly diagnosed with liver cancer, and I watched her—slowly at first and then very suddenly—die. A breeze from the grave suddenly blew across dreams of youth, which lay caked in the patient dust of "someday," and made them gleam again with their original brilliance. I withdrew from any professional obligations, sold everything, and committed to two all-consuming goals: First, to finish the book you are holding, whose initial scribbles dated back to the events described, but whose completion required a year of itinerant writing and editing. Second, to sail around the world alone on a small boat. This was a dream cultivated since childhood, when I raced my Optimist dinghy in Biscayne Bay by day, and read of Robin Lee Graham's adventures by night. Graham was an American sailor whose solo circumnavigation in 1970, on a cramped twenty-four-foot boat named *Dove*, made him the youngest person to ever complete such an ocean passage.

To that end, when I had finally scraped the bare minimum amount of money together, I fitted out two boats, one after another, for such a voyage, and then in turn negligently let them rot at the dock during the events described in this book, one during AdGrok and the other during Facebook. Those boats were in turn sold, as much to hide my embarrassment at the neglect of both ship and personal ambition as to recoup costs.

Shortly before my mother's death, I purchased a stout forty-foot cutter-rigged sailboat. That vessel, like my daughter, named *Ayala* after the first European to enter San Francisco Bay, will not suffer the same fate. Through 2015, I spent marathon writing sessions hunched over a screen, alternated with dusty days splayed on the deck of *Ayala*, installing or fixing one or another piece of overpriced marine hardware. To quote Theodor Herzl, "If you will it, it is no dream; and if you do not will it, a dream it will remain." Willing dreams into existence was what being an entrepreneur and a product manager was about; for once, finally, they'd be my dreams, rather than purely corporate or mercenary ones.

Thus do I bow off this stumbled-upon stage, hopefully forever, and disappear into the heaving swells of the Pacific Ocean, the only such sanctuary from social mediation we'll soon have left.

Orcas Island, Washington

Acknowledgments

Thanks to British Trader, who not only bore most of the burden of raising our children but also provided invaluable counsel during the most trying times. Shame that a household, like a ship, admits only one captain.

Thanks to Israeli Psychologist, my long-suffering mate during the Facebook half of this book, without whose warm ministrations I'd never have survived that infernal experience. As your people once wrote: "A woman of valour, who can find? For her price is far above rubies. She openeth her mouth with wisdom; and the law of kindness is on her tongue." Your endless kindness deserved a worthier target.

Finally on the partner front, thanks to French Architect, who first read the manuscript, and who very patiently dealt with her pregnancy while I dealt with my deadlines. I suspect your take on all this parallels what your countryman Racine wrote: "After such sweetness beyond memory. He who held me so dear, to yet betray! Oh! I have loved him too much not to hate."

To our ever-fluctuating love and hate, always so fiery, and so intoxicating.

Life is a marathon, not a sprint, goes the cliché. This book was both at once. From deal to physical book took ten months, about as long as AdGrok took to found and sell. The breakneck start was thanks to my agent, Sloan Harris, who saw this work's inchoate promise from the first moment. Whether on Wall Street or in Silicon Valley, never have I seen a product better packaged and sold than what came to be known as *Chaos Monkeys* under Sloan's adept representation.

To Jennifer Barth at HarperCollins, my editor, who dealt gracefully and knowledgeably with my intemperate prose and character. *Chaos Monkeys* would be half as readable without her "massive" help (which included removing the dozen uses of the word "massive").

If *Chaos Monkeys* had a single, dramatic conception moment, it was when Kate Lee (then an agent at ICM, now at Medium) emailed me about my first viral AdGrok blog post, suggesting I write a book. Google classified the email as spam, and only my random search for a waylaid email uncovered it. Had I not, you wouldn't be looking at these words. Thanks to Kate Lee for her initial encouragement, gentle goading through these many years, and editing of my early Medium posts (some of whose content ended up here). You truly nurtured the idea from a mere attention-grabbing blog post to a book.

The setting for the writing itself extended from Silicon Valley, usually typed angrily after the event in question, to more contemplative scribbling in Barcelona, Berlin, and Orcas Island, Washington, months or years later.

A special acknowledgment to that emerald jewel in the northwestern crown of the San Juans: Orcas Island. As beautiful as it is bewitching, that horseshoe-shaped haven served as the ideal writer's hideaway, with its craggy peaks, verdant forests, windswept waters, and warm locals. Never change, Orcas; you're the antidote to every illness of our postmodern Internet age.

Special thanks to the master brewers at Aslan Brewing of Bellingham, Washington, whose Batch 15 IPA was the principal psychic sustenance during the dark and rainy Pacific northwestern winter during which this book was mostly written. Without that beer's citrusy bite, *Chaos Monkeys* would have been half as long, and half as entertaining.

I wish I could somehow manage to thank the Silicon Valley ecosystem itself: investors, the tech press, lawyers, informants, advisers, and the various characters I've alternately befriended or maligned in these pages. Let's be blunt: ours was a relationship of pure convenience, and I exploited you as much as you did me. As they say, the ideal deal is one where both parties walk away feeling slightly screwed. Here's to our perfect deal.

Thanks to Matt McEachen and Argyris Zymnis, my fellow comrades in the startup trenches. I told you this Y Combinator thing would be big.

To Paul Graham, Jessica Livingston, Sam Altman, and the rest of the Y Combinator partners and founders involved in the AdGrok saga. In a Valley world awash with mammoth greed and opportunism masquerading as beneficent innovation, you were the only real loyalty and idealism I ever encountered.

Lastly, thanks to my former Facebook colleagues, who provided such an amusing cast for this book, and two years of my life. Many of you will surely excommunicate me following publication. Remember: the only thing worse than being talked about is not being talked about. What do you reckon they'll say of Facebook, if anything, in 2116? Ponder that as you furiously click the Unfriend button.

Index